AGRICULTURE REFRESHER

(An anchor for Undergraduates, Postgraduates, Entrance Examinations, JRF, SRF, aspirants of Civil Services, Various Provincial Services, Agriculture Officer Examinations for Banks, ARS and various other Agricultural Examinations.)

Ram Dutta

2012

JAIN BROTHERS (NEW DELHI)

16/873, East Park Road, Karol Bagh, New Delhi-110005,
Phones: (011) 23618426, 45097398
E-mail: jain_bros@hotmail.com
Website: www.thejainbrothers.com

Published by :

Shri Sunil Kumar Jain
for
JAIN BROTHERS (NEW DELHI)
Ph. (011) 23618426

Distributors :

1. **M/s Sunil Book Service,**
FATIMA NAGAR, KAZIPET-506004
Ph. (0870) 2459617

2. **M/s Jain Brothers**
Vidya Vihar, Pilani (Raj.)
Ph. : (01596) 242144

First Published : Oct., 2005
Reprinted with corrections : 2009
Revised and Updated : Oct., 2011

ISBN : 81-8360-023-9

Price : ₹ 225.00

Laser Typesetting & Diagrams by :

Niyati *Graphics*
754 / 23 Khajoor Road,
Karol Bagh, New Delhi-110005

Printed at :

New Balaji Offset Printers,
Daya Basti, Delhi-110035.

I dedicate
this book to almighty and all those
who inspired me to work hard
and serve the society.

Ram Dutta

Preface

Agriculture from time immemorial is playing an important role in providing food, fibre and helping ever increasing population to start their livelihood. Agricultural scientists, since green revolution till now, are concentrating on investigations relating to production as well as protection technologies. An understanding of the basic information being used in one area of specialization is necessary for scientists of other disciplines because agricultural science calls for an interdisciplinary approach. A specialist dealing in one aspect cannot afford to remain unaware of the other areas. It is, therefore, necessary for a specialist to go beyond his field of specialisation and develop an overall appreciation of the subject of agriculture. This book, therefore, includes several chapters relevant to all areas of agriculture. For better exposition, book has been divided into 47 chapters devoting on well defined information pertaining to agriculture. Attempts have been made to compile the information from various sources including books, journals and presented in a way as to have better understanding of the information.

I hope that this book will impart basics and innovative knowledge of various fields of agriculture. This will serve as the refresher of basic information for undergraduates, postgraduate students and ready reference for graduate students, researchers, extension workers, planners and candidates appearing in various examination concerning to agriculture. I believe that bringing information together in one volume will contribute to the advancement of knowledge on agriculture.

I express my gratitude to the writers/owners/disclaimers of the numerous information, which has been consulted for this manuscript. I am indebted to the individuals for their assistance provided to me at the time of exigencies while preparing this manuscript. In spite of the best efforts, it is possible that some errors may have crept into the compilation. I will be grateful to readers if errors are pointed out so that necessary corrections can be incorporated in the book. I humbly welcome critical suggestions for further improvement of this book. I finally thank 'JAIN BROTHERS' for cooperating and bringing this book in present form.

October 26, 2005 **Ram Dutta**

Dr. Kirti Singh
FNASc. FNAAS
Former Chairman, ASRB (ICAR), New Delhi
Former Vice-Chancellor, NDUAT, Faizabad
HPKV, Palampur and IGKV, Raipur
Former Secretary, NAAS, Delhi
President, Indian Society of Vegetable Science

Foreword

Agriculture has its relevance in the economic and social development of any nation. The present scenario of Indian agriculture is to conserve the natural resources in order to sustain the productivity and protect the produce for livelihood. It is an urgent need that must be addressed to meet the requirement of food, feed, fibre, and fuel for the ever-increasing population. The green revolution has helped us to achieve self-sufficiency in food grain production. Our population has increased enormously, and to feed this population there is an urgent need for not only producing additional food grains, but taking care of food and nutritional security for better quality of life of our people.

The emerging problem has to be handled with new vision and thoughts accumulated with past knowledge and experience. Time has come now to analyze the potentialities of developed technologies and discrepancies to face the challenges ahead.

The present book *"Agriculture Refresher"* is a progressive very timely and appropriate attempt for better understanding of basics of agricultural sciences. I congratulate Dr. Ram Dutta for this comprehensive volume containing updated information on agriculture comprising various fields. I am confident that this publication will be of immense value to the teachers, students, researchers, extension workers, administrators, planners and every one interested in the subject.

(KIRTI SINGH)

Residence: C-9/9766, Vasant Kunj, New Delhi-110-070
Phone : +91(11) 51767608 ; E-mail : kirtisingh1934@yahoo.co.in

Dr. Kirti Singh
FNASc, FNAAS
Former Chairman, ASRB (ICAR), New Delhi
Former Vice-Chancellor, NDUA&T, Faizabad
HPKV, Palampur and IGKV, Raipur
Former Secretary, NAAS, Delhi
President, Indian Society of Vegetable Science

Foreword

Agriculture has its relevance in the economic and social development of any nation. The present scenario of Indian agriculture is to conserve the natural resources in order to sustain the productivity and protect the planet for livelihood. It is an urgent need that must be addressed to meet the requirement of food, feed, fibre, and fuel for the ever-increasing population. The green revolution has helped us to achieve self sufficiency in food grain production. Our population has increased enormously, and to feed this population there is an urgent need for not only producing additional food grains, but taking care of food and nutritional security for better quality of life of our people.

The emerging problem has to be handled with new vision and thoughts accumulated with past knowledge and experience. Time has come now to analyze the potentialities of developed technologies and discrepancies to face the challenges ahead.

The present book "*Agriculture Refresher*" is a progressive very timely and appropriate attempt for better understanding of basics of agricultural sciences. I congratulate Dr. Ram Datta for this comprehensive volume containing updated information on agriculture comprising various fields. I am confident that the publication will be of immense value to the teachers, students, researchers, extension workers, administrators, planners and everyone interested in the subject.

(KIRTI SINGH)

Residence: C-9/9766, Vasant Kunj, New Delhi-110 070
Phone: +91(11) 51762083 E-mail: kirtisingh95@yahoo.com

CONTENTS

1

General Agriculture

Agriculture is the backbone of the country's economy. It contributes nearly 19·67 percent to Gross Domestic Product (GDP), for the year 2007-08, 15% to export and provide livelihood for 53 percent of labour force dependent on it.

Production 2007-2008 (Economic Survey, 2008-2009)

Total food grain production	:	230.8 million tonnes (MT)
Coarse cereals	:	40.7 MT
Pulses	:	14.8 MT
Wheat	:	78.6 MT
Rice	:	96.7 MT
Jowar	:	7.9 MT
Maize	:	19.0 MT
Gram	:	6·91 MT
Bajra	:	10.0 MT
Oilseeds	:	29.8 MT (Groundnut: 9.2 MT, Sesamum: 0.86 MT, Rapeseed and Mustard: 5.80 MT, Sunflower: 1.444 MT).
Cotton	:	25.9 Million bales (1 bale =170 kg)
Jute and Mesta	:	11.2 Million bales (1 bale= 180 kg)
Sugarcane	:	348.2 MT
Potato	:	28.5 MT

Per capita availability of cereals against total food grains: Per capita availability of cereals/day has been at 407.4 g, whereas per capita availability of total food grains was 442.8 g/capita/day during 2006-2007.

Per capita availability of pulses versus requirement: During 2006-2007, the availability of pulses was recorded at 35·5 g per capita, as against the minimum requirement of pulses in balance food was measured to 58 g/capita/day.

Horticulture, including fruits, vegetables, spices and other crops contributed to 30% of agricultural GDP with the production of 17.2 MT from 17.2 (8.5%) Mha area, during 2003-2004.

- **India is the second largest producer of fruits** with 43 MT from 4 Mha area. Mango contributes to 24% of fruit export followed by citrus (24%) and apple (14%). The highest earning in terms of foreign exchange comes walnut (34%) followed by Mango (24%), Grapes (17%) and Citrus (11%).
- **India is the second largest producer of vegetables** also in world after China with production of 80.26 MT accounting for 9.3% world production. However, it is **first in Okra and Vegetable pea** production. Tamil Nadu has the highest productivity of Cabbage (25.5 t/ha) followed by U.P.19.3 t/ha).
- India is the largest producer (0.9 MT) and consumes (0.72 MT) of **tea** in the world and accounts for around 27 per cent of world production and 13 per cent of world trade during 2006-2007.
- **Rubber** is primarily produced in Kerala, Kanyakumari, Tripura, Assam, Megahalaya, Mizoram, Manipur, Goa and Coastal Karnataka yielding 0.9 mil. tonnes from 5.7 lakh hectares of area during 2008. India is fourth largest producer of natural rubber with a share of 8·5% in world production in 2009.
- **Water availability** during 2003-2004 has been measured to 2200 m^3 per capita/person (800 M^3 for south India).
- **Power** availability for carrying out various agricultural operations has touched a level of 1.4 kw/ha in 2003-04 from 0.3 kw/ha in 1971-72. The share of mechanical and electrical power has increased from 40%1971-72 to 84% in 2003-04. The U.P. has recorded the highest (58,102 tractors) average sales of tractors during the five-year period ending in 2003-04.
- "India ranks first in milk production increasing the production from 17 million tonnes in 1950-51 to 112.5 million tonnes in 2009-10. The per capita availability of milk has increased from 112 grams per day in 1968-69 to 263 grams in 2009-10.

Fertilizers (during 2007-2008) India is the third largest producer and consumer of fertilizers in the world after China and USA.

A total of **22570.8** thousand tons chemical fertilizers consumption was recorded during 2007-2008 in terms of nutrients. The consumption among the States was highest in Punjab followed by Haryana and Andhra Pradesh. The all India average consumption of fertilizer at 112.3 kg/ha per hectare in 2006-07 was higher than the preceding year's average of 89.8 kg per hectare.

Estimated Production for 2008-2009 (Economic Survey, 2008-2009)

As per advance estimates on foodgrains production by the Agriculture Ministry, the total foodgrains production in the current year (2008-2009) is expected to be 229.9 million tonnes compared to 230.8 (during 2007-2008) million tonnes last year. The estimated food grain production **for the year 2009-2010** (Final estimate) is as follows,

The production of food grain declared to 218.11 million during 2009-10 (Final estimate)

Rice	: 89.1 MT
Wheat	: 80·7 MT
Maize	: 16·7 MT
Oilseeds	: 24·9 MT
Pulses	: 14.6 MT
Sugarcane	: 292.30 MT
Cotton	: 24.22 MT
Jute & Mesta	: 11.82 Million bales (1 bale = 180 kg)
Food grains in *Kharif*	: 103.8 MT
Food grains in *Rabi*	: 114.4 MT
Total	: 218.2 MT

Consumption of fertilizers (Nutrients) by 2011-12 is projected at 14 million tonnes of NPK.

The domestic production of Urea, Diammonium Phosphate (DAP), and complex fertilizers in the year 2009-10 has increased compared to 2008-09. The production of urea is estimated at 215.37 lakh tonnes in 2010-11 and that of DAP and complexes at 39.58 lakh tonnes and 91.66 lakh tonnes, respectively. Availability of raw material intermediates has been a major bottle neck in the increase of production of fertilizers.

- The village revenue officials keep plot-wise record of crops grown in each season. These are annually compiled district-wise, state-wise and finally on all-India basis. From these records the calculation of the relative abundance of crop (s), production per capita for all crops, are made.
- **International year for rice:** The United Nations General Assembly (UNGA) declared 2004 the International Year of Rice (IYR) with the theme of "**Rice is life**".

Agriculture Development in India At a Glance

- *President of ICAR:* The Union Minister for Agriculture is the *Ex-officio* President of ICAR Society.

- Vice-President of ICAR: The Union Minister of State for Agriculture is the *Ex-officio* Vice-President of ICAR Society.
- *Director General of ICAR*: The Director General of ICAR is the *Ex-officio* Secretary to DARE (Department of Agriculture Research and Education).

1871 Department of Revenue, Agriculture and Commerce was established (chief function collection of statistics, revenue and number of agricultural research) during tenure of Lord Mayo.

1877 India faced severe famine and Government of India (the Imperial Government) resolved to set up a central department of agriculture controlled by Imperial Secretariat.

1881 Department of Agriculture was set up for provinces, following the recommendations of Famine Commission (1881).

1892 Agriculture chemist and an assistant chemist were appointed to look after research and teaching.

1901 Inspector General of Agriculture and an Imperial mycologist were appointed to advice the Imperial and provincial Government in Agriculture matters.

1903 An entomologist was employed.

1901-05 Agricultural Colleges were established at Pune, Kanpur, Sabour, Nagpur, Layallpur and Coimbatore.

1905 Agriculture Research Institute was established at Pusa, Bihar by Lord Curzon.

1919 Constitutional reforms made agriculture a State subject.

1928 Royal Commission on agriculture, headed by Lord Lilinthgow, recommended setting up the Imperial Council Agriculture Research to promote, guide and coordinate Agricultural Research throughout India.

23rd May 1929 Imperial Council of Agriculture Research was established. The governing body was composed of 16 members including following office bearers:
President: Khan Bahadur Sir Mohammad Habibullah
Vice-president: Diwan Bahadur Sir Vijaya Raghavacharya
Secretary: Mr. S.A. Hydari

March 1948 The name Imperial Council of Agricultural Research was changed to Indian Council of Agricultural Research (ICAR). The then President was: **Sir Jogindra Singh**.

1963 Agriculture review team, headed by Dr. Marion W. Parker of USDA, was appointed which recommended the reorganization of ICAR as fully autonomous body.

1965 A policy was made to appoint an agricultural scientist as the Chief Executive of ICAR, with the Designation as Director General. **Dr. B.P. Pal** became the first director General of ICAR in 1965.

1966 ICAR was declared fully autonomous and meanwhile its main institutes, IARI/NDRI/IVRI, were given the status of National Institutes.

June 1972 Gajendra Gadkar committee was appointed to review the recruitment and personnel policies of ICAR and its institutes, which submitted its report in 1973. Accordingly, the Department of Agriculture Research and Education (DARE), Govt. of India was created in 1973 under the Ministry of Food and Agriculture.

1973
- DARE established.
- Agricultural Research Service (ARS) was initiated for the recruitment of Scientific personnel under the name of Agricultural Scientist Recruitment Board (ASRB). The board is currently housed at Pusa Bhavan, New Delhi.

Indian Agricultural Research Institute (IARI)

1905 Agriculture Research Institute was established at Pusa, Bihar by Lord Curzon. For which Mr. Phipps of USA donated the land, after whose name, the place was named as PUSA (P from his name and USA was the country of his native). Phipps laboratory in the division of soil science and agricultural chemistry were also named after him.

1911 The name of Agricultural Research Institute was changed to Imperial Agricultural Research Institute.

1923 Institute started offering diploma in Associateship.

1934 Major earthquake damaged the building at PUSA Bihar hence the Institute was shifted to New Delhi in 1936.

1936 **B. Vishwanath** became the first Indian Director of the Institute.

1946 Diploma of Associateship was recognized as equivalent to M.Sc.

1947 The name of Imperial Agricultural Research Institute was changed to Indian Agricultural Research Institute.

1958 Institute was recognized as Deemed to be University under the UGC Act. of 1956; Post Graduate School was established.

All India Coordinated Research Projects (AICRPs)

1957 AICRP on Maize was established with aid from Rockefeller foundation.

1965 AICRPs on other crops were started as well for the research work.

Awards and Merits in Agriculture

Agricola medal	F.A.O contributes for outstanding work in agriculture.
Boerma Award	F.A.O contributes for focusing attention on world food problems.
Borlaug Award	Coromandal Fertilizers Limited contributes for agriculture development.
Gopal Ratna Award	Ministry of Agriculture and Cooperation contributes for dairy farming and rearing of animals for milk.
Hooker Award	IARI contribute for outstanding research in agriculture to increase food security.
Kidwai Award	NDRI contributes for dairy development.

ICAR Awards

- The Indian Council of Agricultural Research instituted a number of awards, which at present rose to 17 (eight annual and nine biannual) are given in different categories.

Krishi Pandit Award	ICAR for highest production in various crops in agriculture.
Sardar Patel outstanding ICAR Institution Award	Three awards of Rs. 5 Lakh each awarded annually for the best performance in Agricultural Research, Extension and Education.
Choudhary Devi Lal outstanding Project Award	It is awarded annually with cash of Rs. 1 lakh, to AICRP and its coordinating centres.
Rafi Ahmed Kidwai Award (since 1956)	Nine awards of Rs. 3 lakh cash, given biannually, for research work in Agriculture, Animal Husbandry and Allied Sciences.
Fakhruddin Ali Ahmed Award (since 1977)	Rs. 50,000 awarded biannually for Agricultural Research in Tribal Areas.

Hari Om Ashram Trust Award, (since 1972)	Rs. 40,000 awarded biannually to recognize published original research, in Crop Science, Horticulture, Resource Management and Animal Science.
Jawaharlal Nehru Award (since 1969)	Eighteen awards with a cash prize of Rs. 20,000 each with a Gold Medal given annually, for best Ph.D in Agriculture and Allied Sciences.
Vasantrao Naik Award, (since 1994)	The award with Rs. 1 lakh cash, given annually, for published work from extension worker in Water Conservation and Dryland Farming.
Lal Bahadur Shastri Young Scientist Award	The awarded biannually for original research work.
Bharat Ratna Dr. C Subramaniam Outstanding Teacher Award	Eight awards of Rs. 50,000 each, given biannually, to provide incentive in the field of agriculture.
Punjab Rao Deshmukh Woman Agricultural Scientist Award (since 1995)	Two awards of Rs. 50,000 each given, to individual woman scientist, annually to encourage the woman scientists.
Chaudhary Charan Singh Award, (since 2000)	Rs. 1 lakh awarded for outstanding Journalism in Agriculture Research and Development
N.G. Ranga Farmer Award for Diversified Agriculture (since 2001)	Rs. 1 lakh award is given annually to contributions in diversified agricultural activities.
Jagjivan Ram Kisan Puruskar	Rs. 1 lakh awarded annually to individual farmer in the area of Agricultural Productivity and Allied Activities.
Swamy Sahajanand Saraswati Extension Scientist / Worker Award (since 1995)	Four awards of Rs. 25,000 with a citation, given biannually to outstanding and innovative research in developing extension education programmes as well as methodologies.
ICAR Award	Nine awards of Rs. 1 lakh each given biannually for outstanding inter-disciplinary team (usually eight) research in agriculture and allied sciences.

Best Krishi Vigyan Kendra Award	This award is given to institutes running KVKs for best performance. Award carries Rs. 50,000 given biannually.
Dr. Rajendra Prasad Puruskar	Eight awards of Rs. 50,000 each given biannually to promote Hindi authors in agriculture.

- **Film on Agriculture:** "Seed of life" by Director Usha Albuquerque, has been awarded best film in agriculture in 2004.

Cropping seasons

Cropping activities go on round the year in India, provided the water is available.

- In northern India, there are two distinct seasons, *kharif* (July to October), and *rabi* (October to March). Crops grown between March and June are known as *zaid*.
- *Kharif*: It is the monsoon season or rainy season from June-July to October-November.
- *Rabi*: It is the winter season from November-December to March-April.
- *Zaid*: The summer season, crops grown between February-March and June-July.

Rice seasons: Aus Rice: Rice crop sown in April-June and harvested in August-September (the autumn season). **Aman Rice**: Rice crop grown in June-July and harvested in winter from November-December. **Boro Rice**: Rice crop grown in December-January and harvested in May-June

Sugarcane seasons: The planting of sugarcane is done thrice in a year *viz.* **Spring sugarcane** is transplanted in March-April and harvested during February-March; **winter crop** is planted during October and harvested during October-November; Adsali is planted in July and harvested after 18 months in November-December next year.

Composition of plant body: Cellulose 20-30%, Hemicellulose 10-30%, Lignins 10-30%, Proteins 1-15%, Fats and Waxes 1-8%.

Area under different crops and regions

Crop	Area	Region (per cent of total area under crop)
Sugarcane	2.5 Mha	Uttar Pradesh (51), Haryana (6), Bihar (6), Punjab (6), Maharashtra (8), Andhra Pradesh (5), Tamil Nadu (5), Karnataka (3).
Tobacco	0.427 Mha	Andhra Pradesh (48), Gujarat (19.5), Karnataka (8.7), Maharashtra (3.5), Tamil Nadu (3.5).

Potato	0.491 Mha	Uttar Pradesh (33.6), Bihar (20.4), West Bengal (13.3), Assam (5.2), Orissa (4.8).
Jute	0.778 Mha	West Bengal (60), Northeastern Region (18.7), Bihar (17.6), Orissa (6.1), Uttar Pradesh (1.7).
Coconut	1.05 Mha	Kerala (68.3), Karnataka (12.4), Tamil Nadu (9.7), Andhra Pradesh (3.5).
Rubber	0.197 Mha	Kerala (92.8), Tamil Nadu (5.0), Karnataka (1.9).
Cashew	0.264 Mha	Kerala (67.4), Karnataka (12.1), Andhra Pradesh (10.8), Tamil Nadu (9.8), Maharashtra (4.8).
Tea	0.35 Mha	West Bengal, Assam and Tripura (77), Kerala, Tamil Nadu and Karnataka (20).
Coffee	0.138 Mha	Kerala, Tamil Nadu and Karnataka (99).
Fruit-crops	1.8 Mha	Spread all-over India.
Onion	0.16 Mha	Maharashtra (18.5), Karnataka (11.7), Andhra Pradesh (12.8), Tamil Nadu (11.2), West Bengal (7.6), Madhya Pradesh (7.2), Orissa (6.8), Punjab (6.2).
Chillies	0.733 Mha	Andhra Pradesh (26.9), Maharashtra (20.4), Karnataka (14.5), Madhya Pradesh (5.5), Tamil Nadu (10.1).
Coriander	0.283 Mha	Andhra Pradesh (36), Rajasthan (23.6), Madhya Pradesh (11.1), Tamil Nadu (10.0).

Critical Stages for Irrigation

Crop	Critical stage (s)
Cereals	
Rice	Tillering, Panicle initiation, Heading and Flowering
Sorghum	Booting, Blooming and milky Dough stages
Maize	Silking and Tasselling to Dough stages
Pearl millet	Heading and Flowering
Finger millet	Primordial initiation and Flowering
Wheat	Crown root initiation, Tillering to Booting
Pulses	
Chick pea	Late Vegetative phase
Black gram	Flowering and Pod Setting

Green gram	Flowering and Pod Setting
Beans	Flowering and Pod Setting
Peas	Flowering and Early Pod Formation
Alfalfa	After Cutting and Flowering
Oil seeds	
Ground nut	Flowering, Peg Formation and Pod Deve-lopment
Seasmum	Blooming to Maturity
Sunflower	Pre-flowering and Post-Flowering
Soybean	Blooming and Seed Formation
Vegetables	
Onion	Bulb Formation and Pre-Maturity
Tomato	Flowering and Fruit Setting
Chillies	Flowering and Fruit Setting
Cabbage	Head Formation
Potato	Tuber Initiation to Maturity
Carrot	Root Enlargement.
Miscellaneous	
Cotton	Flowering and Boll Formation
Citrus	Flowering, Fruit Setting and Fruit Enlargement
Mango	Pre-Flowering and Fruit Setting

Agricultural Revolutions in India

Revolution	Related to
Green Revolution	Food grain production
Yellow Revolution	Oil seeds production
White Revolution	Milk production
Blue Revolution	Fish production
Grey Revolution	Fertilizer production
Red Revolution	Meat/tomato production
Round Revolution	Potato production
Silver Revolution	Egg/poultry production
Pink Revolution	Prawn production
Golden Revolution	Fruit production
Brown Revolution	Fertilizer production
Red Revolution	Tomato production
Pink Revolution	Onion production

- **William Gadd suggested the term green revolution in 1967.**

Number One States in Crop Production

Crop		State	Crop		State
1.	Wheat	U.P.	2.	Pulses	Madya Pradesh
3.	Groundnut	U.P.	4.	Cotton, Onion	Maharashtra
5.	Tea	Assam	6.	Coffee	Karnataka
7.	Rubber	Kerala	8.	Rice	West Bengal
9.	Cotton	Gujrat			

Number One Country in Crop/Fruit Production

Crop		Country	Crop		Country
1.	Cotton	U.S.A	2.	Tea	India
3.	Tobacco	China	4.	Coffee	Brazil
5.	Rubber	Malaysia	6.	Banana	India

Epithets in Agriculture

Epithet	For
King of fruits	Mango
Queen of flowers	Gladiolus
King of pulses	Chickpea
Fountain tree	*Spathodia campeculata*
Butter bowl	*Ficus kisni*
Butter fruit	Avacado
Food of God	Cocoa
Poor man's fruit	Ber
Green gold	Opium
Queen of milk	Sannen breed of Goat
Blue mountains	Nilgiris Mountains
Garden city of India	Bangalore
Island of Clove	Zanzibar
Sugar bowl	Cuba
White gold	Cotton

Important Dates in Agriculture

March 11	Water Resource day
March 21	World forestry day
March 22	World water day
May 1	Labour day
June 5	World environment day

July 1-7	*Van Mahotsava*
October 6	World food day, world animal day
October 16	World food day
December 4	Agriculture Women day
December 23	Farmers' day

Land use pattern in India

Land use	Million hectare
Total Geographical Area	329.00
Total area suitable for cultivation	305.16
Gross cropped area	185.49
Net sown area	142.51
Area sown more than once	42.98
Forest	68.07
Area to no agricultural uses	21.8
Barren uncultivable land	19.38
Permanent pastures and other grazing lands	11.30
Land under miscellaneous tree crops	3.67
Cultivable wastes	14.64
Old fallows land	9.65
Current fallows	13.91

Conversion factors and units used for different crops

Area	1 acre	= 4840 sq yards = 43,560 sq feet
	1 gutha	= 1/40th acre = 1089 sq ft = 33′ x 33′
	1 acre	= 0.4047 hectare
	1 hectare	= 2.471 acres
	1 sq mile	= 640 acres
Distance	1 mile	= 1760 yards = 5,280 feet
	1 metre	= 1.0936 yards = 39.37 inches
	1 yard	= 0.9144 metre
	1 foot	= 0.3048 metre
	1 inch	= 2.54 centimetres
Weight	1 metric ton	= 1000 kilograms = 2204.6 pounds
	1 maund	= 80 pounds (approx.)
	1 short ton	= 0.9072 metric ton
	1 long ton	= 1.0161 metric ton
	1 pound	= 453.6 grams = 0.4536 kg
	1 kilogram	= 2.2046 pounds
	1 cotton bale	= 170 kg

	1 jute & mesta bale = 180 kg
	1 silk bale = 50 kg (Indian) or 60 kg (International
Capacity	1 gallon (U.S.)= 3.7853 litres
	1 gallon (Imperial) = 0.1604 cubic feet or 4.5461 litres
	1 liter = 0.2200 gallon (Br.)
	1 liter = 2642 gallon (U.S.)
	1 bushel = 56 lb (Potatoes)
	1 bushel = 56 lb (Barley)
	1 bushel = 60 lb (Wheat)
	1 bushel = 42 lb (Oats)

Ratio between raw and processed products of different crops

Crop	Product	Ratio
Paddy	Rice	2/3rd of paddy production
	Husk	1/3rd of paddy production
Cotton	Lint	1/3rd of production
	Seed	2/3rd of production
	Oil	14-18 percent of seeds
	Cake	82-86 percent of seeds
Groundnut	Kernels	70 percent
	Oil	40 percent
	Cake	60 percent
Sesame	Oil	40 percent
	Cake	60 percent
Rape seed and mustard	Oil	33 percent
	Cake	67 percent
Castor	Oil	33 percent
	Cake	67 percent
Coconut	Oil	62 percent of copra
	Cake	38 percent of copra
Soybean	Oil from seeds	18 percent
	Meal	73 percent of seed
Linseed	Oil from seeds	40 percent
	Cake	60 percent
Sugarcane	Jaggery	12 percent from cane
	Juice	60 percent from cane
	Crystal sugar	62.5 percent from Gur
	Crystal sugar	9.8 percent from cane
	Molasses	18 percent from cane
Sugarbeet	Sugar	15-16 percent of production

- Shelling Percentage= $\frac{\text{Weight of grains/kernels}}{\text{Weight of cob/pod}} \times 100$
- Higher values of shelling percentage indicate the superiority of plant type/variety.
- Hulling percentage = $\frac{\text{Weight of rice}}{\text{Weight of Paddy}} \times 100$
- Ginning percentage

$$= \frac{\text{Weight of lint (cotton fibre)}}{\text{Weight of seed cotton taken for ginning}} \times 100$$

- **Ginning** is the separation of lint from seed cotton. Higher the ginning percentage, superior the variety.
- Lint indes = $\frac{\text{Weight of 100 cotton seeds}}{100} \times$ Ginning percentag

Description of some imaginary lines

Name	**Joining point of (Description)**
Contour	Equal elevations
Isopleth	Uniform values of any phenomenon
Isobar	Equal atmospheric pressure
Isohyte	Equal rainfall
Isochrone	Equal time
Isobath	Equal water table
Isohels	Equal sunshine
Isoleuth	Equal evaporation values
Isostere	Constant moisture contents
Isogonals	Same magnetic declination
Isophene	Similar seasonal phenomenon
Isoseismals	Equal seismic activities
Isotherm	Equal temperature
Isotech	Equal wind velocities
Isotope	Equal number of electron and proton

❑❑❑

2

Techniques in Agriculture

Mechanical processing of soil to maintain proper physical condition for planting is referred as **tilling**. Adding nutrients and trace elements is called **fertilization**.

Primary Tillage Equipment

Equipments used to break and loosen the soil for a depth of 15 to 90 cm are called as primary tillage equipments. It includes mouldboard, disc, rotary, chisel, and subsoil ploughs. The mouldboard is well suited for turning and covering crop residues. When a bottom turns the soil, it cuts a trench, or furrow, throwing to one side a ribbon of soil that is called the **furrow slice**. The ridge created by mouldboard is called a **back furrow**.

Hydroponics

The term hydroponics (comprised of two Greek words: *hydro,* means related with water and *ponos,* means labour) denotes soilless culture of plants. In hydroponics plants are grown with their roots immersed in a water solution containing necessary minerals or rooted in a sand medium kept moistened by such a solution.

- Boyle in 1666 first grew *Raphanus aquaticus* (Spearmint) in vials containing only water. Gericke of California University in 1929 was first to promote commercial potential of liquid culture.
- A typical hydroponics technique has plants supported in a bed of peat, wood fibre, or similar material, on a wire screen with the roots dipping into the solution below.
- In another method, the plants are rooted in a medium of sand or gravel contained in a shallow tank into which the solution is pumped at intervals by automatic control.

Greenhouses

The greenhouse is typically, a structure having transparent or translucent roof and sides, permitting a sufficient quality and quantity of solar radiation to enter the structure for photosynthesis. It allows the growing of crops independently of the outside climate, since its interior temperature and humidity can be controlled.

- Hot water, steam, electric cable, or warm-air furnaces provide the heat, which is usually controlled by thermostat.
- Sometimes carbon dioxide is added to the air, if the crop requires it, for extra photosynthetic efficiency.

Phytotrons

Greenhouses with precise environmental controls are known as phytotrons. The first such laboratory dealing with plant materials was established at IARI, New Delhi.

Photoperiodism

The length of a day is a photoperiod, and the response of the plant development to a photoperiod is called photoperiodism. Long-day plants flower only under day lengths longer than 14 hours. Flowering in short-day plants is induced by photoperiods of less than 10 hours. Day-neutral plants form buds under any period of illumination.

Temperature

Three temperature points (minimum, optimum and maximum) are collectively called **cardinal** temperatures for a given plant. Cool-season crops (oats, rye, wheat, and barley) have low cardinal temperatures, whereas, warm-season crops (melons and sorghum) have much higher.

Cardinal Temperature (°C) for Important Crops

Crops	Minimum	Optimum	Maximum
Barley	3.0-4.5	20	38-40
Maize	8-10	32-35	40-44
Oats	4-5	25	30
Rice	10-12	30-32	36-38
Sorghum	8-10	32-35	36-38
Tobacco	13-14	28	35
Wheat	3.0-4.5	25	30-32

- The cardinal temperatures may vary with the stage of development. For instance, cold treatment at zero °C temperature of germinated seeds before sowing can transform winter rye into the spring type, such treatment called vernalization.

- Diurnal temperature is a variation in the temperature during daytime and night time.

Frost

Two types of frost are recognized: (*i*) radiation frost, which occurs on clear nights with little or no wind when the outgoing radiation is excessive and the air temperature is not necessarily at the freezing point; and (*ii*) wind, or advection, frost, which occurs at any time, day or night, regardless of cloud cover, when wind moves air in from cold regions.

Remote Sensing

Remote sensing comprised of any method used to obtain information about an object or area from a distance. Cameras and other instruments that collect and record this information are called **sensors**. Most remote sensors record the amount of electromagnetic energy that objects radiate or reflect. These remote sensing systems are commonly used to survey, map, and monitor the resources and environment of the Earth. Special sensors called **multispectral scanners** provide data electronically for multiple portions of the electromagnetic spectrum. Infrared sensors and microwave sensors record invisible electromagnetic energy. Infrared sensors create images that show temperature variations in an area.

- Scientists use **infrared images** to determine the condition of vegetation, survey temperature changes in bodies of water, locate damage in underground pipelines, and map certain geographic features above and below ground.
- **Microwave sensors**, such as radar, transmit electromagnetic waves towards objects and record the reflection of waves. Such sensors have ability to collect information about an area through clouds. The surface of Venus, which is entirely surrounded by dense clouds, has been mapped in this way.
- **Satellites** have proved extremely useful in the development of remote sensing systems. The United States, the European Space Agency (ESA), India, Japan, and Russia have launched Earth-observing satellites.
- There are four satellites, IRS-1A/1B, IRS-1C, IRS-1D, IRS-P4, launched from India for agricultural purposes.

Gene Bank

The term gene bank applied to a facility where plant germplasm is stored, usually in the form of seeds, also as whole plants, pollen, and cell cultures. Gene banks serve as the collection centres for broad range of plant genes from which breeders may choose to develop new plant varieties with desired characteristics. The first such Gene Bank in India was developed at National Bureau of Plant Genetic Resources (NBPGR), New Delhi

Molecular Techniques in Agriculture

The molecular techniques so called as they are linked to molecule, the DNA, of any individual. Linkage maps of many plant species have been drawn with the help of molecular mapping. The inability to incorporate many markers into a single stock to be used for genetic analysis is primary difficulty in the development of linkage maps. Molecular markers are phenotypically neutral. The three most common types of markers used today are RFLP, RAPD and isozymes. The molecular markers can be classified into several categories based on the molecule they study.

DNA Based Molecular Markers

Molecular marker may be defined as a DNA sequence used for chromosome mapping, as it can be located at a specific site in a chromosome. They may be either **anonymous** (*i.e.,* cloned random DNA fragment whose function and specificity are not known) or **defined** (*i.e.,* contains a gene or some other specific features).

- Molecular markers, which have different structures in different individuals for cut ends, are called **polymorphic markers**.
- **Probe** is a short fragment of DNA that identifies a region of genome by its precise complementary sequence.

Important DNA Based Molecular Markers

- Restriction Fragment Length Polymorphism (RFLPs)
- Random Amplified Polymorphic DNA (RAPDs)
- Variable Number of Tandem Repeats (VNTRs)
- Mini satellites DNAs
- Micro satellites DNAs

Restriction Fragment Length Polymorphism (RFLPs)

It is a variation in the homologous fragment length of DNA on being digested with restriction endonucleases. The main **procedure** involves:

(i) The isolation of DNA;
(ii) Digestion of DNA with restriction endonucleases;
(iii) Separation of fragments on a Agarose-gel-electrophoresis;
(iv) Staining of gel;
(v) Transfers of DNA to the nitro-cellulose membrane (southern transfer);
(vi) Hybridization of restricted DNA with a labelled radioactive probe;
(vii) Washing away the non-specific probes, auto-radiography; and
(viii) Observation of differences in RFLPs.

Random Amplified Polymorphic DNA (RAPDs)

This approach for assaying DNA polymorphisms is based on the use of PCR (Polymerase Chain Reaction) amplification by repeated cycles of DNA Denaturation-Renaturation-DNA replication of random DNA segments with single primers of arbitrary sequence. These polymorphisms are detected as DNA fragments, which amplify from one parent but not the other, are inherited in a Mendelian fashion. Such polymorphisms can easily be visualized in gels stained with **ethidium bromide** and information obtained can be used for linkage mapping in the same manner as in the case of RFLPs.

- RAPDs approach does not utilize restriction enzymes and probes of any kind. It utilizes the PCR, which is resistant to high temperatures (due to *Taq* polymerase) needed for DNA denaturation.
- *Taq*-polymerase is an enzyme extracted from *Thermus aquaticus* bacteria, which resists high temperature (up to 98°C) needed for denaturation and renaturation of DNA.
- RAPDs can be grouped into two types *viz*: AP-PCR (Arbitrary Primer-PCR) and AFLP (Random Amplified Polymorphic DNA).

Variable Number of Tandem Repeats (VNTRs)

VNTRs are dispersed throughout the genome and are made up of a variable number of end-to-end duplications of identical or almost identical sequences of 2-80 bp (based pairs) each. Polymorphism in VNTRs is usually associated with the number of repeats, *i.e.*, different individuals show variations constitute the alleles of VNTRs loci. VNTRs are generally classified into two categories: Mini satellite DNAs and Micro satellite DNAs.

Mini Satellite DNAs

These are usually 0.2-2.0 kb (kilobyte) long and consist of tandem repeats of 15 to 60 bp sequence. Such marker system can only be applied in plant genome.

Micro Satellite DNAs

These are short DNA fragments of usually less than 100 bp and are made up of tandem repeats of 2 to 7 bp; therefore, they are also called **short tandem repeats (STRs), simple sequence repeats (SSRs), simple sequence length polymorphism (SSLP).** STRs are frequently distributed in all eukaryotic genomes (except in yeast). They show a large, stable polymorphisms due to variation in the number of repeat units and are almost ideal as molecular markers for genome mapping.

Application of Molecular Markers in Crop Improvement

Molecular markers **are used** for,

- Tagging genes for indirect selection;
- Assessing somaclonal variation;
- Varietal identification;
- Identification of pathogen races and biotypes;
- Germplasm organization;
- Identification of wide hybrids;
- Protection of plant breeder's rights;
- Tracing back the evolutionary pathways;
- Identification of heterotic cross-combinations;
- Saving time in breeding activities;
- Mapping and selection for QTL;
- Simultaneous transfer of multiple genes from different donors conferring resistance to a particular disease to a recurrent parent; and
- Selection under practically difficult situation.

Achievements in Crop Improvement Using DNA Molecular Markers

The various International Agriculture Research Institutes, particularly those funded by the Consultative Group for International Agriculture Research (CGIAR) have profitably utilized this technology for crop improvement.

- Pyramiding of genes against bacterial blight in rice (Yoshimura *ts al.*, 1995; Huang *et al.*, 1997).
- Cyst nematode resistant soyabean (Danesh *et al.*, 1995).
- Scald resistance variety in barley (Graner and Tekauz, 1996).

- Enhancement of durability of resistance by incorporating multiple resistance genes in a single variety of wheat (Li *et al.*, 1999).
- A major gene for P-deficiency tolerance on chromosome 12 in rice linked to RFLP markers (RG9 and RG241).
- Identification of major gene in rice for submergence tolerance on chromosome 1 and 9.

Protein Based Molecular Markers

The molecular marker systems work on the basis of protein staining with identical function with different electrophoretic mobility.

The Procedures to Identify Isozyme Variation

(i) A crude protein extract is made from some tissue sources.

(ii) The extracts are next separated by electrophoresis in a starch gel.

(iii) The gel is then placed in a solution that contains reagents required for the enzymatic activity of the enzyme to be monitored. In addition, the solution contains a dye that the enzyme can catalyze into a colour reagent that stains the protein.

- In this manner allelic variants of the protein can be visualized in a gel.

Isozyme: Isozymes are protein markers. The technique is based on the principal that allelic variation exists from many different proteins. For example, alleles of maleic dehydrogenase perform the correct enzymatic function, but the electrophoretic mobility of the two alleles may differ, therefore, two alleles would not migrate to the same location in a starch gel.

PCR (polymerase chain reaction): PCR is the amplification of a small amount of DNA into a larger amount. It is quick, easy, and automated process. The technique was developed by Nobel laureate biochemist Kary Mullis in 1984 and is based on the discovery of the biological activity at high temperatures of DNA *Taq*-polymerases found in thermophilic bacteria (*Thermus aquaticus*). Most of DNA polymerases work only in the low temperatures condition at which DNA is tightly coiled, but *Taq*-polymerase works at 98°C, a temperature at which DNA remain denatured in linear form.

Diagnostic Techniques in Agriculture

Enzyme-linked Immunosorbent assay (ELISA): It is method to detect the virus in the plants even at the minute amount. It combines the specificity of antibodies with the sensitivity of simple enzyme assays, by using antibodies or antigens coupled to an easily assayed enzyme. ELISA can provide a useful measurement of antigen or antibody concentration.

- The **procedure of ELISA** completes in five steps *viz.* *i.* Coating the microtiter plate wells with antigen; *ii.* Blocking all unbound sites to prevent false positive results; *iii.* Adding antibody to the wells; *iv.* Adding anti-mouse IgG conjugated to an enzyme; and *v.* Observing reaction of a substrate with the enzyme to produce a coloured product, thus indicating a positive reaction.
- There are many different types of ELISA among which sandwich ELISA is most common. The sandwich ELISA measures the amount of antigen between two layers of antibodies.

Southern blotting: Southern blotting was named after Edward M. Southern who developed this procedure at Edinburgh University in the 1970s. In the technique DNA molecules are transferred from an Agarose gel onto nitrocellulose membrane. The technique is used to locate a particular sequence of DNA within a complex mixture. For example, Southern Blotting could be used to locate a particular gene within an entire genome. The amount of DNA needed for this technique is dependent on the size and specific activity of the probe. Short probes tend to be more specific. Under optimal conditions, one can expect to detect 0.1 picogram of the DNA.

Procedure involves, (*i*) Digestion of DNA with an appropriate restriction enzyme; (*ii*) Running the digest on an agarose gel;

(*iii*) Denaturing the DNA; (*iv*) Transfer the denatured DNA to the membrane; (*v*) Probing the membrane with labelled ssDNA (the hybridization); and (*vi*)Visualization of radioactive labelled target sequence.

Northern blotting: This technique is similar to southern blotting, but it is used for locating RNA sequence. The procedure and theory behind Northern blotting are almost identical to that of Southern blotting, except it is working with RNA instead of DNA.

Western blotting: This is used to detect a single protein in a mixture of proteins. The method is dependent on the use of a high-quality antibody directed against a desired protein. Technique involves:

(*i*) Separation of proteins using SDS-Polyacrylamide gel electrophoresis (SDS-PAGE); (*ii*) Placing a nitrocellulose membrane on the gel; (*iii*) Incubating the nitrocellulose membrane with a primary antibody; (*iv*) Incubating the nitrocellulose membrane with a secondary antibody; and (*v*)Putting X-ray film on gel to detect a flash of light.

Comprehensive Sensitivity of Important Serological Techniques

Technique	Detection range
Double immunodiffusion	2-20 μg/ml
Liquid precipitin	1-10 μg/ml
Radial immunodiffusion	0.5-10 μg/ml
Rocket electrophoresis	0.2-1.0 μg/ml
Compliment fixation	50-100 ng/l
Immuno osmophoresis	50-100 ng/ml
Passive haemagglutination	20-50 ng/ml
Latex test	5-20 ng/ml
ELISA	1-10 ng/ml
ISEM	1-10 ng/ml
Western blotting	1-10 ng/ml
Molecular hybridization	<1 Picogram of RNA/ml
Dot blot (Southern blotting)	5-20 Picogram/ml

The Terminator and Verminator Technology

On the 3rd March 1998, The US Department of Agriculture and cotton seed breeders Delta and Pine Land Company acquired US patent 57,23,765 for their work **"Technology Protection System"** (TPS). Under technology, which works as suicide mechanism into seeds of the next generation forcing seed not to germinate in following season, therefore it is called "terminator" technology. Later, on May 11, 1998, Monsanto took over the Delta and Pine Land Co. after buying it for $1.76 billion. RAFI (a non-profit international civil society organization headquartered in Canada) who originally coined the name terminator call this "**traitor technology**".

- This technology was to force farmers for new seed season after season from the companies producing seed of high quality, rather to use their traditional seed.
- On September 15th, 1998 Astra Zeneca received US patent 58,08,034 on its own terminator type technology. This was branded the "**verminator**" as the genes used to terminate the seed growth were, taken from brown rats.
- Both the technologies were based on the **switchable promoters** which allow particular traits to be switched on or off by application of a special chemical catalysts.

Precision Farming or Precision Agriculture

It is an agricultural concept relying on the existance of in-field variability. It requires the use of new technology, such as global positioning (GPS), sensors, satellites or aerial images, and information management tools (GIS) to assess and understand variations. Collected information may to grow more and to more accurately predict crop yields. It seeks to avoid applying inflexible practices to a crop, regardless of local soil/ climate conditions, and may help to better assess local situations of disease or lodging.

Satellites allow farmers to easily survey their land. Global Poistioning Systems (GPS) monitor can find the location of a field to within one meter. It can then present a series of GIS maps that demonstrate which field are moist or dry, and where there is erosion of soil and other soil factors that stunt crop growth. The data can be used by the farmer to automatically regulate the machine application of fertilizer and pesticide.

The US. Department of Agriculture, NASA, and NOAA are among key agencies contributing to this revolution in large-scale agriculture. The goal is to improve farmers' profits and harvest yields while reducing the negative impacts of farming on the environment that come from over application of chemicals.

In India also this concept is gaining importance at present at Tamil Nadu Agricultural University, Coimbatore Tamil Nadu, a project Precision Farming is running under Director of Ext. Education to provide information about precision farming and its benefits to farmers and society.

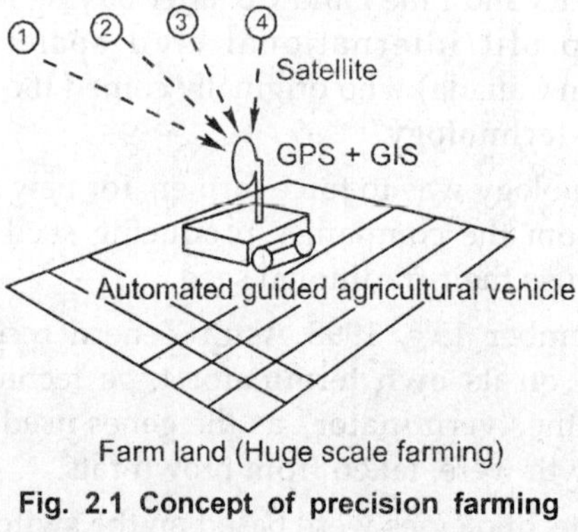

Fig. 2.1 Concept of precision farming

Precision farming is an agricultural system that has the potential of dramatically change agriculture scenario in 21st century. Precision agriculture is doing right thing at the right time. Knowing about the right thing involves data collection to a correct and viable decision.

❑❑❑

3

Meteorology

Meteorology is the science dealing with physical process in the atmosphere that produces weather.

- **Climatology** is the science dealing with the factors that determine and control the distribution of climate over the earth surface.
- **Weather** is a state of atmosphere at a given place at a given time. Weather usually pertains to small area like village, city, district etc. and smaller duration of time like a day or a part of it, *e.g.* hot day, rainy day, cloudy weather, sunny weather etc.
- **Climate** is summation of weather conditions over a region during a comparatively longer period. It is related to a larger area like zone, state, country, and continent; and for longer duration like months, season, year etc. *e.g.* summer season, monsoon season, tropical climate etc.

Meteorology and Climatology (Weather and Climate)

A component of meteorology is the study of weather. Weather is the present condition of the atmosphere at a particular time. It is mainly concerned with its day-to-day effects on life and human activities. Various elements that in combination express weather are air pressure and wind, temperature, relative humidity, precipitation (rainfall, snow, fog, hails, etc.) visibility.

- Climatology is the study of long-term manifestation of the weather represented by a statistical collection of weather conditions over a specific length of period usually at least a few decades.
- The climate is controlled by four factors (climatic controls) called (*i*) Astronomical factors, (*ii*) Geographical factors, (*iii*)Solar factors and (*iv*) Anthropogenic factors. Nine climatic controls are latitude, altitude, and distance from the sea, landsea distribution, semi-permanent pressure system, storm tracks, ocean currents, mountain barriers and air masses.

Sun and the Earth System

The sun is a star and a part of Milky Way Galaxy. Sun rotates in an anti-clockwise direction *i.e.* from west to east. The temperature at the surface of the sun is around 6,000 °C, whereas at the centre it is 165 lakh degree centigrades.

- The earth is at a mean distance of 150 million km from the sun. The mean surface temperature of the earth is 15°C.
- The shortest distance between the sun and the earth is called **perihelion** (147 million km) occurring on 3rd of January and the longest distance is called Aphelion (152 million km) occurring on 4th of July.
- There are four seasons in a year namely **winter solstice** (22nd December), **spring equinox** (21st March), **summer solstice** (21st June) and **autumn equinox** (23rd September).
- With an unconfirmed report, of Dr. S.S. Ojha, Allahabad University through "Amar Ujala (Kanpur edition) dated 29.9.2005", due to change in inclination of earth the **spring equinox** has shown a shift from 21st March to 25th March, **summer solstice**, from 21st June to 23rd June, and **autumn equinox** from 23rd September to 26th September, this year (2005).
- During equinox, the sun is at the equator, during solstices it is at either towards tropic of cancer (summer solstice) or tropic of Capricorn (winter solstice).

Atmosphere and Weather Elements

The vast expanse of air, which envelops the earth all around, is called the atmosphere. It extends up to the height of 1600 km; (but envelop remains mainly up to 40 km) from earth surface. It is divided into four different layers *viz.* (*i*) troposphere (up to 18 km in the equator and 8 km in the poles), (*ii*) stratosphere (8 or 18 km-50 km),

(*iii*) mesosphere (50 km-80 km) and the (*iv*) ionosphere (80 km-400 km) based on vertical temperature differences. All weathers including climate phenomenon pertain to atmosphere.

- Pure dry air constituents mainly of nitrogen, oxygen, argon, CO_2, hydrogen, helium, water vapour, ozone, dust particle, smoke, salts and other impurities.

Composition of Atmosphere

Gases	Volume %	Weight %	Remarks
Nitrogen	78.09	75.53	
Oxygen	20.95	23.14	For respiration
Argon	0.93	1.28	
Carbon dioxide	0.03	0.05	For photosynthesis
Other gases	Traces	Traces	

The atmosphere protects the earth from the harmful radiation of the sun with the help of the ozone (O_3) layer. Like a greenhouse, ozone allows short wave radiation to enter into it and reach the earth's surface but is nearly opaque to long wave terrestrial radiation from sun (greenhouse effect). Some of the important greenhouse gases are CO_2, CFC's, CH_4, Nitrous oxide, etc.

The Troposphere

It is the lowest layer extending up to the height of 8-18 km from earth depending on latitude. It is thicker at equator and thinner at poles. It contributes to 85 per cent of atmospheric mass. In this layer temperature decreases with increase in latitude. Temperature at boundary is $-66^{\circ}C$. Almost all weather phenomena occur in this layer. The tropopause is a thin layer of transition that separates the troposphere from the above lying stratosphere. There is no fall in temperature with height in this transition zone.

The Stratosphere

Stratosphere lies above troposphere beyond the height of 8-18 km up to 50 km depending upon latitude. It contains about 15 per cent of atmosphere's mass of 99 per cent. Temperature increases with increase in latitude making it the warmest layer. The layer is free from dust and clouds. It is the seat of photochemical reactions. Ozone layer lies in this layer, which filtrates the UV radiation. This layer acts as a lid on troposphere keeping convection and weather, below the tropopause. Stratopause separates stratosphere from mesosphere, the layer above to this layer.

The Mesosphere

It lies beyond the height of 50 km extending up to 80 km. Temperature decreases steeply with increase in latitude. Mesopause separates mesosphere from thermosphere.

The Thermosphere

It is the outermost layer of atmosphere. Temperature increases steadily with increase in altitude. The lower layer of thermosphere is called ionosphere, which helps in long distance radio communication by reflecting radio waves.

Weather Elements

The following are the prominent weather elements:

1. Solar radiation
2. Air temperature
3. Atmospheric pressure
4. Wind movements
5. Relative humidity
6. Evaporation
7. Precipitation
8. Clouds

1. **Solar radiation:** It is the source of energy for all the physical processes of atmosphere.

- **Solar constant** is defined as the total amount of solar radiation received per unit area in per unit time in the absence of atmosphere, the radiation being perpendicular and the earth at its mean distance from the sun. Its value 1.94 cal/cm/min × 1.94 Langley/min.
- Solar radiation is received in the form of **electromagnetic waves** and consists of solar particles, called **photons**.
- **Albedo** is the reflected solar radiation without any change in quality. It is very important for **remote sensing**. Cloud and snow are effective reflectors, whereas water surface and sea are poor reflectors. Rocks, sand, soil and vegetation reflect 10-30 per cent of incidental radiation. **Albedo is highest for transpiration.**
- **Terrestrial radiation** is the thermal radiation emitted by earth, which heats the atmosphere.
- **Earth** absorbs solar radiation in short waves and emits back in the form of long waves.
- **Total radiation** coming from solar system of which 43 per cent is absorbed by earth surface, 22 per cent by atmosphere and remaining 35 per cent is reflected back to space. The absorbed radiation is converted into thermal energy and irradiated as long wave radiation.

Measurement in Solar Radiation

Solar radiation is measured in **watts/sq.m** in SI system whereas, it measured in **cal/sq.cm/min** (= 697.93 w/m^2) in CGS system.

- Lux is the oldest unit of radiation.
- **Einstein** unit (Ei) equals to 1 mole of proton, used in photosynthetically active radiation (PAR). **Pyranometers** with quantum sensors are used to measure PAR.
- **Eppley pyranometer** and **Bellani pyranometer** are used for total incoming radiation.
- **Precision pyranometer** is used to continuously record incoming radiation on graph paper.
- **Licor pyranometer** and **Pyrheliometer** are used to directly read radiation with the help of integrator.
- **Albedometer** is a type of pyranometer used to measure reflectivity.
- **Spectroradiometer** is used to measure solar radiation in narrow wave bonds.

2. **Temperature:** Temperature is the degree of hotness or coldness of a substance.

- Heat transfer occurs through conduction, convection or radiation. **Conduction** is the transfer of heat through molecule activity without movement of matter whereas, **Convection** is the transfer of heat through motion of fluid either liquid or gas.
- Solar radiation heats up atmosphere indirectly, not directly. That why there is low temperature in high altitudes.
- Decrease in temperature at higher altitudes in the air is known as **vertical temperature gradient**, as air is heated up by the earth.
- Rate of vertical temperature decrease is called **lapse rate**. The normal lapse rate is **6.5 °C/km**.
- The rate at which the temperature changes as air rises or falls is called **adiabatic lapse rate**. The normal adiabatic lapse rate is **10°C/km**.
- The temperature variation between day and night is called **diurnal variation.** It is less at the equator and more at higher latitudes.
- Temperature decreases gradually from towards the poles due to slanting position of sun's rays.
- Lines joining equal temperature are called **Isotherm**.

Measurement of Temperature

Maximum thermometer (mercury) and **Minimum thermometer** (alcohol) used to measure the highest and lowest temperatures.

- **Soil thermometer** (mercury), **Thermoelectric thermometer** and **Resistance thermometer** are used to measure soil temperature.
- **Thermograph** records air temperature continuously.
- **Infrared thermometer** is used to measure temperature without contact of an object.

3. **The pressure:** Pressure is defined as force per unit area. Atmospheric pressure is the weight of the column of air at any given place and time.

- It is measured by **Aneroid Barometer** in force per unit area. **Barograph** is used to continuously record pressure on graph paper. The unit used for the purpose is called **Millibars**

  (1 millibar = force of one gram on a sq. cm).
- In general, atmospheric pressure is low in areas of high temperature and high in low temperature areas.
- In the lower layers of atmosphere (low altitude) atmospheric pressure is more and with increase in elevation, the pressure decreases.
- A pressure 1,000 mb (millibars) =weight of 1.053 kg/sq. cm. Normal pressure at sea level is 76 cm (1,013.25 mb)
- An isobar is an imaginary line joining paces of equal atmospheric pressure reduced to sea level.
- On the earth surface there are seven pressure belts. They are equatorial low (**the doldrums**), the sub-tropical high.(**horse latitudes**), the sub-polar low and the polar high. Except the equatorial low, all others have matching pairs in the northern and the southern hemisphere.

4. **Wind movement:** Horizontal movement of air is called **wind**, whereas vertical movement is called **air current**. Lines joining places of equal wind speed are called **Isotach**. Winds of high speed are called **Squalls**. Due to horizontal differences in air pressure, air flows from areas of high pressure to areas of low pressure.

- Wind direction is determined with the help of a wind vane and the speed or velocity of the wind by **Robinson's Cup Anemometer**. In a wind vane, the head denotes the direction from which the air is blowing and the tail denotes the direction to which air is blowing.

The two most well understood and significant winds for climate and human activities are the **'trade winds'** (winds blowing from sub-tropical high pressure area, 30°N and S latitude, towards the equatorial low-pressure belts are the extremely steady winds, blowing from west to east) and **'westerly winds'** (wind blowing from the sub-tropical high-pressure belts towards the polar low-pressure belts. They blow from southwest to northwest in the Northern hemisphere and from northwest to southeast in the Southern hemisphere. These winds are best developed between 40 and 60 latitude. These are also called **roaring forties, furious fifties** and **shrieking sixties).** Near the equator, the trade winds clash with each other and on the line of convergence, they rise and cause heavy rainfall. The winds that reverse their directions periodically with season are called **periodic winds.**

- Winds, which blow throughout the year from one latitude to another in response to the latitudinal differences in air pressure, are called **prevailing winds** or **planetary winds** (*e.g.* trade winds). The monsoons are the best examples of large-scale modifications of planetary wind systems.
- The word monsoon is derived from the Arabic word *'Mausim'* which means season.
- In India, 80–90% of the rainfall is obtained from two monsoons namely Southwest monsoon and Northeast monsoon or Retreating monsoon. Normally, the southwest monsoon reaches the Kerala Coast by the end of May, advances along the Konkan coast in early June and extends over the entire country by the end of July. The rains continue up to the end of September, when the southwest monsoon recedes.
- In November and December, northeast monsoon is the main contributor of rain over the southeastern part of the peninsular region especially Tamil Nadu.
- The monsoon depression can be said to be the single factor that controls the distribution of rainfall all over the India. These low-pressure systems, which originate near the head Bay of Bengal, end travel across the country in a west and northwesterly direction. Heavy rainfall mainly occurs to the

south of the tracks of these depressions. At least 3 to 4 depressions are found in a month during these monsoons. When they take a normal Northwesterly track, there is flood in the Northern India and drought in the peninsular parts and drought in the Northern part of India. These depressions terminate in Gujarat and Rajasthan. When a depression reaches these states, they get abundant rains, otherwise they are subject to prolong drought.

- Occasionally there are one or two monsoon breaks during the monsoon seasons. These types breaks normally bring floods in the rivers of Northern Bengal and Bihar.

Thunderstorms and Hails

Sudden change in the weather of a particular place with heavy downpour is called thunderstorm whereas, hail is the rain in form of crystals. Thunderstorms and hails are predominant weather phenomenon before and after monsoon seasons. Important thunderstorms are *Kalbaisakis* in Bengal and *Andhis* over Northwest India. **Nimbostratus clouds indicate thunderstorms.**

Cyclonic Storms

Cyclonic storms are caused due to creation of low-pressure zones. They cause severe damage to the coastal zoos. On an average 2-3 storms may be expected in a year. They are associated with the high wind speeds and tidal winds.

Western Disturbances ITCZ (In)

Series of disturbance in the form of cloudy weather and light rainfall in the plains and snow fall in the hills. These disturbances affect the *rabi* crop.

5. **Relative humidity:** Humidity refers to water vapour content of atmosphere. The amount of water vapour present in the atmosphere depends upon the wind and temperature. Wind distributes the water vapour in the atmosphere. Higher the temperature more is the amount of water vapour that can be held by the atmosphere.

The quantity of water vapour held in the atmosphere at any particular time can be expressed as:

(i) **Absolute humidity** (g/m^2) = wt. of water vapour/volume of air

(ii) **Specific humidity** (w/w) = wt. of water vapour/wt. of air including water vapour.

(iii) **Relative humidity** = water vapour present in the air/ water vapour required for saturation. It denotes the saturation level of atmosphere, which influences evaporation and transpiration. Therefore it is widely used in agriculture.

- **Vapour pressure deficit** is a difference between the saturation levels of the atmosphere.
- **Psychrometer** is used to measure RH, **Assman's Psychrometer** for RH in crop canopy and **Hygrograph** records humidity continuously on paper graph.

6. **Evaporation and evapotranspiration:** Evaporation is the process by which water in a liquid state is converted to vapour and escapes into air. It is expressed in mm/day. It is measured to calculate irrigation requirement.

- **USWB Class 'A' Open pan evaporimeter; sunken screen evaporimeter and can evaporimeter** (for field) are used to measure evaporation. Open pan Evaporimeter
- Evapo-transpiration (Et) = evaporation from the soil surface + transpiration from plant.
- In India area of high annual Et are extremes west including Rajasthan (Jaisalmer) and extreme south of Tamil Nadu, the Tuticorin.
- Evapo-transpiration is measured using **Lysimeters.**

7. **Precipitation:** Falling of any type of condensed moisture to the ground surface is called **precipitation. Rainfall** is the precipitation in the form of liquid drops larger than 0.5 mm in diameter. **Drizzle** is a rain of very light intensity composed fine droplets measuring less than 0.5 mm in diameter barely reaching the ground. **Mist** is the rain of very light intensity even water droplets completely evaporate before falling to ground. **Glaze** is the rain that falls on the ground having subfreezing temperatures and freezes into a coating of rice. **Rime/ Freezing fog** is the rain, which forms frostily deposits. **Snow** is solid precipitation in form of ice crystals formed after sublimation of water vapour at subfreezing temperature. **Sleet** is also a solid precipitation in the form of small particles of clean ice; it is formed when droplets come into contact of freezing temperature. **Hail** is the precipitation that consists of hard rounded pellets of ice coming along thunderstorms from cumulo-nimbus clouds. Lines joining places of equal rainfall are called **Isohyets.**

- **Rainfall is measured with Simple rain gauze** (*e.g.* Symones type, Roorkee type) and **Automatic rain gauze** (*e.g.* Float siphon, Weighing bucket type, Tipping bucket type).

- The constancy by which a place receives rainfall is studied with the help of coefficient of variation (CV). High CV denotes very little or scanty rainfall. In parts of Sourashtra and Kutch the CV of rainfall is 40-50%, whereas in Western Rajasthan it is 80-90% causing severe drought. **Palmer's drought index** is calculated from data on rainfall, Evapo-transpiration and Soil moisture.
- **Cloud seeding technique:** Silver iodide is used for cold clouds and sodium chloride for warm clouds in order to nucleate artificial rain.

8. **Clouds:** Clouds are formed when air mass is the upper atmosphere cools down due to the expansion, caused by low pressure leading to condensation of water vapour. In the clouds, Cirrus refers feathery/fibrous; stratus-stratified; cumulus-heaps; alto- above the normal height; and nimbus to rain. Clouds are classified into ten forms according to international cloud atlas of World Meteorological Department (1956):

Clouds	Characteristics
Cirrus	Fibrous, highest, detached.
Cirro-cumulus	Patches of small globular masses covering considerable portion of sky.
Cirro-stratus	Thin whitish veil of sheet, milky white, halo around the sun.
Alto-stratus	Uniform grey white sheet, large part of sky may obscure, good rainfall in middle and high latitude.
Alto-cumulus	Elliptical globular units.
Stratus	Uniform grey cloud sheet, usually completely cover sky.
Nimbo-stratus	Thick dark grey shapeless clouds sheet with irregular broken clouds associated with steady precipitation.
Strato-cumulus	Large rolls arranged in long parallel bands cover most of the sky.
Cumulus	White clouds of summer usually cauliflower shaped.
Cumulo	Nimbus 3-8 km vertically form thunder-storms.

Observatories: In India there are three kinds of observatories *viz.*

(1) climatic observatories (for studying effect of climate change); (2) synoptic observatories (for the study of weather); and (3) agro-meteorological observatories (for agricultural research).

Agro-climatic Zones of Uttar Pradesh

Uttar Pradesh has been divided into nine agro climatic zones, these include (1) Western Plain zone, (2) Central-Western Plain zone, (3) Southern Western Plain zone, (4) Semi-arid zone, (5) Central Plain zone, (6) Bundelkhand zone, (7) North Eastern Plain zone, (8) Eastern Plain zone, and (9) Vindhyalayan zone.

Agro-Climatic Zones of India

1. **Western Himalayan zone:** Zone includes Himachal Pradesh, U.P. hills, 3 sub-zones of J & K, skeletal soils of cold region including podsols mountain meadow soils, hilly brown soils, silty loam. It is composed of undulating terrain, steep slopes prone to erosion.
2. **Eastern Himalayan zone:** Arunanchal, Nagaland, Manipur, Tripura, Mizoram, Assam, Jalpaiguri and Coochbihar districts of West Bengal. High rainfall and forest cover. Mostly alluvial soils are found. Shifting cultivation is practised. Zone is prone to floods.
3. **Lower Gangetic plains zone:** West Bengal. High rainfall area.
4. **Middle gangetic plains zone:** Eastern U.P. (12 districts), Bihar (27 districts). Potential for exploitation of ground water, canals and tube wells.
5. **Upper Gangetic plains zone:** Include 32 districts of western U.P.
6. **Trans gangetic plains zone:** Punjab, Haryana, Delhi, Chandigarh, Sriganganagar Distt of Rajasthan. Highest net sown, irrigated, crop intensive, water utilization.
7. **Eastern plateau and hill zone:** Eastern Madhya Pradesh, South West Bengal, Inland Orissa. Medium soil depth and undulating topography is the characteristic feature. Tank and tube wells are prominent.
8. **Central plateau and hill zone:** South U.P., Eastern Rajasthan, most of Madhya Pradesh.

9. **Western plateau and hill zone:** Major parts of Maharashtra, parts of Madhya Pradesh, one district of Rajasthan. Only 12.4 per cent area is irrigated. Canal is the main source of irrigation.
10. **Southern plateau and hill zone:** Parts of Andhra Pradesh, Kereal and Tamil Nadu (35 districts). Mostly semi-arid climate.
11. **East coast plains and hills zone:** East coast of Tamil Nadu, Andhra Pradesh and Orissa. Alluvial soils and coastal sand is mainly present. Canal and tank irrigation is main source.
12. **West coast plains and Ghats zone:** West coast of Tamil Nadu, Kerala, Karnataka, Maharastra, Goa. Variety of soil types, rainfall pattern, cropping pattern.
13. **Gujarat plains and hills zone:** 19 districts of Gujarat. Arid climate. Well and tube well irrigation.
14. **Western zone:** 9 districts of Rajasthan. Hot desert, sandy, erotic Rainfall, high evapo transpiration, scanty vegetation, ground water level is low, brackish. Drought is common.
15. **Islands zone:** Andaman and Nicobar, Lakshadweep. Equatorial, more than 300 cm. Rainfall for 8 months. Forest zone.

Institution Involved

- Indian Institute of Tropical Meteorology, Pune
- Central Arid Zone Research Institute (CAZRI), Jodhpur, Rajasthan
- International Crop Research Institute for Semi-arid Tropics (ICRISAT), Hyderabad
- NRC on Medium Range Weather Forecasting (NCMRWF), New Delhi
- Strongest recorded wind : In USA on April, 1934 the record wind speed was 371 kmph (231 mph).

□□□

4

Soil Science

Soil is the fine earth covering land surfaces that has the important function of serving as a substratum of plant, animal, and human life and acts as a reservoir of nutrients and water.

- **Pedology** is a scientific discipline concerned with all aspects of soils, including their physical and chemical properties, the role of organisms in soil production and in relation to soil character, the description and mapping of soil units, and the origin and formation of soils.
- **Edaphology** is the study of soil in relation to growth, nutrition and yield of crops.
- Soil is a natural body of mineral and organic constituents consists of a sequence of chemically and biologically differentiated layers, called **horizons**.
- **Soil profile** is the vertical section of soil through all its horizons and it extends up to its parent materials, whereas layers in a soil profile are called **horizons**. Typically there are **four horizons**: O, A, B and C. 'O' horizon is the organic horizon found in the forest soils. 'A' horizon is beneath the 'O' horizon. A_2 layer of A horizon is called **elluvial horizon**. 'B' horizon is found beneath the 'A' which is called illuvial horizon. 'C' horizon consists of unconsolidated parent materials. Below the 'C' horizon 'R' layer is found which is rightly called **Bedrock**.
- The **horizon A** extends from the ground surface to the unmodified regolith or consolidated rock. In this horizon weathering is most intensive. Accumulation of organic matter including humus having 1 per cent of carbon up to a depth of 15 inches, occur in this horizon.
- The **horizon B** lies immediately beneath the 'A' horizon and may reach a depth of 65 to 90 centimetres. It is a zone of moderate weathering and accumulation of many products removed from the horizon 'A'.

- The **horizon** C contains the parent materials, from which the 'A' and horizons 'B' are formed. The 'R' layer is not the part of the soil proper; it is an underlying layer that has properties much different from those of the horizon 'C' immediately above it and that influences the soil by its position.

Processes of Soil Formation

Weathering is the disintegration and decomposition of parent material. **Disintegration** breaks consolidated rocks into unconsolidated parent materials, which on further breaking and chemical decomposition forms soil. **Physical weathering** involves soil agents such as temperature, water, wind, plants and animals and processes such as exfoliation (surface peeling off of rocks), alternate wetting and drying, freezing and thawing, burrowing of animals, root penetration, etc. **Geo-chemical weathering** is the weathering taking place at the layers down below, whereas pedo-chemical or pedogenic weathering is the one taking place at the surface and subsurface layers.

- Stages of soil formation: **Infancy > Youth >Maturity > Old age**.
- Water on freezing expands 9% by volume.
- **Hydrolysis** is most important chemical weathering process.
- Soils found at the site of formation are called **sedentary soils**, whereas soils found far away from the site of formation are called **cumulous** or **transported soils**.
- **Agents of soils transportation and name of soil formed through them**: River water: Alluvium; Lake water: Lacustrine; Sea water: Marine; Wind: Aeolian (Coarse particle) and Loess (Fine particle); Gravity: Colluviums; Ice: Moraine.
- **Pedon** is the smallest volume that can be recognized as a soil.
- The term **Solum** is used to denote horizon A + B together and **Regolith** means horizon A + B + C together.
- **Dokuchalev**, the **Father of Soil Science**, gave the factors of formation, which later were modified by **Jenny**.
- There are various processes of soil formation out of which two, the **Laterisation** and **Podzolization** are important. Laterisation occurs in warm humid tropical conditions, whereas Podzolisation occurs in the cold humid temperature conditions. In laterisation, silica is removed from 'A' horizon and sesquioxides are left, whereas in podzolisation, sesquioxides are leached from the 'A' horizon and silica is left out in upper

layers. The term Laterite is used for making **bricks**. Laterite is very well weathered soils.

The Clay Formation

The most fundamental soil forming process is weathering, during which crystals of feldspars and other silicate minerals are broken and release chemical compounds such as bases, silica, and oxides of iron and aluminium (specifically the sesquioxides: Fe_2O_3 and Al_2O_3). **Leaching** removes most of the bases and some of the silica, and the remaining silica combines with alumina to form crystalline clays. Rapid leaching leaves little silica to combine with alumina and results in what are known as 1 : 1 clays consisting of a tetrahedral (silica) and octahedral (alumina) layer. Slow leaching leads to the formation of 2 : 1 clays, consisting of one octahedral (alumina) layer sandwiched between two tetrahedral (silica) layers.

- Alumina rich 1 : 1 clays have low cation-exchange capacity whereas Silica rich 2 : 1 clays have higher cation exchange capacity but not higher than that of amorphous clay.
- Soils rich in 1 : 1 clays usually have a stable structure and swell very little when moistened; on the other hand, a soil rich in 2 : 1 clays, more especially **montmorillonite,** has a weak structure, low permeability, and swells easily when moistened. Tropical soils are usually dominated by 1 : 1 clays. Temperate countries contain chiefly 2 : 1 clays.
- Mica is a platy silicate mineral that is directly altered (*i.e.*, changed in mineralogical composition) to clays.
- Weathering is more rapid in a medium containing organic acids. Hence, when soil is covered by raw humus, as in podsolic regions, amorphous clays are formed as a result of the rapid weathering.
- The illuvial horizon of podsols, called the 'spodic' horizon, is rich in amorphous clays and resembles and (volcanic ash) soil in many respects.

Classification of Silicate Clay

It is based on tetrahedral and octahedral layers, silicate clays are classified as:

Kaolinite group (Kaolinite, Deckite, Halloysite, 1 : 1): In this one tetrahedral silica layer is alternating with one octahedral alumina layer, held together by oxygen atoms. The whole unit is held together with hydrogen bonding. On moistening no expansion occurs.

Smectite group (Montmorillonite, Andellite 2 : 1): An octahedral alumina sheet is sandwitched between 2 tetrahedral silicon layers.

Illite (Hydrous mica, 2 : 1): Isomorphous substitution occurs in tetrahedral layers. 'K' is strongly attached between crystal units. 'K' prevents the expansion.

Chlorite (2 : 1 : 1 or 2 : 2): Silicate of 'Mg' with some 'Fe' and 'Al'. 'Mg' octahedral is sandwitched between 2 silicon tetrahedral sheets. It is Mg rich clay mineral.

Vermicullite: Isomorphous substitution at silicon tetrahedral unit. CEC is very high.

Humification

Second best soil constituent after clay is organic matter. Roots die continuously and other vegetation and crop residues transformed by microorganisms into a mixture of organic substances called humus. The humus may be distinguished:

1. **Mild humus** is dark in colour, well saturated with bases, especially calcium, rich in humic acids, and serves to stabilize clay. Grasses produce mild humus rich in humic acids, and conifers produce raw humus rich in fulvic acids. Calcium-rich soils produce milder humus than hydrogen-saturated soils.
2. **Raw humus** is reddish in colour, less basic, rich in fulvic acids, and favours dispersion of clay.

Biological Transport of Elements

Plants absorb various elements from the profile and deposit them, with their residues, on the soil surface, a process that counteracts leaching. In soils rich in bases leaching is more important. This accounts for the fact that base saturation and pH usually increase with depth. In acid soils, leaching is difficult because cations are firmly retained by soil colloids, and biological transport to the surface prevails.

- **Solonization**: Sodium clay is easily dispersible, and in sodium soils it is transported from the surface to some depth. Sodium soils swell when moistened, however, which impedes clay movement, so that clay illuviation takes place near the surface rather than at depth. This process is called **solonization**, or **solonetization**, and results in sodium-saturated soils (solonetz) that have a richer clay horizon at depth than at the surface.

- **Brunisolic soils:** Fulvic acids react with iron and may cause its eluviations. Due to this reason soils formed under forest vegetation produce humus rich in fulvic acids, which is often leached. Soils having fulvic acid and free iron are popularly known as brunisolic soils, as they are brown in colour.
- **Podsolization:** Weathering in a strongly acid medium produces an eluviation of the sesquioxides (Fe_2O_3 and Al_2O_3) in result of weathering. The upper horizon of these soils are rich in sand and illuvial rich in amorphous clays from the spodic horizon. Such soils are called **podsols**.
- The organic matter that produces eluviation of clay or sesquioxides decays and cannot accumulate in the illuvial horizon; but when this horizon is waterlogged or when its temperature is very low, organic matter accumulates and a humus illuvial horizon forms. Such soils are called **humus podsols.**
- **Rubification:** In dried soils precipitates of iron and organic matter cannot accumulate and even organic matter disappears by decay, causing formation of irreversibly dehydrated iron sesquioxides. Process is known as **rubification**, and the resulting soils, called cinnamonic, are rich in fine crystallites of dehydrated iron sesquioxides.
- **Ferrugination:** Iron sesquioxides adhere firmly to sand grains and gravel giving them red colour and may cement them to form an iron pan (fragipans). The process is most common in soils formed from materials that release much iron upon weathering.
- **Gleization:** Under waterlogging conditions, iron becomes ferrous leading to ferrous soils. These soils have gray-blue colour, therefore, sometimes they are called **gley**, and the process is called **gleization.**

PHYSICAL PROPERTIES OF SOIL

Soil is a three phased, particulate, disperse, porous, open and heterogeneous system. An ideal soil contains 50% solid matter (45% mineral matter + 5% organic matter) and 50% pore space (25% air + 25% water).

Size of soil particles

International system		Atterberb system	
Gravel	2 mm or more	Coarse sand	2 mm- 0.2 mm
Very coarse sand	2.0 mm-1.0 mm	Fine sand	0.2mm-0.02 mm
Coarse sand	1.0 mm- 0.5 mm	Silt	0.02 mm- 0.002 mm
Medium sand	0.5 mm-0.25 mm	Clay	< 0.0002 mm
Fine sand	0.25 mm = 0.1 mm		
Very fine sand	0.1 mm = 0.05 mm		
Silt	0.05 mm = 0.002 mm		
Clay	Less than 0.002 mm		

- India follows international classification.

Texture

The relative proportion of the various soils separate is called **soil texture**. There are 12 textural groups. These groups sand, loamy sand, sandy loam, loam, silt loam, silt, sandy clay loam, clay loam, silty clay loam, sandy clay, silty clay and clay. Soil texture is a static property it cannot be changed.

- Gravel is neither a soil separate nor a soil texture. Because particles ^{3} 2.0 mm are included into category of soil.
- Texture of soil is determined by International Pipette and Bouycous Hydrometer method. Stoke's law is applied in the determination of soil texture.

Structure

Soil structure is the arrangement of soil aggregates or primary and secondary particles. Structure is denoted in GRADE-CLASS-TYPE. Structural grade denotes the durability or stability of the aggregate, such as structureless, weak, moderate strong and very strong. Class of soil structure denotes size of the aggregates, *e.g.* very fine, fine, medium, coarse and very course.

- There are four types of soil structures *viz.* platy, prismatic or columnar, angular or sub-angular blocky and spheroidal (granular and crumb structure). Structure of the soil can be easily changed by management practices. Loamy texture and granular or crumb structure is best suited for agriculture crops.
- **Bulk density** (Apparent density) of soil is the mass of unit volume of soil including the pore space, whereas Particle

density (True density) is the mass of unit volume of soil without pore space. Bulk density (*A*) is approximately half that of particle density. So bulk density is always lower than particle density. Value of bulk density is 1.4 to 1.8 mg/m^3. Bulk density increases on compaction whereas it decreases on addition of organic matter. The particle density (*T*) of soils is around 2.65 mg/m^3 due to dominance of quartz whose density is also of the same value.

- Porosity percentage can be calculated by the formula.

  Porosity percentage $=100 \times (T - A/T)$.
- Pore spaces in course-textured soil are filled with air, whereas in fine textured soil are occupied by water.

Types of Structures

1. **Platy:** When particles arranged around a plane, generally horizontal.
2. **Prism-like:** When particles arranged around a vertical axis and bounded by relatively flat vertical surfaces, *e.g.* prismatic and columnar types.
3. **Block-like**: When particles arranged around a point and bounded by flat or rounded surfaces *viz.* angular and subangular types.
4. **Spheroidal:** When particles arranged around a point and bounded by curved or very irregular surfaces that are not accommodated in the adjoining aggregates, *e.g.* granular and crumb types.

Soil Colour

Colour of soil is correlated with Munsell Colour Chart. Three variables are used to denotes soil colours. They are Hue dominant wavelength, value-relative lightness of the colour and chromapurity of the colour.

Plasticity and Cohesion

Plasticity is the capacity of the soil to change its shape under moist conditions. Cohesion is the capacity to stick particles together. Plastic soils are cohesive in nature.

Soil Colloids

Soil colloids are consisting of two phases: the dispersed phase (clay and humus) and dispersion medium (water). Colloids may be of two kinds: inorganic colloids (colloid of clay) and organic colloid (colloids of humus). Particles smaller than one micron are said to exhibit colloidal activity. Colloidal property increases with decrease in diameter of soil particles.

- Colloids exhibit the property of surface activity such as the capacity to hold solid, gases, salts and ions.
- Soil colloids have high exchange capacity, which increases with silica sesquioxides ratio.

Soil Water

Water has maximum density at 4 °C. The diameter of water molecule is 3 angstrom. Water has high dielectric constant of 80. Its surface tension is 7.2×10^{-2} N/m.

- Structure of water molecule is hexagonal lattice with the angle of 104° 5′.
- If water is allowed to drain by gravity after supplying water, some water remains even after drainage due to gravity. It is called **field capacity**. Water at field capacity is held at 1/3rd atm pressure. Water held between 1/3rd and 15 atm is called **available water.**
- **Darcy's law** in soil deals to hydraulic gradient.

Water held in soil in the following forms:

1. **Hygroscopic water:** It occurs as a thin film (4-5 mm) and is held tenaciously with a tension of 31 atm or more. It is not available to plants.
2. **Capillary eater:** It forms a continuous film around soil particles (outside the film of hygroscopic water). Capillary water is held at a tension ranging from 1/3rd to 31 atmospheres.
3. **Gravitational water.** It is free water held at a tension below 1/3 atm pressure. It saturates the soil and percolates downwards under the influence of gravity.

Soil Air

Soil air contains about 90% carbon dioxide, about 10% nitrogen and a trace of oxygen. Ideally 2/3rd soil pores are filled with water and 1/3rd with air. Submersed soils contain less oxygen. **Fick's law** deals about the diffusion of gases in soil, represented into ODR (Oxygen Diffusion Rate).

Soil Temperature

In soils, heat is mainly transferred through conduction. Sandy soils absorb more heats than clayey soils because the specific heat of water is required to heat a substance is 4-5 times that of soil particles. **Fourier's law** deals with conduction in soils.

CHEMICAL PROPERTIES

pH is the negative logarithms of H^+ ion concentration. **Sorenson** gave pH scale. There are two types of acidities in soil *viz.* **active acidity** and **potential acidity**. **pH** measures only active acidity, potential acidity forms the bulk of the soil acidity. It is greater than active acidity. Soil with pH less than 6.5 are acidic, 6.5 to 7.5 are neutral and above 7.5 are alkaline.

- One unit change in pH changes H^+ ion concentration by 10 times, 2 units by 100 times and so on.

Electrical Conductivity (EC)

It is the property of soil to transfer an electrical charge (reciprocal to resistance). It is used for measurement of salt contents of soil (through an extract). It is measured at 25 °C in millimmhos (mmhos)/cm through conductometer.

Ion Exchange

It is the most important process occurring in soil, and measured as sum of total exchangeable cations absorbed by soil. Ion exchange is a reversible process. Soil colloids are the seat of ion exchange.

- CEC (Cation Exchange Capacity) is measured at pH 7 and expressed as milliequivalents (m eq)/100 g of soil. CEC varies greatly with nature and amount of clay and organic matter. Kaolinite has 3-10, Illite 10-30, Montmorillonite 80-150 and organic matter > 200 CEC.

Base Saturation

It is the extent to which the adsorption complex of soil is saturated with exchangeable cations other than hydrogen. It is expressed as a percentage of the CEC. It can be calculated as,

- Base saturation= $\dfrac{Na^{-} + K^{+} + Ca^{++} + Mg^{++}}{CEC} \times 100$
- Fertile soils are saturated with Ca^{++} and Mg^{++} ions. If soil is saturated with more than 15% exchangeable sodium, then that

soil is called alkali soils and those saturated with H^+ ions are called **base unsaturated** or **acidic soils.**

Organic Matter (OM)

OM on decomposition by the process of humification gives rise to humus. Humus is amorphous in nature. In India OM is very less because of tropical and subtropical climate. In hilly and high altitudes, OM is above 1%. In mangrove it is 10-30%. Carbon Nitrogen (CN) ratio of OM is 10 : 1 whereas that of Indian soils is 5 : 1 to 25 : 1 with an average of 14 : 1. Organic soils are called **Histosols.**

- Organic matter **decomposition stages**: First sugars and starch followed by protein, hemicelluloses, celluloses fatty acids and finally lignin and waxes.

BIOLOGICAL PROPERTIES

There are number of microbes presents in soil which includes in order of abundance, Bacteria > Actinomycetes > Fungi > Algae. Bacteria occur in neutral to alkaline pH, fungi in acid pH and algae in shade areas.

- The smell of soils after fresh showers is due to actinomycetes.
- Some of the nitrification inhibitors are N-serve and AM. Field capacity and more than 5.0 pH is the optimum condition for nitrification.

MINERALOGICAL PROPERTIES

There are primary, secondary, accessory and amorphous minerals.

- **Primary minerals** occurs as Feldspars > Quartz > Mica > Limestone > Hornblende and Augite> Olivine and serpentine. Serpentine is the hydrated silicates of Magnesium.
- Secondary minerals:

1. **1 : 1 one silica and one alumina layer:** Kaolinite, Halloysite and Dickite.
2. **2 : 1 two silica and one alumina layer:** Montmorillonite (expanding), Vermiculite (slightly expanding) and Illite (none-expanding and 15% of silica is replaced by Al^3 and K^+ ions). Illite is also called **hydrous mica.**
3. **2 : 1 : 1 or 2 : 2= chlorite:** The crystal unit is composed of one 2 : 1 unit (like mica and montmorillonite) and one octahedral unit, Brucite $(Mg_3 (OH))_6$.

- **Accessory minerals:** B-Tourmaline, F-Topaz, P-Apatite, Ti-Rutile and Anatase.
- **Amorphous clay minerals:** Allophane, found in soil order Andosols.
- Negative charge is due to exposed surface of clay and isomorphous substitution.

SOIL SURVEY, CLASSIFICATION AND SOILS OF INDIA

There are two types of soils survey *i.e.,* Reconnaissance Soil Survey (RSS) and Detailed Soil Survey (DSS). In RSS: 1′ = 1 mile; Toposheets of 1 : 5,00,000 to 1 : 1,00,000 or aerial photo of 1 : 25,000 or 1 : 50,000 is used. Observations are once at 3-6 km. DSS: 1′ = 8 mile or 1′ = 16 mile, cadastral maps of 1 : 5,000 to 1 : 8,000 or aerial photo of 1 : 10,000 is used. Observations are at once 1/4 -1/2 km. Forest area is surveyed by RSS .

Soil Classification

India, from 1969, follows USDA's comprehensive system of soil classification called **soil taxonomy**. It is type of multi-category classifications including soil order, great group, sub-group, family and series.

Soils of India

Soils	Characteristics and distribution
1. Red soils	Red colour is due to various Fe oxide presence; formed *in-situ*; also called **sandy soil** or **red alluvium**; formed from granite and shales; deficient in organic matter; low base exchange capacity; kaolinite present; poor in N, P, K; pH varying 7 to 7.5. Most of the red soils have been classified in the order 'Alfisols'.**Areas**: Andhra Pradesh, Madhya Pradesh., Orissa, Bihar (Chhota Nagpur), Tamil Nadu, Assam, Goa, Parts of Kerala, Maharashtra, Karnataka and West Bengal.
2. Laterite and Lateritic soils	Mostly found in high rainfall area as under high rainfall conditions silica is released and leached downwards and the upper horizons of soils become rich in oxides of iron and aluminium; acidic in reaction; deficient in lime; pH 5-6; low base exchange capacity. Most of the laterite soils

	have been classified in the order 'ultisols' and a few under ' oxisols'.**Areas**: Hilly regions of Deccan Karnataka, Kerala, Madhy Pradesh, Ghat regions of Orissa, Andhra Pradesh., Maharashtra, West Bengal, Tamil Nadu and Assam.
3. Black soils	Formed by the lava ejected by volcanoes several millions year ago. Dark grey to black colour with high clay content; developed from basaltic rocks under semiarid conditions; known as **regur** or **black cotton soils**; well in moistening or wetting; shrink or crack on drying; pH 7.5-8.5; deficient in 'N', 'P'; rich in 'K' and 'Lime'; high base exchange. These soils are classified in the order 'Entisols', 'Inceptisols' and 'Vertisols'.**Areas**: Maharashtra, Gujarat, Andhra Pradesh, Madhya Pradesh, Tamil Nadu, etc.
4. Alluvial soils	Grey in colour; sandy to clay loam texture; deficient in 'N', 'P' and humus; rich in lime; pH 7-8; low base exchange capacity. Most of the alluvial soils have been classified in the orders 'Entisols', 'Inceptisols' and 'Alfisols'.**Areas**: River belt of Indo-Gangetic plains, Brahmaputra valley and almost all states of North and South.
5. Desert soils	Brown to yellow brown colour; sandy to loamy in texture; receive rainfall 10-50 cm; pH ranging 8.0 to 8.5; low nitrogen content; high soluble salts. They are classified in the order 'Aridisols' and 'Entisols'.**Areas**: Desert area of Haryana, Punjab, Rajasthan.
6. Saline and Alkaline soils	Saline soils contain excess of natural soluble salts dominated by chlorides and sulphates; saline soils are formed in arid and semi-arid regions; sodic or alkali soils contain high exchangeable sodium salts. These soils are classified under 'Aridisols', 'Entisols' and 'Vertisols'.**Areas**: Both kinds of salt affected soils occur in different parts of India like U.P., Haryana, Punjab, Maharashtra, Tamil Nadu., Gujarat, Rajasthan and Andhra Pradesh.

7.	Peaty and Marshy soils	Black in colour; occur in humid regions with accumulation of high organic matter; highly acidic having pH 3.5; free aluminium and ferrous sulphate are present; best suited for rice cultivation.Waterlogged soils in the depression of dried rivers and lakes are blue in colour due to the presence of ferrous iron.**Areas**: Peaty soils found in Kerala; marshy soils are found more in coastal tracks of Orissa, West Bengal, Sunderban area and South East coast of Tamil Nadu.
8.	Tarai soils	Found in 30 km sub-belt of Himalaya; dark brown in colour; high humus content; acidic in nature.

- Largest area (75 Mha) is occupied by alluvial soils. Black soils (vertisols mostly) are 72 Mha, and characterized by Gilgal (shining surface), nicro relief (ups and downs), self-churning, smectite (expanding clays).
- 2/3rd part of Tamil Nadu. is consisted of red soils. The parent material for red soils is mostly granite.
- Laterite (bricklike) is older than lateritic soils. Laterites are the oldest or most withered soils.
- Problem soils occupy 10 Mha areas, of which saline soils are 7.2 Mha and alkali soils, 2.8 Mha. These soils are highest in U.P.
- Saline soils are formed mainly in aridand semi-arid regions due to rising of salt level in the watertable. Also it is due to secondary salinisation and poor quality of irrigation water. Saline soils are called **white alkali** and said to cause boron toxicity.
- **Acid sulphate soils**: pH less than 3.5 due to hydrogen sulphide gas production. Found in Kerala and Sunderbans; causes Akiochi disease; cat clays are associated with these soils. Acid soil has very low pH. Reclaimed by addition of lime or limestone or calcite ($CaCO_3$), Dolomite ($CaCO_3$ $MgCO_3.2H_2O$), slaked lime Ca $(OH)_2$ and Burnt lime or quick lime (CaO).

Soils Order and Their Respective Groups

There are 12 orders and the lastly added 11th and 12th orders are andosol and gelisols, respectively.

Order	Soils groups
1. Vertisols	Black cotton soil or regur soil.
2. Mollisols	Dark coloured, based rich soils of steppes, Ca dominates.
3. Aridisols	Desert soils.
4. Alfisols	Non-calcic soils; ochric epipedon; red and laterite soils of India (particularly Kerala).
5. Inceptisols	Soils of humid regions. Indo Gangetic plains and Brahmaputra valley soils.
6. Histosols	Organic soils called bogs, peat, muck. 20 per cent organic carbon present.
7. Oxisols	Having oxic and plinthite horizon. Laterite soils.
8. Ultisols	Clay translocation; intense leaching noticed; found in Assam, Northeast Himalayan region.
9. Spodosols	Cemented by iron that rests on fragipan; placic or albic horizon; also called acid ashy grey sand or dark sandy loams.
10. Entisols	Little; no evidence of development of pedogenic horizons; erosion faster than the soils development. Found in deserts of Rajasthan.
11. Andosols	Found in volcanic eruption areas and contains high content of allophane.
12. Gelisols	Found in arctic regions.

- Inceptisols followed by entisols are mostly found in India.

Estimation of Soil Nutrients

It is done through soil testing. The total soluble salts are achieved by EC; organic carbon by Walkley and Black method; available N by alkaline permanganate method; available Phosphorus by Olsen's or Bray's method; available Potassium by Neutral Normal Ammonium Acetate method.

HORIZON NOMENCLATURE

Usually the upper horizon, which is rich in humus and may be eluvial, is called A; it may be "humic" (**Ah**), eluvial (**Ae**), or "bleached" (A_2).

- The horizon in which clay has been illuviated is called **Bt**; that of amorphous clays produced by podsolization ("spodic horizon) called **Bir**; and that of humus illuviation **Bh**.

- Weathered material that has not been sufficiently enriched in humus to be humic and has not had important illuviation of clay or humus is called C.
- Underlying consolidated rock is called an **R** horizon.
- A horizon of **lime** accumulation is usually called **ca**; an accumulation of **gypsum** is indicated as **cs**; a horizon unusually rich in easily **soluble salts** is represented by **sa**; **cn** designates an accumulation of ferruginous concretions and nodules; **mf** a ferruginous hardpan; **mc** a calcic hardpan; **xa** fragipan (fragile hardpan cemented with iron); **G** denotes strong gleying; **g** moderate gleying.
- Poor soils in nutrient are called **dystrophic**, whereas the term **eutrophic** represents for highly nutritive soils.

SOIL GROUP CLASSIFICATION AND NOMENCLATURE

Seventh approximation system: It is a system based on measurable soil properties of soil formation. The seventh American Approximation System was introduced in 1960. It is the first approach to deliver precise definition of soil groups and pedologic terms.

- **Podsols** are also called ashy soils. Soils with a deep, dark horizon rich in organic matter and well saturated with calcium are termed as **chernozems** or black soils. Soils of rather undifferentiated profile and of red colour are named as **krasnozems** or red soils.
- Soils denoting special features may be **included** in soil nomenclature. For example: clay, loam, sand refer to soil texture; **lithosol** (stony, gravelly); **regosol** (sandy); **aeolian** (formed by wind, dune); and **hammada** (stony desert).
- **Takyr** and **lunettes** are special kinds of saline soils.
- Roof clays and sulphate saline clays (cat clays) are special kinds of clays.
- Prairie, chestnut (kastanozems), and reddish chernozemic are different kinds of chernozemic soils. Podsolized, leached, or degraded chernozems are types of brunisolic or leached soils.

CLIMATIC ELEMENTS OF THE SYSTEM

Although soil temperature and moisture are not intrinsic soil properties, they are used as diagnostic features in the Seventh

Approximation System; *i.e.* soils are classified according to the climate in which they are encountered. Such formative elements include: **bor**, boreal; **cryo**, very cold; **pergelic**, permafrost; **torri**, torrid (usually dry); **trop**, small annual range of temperature; **ud**, usually humid; **ust**, dry but not long dry seasons; and **xer**, for long dry seasons.

ROCKS

Earth crust consists of the Elements, Oxygen, Silicon, Aluminium, and Iron, etc. in the decreasing order of their amounts. Rocks are divided into three categories, *viz.* Igneous, Sedimentary and Metamorphic.

- **Igneous rocks**: These rocks are formed by solidification of molten Magma from the interior of the earth. Granite, Basalt (Deccan trap), Gabbro, Pumice, Rhyolite and Tracheolite. Acidic igneous rocks contain 60-75% quartz, *e.g.* granite whereas basic rocks contains less than 50% of quartz, *e.g.* Granite and Basalt.
- Igneous rocks or primary rocks constitute 18%, in which Granite constitutes 15% and Basalt 3%.
- **Sedimentary rocks:** These rocks are formed by the sediment deposits on the ocean beds. Limestone, Sandstone, Shale, Dolomite and Conglomerate. Gypsom and Chalk.
- **Metamorphic rocks:** Such rocks are formed from igneous and sedimentary rocks *e.g.* Marble, Gneiss, Graphite and Slate.
- Gneiss is formed from Granite, Marble from Limestone, Graphite from Coal, Slate from Shale and Quartzite from Quartz or Sandstone.
- Sedimentary rocks or stratified rocks constituting 74% of total rocks, in which Shales constitute 52%, Sandstone 15%, and Limestone and Dolomite 7%.
- Other rocks constitute 8% of total rocks.
- **Petrology** is a science of rocks. **Petrography** is a description of rocks. **Petrogenesis** is a study of origin of rocks.

Classification of Rocks

1. **Igneous rocks** based on mode of origin, they are classified as:

(*i*) **Intrusive/plutonic** (solidification of magma at moderate depth), *e.g.* Granite

(*ii*) **Extrusive/volcanic** (solidification at the surface of the earth), *e.g.* Basalt.

Based on chemical composition, they are:

(*i*) **Acid rocks** having 65-75% silica *e.g.* Granite, Sandstone (*ii*) **Neutral/ intermediate** has 55-65% silica *e.g.* Andesite, Deorite.

(*iii*) **Basic** has 40-55% silica *e.g.* Limestone.

2. **Sedimentary rocks:**

A. Fragmented/mechanically **formed by deposition and cementation of erosion products, *e.g.* Sandstone, Shales.**

B. Chemically formed: **Chemically formed rocks are further divided into:**

(*i*) **Inorganically formed**: Formed either by (1) Evaporation, *e.g.* Gypsum, Halite or (2) Precipitation and Flocculation, *e.g.* Limestone, Dolomite.

(*ii*) **Organically formed,** *e.g.* Lignite, Anthracite.

3. **Metamorphic rocks:** The chemical and physical transformation of igneous and sedimentary rocks produces metamorphic rocks. Heat and pressure convert rocks as Granite, Rhylite and Andesite develop into Gneiss; Mica into Schist, Shale, Siltstone; Mudstone into Slate; Sandstone to Quartzite; Limestone and Dolomite to Marble.

COMPONENTS OF SOIL

Soil is composed of two phases: the solid phase includes mineral matter and organic matter; pore phase includes water and air; constitutes 50% each. **Solid phase** constitutes 45% mineral matter and 5% organic matter. Rest 50% is a **porous phase,** which has 25% water and 25% air.

1. **Mineral matter** includes rock fragments, colloidal clay particles, etc. Majority of Indian soils are mineral soils.

(*i*) **Primary** minerals include Quartz, Feldspar that have high amount of pyroxine, amphiboles, olivines and micas.

(*ii*) **Secondary** minerals include clay minerals/ hydrated iron and aluminium oxide minerals.

(*iii*) **Amorphous** minerals are allophane (volcanic origin), silicate clay, limonite, hematite (secondary minerals)

2. **Organic matter**: Soils having > 20 per cent organic constituents are designated as organic soils.

- In good soils there has to be at least 10 per cent aeration.

PROBLEM SOILS AND THEIR MANAGEMENT

The problem soils are formed either due to unfavourable condition or man-made causes. These include acid soils and salt affected soils.

Acid Soils: Acid soils are based on unsaturated soils. There are no free H^+ ions. Acid soils absorb exchangeable hydrogen ion leading to lower pH of soils. Such soils have low pH; high proportion of exchangeable H^+ and Al^{3+} ions; dominance of Kaolinite and Illite types of clay minerals; low CEC and high base unsaturation; Fe and Mn toxicity. Based on nature of acidity they are classified as:

(*i*) **Active acidic soils:** In such soils H^+ ions remain present freely in the soil solution and produce limited acidity, *e.g.* acid sulphate soils

(*ii*) **Reserve/potential acidic soils:** In soil colloidal complex, exchangeable H^+ ions are absorbed reducing soil pH lower than neutral.

- In normal soils H^+ ions are replaced by Ca^{++}, Mg^{++} ions.

Development and formation of acid soils: The acid soils are formed due to following reasons:

(*i*) **Leaching:** Due to heavy rainfall lime and other bases like Ca^{++}, Mg^{++} are leached down in lower layers of soil. H^+ and carbonic acid develop to replace the basic cations. This condition occurs where annual rainfall is more than 100 cm.

(*ii*) **Microbial action:** Microbes induce acidity in soil; if it is not neutralized by any means it creates long-term acidity in soil.

(*iii*) **Acidity from parent material:** The parent materials which are acidic in nature, and formation of soil occurs from such parent materials, then the developing soil will certainly be of acidic in nature, *e.g.* Soils from granite rock are acidic in nature.

(*iv*) **Removal of bases from soil:** If any crop removes more bases, then it will increase acidity. *e.g.* Sugarbeet absorbs more bases thereby increasing acidity.

(*v*) **Application of fertilizers:** Some fertilizers, if continuously used, causes acidity in soil, *e.g.* Ammonium sulphate, Ammonium nitrate increase soil acidity.

Management of Acid Soils

(i) **Addition of lime:** In acid soils H^+ ions are more than the OH^- ions. When lime is added the soil solution becomes charged with calcium ions. In turn Ca^{2+} ions exchange with H^+ ions. These H^+ ions combines with OH^- ions in water or CO_2 to form H_2CO_3 (carbonic acid), thus soil becomes neutral. Lime is added according to pH and type of soil, *e.g.* at pH 6.4 sandy soils need 75 kg/ha, loam soil require 112 kg/ha and clay loam 175 kg/ha of lime for reclamation. For every fall of 0.2 pH from 6.4 (say 6.2, 6.0, 5.8 so on), lime is added @ 150, 225, 350 kg for sandy, loam, clay loam soils, respectively plus base amount at 6.4 pH.

- **Lime as reclaiming agent:** Lime is added to neutralize acidity and to increase the pH, so that the availability of nutrients is increased.
- **Fertilizers in reclamation:** Ammonium sulphate and Ammonium chloride should be replaced with Calcium Ammonium Nitrate (CAN). Any citrate soluble phosphate fertilizer is good source of phosphorous for acid soils, *e.g.* Di-calcium phosphate (DCP), Tri-calcium phosphate (TCP). Potassium sulphate is a suitable source of 'K' for acid soils. But MOP is better than K_2SO_4 because Cl of MOP replaces OH^- ions; thereby release of OH^- ions tends to increase the pH.

(*ii*) **Use of basic fertilizers:** Basic fertilizers like sodium nitrate, basic slag reduce soil acidity. Basic slag obtained from iron and steel industry can be substituted for lime. It contains about 48-54% of CaO and 3-4% MgO.

(*iii*) **Growing acid tolerant crops:** The crops like Rice, Potato, Oat, Sweet Potato, Castor, *Echinochloa, Paspalum* (highly tolerant); Barley, Wheat, Maize, Turnip, Brinjal (moderately tolerant); Tomato, Carrot, Red Clover (mild tolerant); are effective in acid soils.

Crops Suitable for Cultivation in Acid Soils

pH Level	Suitable crops
4.5	Citrus, Blue berries
5.0	Tobacco, Apple, Grapes, Plum, watermelon
5.5	Cowpea, Soya bean, Cotton, Wheat, Oat, Peas, Tomato, Sorghum
6.0	Peanut, Cabbage, Carrot, Onion, Radish, Spinach, Cauliflower
6.5	Alfalfa, Sugarbeet

Saline and Alkaline soils: In such soils the exchangeable complex sodium ions predominates.

Saline soils or Solonchak or White alkali: In such soils soluble salts like Na^+, Ca^{2+}, Mg^{2+} as cations and Cl^- , SO_4^{2} as anions are present. The concentration of carbonates, potassium, bicarbonates and nitrate is completely low. Saline soils have (1) High osmotic pressure of soil solution hinders water uptake by roots of plant. (2) Exchangeable sodium percentage is below 15 per cent (3) pH is below 8.5. (4) Electrical conductivity of saturated extract is more than 4 m mhos/cm^2. (5) Total soluble salt (TSS) content is more than 0.1 per cent and; (6) White salt crust appears on the soil surface in the dry season.

Alkali soils or Solonetz: Exchangeable sodium present. These soils are classified as:

(*i*) **Non-saline alkali soils or Black alkali:** In such soils the colloidal complex is saturated with exchangeable sodium (the usar soils). Soil contains sodium carbonate in abundance, which is toxic to roots of plants. Exchangeable sodium percentage is greater than 15 per cent. pH ranges from 8-10. EC of TSS content is less than 4 m.mhos/cm^2. Sodium absorbs organic matter so OM is depleted therefore soils are almost barren.

(*ii*) **Saline alkali soils:** These soils have both saline and alkaline property. The sodium salt is excess in amount. The ESP is more than 15 per cent. pH is around 8.5. TSS more than 0.1 percent. EC greater than 4 m mhos/cm^2.

Formation of Saline and Alkali Soils

1. **Arid and semiarid climate:** In areas of aridand semiarid climate, the rainfall is low and evaporation is high. The soluble salts are not leached down completely and they occur in the surface layer when evaporation takes place.
2. **Poor drainage of soils:** The salts impeded drainage soluble salts occur in the lower layer and come up when water evaporates.
3. **High watertable:** When ground water contains soluble salts. When watertable comes up the salts simultaneously move up through capillary action and accumulate on the surface.
4. **Sea water inundation:** When flow of sea water happens to be on land, the accumulation of salts occurs inside the land.
5. **Irrigation water:** If irrigation water itself is rich in salts upon irrigation adds salts to the soil.
6. **Salts blown by wind:** Near the sea area, the salts are blown with the winds. In Rajasthan the salts blew from sea cause alkali soils.
7. **Excess use of basic fertilizers:** Fertilizers like sodium nitrate and basic slag develop alkalinity.

Reclamation of Saline Soils

1. **Leaching of soluble salts:** Leaching salts below the root zone is done by flooding the land with water and allow water to stand for a week. In the mean time gypsum is applied in the standing water. Drain the standing water, after salts are dissolved.
2. **Scrapping out surface soils:** Scrapping salts from the surface may remove salts.
3. **Use of acidic fertilizers:** Acidic fertilizers like ammonium sulphate can be used.
4. **Growing salt tolerant crops:** Crops like Barley, Sugarcane, Cotton, Sugarbeet, Lucerne (highly tolerant); Wheat, Rice, Sorghum, Maize, Flax, Castor (moderately tolerant); and Beans, Radish, White clover, Pulses, Linseed, Sesamum (mild tolerant).

Reclamation of Alkali Soils

1. **Use of gypsum in leaching:** Gypsum helps in leaching salts below the root zone.
2. **Use of sulphur:** Sulphur is oxidized to sulphuric acid, thereby converting sodium carbonate into sodium sulphate.
3. **Addition of organic matter:** Organic matter supplies food for the bacteria that stimulates oxidation of sulphur to sulphate form.
4. **Growing sodium tolerant crops:**

Highly tolerant	Tolerant	Sensitive
Karnal grass, Rhodes grass, Bermuda grass, Rice, Sugarbeet, Datepalm, etc.	Wheat, Barley, Oat, Senji, Berseem, Sugarcane, Bajra, Cotton, etc.	Cowpea, Gram, Groundnut, Lentil, Peas, Maize, etc.

5. **Use of sulphuric acid:** Sulphuric acid converts sodium carbonate into sodium sulphate, which leached down easily into lower layers of soil.
6. **Addition of molasses:** Molasses provide energy for microbes, which produce organic acid. The organic acid neutralizes bases.

Carbon : Nitrogen (C : N) ratio: It is the ratio of utilizable carbon to total nitrogen, in other words, the ratio of the weight of organic carbon to the weight of the total nitrogen in a soil or organic matter is called

CN ratio

- When fresh plants are added to soil, they are rich in carbon instead of nitrogen resulting wider C : N ratio up to the 40 : 1. Upon the decomposition, this ratio changes into humus, then the C : N ratio is 10 : 1.
- C : N ratio of Legumes is 20 : 1 to 35 : 1; Farm yard manure 100 : 1; Bodies of microbes 4 : 1 to 9 : 1; Arable soils 5 : 1 to 15 : 1; Humus 10 : 1.
- 30 parts of Carbon and 1 part of 'Nitrogen' is essential to start the process of decomposition, *i.e.* 30 : 1 ratio.

Institutions involved

1. Institute of Soil Science, Nabi Bagh, Berasia Road, BHOPAL (M.P.)

❑❑❑

5

Soil Conservation

Soil conservation is the using and managing the land based on its capabilities, involving the application of best practices to result in greatest profitable production without damaging the land. It is accomplished by land use based on its capabilities, conservation of soil and moisture to avoid damage to soil and use of suitable soil and crop management practices.

- H.H. Bennett is known as the **Father of soil conservation.**

SOIL EROSION

Soil erosion is the wearing away of land surface by the action of natural agencies. Nature requires approximately 1,000 years to build up 2.5 cm of topsoil. An extreme example of sand movement from the coast due to wind erosion is to be seen in the Saurashtra region of Gujarat where the once-flourishing ports are now covered with advancing sanddunes. Active soil erosion occurs due to floods over 140 Mha of land resulting into loss of 6,000 MT of fertile soils containing 5.5 MT of NPK.

Losses /Due to Erosion

Loss of rainwater and fertile topsoil: Due to erosion great loss of these important resources occurs. In India it is 16.3 t/ha/yr whereas permissible limits is 11 t/ha/yr.

- **Silting in reservoirs:** In India 29,000 hectare meter (hcm) of sediments forming 64 million hectare (Mha) of catchment goes to 21 major reservoirs.

Types of Erosion

1. **Geologic erosion:** This is a normal feature of any landscape. Geologic erosion takes place to make equilibrium between the removal and formation of soil.

2. **Accelerated soil erosion:** The removal of the surface soil as a result of human and animal interference is called **accelerated soil erosion.** It takes place at a much faster rate than that of formation of soil.

Agencies of Erosion

1. **Wind erosion:** It is the serious problem of barren lands of arid and semiarid zones, where the wind velocity is at the highest.

Mechanism of wind erosion: In wind erosion movement of soil particles takes place through following three stages:

(*i*) **Surface creep:** Rolling of coarse (0.5-3.0 mm diameter) particles of soil by wind along the surface of ground is called **surface creep.** Approximately 5-25% weight of soil loss occurs by surface creep.

(*ii*) **Saltation:** It is the movement of soil particles in series of jumps. These could be of 30-60 cm high and the particle size ranges between 0.1-0.5 mm diameters. Approximately 50-75% weight of soil loss occurs by saltation.

(*iii*) **Suspension:** Floating of dust particles (<0.1 mm size) through the air is called **suspension.** They are carried in suspension up to 100 km. The particles come down only with rains or when wind velocity is decreased. Approximately 3-4% weight of soil loss is by suspension.

2. **Water erosion:** Water can be distinguished in following forms, *viz.* (*i*) Splash erosion, (*ii*) Sheet erosion, (*iii*) Rill erosion, and (*iv*) Gully erosion, (*v*) Landslide or landslip erosion, and (*vi*) Stream bank (torrent) erosion.

(*i*) **Splash erosion:** The splattering of small soil particles caused by the impact of raindrops on wet soils is called **splash** erosion. The loosened particles are subsequently removed by surface run-off.

(*ii*) **Sheet erosion:** Sheet erosion removes a thin covering of soil from large areas, more or less, uniformly during every rain, which produces a run-off. This type of erosion can be detected by the muddy colour of the run-off from the fields.

(*iii*) **Rill erosion:** When after run-off water movement creates small channels, the scrapping off soil takes place, such erosion is called rill erosion.

(*iv*) **Gully erosion:** It is the second (advance) stage of rill erosion. When rill erosion is neglected the tiny grooves develop into wider and deeper channels. The gullies tend to deepen and widen with every heavy rainfall. The gullies are described as,

Symbol	Description	Specifications
G_1	Very small gullies	Up to 3 m deep and up to 18-meter wide bed. Side slopes vary.
G_2	Small gullies	Up to 3 m deep and bed width greater than 18 m. Side slopes vary.
G_3	Medium gullies	Depth between 3 and 9 m. Bed width not less than 18 m. Side slopes uniformly sloping between 8 and 15 per cent.
G_4	Deep and narrow gullies	3 m to 9 m deep. Bed width less than18 m. Side slopes vary.

(*v*) **Landslide or landslip erosion:** A landslide is defined as an outward and downward movement of the slope-forming material like natural rocks, soil etc. The fundamental causes of landslides are topography of the region and geological structure. The immediate cause of a slide may be an earthquake or heavy rainfall, which unduly saturates the ground or a part of a road.

(*vi*) **Streambank (Torrents) erosion:** Streams are characterized by wide-spreading beds on emergence from the hills with ill-defined banks, flashy flows and swift currents.

Factors Affecting Erosion

(*i*) **Rainfall**: High amount and high intensity of rainfall accelerate erosion.

(*ii*) **Vegetation**: Good vegetation reduces erosion by obstructing the beating action of raindrops and providing good infiltration facility to rainwater through root activities.

(*iii*) **Soil types**: Length of slope increase erodibility. If percentages of slope increase is 4 times it doubles the velocity of water flow. Light soils are easily detachable but less erodible, whereas in heavy soils are not easily detachable but run-off is usually more. Erosion increases with increase in fineness of soil. Moist soils are more susceptible to erosion than dry soils. Soil with high CEC is less erodible, whereas soils having high salts and sodium are highly erodible.

(*iv*) Human activities like extracting farming like cultivation on steep slopes and cultivation along slopes, deforestation and excessive grazing causes erosion.

- **Universal Soil Loss Equation: $A = RKLSCP$**

where, A = Predicted soil loss (t/ac/yr);
R = Rainfall and run-off factor;
K = Soil erodibility;
L = Slope length;
S = Steepness (of slope);
C = Soil cover and management;
P = Erosion control practice.

- **Design of composite check dams:** The design discharge (maximum run-off) through the drainage channel is computed from the empirical formula: $Q = 0.0028\ C\ I\ A$.

where, Q = Run-off in cubic metres per second (m^3/sec).
C = Run-off coefficient (a value calculated by constants of slope and soil type)
I = Rainfall intensity in mm/hr.
A = Watershed area in hectare.

- The **length of the spillway** is determined by the formula:

$$Q = 1.70\ LH^{3/2}$$

where, Q = Run-off in cubic metres per second (m^3/sec).
L = Length of the weir notch in metres.
H = Height in metres of water flow above the spillway level.

LAND USE BASED ON ITS CAPABILITIES

Land capability classification: It is a grouping of land based on their capability and limitation. It was first carried out by U.S. Soil Conservation Service. The guiding principles of soils are in combination with climate, landscape, feature, erodibility and other natural hazards. The land capability classification is made into three categories namely, (A) Capability class, (B) Capability sub-class, (C) Capability units.

A. **Capability class:** There are eight classes that are indicated by roman numbers. Class I to IV are suitable for cultivation and V to VIII are unsuitable for cultivation.

Land Suited For Cultivation

Class I (Light green colour): Soils in this class are very good. The soils are deep productive, easily worked, and nearly level. They are not subject to over flow (run-off) damage. However, they are subject to fertility and puddle erosion. Soils of this class have no or only slight risk of damage.

Class II (Yellow colour): Soils of this group are good for cultivation with easily applied practices. They are subject to moderate risk of damage. Soils of this group have gentle slopes, subject to moderate erosion. They are subject to occasional overflows. These soils may require special practices such as contour tillage, crop rotation, and water control devices.

Class III (Red colour): Soils of this class are subject to severe risks. They are moderately good soils. They can be used regularly for crops. These soils have moderately steep slopes, are subject to more severe erosion and low inherent fertility. These soils require cropping systems that produce adequate plant cover. In strip cropping sole crops should be grown instead of cultivated row crops in this class of soils.

Class IV (Blue colour): Soils of this class have severe permanent hazards if used for cropland. The soils are fairly good soils as found on steep slopes which are subject to severe erosion. The soils are shallow or moderately deep, low in fertility. Such soils are usually used as pastureland, although a grain crop may be grown once in five or six years.

Land Not Suited For Cultivation

Class V (Dark green or colourless): Soils of this class should be kept for permanent vegetation. They should be used for pasture or forestry purposes. Cultivation is not feasible, however, because of wetness, stoniness, or other limitations. The land is nearly levelled; therefore it is subject to only slight erosion by wind or water, if properly managed. They have few permanent limitations.

Class VI (Orange colour): Soils of this class should be used for grazing and forestry. They are steep or shallow in topography. Land of this class is either steeper or more subjects to wind erosion than Class IV. Class VI land is too steeps stony, wet for cultivation.

Class VII (Brown colour): Soils of this class are subject to severe permanent limitations (or hazards). They are fair to poor for grazing or forestry. They are steep, eroded, shallow, droughty or swampy and are unsuitable for cultivation.

Class VIII (Purple colour): Soils of this class are extremely rough, arid or swampy and are unsuitable for cultivation. They are not suited for forestry or grazing also. They may be used for wildlife, recreation or watershed uses.

B. **Capability subclass:** Subdivisions of capability classes made on the basis of four limitations namely, risk of erosion (*e*) wetness, drainage or overflow (*w*), rooting zone limitation (*s*) and climatic limitation (*c*).

- Sub classes are mapped by adding the limitation symbols to the capability class number e.*g*. II (*e*) or III (*c*) etc. Subclasses are indicative of the degree and kind of limitation.

C. **Capability units**

These are subdivisions of capability sub classes. Capability units consist of soils, which are sufficiently uniform in their characteristics, potentialities, and limitations requiring fairly similar conservation treatments and management practices.

- Land capability classes can be changed towards classes if the existing limitations are permanently removed. Likewise further deterioration in existing conditions can shift the capability to a poorer class.

Soil and Moisture Conservation Measures

Agronomic measures: Out of agronomic measures the following considerations should be taken care of,

1. **Contour cultivation**: Contour cultivation should be done when slope is less than 2% where ploughing and sowing across the slopes reduces run-off.
2. **Tillage**: Conservation tillage, which includes minimum tillage and zero tillage. Conservation tillage reduces soil loss by 50% over conventional tillage.
3. **Subsoiling**: Disturbing the subsoils by suitable implements increases infiltration and reduces run-off.
4. **Mulching**: Increases infiltration thereby reducing run-off and soil loss.
5. **Cropping system**: Cover crops like Green Gram reduces run-off and soil loss. Multiple cropping reduces soil loss over monocropping.
6. **Strip cropping**: It is a system of growing strips of erosion resisting crops (close growing crops) alternated with strips of

erosion permitting crops (erect growing crops, *e.g.* millets + pulses).

7. **Use of chemicals and amendments**: Chemicals and amendments like polyvinyl alcohol @ 480 kg/ha, Bitumen, FYM, green manures and other organic manures form stable aggregates reduce soil loss.

Mechanical measures:

1. **Contour bunding:** The contour bunds being on the same elevation assures that the depth of water against the bund is uniform throughout its length. It ensures uniform distribution of water above the bunds. Here, cultivation possibilities are better than any other type of bund. As the bunds are at regular intervals they intercept the run-off from attaining erosive velocity.
2. **Graded bunding:** The graded bunding is recommended where rainwater is not readily absorbed either due to high rainfall or low intake of soil. The soil from excavation of channel is formed into a bund on the downstream to guide the water into a grassed waterway. The cross section and grade of the channel are designed for conveying the peak rate of the inter-bunded run-off at non-scouring and non-silting velocity.
3. **Broadbased terrace:** A terrace is a combination of ridge and channels built across the slope on a controlled grade having wide base and low height of ridge. Through these terraces excess water is let at non-erosive velocity into grassed waterways. It is suitable for black soil with higher intensity of rainfall.
4. **Bench terracing:** It consists of transforming steep land into a series of level across the slope of land. The field is made into a series of benches by excavating the soil from upper part of the terrace and filling the lower part. It reduces the slope length thereby reducing the erosion. Bench terracing is suitable for undulated land with steep slope (16 to 33%) and good soil depth (to avoid exposure of unproductive subsoil during levelling). Slopping inwards terraces are maintained in high rainfall (>750 mm) and poor infiltrating soils. Table levelled terracing is maintained in medium (750 mm) rainfall and highly permeable deep soil. Slopping outward terracing is done in low (< 750 mm) rainfall and permeable medium deep soils.
5. **Zing terracing:** In these terracing total field is divided into two, the one donor area and other is the recipient area in the ratio of

2 : 1. The recipient area is levelled and provided with bunds whereas donor area remains unlevelled, creating a zigzag appearance. Zing terracing cuts down the length of slope, harvests run-off from operand for benefit of crops in lower end, ensures adequate drainage during heavy rains and suitable for areas of medium to deep soils, moderate to heavy rainfall and moderate slope (3 to 10%).

6. **Contour trenching:** These trenches are made as discontinuous structure of 60 metre long, 60 cm wide with 48 cm height spaced at a distance of 10 to 30 metre between each trench. The trenches are half filled with diagonally excavated material and remaining half form the spoil bank. Rainwater is held in the trenches, which support the growth of vegetation on the spoil bank. Generally trees and grasses are grown.
7. **Vegetative barriers:** They are closely spaced plantations grown along contour for erosion control in agricultural lands. These barriers check the velocity of overland flow and entrapment of silt load behind them. Trees like vetiver or khus (*Vettiveria zelanica*) and *Tripsacum* spp. are used for the purpose.
8. **Grassed waterways:** These are drainage channels either developed by shaping the existing drainage ways or constructed separately to agricultural lands. Such drainage waterways are made suitable by perennial grasses of deep-rooted and spreading type, which are not edible for cattle and also leave water at non-erosive velocity. Grasses used for grassed waterways are *Panicum repens, Paspalum notatum, Cynodon dactylon, Cynodon plectostachyus* and *Brachiaria mutica*.

WATER HARVESTING TECHNIQUES

Water harvesting is defined as the collection and storage of water on the surface of the soil for subsequent use.

Water Harvesting In Arid Regions

1. **Run-off farming:** It is the farming in which water collected in large areas is let to few fields. The ratio of catchment area to command area is 50–100 : 1. Catchment area is subdivided with individual collection channels. For the purpose spillways, check dams and grassed waterways are used.
2. **Water spreading:** It is the deliberate diversion of flood waters from their natural courses and spreading of it over adjacent plains.

3. **Micro-catchment:** It is the catchment around 16 m^2 area surrounded by dirtwall of 15-20 cm, in the center of which a basin of 40 cm deep is dug and a tree is planted in it. The basin stores run-off from the catchment.

Water Harvesting In Semi-Arid Regions

1. **Dug wells:** Dug wells are used to collect and store underground water. However, the quality of water is poor due to dissolved salts in such water.
2. **Tanks:** Traditional tank system contains the following components, the catchment's area, storage tank, bund, sluice, spillways and command area. The quality of water is good.
3. **Farm ponds:** These ponds are established in low-lying area of farm used for collection of excess rainwater. The seepage loss, in ponds is quite high, which can be minimized by lining walls with bentonite clay, soil cement mixture of red and black soils.
4. **Percolation ponds:** Such ponds are created by obstruction of rivulets or gullies. Water from ponds percolate and raises water level of the region.
5. **Inter-row water harvesting:** Growing maize in beds and Rice in furrows. Excess rainfall in beds drain into furrows, which is helpful for maize and rice crop.

Run-off Induction

Run-off is induced by following ways,

1. **Land alterations**: Cleaning rocks, vegetation, and compacting the soil surface can increase run-off.
2. **Chemical treatment**: Soils can be treated with chemicals that fill pores or make soil repellant to water, *e.g.* Latexes, Asphalts, Wax and sodium salts of Silicon.

MODERN CONCEPT OF TILLAGE

1. **Minimum tillage**: Reduction of tillage to the minimum extent is necessary for ensuring a good seed bed, rapid germination, satisfactory crop stand and favourable growing conditions. It is done by combining operations like sowing and fertilization together. Methods of minimum tillage include:

(*i*) **Row zone tillage**: Primary tillage is done with mouldboard plough and secondary tillage in row zone only.

(*ii*) **Plough plant tillage**: Primary tillage is followed as usual and in secondary tillage pulverization of row zone together with sowing is done.

(*iii*) **Wheel track planting**: Primary tillage as usual and wheels of the tractor use for sowing to pulverize the row zone.

2. **Zero tillage**: In zero tillage the primary tillage is completely avoided and secondary tillage is restricted to seedbed preparation in the row zone only. Such tillage is suitable for areas where wind and water erosion is high.

Institution Involved

- Central Soil and Water Conservation Research and Training Institute (CSWCRT), Dehradun, Uttarakhand.
- Soil Conservation Research Demonstration and Training Centre, Hyderabad, Andhra Pradesh.

❑❑❑

6

Dry Land Agriculture

Comparison among Different Dry Land Farming

Constituents	Dry Farming	Dry land farming	Rainfed farming
Rainfall	<750 mm	<800 mm	>800 mm
Moisture availability	Acute shortage	Shortage	Enough
Growing season	<200 days	<200 days	>200 days
Growing regions	Arid region	Arid, Semi Arid and uplands	Humid and sub humid
Cropping systems	Single crop/ inter cropping	Single crop/ Inter, cropping	Inter/multiple cropping
Crop failure	More frequent	Less frequent	Rare
Constraints	Wind erosion	Wind erosion/ water erosion	Water erosion
Dry spell	Most common	Usual	Rare

- Total arable land in India is 143.00 Mha of which 34.0 Mha is under dry land, 61.0 Mha (15 Mha flood prone area) rainfed and 48.0 Mha under irrigated land.
- In India Dry Land Agriculture contributes to 42% of total food grains; 75% oil seeds and pulses; 70% coarse grains and pulses; > 50% rice; and 50% wheat.

Characteristics of Dry Land

Uncertain, low annual rainfall; extensive climatic hazards like drought, flood; soil surface is undulating due to extensive erosion;

holdings are large due to low density of population; type of agriculture is extensive cultivation; similar type of crops are grown; cropping intensity is 100%; crop yields are generally low; market value of the product is generally poor; and economic condition of the farmer, involved in Dry Land Agriculture is poor.

Problems in Dry Land Agriculture

1. Moisture stress due to uncertain, scarce rainwater, late onset and early cessation of monsoon, prolonged dry spell during the crop period, high evapo-transpiration losses and heavy dry winds causing moisture loss.
2. Soils have the problems of low moisture retention capacity, low fertility and high salinity.
3. Choice of crop is generally limited to drought tolerant crops only, short duration varieties those are suitable for dry farming.
4. Quality of produce from dry land is usually poor; hence there is a problem for marketing.
5. Poverty is endemic problem in dry land agriculture.

Drought: Drought is a condition of insufficient moisture supply under which plants fail to develop and mature properly. It can be easily classified based on moisture condition in three different groups:

1. **Atmospheric drought**: It is the condition caused by excessive evapo transpiration, which is not compensated by water absorbed by the plants. It could be due to high temperature, low humidity, high wind velocity, etc.
2. **Soil drought**: It is the condition caused by poor moisture content of soil that cannot supply the water need for plants.
3. **Physiological drought**: Drought caused by higher concentration of soil solution (like salinity) than plant sap, even though soil moisture conditions and atmospheric factors are conducive.

Effect of Moisture Stress on Plants

1. **Water relation:** Water potential of leaf is reduced resulting in loss of turgor pressure; reduced transpiration; and increased canopy temperature.

2. **Photosynthesis:** Photosynthetic rate is reduced due to reduction chlorophyll contents, leaf area and increase in assimilates saturation in leaves.
3. **Respiration:** Respiration causes mild stress, which increase severe stress decreasing respiration.
4. **Anatomical changes:** These include decrease in cell size and intercellular space; thicker cell wall; greater development of mechanical tissue; and increase in number of stomata per unit leaf area.
5. **Metabolic reactions:** Increase in activity of hydrolytic enzymes, decrease in peroxidase activity and proline accumulation.
6. **Hormonal relationships:** Activity of growth promoting hormones like cytokinin, gibberellic acid and IAA decreases,
   - Activity of growth regulating hormones like abscisic acid, ethylene, butane etc. increases;
   - Abscisic acid acts as water deficit sensor and controls stomata on water stress condition;
   - Ethylene produced during moisture stress causes leaf and fruit drop;
   - Butane is also an indicator of moisture stress.
7. **Protoplasmic dehydration** causes increase in viscosity and density in protoplasm.
8. **Nutrition**: Due to moisture stress NPK uptake is reduced.
9. **Growth**: Moisture stress affects germination, leaf expansion and root development.
10. **Development**: Moisture stress before flowering increases the crop duration whereas after flowering decreases the crop duration.
11. **Reproduction and grain growth**: Moisture stress at panicle initiation reduces number of flowers; during anthesis causes pollen drying; during grain development reduces yield.

Drought resistance: It is the capacity of plants to endure drought condition without suffering any irrevocable injury and to grow successfully and mature properly. It could be achieved either by avoiding stress, escaping from drought or tolerating stress.

1. **Escaping from drought:** There are some plants (usually low yielder and extremely short life of 5 to 6 weeks) that confined to a particular season do not have particular mechanism for overcoming the moisture stress, *e.g.* Ephemerals.
2. **Avoiding moisture stress**: It is the ability of plants to maintain a favourable water balance and turgidity even when exposed to drought conditions, thereby avoiding stress and its consequences. It can be achieved either by conserving water through restricted transpiration or by accelerating water uptake in plants.

Mechanism of Conserving Water in Plants

(*i*) **Stomatal mechanisms**: Stomata are usually open at morning hours and closed during bright sunny hours. In some plants these stomata are found in the deep cavities/ depressions, and reduce the rate of transpiration.

(*ii*) **Increase photosynthetic efficiency:** Some plants conserve water in plants by increasing photosynthetic efficiency, *e.g.* C_4 and CAM plants.

(*iii*) **Reduction in leaf area:** Plants conserve moisture by reducing tillering and leaf size or by foliar movement of leaves like rolling, curling and parahelionastic (parallel to sun rays as in legumes) movement of plants or by dropping senescence of leaf.

(*iv*) **Leaf morphology**: Leaf morphology like thick cuticle, waxy surface, spines, and pubescence of leaf increases reflectance, thus reducing solar radiation incidence.

(*v*) **Lipid deposits**: Lipid deposits on plants surface reduces water loss, *e.g.* soya bean and sorghum.

(*vi*) **Water storage in plants:** Some plants may confer an adaptive mechanism in dry condition by lowering transpiration rate, *e.g.* pineapple.

Mechanism to Accelerate Water Uptake by Roots

Effective root system like vertical growth of roots, deeper roots and higher density of roots/unit volume of soil accelerate the water uptake; high root to shoot ratio; high osmotic pressure of plants to absorb water; increase in liquid phase conductance by increasing either diameter of xylem vessels or their number.

Tolerating Water Stress

Drought tolerance is the tolerance of plants to a level of stress at which 50 per cent of cells die, because water potential of plants is reduced hence the adverse affect is felt. Drought tolerance is achieved by mitigating stress and by showing high degree of tolerance.

Mitigating moisture stress: Under this condition plant get adapted for maintaining turgor pressure even under high drought conditions. Moisture mitigation is as follow:

(*i*) **Resistance to dehydration**: Plants develop morphological adaptation to accumulate sufficient solutes to maintain higher cell pressure (turgor) that prevents internal desiccation.

(*ii*) **Prevention of leaf collapse**: Plants develop morphological adaptations like thick cell wall, sunken stomata, waxy/lipid coating on leaves, and presence of spines to prevent cell collapse by transpiration loss.

High degree of tolerance: The death of plants can be avoided either by reducing metabolic strain or plastic strain during drought. **Metabolic strain** of plants is the adverse influence of drought on metabolism of plants.

- **Photosynthesis**: Moisture stress leads to partial or complete closure of stomata, which affect the process of photosynthesis. Resistant plants are able to keep their stomata open in the condition of stress.
- **Protein synthesis**: Moisture stress leads to the loss of RNA, which results in breakdown of proteins leading to accumulation of amino acids to a toxic level. Resistant plants are able to combat loss of RNA in the adverse conditions.

Plastic strain: It is the irrevocable loss of plant tissue due to severe stress. It can be brought out by killing the transpiring portions and keeping propagation material without desiccation; and killing of above ground parts and keeping underground parts like runners, bulbs, etc. alive and dormant.

Suggestion to Enhance the Productivity of Dry Farming Areas

Success in dry land areas can be achieved by conserving moisture, water harvesting and selecting suitable crop/varieties based on local condition, suitable agronomical methods, considering the available facilities and constraints.

(*i*) **Moisture conservation and water harvesting:** Summer ploughing, contour bunding, compartmental bunding, broad based bunding, ridges and furrows, scooping of land and bedding systems can conserve moisture.

(*ii*) **Reduction of evapo transpiration losses:**

- **Mulching:** Mulching increases soil moisture retention by reducing evaporation, run-off and increasing infiltration. Mulches include soil mulch (loosened surface soil), stubble mulch (crop stubbles as mulch), straw mulch, plastic mulch (polythene or PVC etc.), and vertical mulch (stubbles in trenches across slope).
- **Anti-transpirants:** Some chemicals have property to close the stomata and reducing transpiration. These chemicals include Phenyl Mercuric Acetate, Hydroxy Sulphonates, Alkyl Succinic Acids (ASA), Adol 52 (a formulation of alcohol), OED gree (a combination of docosanol and octadecanal with ethylene oxide), S-600 (a plastic, transpiring spray), hexadecanol and octadecanol. ASA penetrates the lipid layer of root membrane and increases the permeability of water eightfold.
- **Other chemical** *viz.* Mobileaf, Hexadecanol, Silicone form film over the plant surface and reduce transpiration. Chemicals like 5% Kaolinite, Celite (a diatomaceous earth product) works as reflectants of light, thus reduce transpiration.

- **Growth retardants:** Chemicals, like Cycocel, are used as growth retardants.
- **Windbreaks and shelterbelts:** Windbreaks are any structure (plant or wall) that reduces wind thrust. Shelterbelts are rows of trees planted across the direction of wind for protection of crops against wind. Shelterbelts provide protection from winds to the extent of 5 to 10 times of their height in windward side and up to 30 times in leeward side. They also reduce evapo transpiration loss and wind erosion. Trees like Neem, Cassia and Acacia are used as shelterbelts.

(*iii*) **Agronomical approach:** Summer ploughing and interculture; hardening after seed sowing; advance sowing with placement at 8 cm depth; 25% higher seed rate to facilitate thinning; application of bio-fertilizers instead of chemical fertilizers; different cropping system like agro-silvi culture system, silvi-pastoral system, agro-silvi-pastoral system and multi-forestry systems; different cropping pattern like crop rotation (Groundnut - coriander; sesamum - coriander) and intercropping (Groundnut + red gram; Sorghum + red gram); integrated weed control, integrated pest control and integrated disease management should be followed to combat all the pests.

(*iv*) **Selection of drought resistant crops and varieties:** Field crops and varieties suitable for dry lands agriculture:

Crops	Varieties	Crops	Varieties
Sorghum	K 5, K 7, K tall	Bajra	K 2, Co 6
Tenai	K 2	Red gram	Co 1,SA 1, SA2
Black gram	Vamban1, Co 1, Co 2	Green gram	Vamban1, Co1, Co 4
Cowpea	Co 1, Co 3	Castor	Aruna, Bhagya
Cotton	LRA 5166		

(*v*) **Use of specially beneficial chemicals**

- Nutrients spray with Urea, DAP and $ZnSO_4$ mitigate the moisture stress.
- Seed hardening (seed treatment for drought tolerance) with Calcium chloride @ 0.25%; chemicals of Kreb's cycle like Citric

acid, Fumaric acid, Succinic acid, Maleic acid etc.; Purine and Pyrimidine bases, which promote DNA synthesis; and Caffeine, Uracil, Xanthine, Uridine Di-phosphate hardens the seeds through synthesis of RNA.

- Some chemicals are used as soil additive *e.g.* Aluminium-0.05 mg/kg of soil; Cobalt- 0.17 mg/kg of soil; Molybdenum-0.70 mg/kg of soil.

Institution Involved

- Central Institute for Dry Land Agriculture, Hyderabad (Andhra Pradesh).

❑❑❑

7

Manures and Fertilizers

It is now well established that at least 16 (however, unconfirmed report declare 21) plant-food elements are necessary for the growth of green plants, which include Carbon (C), Hydrogen (H), Oxygen (O), Nitrogen (N), Phosphorous (P), Sulphur (S), Potassium (K), Calcium (Ca), Magnesium (Mg), Iron (Fe), Manganese (Mn), Zinc (Zn), Copper (Cu), Molybdenum (Mb), Boron (B) and Chlorine (Cl). Some sources now claim that there are 21 essential elements, adding Sodium (Na), Vanadium (Ve), Cobalt (Co), Silicon (Si) and Nickel (Ni) to the list. Nickel along with Cobalt has been found useful in legumes.

Plant roots take up plant-food elements from the soil in the ionic forms. The positively charged ions are called 'cations' and negatively charged ions are 'anions'. Cations (represented with plus sign) include Potassium (K^+), Calcium (Ca^{++}), Magnesium (Mg^{++}), Iron (Fe^{+++}), Zinc (Zn^{++}), etc. The anions are denoted by minus (-) sign include nitrogen (NO^-_3), Phosphorous ($H_2PO^-_4$), Sulphur (SO^-_4), Chlorine (Cl^-), etc.

Arnon and Stout (1939) proposed necessity of nutrients, and based on requirement they classified nutrients as:

1. **Major or Macronutrients:** The nutrients, which are required by plants **more than 1 ppm** of weight, they are put under this category. They are further classified to:

(*i*) **Primary nutrients:** These nutrients are needed right from the beginning of germination to growth and development; therefore they are called primary nutrients, *e.g.* C, H, O, N, P, K, C, H, O, are abundantly present in atmosphere and N, P, K are supplied through fertilizers and manures.

(*ii*) **Secondary nutrients:** Such nutrients are needed during the growth of plants. These include Ca, Mg, and sulphur.

2. **Minor or Micronutrient:** The nutrients, which are required by plants **less than 1 ppm**. They are also called **trace elements**. Rests of above are trace elements.

- Nicholas in 1963 put Molybdenum and Cobalt under ultra micronutrient category.

Crop and Nutrients Removed from Soil (Kg/ha)

Crop	Yield (grain) kg/ha	N	P_2O_5	K_2O
Rice	2,240	34	22	67
Wheat	1,568	56	24	67
Jowar	1,792	56	15	146
Bajra	1,120	36	22	66
Maize	2,016	36	20	39
Barley	1,120	41	20	35
Sugarcane	67,200	90	17	202
Groundnut	1,904	78	22	45
Mustard	672	22	11	28
Linseed	1,008	19	12	33
Cotton	448	30	17	45
Jute	1,568	67	34	67
Tea	896	45	13	28
Coffee	896	34	11	34
Tobacco	1,456	94	57	91

MANURES

Manures are the organic material used to fertilize land, usually consisting of the faeces and urine of domestic livestock, with or without accompanying litter such as straw, hay, or bedding. Manure is rich in organic matter, or humus, and improves the soil's capacity to absorb and store water, thus preventing erosion.

Farmyard Manure (FYM)

Incorporation of FYM (*i*) improves the soil tilth and aeration, (*ii*) increases the water-holding capacity of the soil, and (*iii*) stimulates activity of microorganisms that make the plant-food elements in the soil readily available to crops. Urine of cow contains 95% of Potassium, 63% of nitrogen and 50% of sulphur, on dry weight basis.

Compost Manure

Composting is the process of reducing vegetable and animal refuse to a quickly utilizable condition for improving and maintaining soil fertility. Development of compost occurs both in aerobic and anaerobic conditions.

1. **Aerobic process:** Aerobic process of composting completes in three different stages, (*i*) the bedding, sweepings from cattle sheds, some urine-soaked earth removed every day is collected, (*ii*) It is mixed with a little cattle dung and 2-3 handfuls of wood ashes, and (*iii*) deposited at well drained site to gradually build up a low pile of 30-35 cm height, and 5 m width. The pile must be built before start of rainy season.
2. **Anaerobic process:** The mixed farm residues are collected in pits of a convenient size. Each day's collection is spread in a thin layer, sprinkled with a mixture of fresh cow dung, ashes and water and compacted. The pit is filled till the raw material stands 38 to 46 cm above its edge, and then it is plastered with a 2-5 cm layer of a mixture of mud cow dung.

Pit Method of Composting

The material brought from the cattle shed is spread into pit. Over each layer, the slurry of dung made with 4.5 kg urine earth and 4.5 kg of inoculum taken from a 15-day-old composting pit, is spread. Finally water is sprinkled.

- **Turning:** The material is turned 3 times during the whole period of composting after every 15 days and in last days after every 30 days.
- **Enrichment of compost with phosphorous:** It is done by adding 5% superphosphate at the filling of the compost pits.
- **Enrichment of compost with potassium:** The materials with potassium if added enriches compost. Water hyacinth for example, is a rich source of potassium and other elements required by plants; potato peel is rich in trace elements; and dry potato vines contain 1% potassium, 4% calcium and 1% magnesium.

Vermi composting

Vermi-composting is the use of earthworms for composting of organic residues. It is well established that 300 tonnes of compost is produced from 1,000 tonnes of moist organic matter. The casting (excreta of earthworms) of earthworms is rich in nutrients, *viz.* N, P, K, Ca and Mg, and bacterial and actinomycetes population as well.

- **Species of earthworms for vermi-composting:** Compost worms are found on surface and are reddish brown in colour, *e.g. Lumbricus rubellus* (red worms), *Eisenia foetida, Eudrilus eugeniae* and *Perionyx excavatus*.
- **Rearing of earthworms:** The worms are reared and multiplied in shallow wooden boxes of 45 × 60 cm size, provided with drainage holes and stored on shelves and tiers. A bedding material is compounded with sawdust, cereal straw, rice husks, sugarcane trash, bagasse, paper, cardboard, coir waste, grasses etc. and moistened well with water. Mixture is stored for 30 days covered with a damp sack and is thoroughly mixed several times. After fermentation is complete, chicken manure and green matter, *e.g. Leucaena* leaves or water hyacinth is added. For each 0.1 m^2 of surface area 100 g of breeder worms are added to the boxes. Within 60 days about 10 kg of casting is produced from a one kg of worms.
- The average **nutrient content of vermi-compost** is N 0.6-1.20%, P_2O_5 1.34-2.20%, K_2O 0.4-0.67%, CaO 0.44% and MgO 0.15%.
- ***In-vitro* vermi-composting:** This is also called as bio conversion in soil, involves the application of the basal dose (5 tonnes/ha) of vermi-castings and covering with 2.5 cm layer of organic matter followed by 10 cm layer of any crop waste. The worms hatch out within 10 days.

'Night Soil' or Poudrette

Human excrements are a potential source of soil improvement, upon conversion into usable form of manure. The dehydration of 'night soil' with absorbing materials like soil, ash, charcoal and sawdust produces a poudrette that can be easily used as manure. The mixing of 'night soil' with an equal volume of ash and 10% powdered charcoal produces an odourless material, containing 1.32% potash. The addition of 40-50% of sawdust in 'night soil' yields straightway a dry, acidic poudrette.

Green Manures

Green manuring is the practice of ploughing or turning into the soil undecomposed green plant material for improving the physical condition of the soil. There are several crops, which are used for green manuring, Sunnhemp (*Crotolaria juncea*), Dhaincha (*Sesbania rostrata*), Clusterbean (*Cyamopsis tetragonoloba*), Senji (*Melilotus parviflora*), Cow pea (*Vigna catjang, V. sinensis*), Horse-gram (*Dolichos biflorus*), Pillipesara (*Phaseolus trilobus*), Berseem or Egyptian clover (*Trifolium alexandrinum*).

- **Lentil** (*Lens esculenta*) is recommended in Kashmir for green manuring in paddy. **Dhaincha** works well on alkaline and waterlogged soils. **Berseem** is well suited for orchards and the irrigated crops of cotton and sugarcane sown in spring or early summer. *Glyricidia maculata* and *Sesbania speciosa* are planted on the borders of paddy crop.

Important Crops Used for Green Manuring

	Green manure crop	Seed rate	Remarks
1.	Dhaincha		
(*i*)	*Sesbania speciosa*	15 kg/ha	Seedlings are raised and planted in rice field bunds. Yield 2-3 t/ha.
(*ii*)	*Sesbania rostrata, Sesbania aculeate*	15-20 kg/ha	Both stem and root nodules present. It can be raised in flooded condition in rice field. Yield of 22 t/ha biomass.
2.	Wild indigo (*Typhrosia purpurea*)	15-20 kg/ha	Hardy and drought resistant plant with duration of 6-8 months for single crop both for sandy and wetland soils.
3.	Indigo (*Indigofera tinctoria*)	15 kg/ha	Suitable for clay soil. It is long duration crop.
4.	Pillipesara (*Phaseolus trilobus*)	10-15 kg/ha	Its seeds are occasionally used in place of green gram as pulse. Yields 3-10 t/ha biomass.
5.	Sunnhemp (Crotolaria juncea)	25-35 kg/ha	Yield 15-20 kg/ha.

Some Green Manure Crops and Nitrogen Accumulation

	Crop	Nitrogen (%) in their parts	N accumulation (kg/ha)
1.	Dhaincha (*Sesbania rostrata*)	3.2-3.37	170-220
2.	Daincha (*Sesbania aculeate*)	2.55-3.21	130-185
3.	Sitha agathi (*Sesbania speciosa*)	2.99-3.10	115-160
4.	Sunnhemp (*Crotolaria juncea*)	2.80-3.15	80-130
5.	Pillipesara (*Phaseolus trilobus*)	2.16-2.77	85-125
6.	Wild indigo (*Typhrosia purpurea*)	2.90-3.22	70-115

Green Leaf Manures and Nitrogen Contents

	Green leaf manures	Nitrogen content (%)
1.	Neem (*Azadirachta indica*)	0.97-1.15
2.	Glyricidia (*Glyricidia maculata*)	2.25-2.75
3.	Madar (*Calotrophis gigantia*)	1.35-1.49
4.	Subabul (*Leucaena leucorcephala*)	3.50-3.70
5.	Pongam (*Pongamia pinnata*)	1.30-1.54
6.	Cassia (*Cassia florida*)	1.40-1.60

Important Manures and Their Composition

Manures	Nitrogen	Phosphate	Potash
Organic manures			
Farmyard manure	0.5-1.5	0.4-0.8	0.5-1.9
Compost	1.0-2.0	1.0	1.5
Green manures	0.5-0.7	0.1-0.2	0.6-0.8
Oil cakes			
Non-edible cakes	5.5-5.8	1.8-1.9	1.0-1.1
Castor cake	2.5-2.6	1.8-1.9	1.8-1.9
Mahua cake	3.9-4.0	0.9-1.0	1.3-1.4
Safflower cakes	4.8-4.9	1.4-1.5	1.2-1.3
Edible cakes			
Coconut	3.0-3.2	1.8-1.9	1.7-1.8
Groundnut	7.0-7.2	1.5-1.6	1.3-1.4
Linseed	5.5-5.6	1.1-1.5	1.2-1.3
Rapeseed	5.1-5.2	1.8-1.9	1.1-1.3
Sesamum	6.2-6.3	2.0-2.1	1.2-1.3
Niger	4.7-4.8	1.8-1.9	1.3-1.4

Animal manures			
Dried blood	10.0-12.0	1.0-1.5	0.6-0.8
Fish manure	4.0-10.0	3.0-9.0	3.0-15
Bonemeal	3.0-4.0	11.0-14.0	2.0-3.0
Fish meal	4.10-4.45	3.9-4.0	0.3-1.5
Horn and hoof meal	13	N	N
Cattle dung mixed with urine	0.6-0.7	0.14-0.15	0.45-0.50
Sheep dung mixed with urine	0.95	0.35	1.0
Horse dung mixed with urine	0.70	0.25	0.55
Poultry manure, fresh	1.0-1.8	1.4-1.8	0.8-0.9
Cattle dung, fresh	0.3-0.4	0.1-0.2	0.1-0.3
Human manures			
Night soil	1.2-1.3	0.8-1.0	0.4-0.5
Human urine	11.0-12.0	0.1-1.2	0.2-0.3
Plant residue			
Rice hulls	0.3-0.5	0.2-0.5	0.3-0.5
Groundnut husks	1.6-1.8	0.3-0.5	1.1-1.7
Straw and stalks			
Bajra	0.65	0.75	-
Banana, dry	0.61	0.12	1.00
Cotton	0.44	0.10	0.66
Jowar	0.40	0.23	2.17
Maize	0.42	1.57	1.65
Paddy	0.36	0.08	0.71
Tobacco	1.12	0.84	0.80
Tur, arhar	1.10	0.58	1.28
Wheat	0.53	0.10	1.10
Sugarcane trash	0.35	0.10	0.60
Tobacco dust	1.10	0.31	0.93
Dry tree leaves			
Calotropis gigantea	*0.35*	*0.12*	*0.36*
Careya arborea	*1.67*	*0.40*	*2.20*
Cassia auriculata	*0.98*	*0.12*	*0.67*
Dellinia pentagyana	*1.34*	*0.50*	*3.20*
Madhuca indica	1.66	0.50	2.00
Pongamia pinnata	3.69	2.41	2.42
Pterocarpus marsupium	*1.97*	*0.40*	*2.90*
Terminalia chebula	1.46	0.35	1.35
Terminalia paniculata	1.70	0.40	1.60
Terminalia tomentosa	1.39	0.40	1.80
Xylia dolabriformis	1.37	0.30	1.61

FERTILIZERS

Fertilizers are natural or artificial substances containing the chemical elements that improve growth and productiveness of plants. Fertilizers enhance the natural fertility of the soil or replace the chemical elements taken from the soil by previous crops.

- Government of India issued Fertilizer Control Order (1957) under the Essential Commodity Act, 1955. The order was revised in 1985 and issued on 25.09.1985.
- **Complete fertilizers** are those fertilizers, which have at least three major nutrients.
- **Straight fertilizers:** Fertilizer which contains only one primary or major nutrient, *e.g.* Urea.
- **Complex fertilizers:** Such fertilizers contain more than one primary or major nutrient elements, which are produced by the process of chemical reaction, *e.g.* DAP, Nitro-phosphate, Ammonium phosphate.
- **Low analysis fertilizers** contain less than 25% of primary nutrient, e.g. Superphosphate (16% P_2O_5), Sodium nitrate (16% N).
- **High analysis fertilizer** contain above 25% of primary nutrients, *e.g.* Urea (46% N), Anhydrous Ammonia (82.2% N), DAP (18%N, 46% P_2O_5).

Recommendations of Fertilizers for Major Crops

Crop	FYM/ Compost (t/ha)	Fertilizer nutrients (NPK kg/ha)			Micronutrients/ Remarks
Paddy transplanted for short duration	12.5	120	38	38	25 kg $ZnSO_4$
Paddy medium and long duration	12.5	150	50	50	25 kg $ZnSO_4$
Direct seeded paddy	12.5	90	45	45	12.5 kg MNM
Sorghum irrigated	12.5	40	20	0	12.5 kg MNM
Maize irrigated	12.5	135	63	50	12.5 kg MNM
Groundnut irrigated	12.5	17	34	54	10 kg Borax
Groundnut non-irrigated	12.5	23	10	45	200 kg Gypsum
Cotton	12.5	80	40	40	12.5 kg MNM
Cotton hybrid	12.5	120	60	60	5% $MgSO_4$
Cotton rice fallow	12.5	60	30	30	1% Urea + 0.1% $ZnSO_4$ for leaf reddening

Sugarcane	12.5	275	60	113	
Tobacco-chewing	12.5	85	100	50	
Chillies	25	75	35	35	
Tomato	25	150	100	50	10 kg Borax + 50 kg $ZnSO_4$
Brinjal	25	100	50	. 30	
Bhindi	25	40	50	30	
Onion	25	60	60	30	

Conversion Factors for Determining Quantities of Fertilizers: Quantity necessary for application of nutrient from fertilizers can easily be calculated by multiplying with conversion factor. For instance, if 120 kg of nitrogen is needed for application, multiply 120 with conversion factor, say 120 × 4.854 will give rise the amount of Ammonium sulphate (520.48 kg), and so on.

Nutrient	Conversion factor	Fertilizer
Nitrogen	4.854	Ammonium sulphate
Nitrogen	2.222	Urea
Nitrogen	3.846	Ammonium sulphate nitrate
Nitrogen	4.000	Ammonium chloride
Nitrogen	3.030	Ammonium nitrate
Phosphoric acid (P_2O_5)	6.250	Superphosphate, single
Phosphoric acid (P_2O_5)	12.222	Superphosphate, double
Phosphoric acid (P_2O_5)	2.857	Di-calcium phosphate
Phosphoric acid (P_2O_5)	5.000	Bonemeal, raw
Potash (K_2O)	1.666	Muriate of potash
Potash (K_2O)	2.000	Sulphate of potash
Ammonium sulphate	0.206	Nitrogen
Sodium nitrate	0.155	Nitrogen
Urea	0.450	Nitrogen
Ammonium sulphate nitrate	0.260	Nitrogen
Ammonium chloride	0.250	Nitrogen
Ammonium nitrate	0.330	Nitrogen
Superphosphate, double	0.450	Phosphoric acid (P_2O_8)
Di-calcium phosphate	0.350	Phosphoric acid (P_2O_8)
Bone meal, raw	0.200	Phosphoric acid (P_2O_8)
Muriate of potash	0.600	Potash (K_2O)
Sulphate of potash	0.500	Potash (K_2O)

Nitrogenous Fertilizers

Nitrogenous fertilizers are obtained from synthetic ammonia. The ammonia (NH_3) is used either as a gas or in a water solution, or it is converted into salts such as Ammonium Sulfate, Ammonium Nitrate, and Ammonium Phosphate, etc.

Nitrate fertilizers	Ammonical fertilizers	Nitrate and ammonical fertilizers	Amide fertilizers
Obtained naturally and synthetically. Reduce soil acidity. Contain 27% of 'Na' suitable for Cotton, Sugarbeet.	Acidic in nature. Readily soluble. Paddy is an exception, preferring in early stage of growth.	Readily soluble in water. Ammonical form resists leaching. They are acidic.	Called organic fertilizers. Readily soluble and decomposable in soil.Synthetic, non-protein in character
Sodium or Chilean nitrate (16% N). 27% of Na suitable for Cotton, Sugar beet	Ammonium sulphate (20% N + 24%S). Quick acting. Suitable for paddy	Ammonium nitrate (34-36%N), hygroscopic in nature	Urea (46% N). hydrolised by urease enzyme secreted by microbes in field.
Calcium nitrate (15.5% N)	Ammonium chloride (25%N + 66%Cl).	CAN (25%N +25%Ca)	Calcium cyanamide (20.6% N). Reduces acidity in soil.
Potassium nitrate (13%N + 36.5% K)	Anhydrous Ammonia (82% N).	Ammonium Sulphate Nitrate (26% N + 12% S)	

- Urea comes in different forms and coatings, called slow release urea or efficient urea, these include, Urea formaldehyde (38% N), Urea super granules (44% N), Plastic coated urea (44% N), Thiourea (36.8% N), Gypsum Coated Urea (32% N) and,

1. **Mud bal urea:** It is prepared with moist soil by mixing 1 Kg urea in 5 Kg of moist soil and kept in shaded place for 36-48 hrs and then applied.

2. **Neem coated urea:** Urea is coated with Neem cake. The neem cake is used @ 15-20 per cent of urea.
3. **Sulphur coated urea:** It is prepared with sulphur coating, which is used to prolong flooding situation.

- Friedrich Wohler synthesized urea for the first time in laboratory in 1828.
- Sodium Nitrate (1st nitrogenous fertilizer), and Chilean nitrate (16% N) are nitrate forms of nitrogenous fertilizers, used in acid soils.
- Ammonium sulphate 20.6% and 24%, when applied close to seed affect germination.
- Anhydrous ammonia contains highest N contents of 82%. It is dissolved in water, it is called **Aqueous Ammonia**.
- **Nitro-chalk** is obtained by mixing Ammonium nitrate with 40% Limestone or Dolomite, has 20.5% (50% in ammoniacal form and 50% in nitrate form) of nitrogen.
- Ammonium sulphate nitrate (Ammonium nitrate + Ammonium sulphate) contains 26% N of which 3/4th in ammoniacal form and 1/4th in nitrate form.
- Ammonium chloride has 26% N, possess good physical condition. Action is as similar to Ammonium sulphate but not recommended for Tomato, Tobacco, etc.
- CAN also called *Kisankhad* has 25-28% N (1/2nd ammoniacal form and 1/2nd nitrate form).

Phosphatic Fertilizers

Phosphatic fertilizers are derived from phosphate rock or bones. The more soluble Superphosphate and Triple Superphosphate preparations are obtained by the treatment of Calcium phosphate with sulphuric and Phosphoric acid, respectively. Solubility is basic problem in phosphatic fertilizers. Based on solubility they are classified as:

Water soluble **Superphosphate single, Superphosphate double, Concentrated triple super- phosphate, Mono-ammonium phosphate.**

Citrate soluble Basic slag or Thosma slag, Di-calcium phosphate.

Insoluble both in water and citric acid Rock phosphate, Bone meal.

- Rock phosphate has 25-35% water insoluble P_2O_5. Phosphoric acid and bone meal contains 20-25% P_2O_5. Citrate soluble P and Calcium phosphate have 35-38% P_2O_5. Basic slag, by product of steel industries, has 14-18% P_2O_5. Gypsum has 20% S and 23% Ca. Superphosphate single (16-18% P_2O_5), double (32% P_2O_5) and triple (44-49% P_2O_5) are the most widely used watersoluble phosphatic fertilizers in India.

- **Bio-super**, granular material, is a mixture of rock phosphate and finely ground elemental sulphur inoculated with *Thiobacillus thiooxidase.*

Potassic Fertilizers

Potassium fertilizers, namely Potassium chloride and Potassium Sulphate, are mined from potash deposits. Based on availability potassic fertilizers are classified into following categories:

Natural Potassium minerals

Processed Potassium chloride, Muriate of potash, Potassium sulphate (K_2SO_2), Sulphate of potash

Synthetic Potassium nitrate, Potassium phosphate

- India imports K fertilizers mainly from Germany and France.
- Muriate of Potash (MOP) has 50-63% K_2O in the form of Potassium chloride and 47% Cl. This fertilizer should be avoided in potato, iomato and tobacco, as Cl creates hindrance in starch conversion from leaf to other parts of plants. Sulphate of Potash (SOP) has 48-52% K_2O in the form of Potassium Sulphate. It is safest for potato, tomato, rice and tobacco. Wood ash has 5-6% Potassium carbonate.
- **Schoenite** or Potassium magnesium sulphate ($K_2SO_2.MgSO_4.6H_2O$). It is byproduct of salt industry, contains 25-30% K_2O and 10-12 MgO. Suitable for Cashew nut, Arecanut and Coconut.

Sulphur Fertilizers

In several fertilizers other nutrients are as primary and sulphur is present as secondary. Ammonium sulphate contains 24% of Sulphur, Ammonium sulphate nitrate (15%), Potassium sulphate (18%), Magnesium sulphate (13%), Gypsum (16.5%), Zinc sulphate (17%), Basic slag (3.4%), Urea sulphur (10%), Urea gypsum (14.8%), etc.

Iron sources: Ferrous sulphate (19%), Ferric sulphate (23%), Ferrous oxide (77%), Ferrous ammonium sulphate (29%), etc.

Manganese sources: Manganese sulphate (41%), Manganese oxide (63%), Manganese chelates (12%), etc.

Boron Fertilizers: Borax (11%), Sodium penta-borate (18%), Sodium tetra-borate (14%), Boric acid (17%), etc.

Zinc sources: Zinc sulphate monohydrate (35%), Zinc oxide (78%), Zinc sulphide (67%), Zinc phosphate (51%) and Basic zinc sulphate (55%), etc.

Copper sources: Copper sulphate (21%), Copper ammonium phosphate (30%) and Copper chelates, etc.

Complex fertilizers: Di-ammonium phosphate (DAP) has 18 : 46 : 0 NPK and **Suphala** (nitrophosphate) comes in 20 : 20 : 20, 15 : 15: 15, 18 : 18 : 9 NPK.

Difference Between Manures and Fertilizers

	Attributes	Manures	Fertilizers
1.	Composition	Moisture content and nutrient content vary greatly.	They have constant composition.
2.	Nutrient availability	Release of nutrient is very slow. Residual effect remains for 2-3 years.	Rapidly available and used mostly for single crop only.
3.	Completeness	Complete with respect of all essential nutrients.	Not complete
4.	Analysis value	Very low, *e.g.* FYM has 0.5%N	Very high, *e.g.* Urea has 46% N
5.	Effect on physical/ biological conditions of soil	Improve both physical and biological conditions of soil.	It deteriorates if applied unbalanced.

BIOLOGICAL NITROGEN FIXATION

Nitrogen fixation is a reductive process where nitrogen gas (N_2) is converted into inorganic nitrogen compounds, is mostly accomplished by certain bacteria and blue-green algae. A much smaller amount (10%) of free nitrogen is fixed by abiotic means (*e.g.*, lightning, ultraviolet radiation, electrical equipment) by conversion to ammonia through the Haber-Bosch process.

The Haber-Bosch (after German chemist Fritz Haber and Carl Bosch, 1909) process directly synthesizes ammonia from nitrogen and hydrogen. It is the most economical nitrogen-fixation process known so far.

- Nitrogen is fixed in nature as ammonia, nitrites, and nitrates by soil microorganisms, which carry out more than 90% of all nitrogen fixations (10% is carried out as nitric oxide by lightning and ultraviolet rays).
- Two kinds of nitrogen-fixing microorganisms are recognized,

1. **Mutualistic** (symbiotic) bacteria (*e.g. Rhizobium* spp.) invade the root hairs of host plants, multiply there and stimulate the formation of root nodules. Within the nodules the bacteria convert free nitrogen to nitrates, which the host plant utilizes for its development.
2. **Free-living** (non-symbiotic) bacteria, including cyanobacteria (or blue-green algae) *Anabaena, Nostoc* and *Azotobacter* spp. (aerobic), *Beijerinckia, Azomonas, Mycobacterium,* and *Clostridium* spp. (anaerobic) fix nitrogen.

- **Associative symbiotic** nitrogen fixation occurs without formation of nodules. Associative symbionts like *Azospirillum bransilense, Pseudomonas azotogensis, Enterobacter, Bacillus, Klebsiella* etc. associate with the roots of grasses and cereals. These microbes grow in rhizosphere region of plants in close contact to roots and fixes nitrogen.
- *Anabaena* fixes ten times more nitrogen than bacteria. There are reports that soil fertility of rice field is maintained due to *Anabaena* and *Nostoc.*
- **Nitrification**: It is a process where plants can assimilate ammonia as well as nitrates; most of the ammonia in the soil is converted to nitrites (NO_2^-) by *Nitrosomonas, Nitrosospira, Nitrosococcus, Nitrosolobus,* etc. and then to nitrates by certain nitrifying aerobic bacteria (*Nitrobacter, Nitrospina,* and *Nitrococcus*) through the oxidative process.
- **Nitrification inhibitors** inhibit the process of nitrification, which include Nitrapyrin (N-serve), Potassium azide, Sulphathiazole, Etridiazone (Dwell), Thiourea, Caffeic acid, etc.
- Once plants have assimilated nitrogen, it can be converted to organic forms, such as proteins following proteolysis to amino acids. The organic nitrogen, which is only usable, form for animals obtains by consuming plants or other animals.
- **Ammonification:** As the organisms die, certain microbes such as detritivores are able to participate in the decomposition of organic nitrogen into ammonia, called **ammonification**, providing a constant supply of ammonia to be used in the process of nitrification.

- **De nitrification:** Some nitrogen does return to the atmosphere, as denitrifying bacteria (*Thiobacillus denitrificans, Micrococcus denitrificans* and some species of *Serratia, Pseudomonas,* and *Achromobacter*) break down nitrates in order to obtain oxygen, thereby releasing gaseous N_2.
- *Pseudomonas aeruginosa* can, under anaerobic conditions (as in swampy or waterlogged soils), reduce the amount of fixed nitrogen (as fertilizer) by up to 50%.

BIO FERTILIZERS (MICROBIAL INOCULANTS)

Bio-fertilizers are carrier-based inoculants containing cells of efficient strains of specific microorganisms used by the farmers for enhancing productivity of the soil either by fixing atmospheric N or by solubilizing soil phosphorus or by stimulating plants growth through synthesis of growth promoting substances, *e.g. Rhizobium* for nitrogen, phosphobacteria for phosphate and Blue green algae for plant growth promotion. Bio-fertilizers release growth-promoting substance including auxins and vitamins, which improve germination of seeds and growth of seedlings.

Rhizobium, a Bacterium

Rhizobium is an important nitrogen-fixing organism. It was isolated for the first time by **Biejerinck** in 1888. Fred Baldwin and Mc Cov established the crossinoculation concept of *Rhizobium.* In carrier-based inoculants of *Rhizobium* a minimum of 10^8-cells/ gram of carrier must be present on dry mass basis. It can be kept for a maximum of 6 months after manufacturing but effectively it should used within 15 days of development. The pH of inoculants must be maintained between 6-7.5. Packing should be done in polythene bags.

Azoll, is the free-floating fern

Azolla (Mosquito fern) has become a valuable plant. Azolla has bi-lobed leaves and long suspended roots. *Azolla mexicana, Azolla nilotica,* and *Azolla pinnata* are common species of Azolla in India. Fleshy upper leaves of Azolla have cavities, which have aerial chlorophyll and contain the BGA *Anabaena azollae,* which help convert nitrogen to a form usable by other plants, thus greatly increasing the productivity of rice. Azolla forms a green mat over water, which often becomes reddish due to the accumulation of anthocyanin pigments.

- Azolla is susceptible to parasites and fluctuations of temperature. One month pre-flooding is necessary for *in-situ* multiplication of Azolla.

Mycorrhiza: The symbiotic association of roots of higher plants and endophytic fungal association are known as Mycorrhiza (Myco from *Myke* = fungus, *rhiza* = roots). The fungus enters into the cortex and remains outer cortical cells to form a network popularly known as hartignet, as Robert Hartig discovered it. The fungus requires thiamine, carbohydrates from the plant roots; in turn fungus supplies growth substances like IAA and other metabolites to the plants.

- The disintegration of hyphae within the cell is called as **Tolypophagy/Ptyophage**.

Mycorrhiza are classified into two *viz.* ecto and endo Mycorrhiza.

- **Ecto-mycorrhiza**: In this mycorrhiza fungus completely encloses each feeder rootlet in a sheath or mantle of hyphae. Mostly basidiomycetous fungus like *Amanita, Boletus, Russula, Scleroderma* and *Cenococum* are associated with hosts like *Quercus, Fagus, Alnus,* etc.
- **Endo-mycorrhiza**: In endo-mycorrhiza fungal hyphae penetrates the host tissue and remain in intracellular spaces. Fungi like *Marasmium, Armilaria, Corticium* are associated with hosts like *Orchids, Vanilla, Epipogon, Corolliorrhizae,* etc.
- **Vesicular, Arbuscular Mycorrhizae (VAM)** develop arbuscules and vesicles. The arbuscules help to transfer phosphate from the soil into the roots system and it is deposited into vesicles. The host plant provides carbohydrate for fungi. VAM are maintained only on growing plants inoculated with spores of fungi (*e.g. Glomus, Gigospora, Sclerocystis*). VAM help in absorbing both immobile (P, Zn, Cu) and mobile (S, Ca, K, Fe, Mn, Cl, Br, N) elements to plants.
- **Mycorrhizal inoculum** is necessary for establishment of certain plant species like **pines**. VAM increases resistance in plants against *Pythium, Phytophthora,* and *Rhizoctonia* etc.

Bio-fertilizers at a Glance

Bio-fertilizers	Method of application	Doses	N fixation	Remark
Symbiotic				
Rhizobium spp.	Seed treatment or direct appli-cation	20 gm/ kg of seed. 10 packets (200 gm each) for soil appli-cation.	50-100 kg N/ha, increases 10-35% of yield	Work only with legumes. Need optimum P and Mo.

Azolla	Direct field application	200 gm/m^2	30-100 Kg N/ha 10-25% yield increase	Survival is difficult at high temp. Need high Phosphorus. Exploited only in flooded rice.
Mycorrhiza	Placing inoculum below seed/ seedling. Seed treatment	2 kg/ha soil based culture	Absorb im-mobile (P, Zn, Cu) and mobile (S, Ca, K, Fe, Mn, Cl, Br, N), elements	Culture cannot be maintained. Exploited in Wheat, Maize, Potato, Clover, Lucerne, Cowpea, Soybean, Citrus, Redgram, Coffee, Papaya, etc.
Associative symbiotic				
Azo-spirillum	Seed treat-ment as dipping of seedling roots. Direct appli-cation with FYM.	2 kg/ha in soil. 600 g/ha for seed. 1 kg/ ha for seedling	20-40 kg N/ ha15-30% Yield increase	Exploited in Rice, Millets, Maize, Wheat, Sorghum, Sugarcane etc.
Non-symbiotic				
Cyano-bacteria (BGA) *e.g. Anabaena, Nostoc*	Direct field application (Broad casting)	10 kg/ha dried algal flakes	20-30 kg N/ ha10-15% yield increase. Produce IAA, etc.	Effective only in submerged rice.Demand bright sunlight.
Azotobacter chrococum	-do-	-do-	20-25 kg N/ha	Demand high inorganic matter. Exploited in cereals, Cotton, Vegetable, and Sugarcane.
Phospho-bacteria	-do-	2 kg/ha peat based culture	No nitrogen fixation	Exploited in Beet, Cabbage, Tomato, and Groundnut.

Phosphate Solubilizing Organisms

Many fungi and bacteria solubilize the insoluble phosphate into soluble form by secreting organic acids like formic, acetic, lactic, fumaric, succinic acids, etc. These acids lower the soil pH thereby bringing dissolution of phosphates. Bacteria of this group include *Pseudomonas putida, P. striata, Bacillus megaterium* var. *phosphaticum, Bacillus subtilis, B. polymyxa* etc. Fungi include *aspergillus flavus, A. fumigatus,* and *Penicillium digitatum.* Actinomycete-*Streptomyces* spp.

- The Phosphobacteria applied as seed treatment (3 packets of Phosphobacteria + 700 ml of rice gruel), seedling treatment (dip seedling in solution of 3 packets in 30 liters of water for Paddy, Ragi) and soil application (10 packets + 25 kg soil + 40 kg sand).

Biodynamic Farming

Biodynamic farming is the use of certain principles and practices of farming performed as per zodiac principles, *e.g.* sowing or transplanting date, management at appropriate time etc.

- It involves the application of NADEP/vermi/biodynamic compost (BD)/microbe mediated compost (MM compost) and use of Neem, Karanj, Castor, Groundnut, etc. cakes.
- Mulching after the application of 5-20 kg vermi/BD compost, 100 g CPP and release of earthworms in basin.
- Regular use of cow pat pit (CPP) and cow horn manure (BD-500) to refurnish biological properties of soil.
- Use of liquid manures prepared from cow dung; cow urine, leguminous leaves to promote growth and fruiting.
- Spraying of biodynamic pesticides prepared through fermentation of cow dung, cow urine, Neem, Karaṇj, Caliotropis, Castor or Neem leaves.
- Two sprays of cow horn silica (BD-501) at flowering and fruit development stages.

□□□

8

Irrigation and Water Management

Irrigation is the artificial application of water to the soil in order to supplement water requirement for crop production. In the irrigation water most of the cations (Calcium, Magnesium, Sodium and Potassium) and anions (Chlorides, Carbonates and Bicarbonates, Sulphates) are present. Fluorine content beyond 10 ppm in irrigation water is harmful indirectly to animals feeding on plants irrigated with high fluoride waters. Total Irrigation potential in the country has increased to 108·2 million hectares upto March 2010.

Quality parameters of irrigation waters: Suitability of irrigation water mainly depends on the amount and type of salts present into it, which can be measured in three ways, *viz.* total salt concentration, sodium adsorption ratio and bicarbonate and boron content.

1. **Total salt concentration:** Salt contents of irrigation water are measured as electrical conductivity. Water containing total dissolved salt to the extent of more than 1.5 m mhos/cm has been classified as saline water.

- **Saline water** has sodium chlorides as the prominent dissolved salts, whereas **Brackish water** contains more of salts other than sodium chloride such as acids, bases, salts of organic matter.

Classification of irrigation water based on total salt contents: Electrical conductivity (EC) serves as a guide to know the extent of soluble salts present in irrigation water. Natural water has EC value of much less than one unit. These values are reported as milli mhos (EC × 10^{-3}) or micro mhos (EC × 10^{-6}) at 25°C. Irrigation water classified based on EC, is as:

Class	EC	Quality characterization	Suitable Soils
C1	<1.5	Normal waters	All soils
C2	1.5-3.0	Low salinity waters	Light and medium textured soils
C3	3-5	Medium salinity waters	Light and medium textured soils for semitolerant crops
C4	5-10	Saline waters	Light and medium textured soils for tolerant crops
C5	>10	Highly saline waters	Not suitable

2. **Sodium adsorption ratio:** This ratio should be low for good quality of water.
3. **Boron contents:** Irrigation water that contains more than 3-ppm boron is harmful to crops, especially on light soils. Boron containing water is classified as:

Class	Boron Content (ppm)	Quality Character	Suitable Soils
B1	<3	Normal waters	All soils
B2	3-4	Low boron waters	Clayey soils and medium textured soils
B3	4-5	Medium boron waters	Heavy soils
B4	5-10	Boron waters	Heavy soils
B5	>10	High boron waters	Not suitable

IRRIGATION SYSTEMS

In India various types of irrigation systems are in practice. The following are some important systems, *viz*. Gravity irrigation, Tank irrigation, Lift irrigation,

1. **Gravity irrigation:** In this system the water is supplied to the land by gravitational flow. It is done in two ways:
   (*i*) **Perennial:** In this system water is assured throughout the crop period from the reservoir with diversions. During monsoon period water is stored reservoirs and directed to crops during cropping season.
   (*ii*) **Inundation:** In inundation water is directed from canal without any diversion. It depends on the periodical rise in water levels in the river.
2. **Tank irrigation:** It is the oldest system of irrigation in India where water is stored by forming a big bund across the natural drainage to avoid the surface run-off loss through natural streams. The tank size varies according to the drainage capacity. It is further classified as:
   (*i*) **System tank:** These tanks receive allotted quantity of water from the river system during the cropping period for its command.
   (*ii*) **Non-system tanks:** The non-system tanks depend upon rainfall in their catchments area and do not have any link to river system to get water.
3. **Lift irrigation:** In this system water is lifted from a reservoir, river, canal, well by using mechanical or electrical power to irrigate the field.

IRRIGATION METHODS

Different methods (surface, sub-surface, sprinkler, drip etc.) of irrigation are followed depending upon the crop, method of cultivation, slope of the land, quantity of water available and equipments needed.

1. **Surface irrigation methods:**

(*i*) **Flooding**: Flooding is followed for low land rice where water is allowed from the channel into entire field.

(*ii*) **Check basin method**: Suitable for groundnut and most of the cereals. In this case field is divided into small plots surrounded by bunds on all four sides. Head channel supplies water to the check basins in the row one after another. Size of basin depends on stream size and soil types.

(*iii*) **Basin method**: Method is suitable for tree crops. In this case water is given only to the basins around the trees, as basins are round or square in shape. These basins are connected with main channel.

(*iv*) **Border strip irrigation**: Method is suited for close growing crops in heavy soils. In this method field is divided into long, narrow strips, bordered with small bunds. Size of strips is 30-300 m× 3-15 m. Borders are made along the slope.

(*v*) **Furrow irrigation**: This method is suitable for crops like Sugarcane, Sorghum, Maize, Cotton, Tobacco, Brinjal, Tomato and Potato. In this case water is allowed in 3 to 5 furrows at a time. Length of the furrow varies from 30 to 300 m.

(*vi*) **Corrugation irrigation**: It is the application of irrigation through shallow furrows formed by inter-cultivation in rainfed crops.

(*vii*) **Alternate furrow irrigation**: It is the application of water to one side of each crop row, which will seep through lateral movement and make the entire surface wet. Water requirement is reduced by 25 to 35%.

(*viii*) **Wide spaced furrow irrigation**: It is the application of water to furrows, which are 3-5 m apart. Water requirement is reduced by about 50%. It is suitable for widely spaced crop like Cucurbits.

(*ix*) **Surge irrigation**: It is the intermittent water supplied to the field surface under gravity flow, which results in a series of 'on' and 'off' modes of constant or variable time spans. The process is continued until the end of irrigation advance phase. The infiltration is nearly uniform and deep percolation is reduced.

(*x*) **Cablegation**: It is a form of gated pipe system. Pipes have outlets on the topside and they are space based on spacing of rows of crops. The flow of water in pipe and flow through outlets is controlled by a plug operated by cable through forward and backward movement. The pipe is placed on the higher reach of the field.

2. **Sub-surface irrigation:** Water is applied through underground-perforated pipes or through deep trenches at 15 to 30 m intervals. Water gradually wets root zone through capillary movement. Evaporation loss is minimum; weed problem is less due to dry surface soil; and trenches are useful for drainage purpose in sub-surface irrigation. Method is usually practised in Kerala and Kashmir for coconut garden and vegetables, respectively.
3. **Sprinkler irrigation:** It is a method of application of water as a spray or raindrops over the crop. Components of irrigation system are pumps for sending water with pressure; main pipeline for conveying water; lateral pipeline for conveying water to risers; riser pipes for vertical conveying of water as high as the crop height; sprinkler heads and fixed pipes which has perforation round the head that too of rotating type. Method works at delivery pressure of >2.5 bars, with distance throw of >10 m and volume of delivery is >1,000 litre/hr. It requires power of 0.5 to 1.0 kg/cm^2.
4. **Drip irrigation:** It is defined as the precise and slow application of water in the form of discrete or continuous or tiny streams or miniature sprays through mechanical device called **'emitters'** located at selected points along water delivery lines. The components of this method are pump, head unit, central distribution system, fertilizer tank, filtration system, screen filter, sand filter, main line, sub-main line, laterals and emitters.
5. **Other methods:**

(*i*) **Pot irrigation**: In this system, mud pots of 10 to 20 liters capacity with pencil size hole made a little above the bottom are kept buried neck deep in the basins of fruit trees. Water filled in the pots wet the root zone slowly. The method is suitable for young trees.

(*ii*) **Typhoon system**: It is a slight modification of drip irrigation system. The typhoon laterals are thin wall dripper lines and the single chambered polyethylene tubes with injection moulded emitter welded to the inner tubes. They eliminate clogging, provide for extra filtration and prevent dust particles from entering the water passages. They are suitable for crops planted rows. In India, it is used for sugar plantation in Maharashtra.

(*iii*) **Low energy precision application system**: It is a modification of sprinkler system in which water is applied directly to the furrow at very low pressure through drop-tubes and orifice controlled emitters.

(*iv*) **Micro inject irrigation:** It is a form of micro irrigation, where water leaves the jets with pressure of 1 bar. Distance of throw is 1 to 4 m. Volume of discharge is 5 to 160 littres/hr.

(*v*) **Micro sprinkler irrigation:** In this system water delivery is by rotating jet of water, with the pressure of 0.8 to 4.0 bars. Distance of throw is 0.9 to 4.0 m. Volume of discharge is 28 to 225 litres/hr.

(*vi*) **Bubbler irrigation:** Water bubbling occurs from open vertical tubes; therefore it is called **bubbler irrigation**. This system is designed to reduce energy requirements of drip irrigation system. It is suitable for widely spaced crops like Mango, Sapota, Orange, and Coconut etc.

SOURCES OF IRRIGATION

Canals: These are artificial waterway constructed for the purpose of irrigation in connection with a hydroelectric dam. The loss of water is high (up to 50%) in canal water. Canals are the major source of irrigation in India.

Wells: A well is a hydraulic hole to the water strata. Water in the well stands at a height equal to the static waterlevel. The wells are classified as:

(*i*) **Open wells:** The wells dug up to water strata of the aquifer are called **open wells**. The large diameter of the open wells permits the storage of water.

(*ii*) **Tube wells:** These are sunk by inserting pipes below ground surface and passing through different geological formations of water bearing and non-water bearing strata.

(*iii*) **Artesian wells:** Due to pressure, water from well comes to the ground without pumping, are generally known as artesian wells.

(*iv*) **Bore wells:** When ground water availability is at deeper layers exceeding 16 to 20 m with hard strata, at this situation only bore wells work.

- **Filter points:** These are shallow tube wells consisting of a well and a short length of casing pipe. Filter points are generally bored in deltaic regions.
- **Rainfall:** Rainfall is dependent in different degrees, on the southwest monsoon and northeast monsoon. India receives most of its rainfall from the southwest monsoon originating in the Indian Ocean. About 75-80% of the rainfall is received in four months *i.e.,* June to September deciding the fate of the *kharif* crops.

Water Requirement (mm) of Different Crops

Crop	Water Requirement (mm)	Crop	Water Requirement (mm)
Rice	900- 2,500	Chillies	500
Wheat	450- 650	Sunflower	350-500
Sorghum	450- 650	Castor	500
Maize	500- 800	Bean	300-500
Sugarcane	1,500-2,500	Cabbage	380-500
Groundnut	500-700	Pea	350-500
Cotton	700-1300	Banana	1,200-2,200
Soya bean	450-700	Citrus	900-1,200
Tobacco	400-600	Grape	500-1,200
Tomato	600-800	Pineapple	700-1,000
Potato	500-700	Ragi	400-450
Onion	350-550	Gingelly	350-400

Crop Irrigation Stages

During the growth span, the plant passes through various phases and the stages of growth. The growth rhythm of plant is slow during some stages and fast during some other stages. Accordingly plant demands variable supply of water.

- **Vegetative phase:** The early vegetative phase consists of crop establishment or initial stage during the first 2-3 weeks after sowing. This is followed by **crop development stage,** which last for 2-6 weeks in different crops.
- **Reproductive or flowering phase:** The reproductive or **flowering phase** comprises the period from initiation of buds to 75% flowering. This period is most of the seasonal crops last for 2-3 weeks and in perennial crops it lasts for 4-6 weeks or more.
- Some crops like cotton, groundnut and pulses even prefer stress during early vegetative growth to suppress excessive vegetative growth. In many crops the initial establishment and flowering stages are highly sensitive to excess water conditions resulting in poor performance of the root system and also shedding of flowers, in addition to lodging at maturity in some crops.

Water Potentials

Potential energy: Any matter in equilibrium has the potential to do the work and consequently the energy is called **potential energy**.

- **Water potential:** The potential energy of water when expressed per unit amount (weight or volume basis) is called **water potential**.

- **Soil water potential:** The difference between the energy state of soil water and pure free water is known as **soil water potential**.
- **Total soil water potential:** Total water potential is the sum of the contributions of gravitation potential, metric potential and the osmotic potential.

Important Irrigation Projects in India

State	Name of project
Andhra Pradeh	Godavari Delta System, Krishna Delta System, Nagarjuna Sagar (Krishna)
Bihar	Gandala
Punjab	Western Jamuna, Bhakranagal, Sutlej, Beas
Gujarat	Kakrapare, Tapti, Narmada
Madhya Pradesh	Gandhi Sagar (Chambal, Ranapratap Setu Sagar)
Maharashtra	Bhima Jayakwadi (Godavari)
Kerala	Kalada, Mullai Periyar
Orissa	Hirakund and Mahanadi
Uttar Pradesh	Upper Ganga Canal, Ramaganga
West Bengal	Damodar Valley
Rajasthan	Rajasthan Canal (Sutlej)
Tamil Nadu	Mettur-Lower Bhavani Project, Parambikulam Alliayar Project, Periyar Vaigai, Cauvery delta, Tamirabarani

WATER USE EFFICIENCY

- **Water use efficiency** (WUE) is the yield of marketable crop product produced per unit of water used in evapo transpiration.

  It is calculated as, $\text{WUE} = \frac{\text{Yield}}{\text{Evapo transpiration}}$
- Water use efficiency is also known as crop water use efficiency or consumptive water use efficiency (ECU), if the water use for metabolic purpose of the crop (G) and is included with Evapo transpiration (ET). Then, it is calculated as, $\text{ECU} = \frac{\text{Yield}}{\text{G}+\text{ET}}$.
- There are considerable differences between plant species to produce a unit dry matter per unit amount of water used resulting in widely varying values of water use efficiency. The water use efficiency for few crops is listed below:

Crop	Water requirement (mm)	Grain yield (kg/ha)	WUE (kg/ha mm)
Rice	2,000	6,000	3.0
Sorghum	500	4,500	9.0
Pearl millet	500	4,000	8.0
Maize	625	5,000	8.0
Groundnut	506	4,680	9.2
Wheat	280	3,534	12.6
Finger millet	310	4,137	13.4

Water Resources in India

Catchments area of the rivers	252.8 Mha (from 20 river basins)
Precipitation	400 Mha m (million hectare metre)
Water flowing back to sea	92 Mha m
Percolation	215 Mha m
Evaporation	70 Mha m
Surface run-off	155 Mha m
Ground water	42.3, Mha m
Surface water	80 Mha m
Water in reservoirs	73 Mha m
Water used for irrigation	27.19% of total water reserve

AIBP (Accelerated Irrigation Benefit Programme) : Programme was initiated by Govt. of India in the year 1996-97 to extend assistance from the completion of incomplete irrigation fall under this scheme. AIBP guideline are modified in the year Dec. 2006 to provide enhanced assistance at 90% of project cost as grant to special category states, Drough Prone Area Programme (DPAP) states,/tribal areas/flood-prone areas, and Koraput-Balangir-Kalahandi (KBK)distrticts of Orissa. As on 31 March 2010, 281 projects have been covered under the AIBP and 120 completed : Irrigation potential of 9·82 lakh ha is estimated to have been created from major/medium/minor irrigation projects during 2009-10.

Micro Irrigation : The centrally sponsored National Mission on Micro Irrigation (NMMI) was launched in June 2010 in addition to the earlier Micro Irrigation Scheme launched in January 2006. The mission is being implemented during the Eleventh Plan period for enhancing water-use efficiencyby adopting drip and sprinkler irrigation systems in all States and Union Territories for both horticulture and agricultural crops. The scheme provides assistance at 60 per cent of the system cost for smalland marginal farmers and at 50 per cent for general farmers. Since 2005-06, a sum of Rs. 2739 crore has been released by the Govt. of India under the scheme and 2.27 lakh ha brough under micro-irrigation. (*Source* : Economic Survey)

❑❑❑

9

Energy in Agriculture

Agriculture is both energy consumer and energy producer. **Conventional** energy sources include fossil fuels (Coal, Petroleum and Natural gas), water (hydel energy) and nuclear energy. **Non-conventional** energy sources include solar energy, bio-energy, wind energy, ocean (tidal) energy, hydrogen energy and geothermal energy. **Renewable** sources are those, which can be further utilized for energy production again and again. These include sources from solar, biomass, wind, ocean (tidal), water and soil (geothermal). **Non-renewable** sources are those sources, which are being exhausted upon their use. Such energy sources are from fossil fuels and nuclear sources.

COAL

- India ranks fourth in coal production in world having 186 billion tonnes of coal reserves.
- Sixty per cent of total electricity produced in India comes from thermal power stations.
- Anthracite coal is not available in India. Important coalmines are Jharia, Bokaro and Barakar, etc.

OIL AND GAS

Any combustible material either gaseous oil mixture used as fuel to provide energy. Petroleum is the naturally occurring oily, bituminous liquid composed of various organic chemicals. It consists of principally hydrocarbons, although a few sulphur-containing and oxygen-containing compounds are usually present (the sulphur content varies from about 0.1 to 5 per cent). Petroleum contains gaseous, liquid, and solid elements.

- In India main area of oil exploration are Bombay High, Gandhar and Krishna basin, Godavari and Cauvery basin, Cachhar, Arunachal, and Rajasthan.
- Recently several explorations have explored oil deposits in India, *viz.* Cauvery basin, Cambay basin and Krishna-Godavari basin by Oil and Natural Gas Corporation and Bikaner-Nagar, Kathaloni, Hoilai, Dhuliagin by Oil India Limited.

- Oil reserves have been discovered in the various places, *viz.* Khoraghat (Assam); Tanot (Rajasthan); Kutch offshore and Audada (Gujarat); South basin (West coast); Bombay offshore; Nada (Cambay basin); Adaikamangalam (Tamil Nadu); and Lingala (Andhra Pradesh).

HYDROPOWER

Hydropower is the power produced by the fall of water from a higher to a lower level, and extracted by means of waterwheels or hydraulic turbines. It is the cheapest source of electricity generation in the country.

- Present hydel power potential in India is 600 billion units, of which only 14% has been exploited.

NUCLEAR ENERGY

Nuclear energy is produced by fission or fusion of atomic nuclei in a nuclear reaction. Presently minerals like Uranium, Thorium, Radium and Lithium are used to produce energy. Production of uranium in India at present is mainly confined to the mines of Jaduguda in Singhbhum district of Bihar.

Uranium reserves:

Bihar	Pichli (Abrakipahar in Gaya district), Jaduguda and Dalbhum in Singhbhum district
Rajasthan	Bisundi (Ajmer) and Umra (Udaipur)
Andhra Pradesh	Sankara mine in Nellore district
Karnataka	Yadyur (Bangalore)
Meghalaya	Dominsat in West Khasi hills

- **Thorium is derived from monazite and upon irradiation produces Uranium-233.**

Monazite reserves:

Kerala	Ilmenite beach sands in Palghat and Quilon districts
Tamil Nadu	Melur taluka of Madurai district
Andhra Pradesh	Medak, Karimnagarm Warrangal, Nalgonda and Hyderabad
Bihar	Hazaribagh district
Rajasthan	Pali district

- Nuclear power stations are located at Tarapore (Maharashtra), Rawatbhatta (Rajasthan), Kalpakkam (Tamil Nadu) and Narora (Uttar Pradesh). Some stations which are under construction include Kudankulam, Kakrapar and Kaiga, etc.

Energy in Different Fuels

Fuels	Energy Kcal/kg	Fuels Kcal/kg	Energy
Hard coal	5,000	Lignite brown coal	2,310
LPG	10,800	Gasoline	10,500
Kerosene	10,300	Diesel	10,200
Natural gas	8,000-9,480	Electricity	860

SOLAR ENERGY

Solar energy is the radiant energy produced in the sun as a result of nuclear fusion reactions. It is transmitted to the earth through space by electromagnetic radiation in quanta of energy called **'photons'**, which interact with the earth's atmosphere and surface. Solar system is the enormous source of energy of which only 0.1% reaches to the earth.

- **Solar energy is utilized by two ways:** (1) by converting into thermal energy, and (2) by converting into electricity. Thermal energy can be obtained by using a solar collector.
- From the solar energy electricity generation is done with the help of **solar photovoltaic technology.** In the technology, when light falls on certain metals, the electrons gets excited and boiled off. These boiled off electrons are collected by another metal and passed through wires in a steady stream. This continuous process constitutes the electric current.
- **Solar pond** is a large energy collector with integrated heat storage device for thermal application. To the pond a large quantity of salts is added to stop the boiling of water. The sides of the ponds are made up of synthetic material to check seepage.
- India is the first Asian country to have solar pond in Bhuj (Kutch district of Gujarat). Kutch also have Asia's **first wind form project** at Mandvi and **first tidal** (ocean) power project **at Kandla.**
- In most part of India the daily average direct radiation is about 5.7 kwh/m^2.

WIND ENERGY

Energy present in a moving mass of air (wind) harnessed and converted into a useful form of power, usually electricity.

- Asia's first wind form project was established at Mandvi whereas the largest being at Lamba (Gujarat) with capacity of 10 MW.
- The total installed capacity of wind power in India is 114 MW.
- A total of 50 MW wind power generation is exploited so far at 27 locations, of which 12 in Tamil Nadu, 6 in Gujarat, 7 in Andhra Pradesh and 2 in Maharashtra.
- For wind power generation, the ideal wind speed is 8.23 metres/. second.

BIO GAS (CH_4 + Co): Bio gas is a sustainable source of energy by virtue of its production from vastly available cattle dung. The biological conversion process involves enzymatic or bacterial breakdown of dung by microorganisms at relatively low temperature. Both Methane and Carbon monoxide are combustible and can be used directly in the gaseous form.

Bio-gas Technology

Biogas production is a microbial process which takes place with organic residues and water in absence of air/or oxygen. Researchers have noted that different groups of bacteria act upon complex organic material to produce biogas rich in Methane. The entire precess involves the action of bacteria in four stages in a biogas plant. The stages are shown on next page and described as below :

(*i*) Degradation of organic materials into fatty acids, amino acids, carbon dioxide and hydrogen by hydrolytic group of bacteria.

(*ii*) In second stage the products like acetate and hydrogen are produced.

(*iii*) In the third stage, more acetate is produced from the products of first and second stage.

(*iv*) The fourth and the final stage offers opportunity to produce the methane from the different product formed in the previous stages. Methanogens like organisms act to product the light weight gas 'methanes.

It is interesting to note that any biological material (nightsoil, animal excreta, poultry and other droppings) can be used as feedback. However, the volume of gas produced in different stocks in not the same. Pig dung can produce 2½ times the quantity of gas as compared to the animal dungs. As the cattle feed has passed through a microbial fermentation process in the rumens and a further microbial action in caecum, facial residues contain little material easily digestible by bacterias in the digester and the gas production would be expected to be lower than the droppings from polity and pigs which do not have rumen fermentation.

Influence of biomass size, mechanical stirring and solid-water ratio have been studied by Pawar *et al* while using. 'Water Hyacinth' and 'Rice straw' as feed stock: Since fermentation is the result of the action of many anaerobic microorganisms, the better the living environment of these organisms, the faster the production of biogas. The gas contains 60% - 80% methane depending on various factors. The discharge from the biogas digester is a good organic fertilizer and soil conditioner similar to compost.

BIOMASS

Biomass either terrestrial (organic residue and higher plants) or aquatic (fresh water aquatic plants, weeds, micro-algae, floating marine plants) and salt tolerant species are used to exploit energy.

- **Energy plantation:** Growing of selected species of trees and shrubs for fuel and firewood.
- In India there is approximately 7 Mha usar land (1.3 Mha in U.P. alone), the trees resistant to calcareous soil are suitable for planting. The important species are *Prosopis juliflora, Azadirachta indica, Butea monosperma, Terminalia arjuna, Pongamia pinnata, Acacia senegal.*
- *Acacia senegal, A. modesta, A. tortilis, P. cineraria* and *Dichrostachys cineraria* have been found to grow successfully in alkaline soils with a mixture of *Kankar. A. nilotica* has been found to be a valuable species for planting in collar soil. *Eucalyptus tereticornis* is reported to grow well in soil having pH 9 and soluble salts up to 0.3 per cent.
- *Parthenium argentatum*, a competitor of rubber plant (*Hebea brasiliensis*), produces rubber as identical to *Hebea brasiliensis* and can be grown in desert conditions. Thus such plants can be exploited for biomass production simultaneously with economic yield.
- **Aquatic biomass:** Green plants like Hydrilla, Potamageton, Vailisneria, Eichhornia crassipes, Trapbispinosa, Pistia, Salvinia, Wolfia, Azolla, Typha, Renunculus, Hygrophila,

Sagitaria can be used for production of aquatic biomass. These also serve as the source of compost, as their leaves contain about 25-35% protein.

Energy in Different Biomass

Type of biomass	Energy Kcal/kg	Type of biomass	Energy Kcal/kg
Paddy straw	3,000	Rice husk	3,440
Mango leaves	3,390	Groundnut straw	4,200
Sugarcane bagasse	3,800	Wheat straw	3,800
Cotton stalks	3,300	Maize stalks	4,700
Maize cobs	3,500	Bajra stalks	3,850
Gram stalks	3,950	Moong straw	3,980
Wood wastes	2,500-3,850	Bark of trees	2,500-2,850

Biomass Based Achievements

- A 10 MW rice straw based thermal plant has been commissioned by BHEL at Jalkheri in Punjab.
- A pilot project to generate electricity from garbage and municipal waste has been installed at Timarpur, Delhi.
- A 100 kW Gasifier system has been established at Port Blair.

ALTERNATIVE SOURCES OF ENERGY

India consumes about 111 MT of petroleum products annually, of which only 33 MT is produced in country as crude oil meeting only 30% of domestic requirement (rest 70% being imported). Approximately, 40 MT High Speed Diesel (HSD) is consumed in India, which represents 36% of total consumption of all petroleum products. Thus efforts to improve the self-sufficiency definitely call for initiatives to explore alternative sources of diesel. The diesel from plants, which can serve the alternative source, is called bio-diesel (chemically Methyl esters). At present Government of India has permitted for blending of 5% such oil in HSD for acclimatization. Ministry of Petroleum and Natural Gas has offered for bus and rail services to be run with bio-diesel.

- Petroleum Conservation and Research Association (PCRA) has opened its centre at New Delhi to create awareness on alternative bio-diesel crops including Jatropha.
- Indian oil with its R & D in Faridabad has started experimenting with *Jatropha curcus* and other sources. It has examined and found

that oils from rice bran, *Jatropha curcus*, Palm, Karanjia, Sunflower, etc. can serve the source of bio-diesel. For the same technology has been transferred to M/s Venus Ethoxyethers, Goa.

Jatropha curcus, the Chief Source of Bio-diesel

Jatropha is, commonly called Physic nut, Ratanjot, Jamalghota, Jangaliarandi or Kala arand, native to Mexico and tropical South America belongs to family Euphorbiaceae, produces yellow-green flowers and 3-5-lobed leaves goes up to 3-4 m height. Portuguese introduced the plant in India. The plant flowers during July-August and produce seeds (mature in September-October), which are the chief source of bio-diesel. Seeds resemble to that of castor having 63.01 g of test weight (weight of 100 seeds). Plants start yielding after second year of planting. On an average 30-35% of oil can be extracted from Jatropha seeds. Jatropha yields 3.5-3.75 t/ha oil.

- **Trans esterification**: It is the process of converting the triglycerides of oil into methyl esters (bio-diesel). Sodium Hydroxide (NaOH) is most commonly used as catalyst of process. The methanol and NaOH are mixed with Jatropha oil and left for 8 hrs; bio-diesel comes at the top of mixture leaving glycerine at the bottom. 100 kg Jatropha oil + 24 kg Methanol + 2.5 kg NaOH, produces 100 kg bio-diesel + 26 kg glycerine.
- Efforts are underway to utilize Coconut oil as a supplement to diesel.
- Bio-diesel reduces emission of carbon dioxide by 44%, sulphate by 100%, unburnt hydrocarbon by 68%, particulate matter by 40%, polycyclic aromatic hydrocarbons by 80% and carcinogenic-nitrated polycyclic aromatic hydrocarbons by 90%, in comparison to petroleum diesel.
- Bio-diesel is traded as B grade oil, *viz.* B5 (5% bio-diesel), B10 (10% bio-diesel). It is now used in several vehicles including railway engines (Shatabdi from Delhi to Amritsar), buses (Minister of Petroleum and Natural Gas has flagged of buses from Gujarat state on March 12, 2005), cars (Mercedes Benz C 220 CDI) etc.

Potential Ingredient for Bio-fuel Production

Ethanol is a renewable source of energy, which can be produced from feedstocks like Molasses, Corn, and Sweet Sorghum. Ethanol used for the blending purpose into petrol is called 'bio-fuel'. Brazil is pioneer in blending ethanol successfully with petrol up to 24%. In

India 5% blended petrol is sold in 9 states, U.P., A.P., Karnataka, Haryana, Maharashtra, Gujarat, Tamil Nadu, and union territories from June 1, 2003.

- Presently India needs approximately 3.9 lakh kilolitres of ethanol for blending in petrol, and ethanol production is quite low, two lakh kiloliters from molasses. Now **sweet sorghum** variety **SSV-84** is exploited for production of ethanol, which yields 4.5 kilolitre of ethanol per hectare.
- **Liquid fuel containing plants**: Jojoba (*Simondsia chinensis*) is a source of carbon molecules and alternative to hydrocarbons particularly as lubricant. Oil extracted from seeds of jojoba is liquid at room temperature. This liquid oil is used in brake systems.

Institutions Involved

- Tata Institute of Fundamental Research (TIFR), Mumbai.
- The Atomic Energy Commission (DAC) 1948, is responsible for policy formation in energy. The Department of Atomic Energy (DAE) was set up in 1954 to execute policies.
- The Indian Rare Earths Limited was incorporated in 1950 for processing and producing radioactive elements explored from sand beaches of Kerala and Orissa. It has several plants in Tamil Nadu, Kerala (Chavara, Alwaye), Orissa (Chatrapur) and thorium plant at Trombay (Mumbai).
- Uranium Corporation of India Limited (UCIL), Trombay, is responsible for locating and mining uranium.
- Bhabha Atomic Research Centre (1957) was set up for research in the application of atomic energy through research reactors.
- Indira Gandhi Centre for Atomic Research, Kalpakkam, Tamil Nadu, was set up in 1971 for research and demonstration in fast breeder technology.
- Nuclear Fuel Complex, Hyderabad (1971) is responsible for fabricating nuclear fuel for power reactors.
- Nuclear Power Corporation is responsible for design, construction and operation of Nuclear Power Stations.
- Atomic Energy Regulatory Board was formed in 1985 for safety and regulatory functions. It reports to Atomic Energy Commission.

10

Farm Management

Farm Management utilizes the basic principles of economics. The term economics has been derived from two Greek words, *viz. Oikas* = home, and *Nomos* = law. The literal meaning of economics is the 'Law of House Hold Management'.

- Agricultural price commission was set up in 1965. In the same year Food Corporation of India came into existence.
- Banks were nationalized on 19.07.1969.
- NABARD (National Bank for Agricultural and Rural Development) was set up on 12 July, 1982, with aims to fund and develop rural agriculture. Previously it was a branch of Reserve Bank of India, called Agriculture Refinance Corporation (ARC).
- In Uttar Pradesh the work on *Zamindari Unmulan* formally started on 1st July, 1952.

Definitions

Farm management is the study of ways and means of organizing land, labour and capital, application of technical knowledge and skills in order that the farm may be made to yield greater continuous profit.

Farm management is the science, which deals with the analysis of the farnring resources, alternatives, choices as well as opportunities within the framework of resource restrictions including social and personal constraints of farming business. It helps to decide about the basic course of action of the farming business.

Farm management **performs five unique functions**

1. Management makes observations on resources, etc.
2. Analyses these observations,
3. Makes decisions,
4. Acts on decisions, and finally
5. Takes financial responsibility.

Farm management is concerned with decision making, which involve:

1. **What to produce:** Management decides about what product to produce. This decision is called **product-product relationship**.
2. **How to produce:** It involves the choosing methods of cultivation for effective production. This relationship is known as **factor-factor relationship**.
3. **How much to produce:** It relates to convert several farm resources to final product. Such relationship is referred as **factor-product relationship**.
4. **Time relationship:** It relates that when farmer makes investment and after how long his money comes back.
5. **How, when and where to deal:** Farm management finally deals simultaneously with all the probable situations for better profit from the farm business.

Management of a Farm

The farm management indeed is the emphasis on the decision-making function of evaluating and choosing between alternative strategies. A major concern is about adjustments, which are more suitable as well as profitable, in the new situations and opportunities.

- It is the approach under which the opportunity costs of the various resources are evaluated and the adjustments are made for better use of available resources with enterprise mixing in order to maximize and secure higher levels of farm income.
- **Farm Planning** is the decisions making in advance followed by actual work. It involves thinking, understanding with challenges of the farmer to move forward.

Different Types of Farm Budgeting and Planning

Farm budgeting may be classified into categories:

1. **Enterprise budgeting:** Enterprise budgeting is the input-output relationship for individual enterprise. An enterprise budget includes all the variable resources required per unit (a hectare/ animal/tree, etc.) of an enterprise, its cost, the expected output, gross returns, etc.
2. **Partial budgeting:** Partial budgeting is a method of making a comparative study of the cost-and-return analysis resulting from a change in business organisation. Partial budgeting cannot be used to change to whole structure of planning. For example,

(1)The economic combination of CAN and superphosphate versus DAP with a basal dose of CAN; (2) The mechanical thinning of fruits like plums and grapes versus chemical thinning; (3) The substituting more economical dairy ration for a costlier one (a single or two nutrients); and (4) American cotton versus desi cotton and hybrid maize versus hybrid cotton, etc.

3. **Full or complete budgeting and planning:** Full budgeting takes care of all the alternatives available. Entire break-even points are provided. Full budgeting always provides better solution over the partial budgeting.

Budgeting Requires Following Steps

1. **Farm map**: The farm is carefully mapped understanding its salient features, like soil type, soil-fertility and cropping patterns, etc.
2. **Inventory of farm resources**: Every asset on the farm, ranging from hand-tools to sources of power, etc. is inventoried, whether they need to be replaced or to be kept.
3. **Examining the existing organisation**: A careful analysis of the restrictions and weaknesses of the farm organisation based on inventories is made.

- **Farm-efficiency** is the ratio of the output against input. It is measured to establish profitability of a farming business. The efficiency of farms is calculated in terms of costs versus returns.

Rules of Success in Farming Business

(*i*) Ability of doing farm practices,

(*ii*) Knowledge of scientific principles related to crop/ livestock production,

(*iii*) Use of basic business principles in farming business.

Investment analysis (Capital budgeting)

1. **Future value of present money**, is calculated with the formulae,

$$A = P\ (1 + i)^{t}$$

where,

A = future value of present sum invested in the project,

P = principal amount invested in the project,

i = applicable rate of interest, and

t = number of years of life of the project

2. **Present value of future money (PW),** is calculated with the formula,

$$PW = \frac{A}{(1+i)^t}$$

where, A = future value of present sum invested in the project,
P = principal amount invested in the project,
i = applicable rate of interest, and
t = number of years of life of the project

Principles of Economics Applied to Farm Management

The principles applied to farm management fundamentally belong to the concepts and law of economics either directly or indirectly. These principles are applicable to crop production, livestock production, farm building, labour and farm practices including machinery etc.

1. **Law of diminishing returns**: It is a practical experience of every farmer that after a certain stage in cultivation, the application of successive doses of labour and capital to a given area of land doesn't bring about as much return as the previous dose. Any additional dose supplied to the same plot gives diminishing return, the situation is known as **diminishing return,** therefore input beyond this stage should not be increased.
2. **Law of comparative advantages**: Farmers tend to produce those items, which give more income at the lowest relative cost. Specialized and Diversified Farming are based on this principle. Sugarcane cultivation near Sugar Mill, Vegetables near city, Sheep and Goat rearing near hills etc., give more profit than others.
3. **Law of equi-marginal returns:** This law states that profit will be greatest provided, each unit of labour, capital and land, is used where it adds the most to the return.
4. **Law of substitution**: The principle, which helps selection from a number of alternatives, is called the law of substitution. According to this law the least cost combinations of inputs or practices are obtained; cheaper inputs in a bid to earn more profit replace costly inputs. Only partial substitution is possible in farming.

Procedure for Finding Least Cost Combination

(i) Computation of marginal rate of substitution (MRS) by dividing the number of units of the replaced input (X_1) by the number of units of added input (X_2).

$$\text{Substitution ratio} = \frac{\text{No. of units of relaced input}}{\text{No. of replaced units of added input}}$$

Or $$\text{MRS} = \frac{\Delta X_1}{\Delta X_2}$$

(ii) Computation of price ratio by dividing the price of added input (PX_2) by the price of replaced input (PX_1), as,

$$\text{Price ratio} = \frac{\text{Price of added input}}{\text{Price of replaced input}}$$

Or $$\text{Price ratio} = \frac{PX_2}{PX_1}$$

(iii) Computation of least cost combination by equating MRS and Price ratio $= \frac{\Delta X_1}{\Delta X_2} = \frac{PX_2}{PX_1}$.

- The least cost is realized at the point where the ratio of the input prices is inversely equal to their marginal rate of substitution.
- If the substitution ratio is greater than the price ratio, then we can lower the costs by using more of the added inputs, as

When, $= \frac{\Delta X_1}{\Delta X_2} = \frac{PX_2}{PX_1}$ Least cost combination

If, $\frac{\Delta X_1}{\Delta X_2} > \frac{PX_2}{PX_1}$, use X_2 input to lower the cost,

If, $\frac{\Delta X_1}{\Delta X_2} < \frac{PX_2}{PX_1}$, use X_1 input to lower the cost.

5. **Principle of opportunity cost and combining enterprises:** An enterprise in farm business is defined as the production of a single crop or kind of livestock. Generally farmers take more than one enterprise on their farms with view to get the maximum profit in minimum expenditure by combining enterprises. Farmers avail the opportunity by increasing the amount of an enterprise whose output is raised due to creation of some infrastructure, *e.g.*, cold storage, sugar mill or other agro-industry in the area, in their farming combination.

Different Ratios in Farm Management

Capital ratios

1. Net capital ratio $= \frac{\text{Total assets}}{\text{Total liabilities}}$

2. Working capital Ratio $= \frac{\text{Working assests + Current assets}}{\text{Intermediary liabilities + Current liabilities}}$

3. Current ratio $= \frac{\text{Current assets}}{\text{Current liabilities}}$

4. Debt equity ratio $= \frac{\text{Different liabilities}}{\text{Net worth}}$

Cost ratios:

1. Gross ratio $= \frac{\text{Total expenses}}{\text{Gross income}}$

2. Fixed ratio $= \frac{\text{Fixed expenses}}{\text{Gross income}}$

3. Operating cost $= \frac{\text{Operating expenses}}{\text{Gross income}}$

Cost Concepts in Farm Management

Costs in general refer to the expenses incurred on productive services and physical productivities, are depend upon the cost of various input factors. It is an outlay of funds for product service.

(*i*) **Fixed cost**: Fixed cost present farming expenses of an overhead nature and do not change with the output, *e.g.* interest on fixed capital, depreciation, revenue, etc.

(*ii*) **Variable cost**: This cost varies with the level of output. It includes changes of hired human labour, seed, manure and fertilizer, irrigation, insecticides and pesticides etc. Such costs are classified into following categories:

(*a*) **Total variable cost** (TVC): It is obtained by multiplying the amount of variable input by the price per unit of output.

(*b*) **Average variable cost** (AVC): It varies with the level of production. It is computed by dividing total variable cost with amount of output, *i.e.* $TVC = \frac{TVC}{\text{Output}}$

(*c*) **Marginal cost** (MC): MC is the change in total cost as related to change in output. It is calculated by dividing the change in total cost by the corresponding change in output, as

$$MC = \frac{\Delta TC}{\Delta Y}$$

(*d*) **Total fixed cost** (TFC): TFC is the total fixed cost showing the sum of expenditure incurred irrespective of output.

(*e*) **Average fixed cost** (AFC): It is calculated by dividing total cost with amount of output, as

$$AFC = \frac{TFC}{\text{Output}}$$

(*f*) **Total cost** (TC): It is the sum of total fixed cost and total variable cost, as

$$ATC = \frac{TC}{\text{Output}}$$

(*g*) **Average total cost** (ATC): It is worked out by dividing TC with output.

Types of costs and their components

Costs	Components
Cost A_1	Value of casual labour + attached labour + hired bullock labour + input value of owned bullock labour + hired machine labour + input value of owned machine labour + seeds + manure and fertilizers + plant protection chemicals + irrigation charges + interest of working capital + depreciation + land revenue.
Cost A_2	Cost A_1 + rent paid for leased in land. If any,
Cost *B*	Cost A_2 + imputed rental value of owned land+ interest on own land and capital.
Cost C	Cost *B* + imputed value of family labour. Cost C is also called Gross cost or total cost of cultivation.

Measurement of income (Aggregate Measures)

Net operation income	=	Gross income - (operating expenses + depreciation on working assets)
Net farm income	=	Net operating income - (fixed expenses + depreciation on fixed assets)
Net family income	=	Net farm income + off farm income

Income Measures in Relation to Different Cost Concepts

1. Farm business income + Gross income – Cost A_1
2. Owned farm business income = Gross income – Cost A_2
3. Family labour income = Gross income – Cost
4. Net income = Gross income – Cost C
5. Farm investment income = Net income + rental value of own land + interest on owned fixed capital

Input-output Ratios

1. $\text{Operating ratio} = \dfrac{\text{Operating expenses}}{\text{Gross income}}$

2. $\text{Fixed ratio} = \dfrac{\text{Fixed expenses}}{\text{Gross income}}$

3. $\text{Gross ratio} = \dfrac{\text{Total expenses}}{\text{Gross income}}$

Investment to Income Ratios

1. $\text{Capital turn over ratio} = \dfrac{\text{Gross income}}{\text{Average capital investment}}$

2. $\text{Rate of return on investment} = \dfrac{\text{Net return to capital}}{\text{Average capital investment}}$

Important Abbreviation Related to Farm Economics and Management

- **CACP:** Commission of Agriculture cost and Prices
- **WTO:** World Trade Organisation
- **GATT:** General Agreement of Tariff and Trade
- **CI:** Crop Insurance
- **EEC:** European Economic Community
- **UNDP:** United Nations Development Project
- **FAO:** Food and Agricultural Organisation
- **DMI:** Directorate of Marketing and Inspection
- **NCDC:** National Cooperative Development Programme
- **KCCS:** Kisan Credit Cards Scheme
- **SFCI:** State Farms Corporation of India
- **NCAP:** National Centre for Agricultural Planning
- **NCAER:** National Centre for Agricultural Economics and Research
- **IMF:** International Monetary Fund
- **STC:** State Trading Corporation of Indian
- **WB:** World Bank

□□□

11

Farming System

System: It is defined as a set of elements/components those are interrelated and interacting among themselves. A system consists of several components, which depends upon each other.

System approach: An approach, which considers, these interrelations among the components of a system are called **system approach**.

Farming system: A farming system is a complicated interwoven mesh of soils, plants, animals, implements, workers, inputs and environmental influence with the strands held and manipulated by a person called **farmer**, who gives his preference and aspirations, attempts to produce outputs from the inputs and technology available with him.

Types of Farming

An area in which many farms have a general similarity in size, products sold and methods followed is called a type of farming. Determination of type of farming is completely based upon the concept of comparative advantage. Types of farming is classified as under,

Basis of classification	Type of farming
1. According to proportion of land, labour and capital investment.	(*a*) Extensive farming (*b*) Intensive farming
2. According to value of products or income.	(*a*) Specialized farming (*b*) Mixed farming (*c*) Diversified farming
3. According to the supply of irrigation.	(*a*) Irrigated farming (*b*) Unirrigated farming
4. According to the nature of produce.	(*a*) Crop farming (*b*) Livestock farming

Extensive Farming and Intensive Farming

A farmer obtains more or less a definite quantity of yield at any particular time on a given plot of land. If he wishes to increase his output, he may either by,

(*a*) Increasing more land for cultivation (the extensive farming), or

(*b*) Applying more labour and capital to the same piece of land (the intensive farming).

- **Extensive farming:** When more land is brought under cultivation in order to increase output, it is termed as extensive cultivation or extensive farming. In extensive farming it is the only land, which is increased to get more yield, other factors remain unchanged.
- **Intensive farming:** Under such farming, in contrast to extensive farming, more labour and capital is used in the same plot of land to get more yields.
- **Specialized farming:** The farm from which 50% or more income is derived from a single enterprise, *viz.* crops, livestock, dairy, poultry, etc., such farm is called **specialized farm** and farming is called **specialized farming.**
- **Mixed farming:** Mixed farming is one where crop production is combined with the rearing of the livestock. If a farm produces at least 10% (at most 49%) of produce from livestock, the said farm would be called as mixed farm. Here, in case of mixed farming the meaning of livestock is cow and buffalo only.
- **Diversified farming:** A diversified is one that has several production enterprises or sources of income. But no source of income should produce more than or equal to 49% of income.
- **Dry farming:** Dry farming is done in areas having average rainfall of less than 50 cm. According to **Widstoe,** "Dry farming is the profitable production of useful crops without irrigation on land that receives annual rainfall of 20 inches or less".

System of Farming

System of farming refers to the nature of production or combination and type of ownership of resources. The combination of products on a given farm and the methods or practices are used in the production are collectively known as system of farming. Such farming systems include:

1. **Family farming:** In the family farming all agricultural operations are carried out by family members. Capital and

management also exclusively belongs to the family alone. The Head of the family distributes the income of farm.

2. **Institutional farming:** It is the farming where generally farms are used by an institution for conducting Research and Demonstration. The farm is well aided and equipped in respect to road, channels, drainage etc.

3. **Cooperative farming:** In this type of farming all the members have the right of ownership in the business. The members voluntarily pool their resources for running the business and there is no pressure other than cooperative members. All the members are free and can leave the society at any time without losing the ownership right of the land and resources pooled by them. The income is distributed according to the share of land, labour and capital of the members. This farming type is further classified as:

(i) **Cooperative better farming**: In such farming members do farming independently and have the right of ownership on land. Each member follows a recommended plan of cultivation. The members obtain credit, seed, manure, fertilizers, and specific services such as marketing and use of machinery etc. from the society. The members pay money for the facilities they get from the society. After the end of the year a portion of the profit is distributed to the members of the society.

(ii) **Cooperative joint farming**: In this farming the members have the right of ownership of land. The members do the cultivation practices jointly. The managing committee prepares plan of cultivation and accordingly work is carried out jointly by the members for which they get wages. The net profit is distributed among the members according to the resources pooled by them.

(iii) **Cooperative tenant farming**: In this farming the cooperative society owns land in freehold or leasehold. The whole area is divided into different plots, and distributed among the members on rent. The members have got no right of ownership on the land. The cultivation plan is prepared by the cooperative society and members follow it. The society undertakes to supply credit, seed, fertilizers, and machinery as well as arrange for the marketing of produce. The profit is distributed amongst the members in proportion to the rent paid by them to the society.

(iv) **Cooperative collective farming**: In such farming the land is acquired by the cooperative either as freehold or leasehold, but

farming is done collectively by the members. There is no ownership right of the members on the land. The profit is distributed amongst the members according to labour and capital invested.

Comparison Amongst Cooperative Farming

Types of cooperative farming	Right of ownership	Mode of operation
Cooperative better farming	Individual	Individual
Cooperative joint farming	Individual	Jointly
Cooperative collective farming	Collective	Collective
Cooperative tenant farming	Collective	Individual

- Cooperative farming is most suitable for arable wasteland. It is most suitable for marginal farmers where land holding are small. Resources those are not available could be availed from cooperative society.

4. **Capitalistic farming:** In capitalistic farming the investment of land and capital is done by big businessperson or capitalist. Wages are paid to the labourers employed. Intensive farming and improved methods of cultivation are adopted. Farms are generally mechanized. Workers are better paid. The profit or loss of the business is borne by the capitalist or businessperson.
5. **Corporate farming:** It has the characteristics just like capitalistic farming, but the right of ownership is on the basis of shares taken by the member. Profit is distributed according to share of members. Workers are generally better paid.
6. **State farming:** Government carries out state farming. Farm managers are employed for conducting day-to-day agricultural operations. The farm may be mechanized or unmechanized depending upon the size of the farm. The Government provides finances as well as other facilities and also fixes the policy to be adopted. The profit or loss is entirely borne by the Government.
7. **Personal farming:** In such farming farmers have the ownership right on the land and do farming independently. The right of ownership is heritable and transferable. The farmer generally serves as a manager, labourer and also as organizer of the farming business. The farm is generally small. The profit and loss is borne by the farmer alone.

8. **Collective farming:** It is also called **Kholkhoz**. Collective members surrender their land, livestock and implements to society. Members elect a managing committee, which is responsible for allocation of work, distribution of income and marketing of surpluses.

Cropping System

The cropping carried on a farm and their interaction with farm resources, other farm enterprises, available technology and environment, which determine their make-up. Cropping system is as unit comprising soil, crop, weed, pathogen and insect sub-system that transform solar energy, water nutrients, labour and other inputs into food, feed, fuel and fibre.

Cropping Pattern

Cropping pattern is the yearly sequence and spatial arrangement of crops or fallow on a given area:

1. **Sole cropping:** In such cropping one crop or variety grown alone in pure stands at normal density.
2. **Patch cropping:** In the patch cropping the component crops are planted in patches.
3. **Monocropping:** A crop system in which the population of **crops**, other than the main crop, grown in relay, sequential or intercropping with the main crop. However, **monoculture** is the repetitive growing of the same crop on the same land.
4. **Multiple cropping:** The intensification of cropping in time and space dimensions, growing two or more crops on the same field in a year.
5. **Sequential cropping:** Growing two or more crops in sequence on the same field in a farming year. The succeeding crop is planted after the preceding crop has been harvested. Crop intensification is only in time dimensions. There is no intercrop competition. The crop grown in sequential cropping, are called a crop sequence.
6. **Skip cropping:** It is a kind of cropping in which a line is left unsown in the regular row series.
7. **Double, triple and quadruple cropping:** Growing two, three or four crops respectively on the same land in a year in sequence.
8. **Ratoon cropping:** Cultivation of crop as re-growth after harvesting of crop, *e.g.* Sugarcane.

9. **Multi-storeyed cropping:** It is the growing of varying heights in the same field in order to maximize the use of solar energy for crop production, *e.g.* Papaya planted with Mustard and vegetables.

10. **Intercropping:** Growing two or more crops simultaneously on the same field. Crop intensification is in both time and space dimensions. In other words, intercropping is the cultivation of two or more crops simultaneously on the same field with or without a row arrangement (row intercropping or mixed cropping).

(*i*) **Mixed intercropping**: Growing two or more crops simultaneously with no distinct row arrangement, sometimes called mixed cropping.

(*ii*) **Row intercropping**: Growing two or more crops simultaneously where one or more crops are planted in row. It is often referred as intercropping.

(*iii*) **Strip intercropping**: Growing two or more crops simultaneously in strips wide enough to permit independent cultivation but narrow enough for the crops to interact each other.

(*iv*) **Relay intercropping**: Growing two or more crops simultaneously during the part of life cycle or each crop. A second crop is planted after the crop has reached its reproductive stage of growth but before it is ready for harvest. The relay intercropping is also referred as relay cropping.

Relationship in the Intercropping Systems

Allelopathy: Allelopathy is any direct or indirect harmful effect that one plant has on another plant through the production of chemical substances that escape into the environment.

Competition: Competition among the crops may be classified as;

(*i*) **Mutual inhibition**: The actual yield of each crop is less than the expected under sole crop system.

(*ii*) **Mutual co-operation**: The yield of each crop is greater than expected under sole crop system.

(*iii*) **Compensation**: One crop in cropping system yields less and the other yielding more than expected under sole crop system. This is the most common type of situation reported from the cropping systems. More yield producer in compensation is called dominant crop.

Assessment of Competition

1. **Land equivalent ratio** (LER): It denotes the relative land area under sole crop required to produce the same yield as obtained under a mixed or intercropping system at the same management level. It is calculated as sum total of the ratios of yield of each component crop in an intercropping or a mixed cropping system to its corresponding yield when grown as a sole crop. Therefore, it is expressed as,

$$\text{LER} = \frac{Yab}{Yaa} + \frac{Yba}{Ybb}$$

where,

Yaa: Yield of component '*a*' in sole stand

Ybb: Yield of component '*b*' in sole stand

Yab: Yield of component '*a*' in mixed stand with '*b*'

Yba: Yield of component '*b*' in mixed stand with '*a*'

For example, in a system of Sorghum and Pigeon pea the yield of Sorghum under sole crop is 2,000 kg/ha whereas, Pigeon pea, if grown alone produces 1,000 kg/ha, then

$$\text{LER} = \frac{1{,}500}{2{,}000} + \frac{5{,}00}{1{,}000} \text{ or } = 0.75 + 0.5 = 1.25$$

- If LER is equal to 1.00, it denotes the mutual cooperation, if it is more than 1.00 it is compensation and if it is less than 1.00 then it is mutual inhibition.
- LER could only be calculated only after the harvest of the crop and hence not predictable by the farmer at the time of sowing.

2. **Relative yield total** (RYT): It is the mean of plant relative yield *i.e.* ratio of the yields per plant if grown in mixture. It is expressed as:

$$\sum_{i=1}^{Z} \frac{Yab}{Yaa} + \frac{Yba}{Ybb} = \left(\frac{Yab}{Yaa} + \frac{Yaa}{Ybb}\right)$$

where,

Yaa: Yield of component '*a*' in sole stand

Ybb: Yield of component '*b*' in sole stand

Yab: Yield of component '*a*' in mixed stand with '*b*'

Yba: Yield of component '*b*' in mixed stand with '*a*'

(i) **Income equivalent ratio (IER):** It is the ratio of the area needed under sole cropping to that of intercropping. At the same management level to produce the same amount of gross income. In other words if instead of crop yield, the monetary value is taken into consideration and worked out as in the case of LER it gives the IER.

(ii) **Relative crowding coefficient (RCC):** This coefficient was proposed by **de Wit** in 1960 and used in replacement series experiments. Each component has its own coefficient (*K*), which gives a measure of whether that component has produced more or less than the expected.

$$Kab = \frac{Yab \times Zba}{(Yaa - Yab) \times Zab}$$

where,

Yab: Yield of *'a'* intercropped with *'b'*

Yaa: Yield of sole stand crop *'a'*

Zab: Sown proportion of component *'a'* in combination with *'a'*

Example, If sorghum and black gram is sown in the proportion of 75 : 25 and yield of sorghum as sole crop is 2,000 kg and if intercropped its yield is 1,500 kg.

Given, *Yab* = 1,500, *Yaa* = 2,000, *Zab* = 75 per cent and *Zbá* = 25 per cent

$$\text{Then, } Kab = \frac{1{,}500 \times 0.25}{(2{,}000 - 1{,}500) \times 0.75} \text{ or } \frac{375}{375} = 1.00$$

- If a component has the coefficient less than 1.00, it means it has produced less than expected yièld. If it is equal to 1.00, the yield is as per the expectations and if it is greater than 1.00 means it is more than expected.

(i) **Aggressivity** (*A*): Aggressivity, was proposed by **Mc Gilchrist** in 1965, gives a simple measure of relative yield increases, in component *'a'* than the component *'b'* in a intercropping system. It is expressed as,

$$Aab = \frac{\text{Mixture yield of } 'a'}{\text{Expected yield of } 'a'} - \frac{\text{Mixture yield of } 'b'}{\text{Expected yield of } 'b'}$$

$$\text{Or } Aab = \frac{Yab}{Yaa \times Zab} - \frac{Yba}{Ybb \times Zab}$$

- If the value of A is zero that means both the components '*a*' and '*b*' are competitive to each other. If it is in positive, it shows dominant component and if it is negative, it means it is dominated component.

(*ii*) **Competition index** (CI): **Donald** proposed the Competition Index in 1968. It measures the competition based on product of two equivalence factors, one for each component crop in mixed stand. The equivalence factor denotes the number of plants of one crop, which is as competitive as one plant of the other crop. If a given crop has an equivalence factor of less than one, it means it is more competitive on plant-to-plant basis than other crop.

(*iii*) **Competition ratio** (CR): **Willey and Rao** proposed CR in 1980, it is the ratio of individual land equivalent ratio of the two component crops. It is measured for correction of the proportion in which they were initially grown.

Assessment of Land Use and Productivity in Multiple Cropping

(*i*) **Cropping index or cropping intensity**: It is the ratio between total cropped area and actual net cultivated are expressed in percentage. It does not consider the growing period of crop. It is measured as the sum of area planted under different crops harvested in a single year divided by the total cultivated area multiplied by 100. The intensity is expressed in percentage, as

$$\text{Cropping intensity} = \frac{\text{Total cropped area}}{\text{Farm area}} \times 100$$

(*ii*) **Cropping intensity index** (CII): **Menegay,** *et al.* proposed cropping intensity index in 1978. It assesses a farmer's actual land use in terms of area and time relationships for each crop or group of crops compared to the total available land area and time, including the land available for production.

Crop Rotation

Crop rotation is a process of growing different crops in succession on a piece of land in a specific period of time, with an object to get maximum profit from least investment without impairing the soil fertility. Farming year is 12 months, one cycle may take one or more farming years to complete.

Basis of Crop Rotation

- The crops with tap roots should be planted followed by crops having fibrous root system.
- The leguminous crops should be grown after non-leguminous crops because legumes fix atmospheric N into the soil and add more organic matter to the soil.
- More exhaustive crops (in terms of nutrition, irrigation and tillage) should be followed by less exhaustive crops.
- Selection of the crops should be demand based.
- The crop of same family should not be grown in succession because they have common pests and as such they intensify.

Rotational intensity: This is calculated by counting the number of crops in a rotation, multiplied by 100, and then divided by the duration of rotation, as

$$\text{Rotation intensity} = \frac{\text{Number of crops in the rotation}}{\text{Duration (years) of rotation}} \times 100$$

Cropping Scheme

The cropping scheme is a plan according to which crops are grown on individual plots of a farm during a given period of time with the object of obtaining maximum return from each crop without impairing the soil fertility. Thus a cropping scheme is related to the most profitable use of resources, land, labour and management.

Principles of Cropping Scheme

- **Area under building and layout:** A proportionate area is allocated for building and layout. Generally 8-10 per cent of area is allocated in case farm size is less than 50 hectares, however, if the farm size is more than 50 hectares, land allocation is done @ 5 per cent only.
- **Number of plots:** The number of plots should be equal to the duration of rotation or in multiple of that.
- **Selection of crops** should be done as per the situation of farm. If farm is: (1) **Near a city** the allocation should be at least 60 percent of area for vegetables; (2) **Near sugar factory**, at least 60 percent area to sugarcane or sugar beet; (3) **Near canning factory**, at least 60 percent area to peas, tomato etc.; (4) Near *vanaspati* **factory** provide reasonable area to oilseed crops like groundnut, sunflower and so on.

❐❐❐

12

Cereal Crops

The term "Cereal" has been derived from "Ceres", the name of the Roman goddess of Grains and Agriculture. Cereals comprised of various species of the grass family, cultivated for their seed used as food.

Wheat (*Triticum* spp.) $2n$ = 14, 21, 42

Wheat is a self-pollinated crop having two sets of roots *viz.* seminal or seedling roots and coronal, nodal, or adventitious roots. Tillering mostly occurs over the coronal roots. The stem of wheat is in the form of culms. Leaves are arranged alternatively on the culms, and uppermost leaf is called **flag leaf**. The inflorescence is called **spike**, consisting of several florets called **spikelets**. Each spikelet consists of flowering glumes having lemma and palea. The grain of wheat is called **caryopsis**.

There are 18 species under genus *Triticum*, but a few are important for agricultural point of view. In India only three species are cultivated, which include (in order of acreage from highest to lowest),

1. ***Triticum aestivum*** (Bread wheat or common wheat) $2n$ = 42: This species of wheat is mostly used for *Chapati* making and bakery purpose. Developed through natural cross among other genus (for detail refer Chapter 18, Plant Breeding).
2. ***T. durum*** (Macroni wheat) $2n$ = 14: It is used for *Suji*, Vermicilli (*Semya*) and Macroni purposes.
3. ***T. diococcum*** (Emmer wheat) $2n$ = 14: It is mostly cultivated in Tamil Nadu for the purpose of *Uppumav* dish.

   The Indo-Gangetic plains form the most important wheat area in India. The cool winters and the hot summers are very conducive for good crop. Based on agro climatic conditions, the country is broadly divided into five wheat zones, which include:

1. **The north-western plains zone:** This zone consists of the plains of Punjab, Haryana, Jammu, parts of Rajasthan and western

U.P. In this zone irrigated wheat is planted in November and the rain-fed wheat in October, and harvested in the month of May. Exclusively *T. aestivum* is cultivated throughout the zone.

2. **The northeastern plains zone:** Eastern U.P., Bihar, West Bengal, Assam, Orissa, Manipur, Tripura, Nagaland, Meghalaya, Mizoram, Arunachal and Sikkim. Crops planted during November-December and harvested in March-April. *T. aestivum* is cultivated throughout the zone.
3. **The central zone:** This zone consists of M.P., Gujarat, southeastern Rajasthan (Kota and Udaipur divisions) and the Bundelkhand area of U.P. Most of the wheat area (75%) in this zone is rainfed. Both *T. aestivum* and *T. durum* are grown in this zone; however, *T. dicoccum* is grown in Gujarat. Sowing commences during October and crop is harvested in February-March. The best quality *durum* wheat is produced in this zone.
4. **The peninsular zone:** This zone consists of the southern states of Maharashtra, Andhra Pradesh, Karnataka and Tamil Nadu. All the three species *aestivum, durum, dicoccum,* are grown in this zone. Sowing commences during October (Rainfed) and November (Irrigated), and crops harvested in February.
5. **The northern hill zone:** The zone includes hilly areas of Kashmir, Himachal Pradesh, Uttranchal, West Bengal, Assam and Sikkim. Crops are sown in October and harvested in May-June. The Wheat plants remain dormant during the cold months from November to March and runs as temperature rises in April, therefore **wheat is mostly grown in summer instead of in winter,** in April-May and harvested in September-October. Only *T. aestivum* is grown in this zone. In the southern hills of Tamil Nadu, two crops of wheat are raised in a year. The first crop is taken between October-April and the second crop in May-September.

Varieties: Irrigated: Sonalika, Kalyansona, Arjun (HD-2009), Janak (HD-1982), U.P. 368 (Karnal bunt resistant), U.P. 262 (resistant to all major diseases), U.P. 215, WL-711, U.P. 319, U.P. 301, U.P. 115, HD-2135, Jairaj, Malaviya 234, HD-2204, 2117, 4530, 2189, H.P. 1209, IWP-72 (resistant to brown rust), K-68; **rainfed:** VL 421, 401, 404, Hy 65, Meghdoot, WL 410, Pratap (HD 1981), K-65, C-281.

- Throughout India, only spring wheats are grown, although they are raised mainly during winter.

Rice (*Oryza sativa*) $2n = 24$

Rice is the self-pollinated crop needs short photoperiod (short day plant). It has fibrous roots systems comprising seminal and secondary adventitious roots. The inflorescence of rice is called **panicle**, which is further composed of spikelets. Plumule and radicle are covered by coleoptyle and coleorhiza in embryo, respectively. The rice grain is botanically **caryopsis**. Kernel is enclosed by the husk or hull or lemma and palea. The outer layer of the kernel is the pericarp and beneath the pericarp there is a thin layer called **testa** and below it, is the **aleurone** layer. The protein (7-8%) found in rice is concentrated in this aleurone layer and scutellum.

- *Oryza sativa* (Asian rice) is present throughout the world and *O. glaberrima* is limited to Africa only.
- The carbonized grains found in the samples from Lothal excavations in India revealed the use of paddy husk in potteries, bricks, in 2300 BC. There is mention of *nivara*, a wild form of rice, in Vedic literature.
- Two major sub-species or races, i.e. indica and japonica, are recognized.

The country has been classified into **eight agro-climate zones of rice.**

1. **The humid western Himalayan region:** The region consists of J & K, Himachal Pradesh, Kumaon, and the Garhwal Division of Uttranchal. The region is composed of both *tarai* and submontane soils.
2. **The humid Bengal-Assam basin:** This region consists of W.B. and Assam. Riverine alluvium, *tarai* soils, lateritic soils, red-yellow loams and red sandy soils are found.
3. **The humid eastern Himalayan region and the Bay Islands:** A.P., Nagaland, Manipur, Mizoram, Tripura, Meghalaya and the Andaman and Nicobar Islands. Soils like red loamy, lateritic, red-yellow, and alluvial are found.
4. **The sub-humid Sutlej-Ganga plains:** This region consists of Punjab, U.P., Bihar and the Union Territory of Delhi. Soils like Calcareous Alluvial, Riverine alluvium, red-yellow loams, mixed red and black, red sandy and both saline and alkaline, are characteristically present.
5. **The sub-humid to humid eastern and southeastern uplands:** Orissa, Andhra Pradesh and eastern M.P. lateritic, red-yellow loams, mixed red, black, deltaic alluvium, deep and medium deep black, red loamy and coastal alluvium are the major soil types found.
6. **The arid western plains:** The zone includes Haryana, Rajasthan and the Union Territory of Dadra and Nagar Haveli. Soils are alluvial, red-yellow, and medium to deep black in nature.

7. **The semi-arid lava plateau and central highlands:** Maharashtra, western and central M.P., and the union territory of goa, daman and diu. riverine alluvium, coastal alluvium, mixed red and black and red sandy soils are found in majority.
8. **The humid to semi-arid western ghats and the Karnataka plateau:** This region consists of Karnataka, Tamil Nadu, Kerala, the Union Territory of Pondicherry and the Lakshadweep Islands. Major soils are lateritic, red sandy, deltaic coastal alluvium and red loamy.

- **Dapog method of nursery:** In India mostly wet nursery was practised but recently Dapog method introduced from Philippines is also in practice. The method was practised primarily in Andhra Pradesh. In Dapog method nursery raising consists of growing seedlings on a concrete floor covered with polythene sheets. A small area is required for raising this type of nursery, 30-40 m^2 being enough to raise seedlings for transplanting one hectare. The seedlings are ready after 14 days for transplanting.
- **Varieties**: **Drought-tolerant:** N 22, Bala, Brown Gora, White Gora, Black Gora, IET 1444 (Rasi), Lal Nakanda, CR 143-2-2 Kanchan, Kiran, Bhavani; **Deep water**: Jaisuria, Jalnidgi Jalmagna; **Aromatic:** Basmati 370, Type 3, Rusa RH 10; **Blast resistant**: CO 14, K 332, K 333, BJ 1, Jaya, Vani, ARC 6087, ARC 6633; **Helminthosporium resistant:** BAM 10, T 141, ARC 11253 ARC 11073, ADT 31; **Bacterial leaf blight resistant**: IET 4141 BJ 1, TKM 6, Ajaya; **Tungro virus resistant**: Kataribhog, PTB 2 Vikramarya; **Grassy-stunt virus resistant**: IR 362; **Green leaf hopper resistant:** Vani, PTB 2, PTB 7, RP 5-12, Pankhari 203 PTB 18; **Gall-midge resistant**: Eswarakora, Surekha, CR 94 MR 1523, PTB 18, PTB 21, RPW 6-17; **Brown plant-hopper resistant:** PTB 21, PTB 33, IET 5118, IET 5119, RP 1045-6-10-1 T 1425, T 1432, Ennapatta, T 1421, Sonnamukhi, Pandi, ARC 6650; **White-backed plant-hopper resistant:** 1471, Lal Basmati Eswara-mangalam, Kodiyan; **Stem-borer tolerant**: TKM 6, W 1263, IET 2812, IET 2815, IET 2845.

Maize (*Zea mays*) $2n = 20$

The maize, popularly called **queen of cereals**, is a monoecious cross-pollinated crop. The male inflorescence is known as **tassel** and located at the top of the plant. Female inflorescence is called **cob or ear** located laterally to the culms. There are three kinds of roots, *viz.* seminal roots, crown or coronal roots and brace or aerial or prop roots. It is anemophily plant. Protein from maize is called **zein**.

The crop is native of America, introduced to India by Portuguese during the 17th century. In terms of world acreage, India stands next to the USA, Brazil, China and Mexico. In India it ranks only next to rice, wheat, *jowar,* and *bajra* both for area and production. It is mostly cultivated in U.P., Bihar, M.P., Rajasthan and Punjab, accounting 75% of the area and production.

- Maize is cultivated in all the seasons *viz. kharif, rabi* (Peninsular India and Bihar), and spring season (Northern India).
- **Varieties: Doublecross hybrids**: Ganga -1, 101, Ganga-3, 4, 5, Ranjit, Himalayan-123; **Topcross**: Ganga safed-2; Hi-starch; **Composites**: Amber, Jawahar, Kisan, Vikram, Vijay, Sona, Laxmi; **Opaque (gene consisting) composites**: Shakti, Rattan, Proteina.
- Simazine or Atrazine (@ 1-1.25 kg/ha of 50% W.P.) as pre-emergence is used for weeds.
- **Baby corn** is a type of maize whose unfertilized cobs are used as vegetables, for making pickles, etc.

Based on its endosperm type, maize is classified (by **Sturtevant, 1899**) into seven groups:

1. **Dent type** (*Zea mays indentata*): It is known so because of dent formation at the top of kernel.
2. **Flint type** (*Zea mays indurate*): Kernels are round on the top. It is principal type of maize grown in India.
3. **Pop type** (*Zea mays everta*): Pop type has small kernels with hard corneous endosperm. Used for popcorns and pop confectioneries.
4. **Flour type** (*Zea mays amylacea*): It resembles to the flint corn. Grains are composed of soft starch with almost no dent on top.
5. **Sweet type** (*Zea mays saccharata*): More amounts of starch and other carbohydrates are present making sweet taste. Green cobs are used for canning and table purposes.
6. **Waxy type** (*Zea mays cerabina*): Kernels have waxy appearance because of amylopectin. The kernels composed of 78% amylopectin and 22% amylose.
7. **Pod type** (*Zea mays tunicata*): The kernels of pod type are enclosed in husk.

Barley (*Hordeum vulgare*)

In addition to direct consumption it is used to prepare malt for manufacturing beer, whisky and other industrial products including alcohol and vinegar. Malt syrup is also utilized for making candies, breakfast cereals, medicines and textile products. Gurgaon and its adjoining areas produce better-quality barley for malt industry. It is also cultivated in U.P., Rajasthan and Bihar, M.P., Haryana, Punjab, West Bengal, Himachal Pradesh and Jammu and Kashmir.

- **Varieties**: **Huskless varieties**: Karan-3, Karan-16 for diara land, Karan-18, 19; **Hulled**: Karan-15; **Malting**: C-138, RD-57, 137, RS-6; **Salt tolerant**: Jyoti, Amber, Vijay, Azad, Ranjit; **Rainfed**: Kailash, Dolma; **Chapati making**: Karan-16 (Neelam); **Nematode resistant**: Raj Kiran; Suited for **High altitude**: LBS-1.

Sorghum or Jowar (*Sorghum vulgare*) 2*n* = 20

It is often cross-pollinated crop most important for food and fodder in dryland areas. Inflorescence is called **panicle**. The grains are rich in leucine contents. It is cultivated in Maharashtra, Karnataka, Andhra Pradesh., Madhya Pradesh., Gujarat, Rajasthan, U.P. (Bundelkhand) and Tamil Nadu. Sorghum is grown in all seasons during *kharif*, *rabi* and summer (only on 4-5% of total area under Sorghum).

- **Varieties** resistant to downy mildew (CSV-5, CSV-4); shoot fly (CSV-6, CSV-5); leaf spot (CSV-5). CSH-1 is suited for rice-based cropping systems. CSH-1 Dwarf hybrid, CSH-2, 4, 5, 6, 9; CSV-1 (Swarna), Co-20 fodder, Co-26, APK-1; **Three way cross**: Co-25. **Ratooning** is done with CSH-1, Co-20.
- Seed treatment with Carbofuran (5 parts a.i. for 100 parts of seed) gives effective control against shoot fly. The midge is effectively controlled by spraying the ears before flowering with Endosulfan (35% EC) 1 litre or Carbaryl (50% WP) 3 kg or Lindane (20% EC) 1 to 2 litres in 500 to 600 litres/ha of water.
- The pre-emergence applications of Atrazine (0.5 kg a.i./ha), followed by a late-weeding control weeds.
- Intercropping systems include sorghum + pigeon pea; sorghum + soya bean; sorghum + groundnut.

Pearl Millet (*Pennisetum typhoides*)

It is also called **cattail** millet, **bulrush** millet. Inflorescence is a compound spike tapering to the central axis, composed of two types of flowers, *viz.* hermaphrodite and staminate. The flowers are cross-pollinated in nature. The grains contain 11.6% protein, 5% fat, 67% carbohydrate, and vitamins A and B. This crop is cultivated for grain as well as for fodder. It is grown all over India except some hilly tracts.

- During largest producing stat in India Rajasthan, the pearl millet production was 11.79 MT from the area of 10.39 MHa.
- **Varieties: Composite**: Composite-3, dwarf composite; **Hybrids**: HB-1, 2, 3, 4, 5 (all from Tift-23A), PHB-10, 14 (with Bristles), MBH-10; Co-8 for fodder; ICMS-7703 synthetic; WCC-75 multiple cross.

Package and Practices

Crop and duration (days)	Season	Seed rate (kg/ha)	Fertilizer N:P:K (kg/ha)	Spacing (cm)	Method of planting	Critical stages	Yield (kg/ha)	Varieties /special information
Rice SD < 120 MD 120-135 LD>140	*Kharif*	60 40 30	100:40:40 120:50:40 150:60:40	15 × 10 20 × 10 20 × 15	Trans-planting 21 DAS 30 DAS 35-40 DAS	Seeding/ Trans-planting Tillering Panicle-initiation Soft dough	4,500-5,500 6,000-7,000	IR-36, 50,64, Co-33 (Karuna); Add 25 kg/ha $ZNSO_4$Ratooning is popular in Southern India, where three crops are taken.
Wheat 15 October-March	*Rabi*	100 125 Bold 25-30 Dibb-ling	120:60:40 Irrigated 60:30:20 Rainfed	20 × 23 15 × 18 Late sowing	Broad-casting, Behind the plough, Kera method, Pora method, Seed drill, Dibbling	Crown root initiation Tillering Jointing Flowering Milking	4,500-5,000 Irrigated 2,000-2,500 Rainfed	With one dwarfing geneSonalika, Safed Lerma;With two genes Kalyan Sona, Sonora-64, Chhoti Lerma, Arjun, Sarbati Sonora, Janak; With three genes-Hira, Lal Bahadur, Moti, Malvika are
Maize 85-105	July-Aug., Sep., Oct., Jan., Feb.	18-20 Compo-site 20 Hybrid	80:30:0 Composite 120:60:40 Hybrid	60-75 × 25-30	Broad-Casting Behind the plough Seed drill Dibbling	Seeding, Tasselling Silking Soft-dough Hard -dough	Irrigated 5,000-6,000 Hybrids 5,000 Compo-site half in rainfed	Called queen of cereals. Ganga -1, 101, Ganga-3, 4, 5, Ranjit, Himalayan-123, Ganga safed-2, Hi-starch, Amber, Jawahar, Kisan, Vikram, Vijay, Sona, Laxmi, Shakti, Rattan, Proteina

Crop and duration (days)	Season	Seed rate (kg/ha)	Fertilizer N:P:K (kg/ha)	Spacing (cm)	Method of planting	Critical stages	Yield (kg/ha)	Varieties /special information
Jowar 90-110	*Kharif*	8-12	80:40:40 Composite 120:50:40 Hybrids; Apply Kaolin for stress	40-45 × 15-20	Broad-casting Trans-planting	Seeding Pre-flowering Grain formation	Irrigated 5,000 Rainfed 2,500-3,000	HCN produced due to drought is poisonous to cattle and seed hardening with 2% KH_2PO_4 or CCC-500 ppm. Apply 12.5 Kg/ ha MNM or 25kg $ZnSO_4$
Bajra 80-90	*Kharif*	4-5	100:40:30 Irrigated 70:35:20 Rainfed	45 × 15	Broad-casting Seed drill Dibbling	Seeding Pre-flowering Grain formation	3,000-3,500 Irrigated 1,200-1,500 Rainfed	ICMS-7703 syntheticWCC-75 multiple cross;HB1, 2, 3, 4, 5; Most drought tolerant crop.
Barley 120-140	Rabi 15 Oct., 15 Nov.,	90-100 normal 120 late	60:30:0 Irrigated 30:20:0 Rainfed	23-25 row to row	Pora method Kera method	Seedling Sprouting Active tillering Flag leaf Milk or soft dough	2,500-3,500	**Malting:** C-138, RD-57, 137, RS-6; Salt tolerant: Jyoti ,Amber, Vijay, Azad, Ranjit; **Nematode resistant:** Raj Kiran; Suitable for high **altitude:** LBS-1.

13

Minor Millets

Millet is a common name for various species of plants of small-seeded grain. They are widely cultivated in poorer agricultural areas and contain less protein than wheat or rye, and more protein than rice. These millets include:

Barnyard Millet or Sawan (*Echinochloa frumentacea*)

This millet resembles largely with rice weeds found in dryland areas. It is mostly grown in Madhya Pradesh, Uttar Pradesh, Tamil Nadu, Andhra Pradesh, Karnataka, Maharashtra and Bihar. It is drought resistant and, simultaneously, capable of withstanding waterlogging. Sowing for *kharif* crop commences in June with the onset of the monsoon and harvested in September, whereas *rabi* crop is sown in October-November and harvested in January-February. This millet is used mainly for rice pudding (*kheer*). It contains 6.2% protein, 9.8% crude fibre, 65.5% carbohydrates and 4.4% ash.

- **Varieties:** VL-8, VL-11, VL-29, Anurag, RAP 2, RAP 39.

Finger Millet or Ragi or Madua (*Eleusine coracana*)

It is an important plant growing erect, tuft up to 60-122 cm, in Karnataka, Tamil Nadu, Andhra Pradesh, Orissa, Bihar, Gujarat and Maharashtra, Uttar Pradesh (hills) and Himachal Pradesh. It is extensively cultivated in areas of rainfall (50-100 cm) as *rabi* crop in southern India and *kharif* in northern India. It is mostly grown on clay and heavy black cotton soils with poor fertility.

- Finger millet contains 9.2% protein, 1.29% fat, 76.32% carbohydrate, 2.24% minerals, 3.90% ash, etc.
- **Varieties:** Indaf-1, Indaf-5, EC-4840, IE-28, Sharda, PR-202, VL-101, VL-204, HR-374, Nirmal, K-5, 7, Co-7, 11, 13 Co 1, Co 7, Co

8, Co 9, K 1, K 2, AKP 1, AKP 2, AKP 7, Poona, Cavery, Hansa, Annapurna, PR 202, I.E 28, Hagari-1, etc.

Italian or Foxtail Millet or Kankun (*Setaria italica*)

It is cultivated in tropical and temperate regions, mostly in Karnataka, Andhra Pradesh, Madhya Pradesh and Uttar Pradesh under rainfed conditions. Normally, it is sown in June-July (rainfed) and February or March (irrigated). The grains contain, 12.3% protein, 4.7% fat, 60.6% carbohydrates and 3.2% ash.

Varieties: Arjuna, MS 1844/2, I.Se.700 and I.Se.701.

Kodo Millet (*Paspalum scrobiculatum*)

This is a highly drought-resistant crop grown in Andhra Pradesh, Uttar Pradesh., Maharashtra, Karnataka and Tamil Nadu It is sown in June-July (September-October in Andhra Pradesh and Tamil Nadu). The grain is very coarse with a horny seed coat, which is normally removed before cooking. The grains contain 8.3% protein, 1.4% fat, 65.6% carbohydrates, and 2.9% ash.

- **Varieties:** Niwas-1, PLR-1, Co-1, Co-2, Co-3, IPS-158, PAC-1, PAC-2, PAC-3, PAC-4.

Common Millet or Cheena or Proso Millet (*Panicum miliaceum*)

It is mostly grown in Uttar Pradesh, Madhya Pradesh, Maharashtra, Andhra Pradesh, Karnataka and Tamil Nadu. It is mostly cultivated in *Kharif* season. Cheena has 12.5% protein, 4.5% lycine, 1.1% fat, and 68.9% carbohydrates.

- Varieties: P.V. 14, P.V. 36, BR-7 and Co-l

Little Millet (*Panicum miliare*)

Little millet is grown on a limited scale as a poor man's crop in Tamil Nadu, Andhra Pradesh. and Uttar Pradesh. The crop flowers in 40-50 days and matures in 75-80 days, depending on the variety. It is resistant to drought and withstands water logging.

- Varieties: PM-2 and PM-296, Dindori-l.

Package and Practices

Crop and duration (days)	Season	Seed rate (kg/ha)	Fertilizer N:P:K (kg/ha)	Spacing (cm)	Method of planting	Critical stages	Yield (kg/ha)	Varieties/Special informations
Madua/ Ragi/ Finger millet 110-120	*Kharif* *Rabi* *Zaid*	8-12 Trans- planting	60:30:30	15 × 15	Broad- casting, Line sowing, Trans- planting	Tillering, Flowering	2,000- 2,500	Indaf-1/5, Sharda, Nirmal, B-1, E-31, A-16, TRY-1 saline/alkaline soil resistant.
Cheena/ Proso/ Common millet 60-90	*Kharif* *Zaid*	8-12	50:30:20	25 × 10	Line planting, Seed drill	Flowering	2,000- 2,500	Co-2 (55 days), K-1 (100 days); Drought tolerant crop.
Sawan/ Barnyard millet 75-90	*Kharif*	8-10	40:30:20		Direct sowing	Tillering, Flowering	1,000- 2,000	Co-1, K-2 (lodging, drought tolerant).

Crop and duration (days)	Season	Seed rate (kg/ha)	Fertilizer N:P:K (kg/ha)	Spacing (cm)	Method of planting	Critical stages	Yield (kg/ha)	Varieties/Special informations
Kodo millet 100	*Kharif*	10-15	40:20:20	45 × 10	Line planting	Tillering, Flowering, Seed drill.	800-1,100	Most droughts tolerant; Immature grains poisonous; Best for diabetic persons.
Little millet 75-80	*Kharif*	8-10	40:30:20			Tillering, Flowering	1,500-1,800	Co-3, K-1, 2.
Kankun/ Foxtail millet 80-85	*Kharif*	8-10	50:35:25	Line planting 22 × 10	Line planting, Seed drill	Tillering, Flowering	1,000-1,600	Co-45, K-32, Arjuna, H-1, N-1; Co-4 can be raised in Rabi season.

14

Pulse Crops

Pulses form an important part of Indian dietary. They are, important source of protein, essential adjuncts to a predominantly cereal-based diet, enhancing the biological value of the food consumed. Pulses contain more vitamins including B_1 (Chickpea 100 I.U., Urd 130 I.U., Mung 155 I.U., Soybean 300 I.U., C (sprouting pulses 10-15 mg/100 g), and Calcium (0.19% in Chickpea, 0.21% in Urd, 0.15% in Mung).

During 2003-2004, the minimum requirement of pulses in balanced food was 50 g/capita/day; but presently the availability of pulses is quite low (37 gm per capita) in comparison to the dawn of independence (71 gm per capita).

During 2003-2004, the pulse production has increased drastically from 8.41 MT with the productivity of 441 kg/ha (1951) to 15.24 MT with 623 kg/ha productivity in 2003-2004.

Causes of Low Yield of Pulses

- Uneven distribution of rainfall is attributed to poor crop stand.
- Lack of high yielding varieties (only after the initiation of All India Pulse Improvement Project in 1965, varieties could be developed for cultivation).
- Improper agronomic management.
- Non-availability of suitable *Rhizobium* culture, etc.

Chickpea or Bengal-Gram (*Cicer* spp.) $2n = 14$ (Desi), $2n = 16$ (Kabuli)

Two type of chickpea, *viz.* Desi type (*Cicer arietinum*) and Kabuli type (*C. kabulianum*), generally contains 21.1% Protein, 61.5% Carbohydrates, and 4.5% Fat; rich in minerals like Ca, Fe, and Vitamin C. It was originated in Southwestern Asia. In India it ranks first in production. Crop is sown during mid-October with the onset of cool weather having average temperature of 25°C. Early sown crop suffers from wilt disease owing to higher temperatures at the time of sowing. Chickpea thrives best on well-drained, coarse-textured/loamy soils with pH 5.5-8.6 but very sensitive to saline and alkaline soils.

- **Varieties: Desi types**: Avarodhi, Pant G-186, Pant G-114, Gaurav, H-208, Uday, Pusa 362, Pusa 372, Radhey, JG 315, Haryana Chana 1, K-850; **Kabuli type:** C-104, L-550, L-144, Pusa-1003, Hare Chhole 1, Pusa-1053, and Sadabahar. C 214, C 235, H 355, G 130, G 543, RS 10, RS 11, RSG 2, GL 769, GNG 146, Pusa 209, Pusa 212, Pusa 261, Pusa 408, L 144 are other varieties of chickpea.
- **Nipping** is the process of plucking the apical buds after 30-40 DAS, in order to stop apical growth for promotion of lateral branching; yielding more pods, and yields.
- The irrigation is avoided at the flowering stage.
- In addition to weeding, Basalin @ 1.0 kg a.i./ha or Stomp (0.75 kg a.i./ha) or Ronstor (1.5 kg a.i./ha) are used for weed control.

Black-gram or Urd (*Phaseolus mungo*) 2*n* = 14

Black-gram is very rich in phosphoric acid and contains 24% Protein, 60% Carbohydrates and 1.3% Fat. It is indigenous to India and grown in M.P., U.P., Punjab, Maharashtra, West Bengal, Andhra Pradesh, and Karnataka contributing to 13% of total pulse production. *Kharif* crop is sown in June-July; summer crop during February-April.

- **Varieties: Black seeded:** Type 9, Pusa 1, Number-55, Khargone-3, Ujjain-4; **Green seeded:** Type 56, Mash 48, Pant U-35, Narendra Urd-1, Azad 1, Type-27, Pant Urd 19, Naveen, Pusa 1, Krishna, Kulu-4, HPU-6, KM-2, ADT-2, PDU-1 are other varieties.
- The pre-emergence application of Lasso @ 1.5 kg a.i./ha keeps the field free from weeds for the first 50 days and thereafter crop itself smother the weeds.

Pigeon Pea (*Cajanus cajan*) 2*n* = 22

Red gram/ Pigeon pea C. *cajan* var. *flavus* (early maturity) and *Cajanus cajan* var. *bicolor* (late maturity). Both species bear tap roots with well, developed lateral or secondary root system consisting nodules on them. Leaves are pinnately compound and trifoliate with oblong, lanceolate leaflets.

- The crop is best cultivated in moist and warm weather having 15-18°C temperatures for growth and a little high for maturity in sandy loam to clay loam soil. It is mostly cultivated in Uttar Pradesh, Madhya Pradesh, Maharashtra, Bihar, Andhra Pradesh, Punjab, Haryana, and West Bengal, etc. Uttar Pradesh produces about 20% of total production of pigeon pea.
- **Varieties:** Gwalior-3, Pusa 75, Pusa 84, Pant A-2, HPA-1, Sagar, B.S.1, Sweta, BDN-1, BDN-2, Co 2, Co 4, Co 5, Pusa-855, Azad, Manak, Paras, Pusa Ageti, Laxmi, A.L.-15, etc. I.C.P.H. 8 is first hybrid released from ICRISAT. Amar, Azad, Asha, and Maruthi are wilt resistant varieties. Pusa-855, Asha, Sharad, Narendra Arhar–1, and Bahar are Sterility mosaic resistant varieties.
- Application Lasso (Alachlor) @ 3.0 kg/ha as pre-emergence or Basalin @ 1.0 litre/ha as pre-sowing, manage several weeds in pigeon pea field.

Green Gram (*Vigna radiata*) 2*n* = 24

Mung is cultivated in both the seasons *Kharif* (Northern India) and *rabi* (South and Southwest India). Mung contains 25% Protein with high digestibility. It is hardiest of all the pulses grown in drought prone areas during *kharif* and summer (North India). The crop requires well drained loamy to sandy loam soil. It is cultivated in Madhya Pradesh, Maharashtra, Uttar Pradesh, Punjab, Andhra Pradesh, Rajasthan, Karnataka, and Tamil Nadu.

- Sowing for *kharif* crop commences during 15 June to 15 July; *Rabi* crop is sown during 15 October to 15 November; and summer from 15 March to 15 April.
- **Varieties**: Pusa 9072, Pusa Vishal, Asha, Narendra mung-1, PDM-11, Pant mung-1, 2, 3, 4, K-851, Varsha, Krishna-11, Jawahar-45, R.S.-4, M.L.-267, Kopergaon, Co-3, KM-1, B-105, T 1, T 44, G 65, Pusa Baisakhi, Pusa 16, Pusa 101, Pusa 105, C 65, PS 16, Pusa 7, Pusa 10, Pant Mung 3, D 66, ML 131, G 65, Jawahar 45, Shining Mung 1, S 8 (Mohini), ML 1, S 9, ML 5, ML 9, T 51, R 288-8.
- No irrigation is given at the full-grown stage of crop, but during summer it is necessary to irrigate the crop at the interval of 15 days.

- **Weed control:** Pre-emergence application of Lasso or Tok E-25 @ 2 kg a.i./ha in 1,000 litres of water ensures complete weed control.

Lentil (*Lens esculentus*) 2*n* = 14

It was originated in Asia Minor, Greece and Egypt; presently India ranks first in the lentil production and mainly cultivated in M.P., U.P., Bihar, etc. Lentil contains 25% Protein, 60% Carbohydrates and contributes to 6% of total pulse production in India.

- **Varieties**: Sivalik, Malika, Pant L-4, Sapna, Priya, Narendra Lentil-1, V.L. Lentil-4, 103, IPL-81, Pusa Vaibhav, Pant Lentil-406, Pusa-6, C-31, JLS-1, etc.
- Weeds like *Chenopodium album, Fumaria parviflora, Lathyrus* spp. can be managed using Basalin @ 0.75 kg a.i./ha as pre-sowing of the crop.

Pea (*Pisum* spp.)

Two species of pea are cultivated in India, *viz. Pisum sativum* var. *hortense* (Garden pea/Table pea), and *P. sativum* var. *arvense* (Field pea/Coloured flower pea). Plants of garden pea are erect whereas it is climbing type in field pea. Plant bear tap root system with nodules. The terminal leaf is modified into tendril. Flowers are arranged in axillary raceme. The crop is self-pollinated.

- It was originated in Italy and Southwestern Europe now it is cultivated in India on sizeable account in U.P., M.P., Bihar, Punjab, etc.
- **Varieties: Field pea:** T-163, Hans, Rachna, V.L. 1, DMR 11, Kinnauri, Pant-5, P.G. 3, B.R. 12, Aparna; **Garden pea:** Type-19, Punjab-87, Early Badger, Early December, Arkel, Bonneville, Asaunji, Jawahar pea-4, Madhu, Type-56, Meteor C.C. -141, Meteor C.C. -195, Swarn Rekha, Rachna, L-116.
- Sowing is done from 15 October (field pea) and 1 November onwards (Garden pea) in North India.
- Weeds like *Chenopodium album* is controlled with the application of Basalin @ 0.75 kg a.i./ha as pre-sowing of the crop.

Soya Bean (*Glycine max*)

It was originated in Eastern Asia including China and now it cultivated in India on 6 Mha of land, in moist and warm conditions from 26.5 to 30°C temperature. Crop better runs on well-drained fertile loam soil with pH 6.0-7.5. Planting is done in third week of June to first fortnight of July.

- **Varieties**: Bragg, Lee, Improved Pelican, Ankur, Alankar, Shilajeet, PK-262, PK-327, Birsa Soya bean-1, Co-1, Clark, Durga, Gaurav, Gujarat Soy-1, Ahilya 143, Pooja, Monetta, Shivalik.

Chickling Pea (*Lathyrus sativus*)

Crop is chiefly cultivated for fodder but poor people use the grain as pulse and unripe pods are used as a green vegetable. The grain and other plant parts contain neurotoxin. **BOAA** (b-N-Oxalyl amine alanine), which has been shown to be the inciting agent of lathyrism, a kind of paralysis of the lower limbs in human beings. The crop is mostly cultivated in M.P., Bihar and U.P. It is a cold weather crop, which thrives best on low-lying deep black soils.

- Steeping the pulse overnight in water and rejecting the water effectively detoxifies the pulse.
- A variety P 24 (developed at IARI) has very low BOAA content.
- The crop is sown in September-October and harvested in February-March.
- **Seed rate:** 10 to 35 kg/ha.
- **Varieties:** No. 9, Rewa-2, No. 11, T-2-12, etc.
- The average **yields** 3 to 4 q /ha.

Cow Pea (*Vigna sinensis*)

Cow pea is used as a fodder, vegetable, pulse and green manure crop. It prefers warm and humid season and grows well on a wide range of soils. However, saline and alkali soils are not suitable for growth.

- Summer crop in Northern India is sown mid-April. Sowing for *kharif* crop commences from early June to the last week of July.

- **Varieties**: Pusa Phalguni, Pusa Barsati, Pusa dofasali, Pusa rituraj, FS-68, Cow pea-74; **Fodder**: FOS-1, FS-145, and IPC-5286. Bacterial blight resistant S 488 (Bangalore); K 11, T 26 and T 5826 (Uttar Pradesh).

Horse-gram (*Dolichos biflorus*)

Horse-gram is extensively grown in peninsular India, including Andhra Pradesh, Karnataka and Tamil Nadu. It is sown during late August-November, however, as a fodder crop it is sown during June to August.

- Seed rate is 25 kg/ha for grain and 40 kg/ha for fodder if spacing is kept at 30 cm between rows.
- **Varieties:** Co-1 Hebble Hurali-1 and Hebble Hurali-2.

Rajmah (*Phaseolus vulgaris*)

It is grown only in Maharashtra, Himachal Pradesh, Uttar Pradesh, and Jammu and Kashmir. Rajmah is grown as a *kharif* crop in the hilly tracts and sown during 15-30 June. However, the determinate and early-maturing varieties can also be grown in the spring season from February to April in the subtropical belt and during March-May or August-October in sub-temperate areas. In plains like those of Maharashtra rajmah is raised as a *rabi* crop.

- **Varieties**: HIM 1, Jawala, Hans, Jampa, Manus, Vaghya and VL Rajamash 63, PDR 3, PDR 14 and PDR 20. Jawala has attractive scarlet-red seeds, Hans has bold white seeds, and HIM 1 has medium bold, light pink seeds with red spots.
- **Seed rate and spacing:** 35-40 kg/ha (small seeded) and 45-50 kg/ha (bold seeded) with spacing of 25-30 cm.
- Since, rajmah is the only legume which do not form nodules for fixation of nitrogen, therefore, application of 80:60:40 kg/ha NPK at the time of sowing gives good results.
- Spraying with 1.5 kg Carbaryl-50 WP or Endosulfan-35 EC in 625 litres of water per hectare is useful for Hairy caterpillar, Blister beetles and Bean-bugs.

Package and Practices of Important Pulse Crops

Crop and duration (days)	Season	Seed rate (kg/ha)	Fertilizers N:P:K (kg/ha)	Spacing (cm)	Method of sowing	Critical stages	Yield (q/ha)	Special features and varieties
Gram/ Bengal gram/ Chick pea 90-105	*Rabi*	75-100	Irrigated 25:50:0 Rainfed 12.5:25:0	30 × 60 (Desi) 45 × 60 (Kabuli)	Seed drill, Behind plough	Grain-development	25-30 Grains, 50-60 Stick, 10 Dried leaves	**Nipping**: Plucking of apical top (30-40 DAS).
Pigeon pea 100-180	*Kharif*	10-15	25:50:0 Irrigated 12.5:25:0 Rainfed	90 x 30 (SA-1,3,4) 45× 30	Line sowing, Dibbling	Flowering Pod filling	15-25	UPAS-120, Pusa Ageti, Sharda, Mukta, Prabhat, BSR-1 (as border crop, shade crop for turmeric).
Urd/ Black gram 60-75	*Kharif* *Zaid*	15-20 25-30	25:50:0 Irrigated 12.5:25:0 Rainfed	45 × 10 20 × 10	Line sowing, Broadcasting	Flowering, Pod formation	10-11 Irrigated 6.5-7.5 Rainfed	KCl @ 0.5% for moisture stress; Type-9, Sindkhera, Pusa-1, Mash, Naveen, Pant U-30, ADT-2
Lentil 80-90	*Rabi*	50-60	25:50:0 Irrigated 12.5:25:0 Rainfed	20 × 45	Seed drill, Behind plough.	Flowering, Grain-development	20-25	Sivalik, Malika, Pant L-4; Runen $ZnSO_4$ 25 Kg/ha.

Crop and duration (days)	Season	Seed rate (kg/ha)	Fertilizers N:P:K (kg/ha)	Spacing (cm)	Method of sowing	Critical stages	Yield (q/ha)	Special features and varieties
Cow pea 70-90	*Kharif* Summer	18-20	25:50:0 Irrigated 12.5:25:0 Rainfed	30-45 × 15	Line sowing; Dibbling	Flowering Pod formation	9-11 Irrigated 8-9 Rainfed	Grown for pulse, vegetable, fodder.
Soya bean 20% Oil, 40% Protein 85-90	*Kharif*	90-100	20:80:40 200 kg Gypsum.	30 × 5	Dibbling	Flowering Pod filling	13-15 Irrigated 11 Rainfed	Kaolin @ 3% for moisture stress;Foliar spray of DAP (2%)+ 0.5% $ZNSO_4$.
Mung/ Green gram 65-90	*Kharif* Summer	15-20 20-25	Irrigated 25:50:0 Rainfed 12.5:25:0	30 × 10	Line sowing, Broad-casting, Dibbling.	Flowering Pod filling	10-11 Irrigated 6.5-7.5 Rainfed	Soak seed in $MnSO_4$ solution; Spray DAP @ 2% at the time of flowering.
Pea 60-90	*Rabi*	60-80 Field 75-125 Garden	25:70:20 25 t FYM	40 × 10	Seed drill Dibbling	Growth Flowering Pod formation	20-25 Field 100-125 Garden	T-163, Hans, Rachna, V.L.1, DMR 11, Kinnauri, Pant-5, P.G. 3, B.R. 12, Aparna.

□□□

15

Oilseed Crops

Oilseeds are cultivated with an annual production of 10 MT on about 16.5 Mha of land constituting approximately one-tenth of the total cultivated area of India. The important oilseed crops grown in India in order of importance include groundnut, rapeseed and mustard, sesame, linseed, safflower, castor, sunflower and niger.

Groundnut (*Arachis hypogaea*)

Arachis hypogaea consists of two sub species, *viz. A. hypogaea* sub sp. *hirsuta* and *A. hypogaea* sub sp. *fastigiata*.

Groundnut or Peanut, or Earthnut, or Monkeynut is a native of Brazil. It was introduced into India during the first half of the 16 th century from one of the pacific islands of China, where it was introduced earlier from either from Central America or South America. It is a self-pollinated crop and pollination takes place early in the morning. Groundnut is a tropical crop requiring warm growing season and sandy or sandy loam soil for cultivation.

- Kernel contains 44-50% oil and, are rich source of Protein (26%) and Vitamins A, B making its calorific value to 349 per 100 g. Oilcake contains 7-8:1.5:1.2 per cent NPK.
- 70% of the area and 75% of the production is concentrated in the four states (Gujarat, Andhra Pradesh, Tamil Nadu and Karnataka). It is raised mostly as a rainfed *kharif* crop, sown during May-June. The critical stage for irrigation is **flowering and pegging** of the crop.
- Groundnut field conserve nutrients in soil, therefore, following cereal crops grown after groundnut give 25% more yield.
- **Varieties:** Ah. 32, Junagadh-11, GAUG-1, GAUG-10, MH-374, Junagadh-113, TMV 1, TMV 2, TMV 3, TMV 7, TMV 8, TMV 9, TMV 10, Pol. 1, Pol. 2, S-206, 230, A.K.10-24, R.S. 1, Chandra, Faizapur-1, P.G.1, Kopergaon-1 and Kopergaon-3.

- Groundnut crop requires 6.25 t/ha FYM plus 10-20:20-40:20-40 kg/ha NPK (Rainfed); and 12.5 t/ha FYM plus 20-40:40-90:20-40 kg/ha NPK for irrigated crop. Inoculation with *Rhizobium* as seed treatment and application of gypsum @ 500 kg/ ha at the pegging stage, enhances yield remarkably.
- **Seed rate and spacing:** 110 kg/ha (spreading type) and 120 kg/ha (bunch type) of seed with the spacing of 10-20 × 20-30 cm.
- **Weed control:** The first hoeing at 21 DAS, the second, and the third about a fortnight and a month later; and application of Lasso or Tok-E-25 @ 5 lit./ha in 500 litres of water as a pre-emergence soil spray within two days of sowing. **Interculture should be avoided after the pegs start going underground.**
- Safe moisture content is not more than 5% for storage. More moisture attracts *Aspergillus flavus* causing aflatoxins.
- **Diseases:** Tikka disease caused by *Cercospora arachidicola* (early) and *C. personata* (late); collar rot (*Aspergillus niger* and *A. pulverulentum*); Rust (*Puccinia arachidis*). Thiram or captan @ 4 g/kg of seed as seed treatment and Hinosan @ 0.02% is recommended to check the spread of the pathogens.
- **Yield** for spreading type (1,200-1,400) and bunch type (800-1,000) is kg/ha. The shelling percentage is 70-75%.

Rapeseed and Mustard (*Brassica* spp.)

Rapeseed and Mustard originated in China and now India is the largest producer of these crops in the world. In India they cultivated mostly in U.P., Punjab, Rajasthan, M.P., Bihar, Orissa, W.B. and Assam.

- Rai and Yellow sarson are self-fertile and the rest of the cruciferous oilseeds, *viz.* Brown sarson, Toria, Taramira, Banarasi Rai and White mustard, are self-incompatible.
- Rapeseed and Mustard yield 30-48 per cent of edible oil and 24-30% protein.
- But the Indian mustard is not accepted in international market due to presence of high erucic acid and glucosinolate contents. However, now a days efforts are going on for minimization of both erucic acid and glucosinolate contents, through development of single or double zero varieties (for detail refer Chapter 18, Plant Breeding).

Common species rapeseed and mustard grown in India include,

1. Brown mustard, commonly called Rai/Raya/Laha (*Brassica juncea*).
2. Sarson includes Yellow sarson (*B. campestris* var. *sarson*), Brown sarson (*B. campestris* var. *dichotoma*) and Toria/Lahi/Maghi Labi (*B. campestris* var. *toria*).
3. Banarsi rai/Black mustard (*B. nigra*).

- It is a *rabi* crop grown from September-October to February-March. Crop requires 25-40 cm of rainfall if grown as rainfed.
- **Varieties: Toria:** Sangam, Type-9, Type 36, TL 15, PT 303; **Brown sarson:** BSH–1, Pusa Kalyani, Suphala, KBS 1; **Yellow sarson:** Thumka; **Mustard:** Varuna, Laxmi, Pusa Jaikisan, Rajat, Pusa Basant, Pusa Bahar, Vardan, Kranti, Prakash, Varuna, B-85.
- **Seed rate:** 5-6 kg/ha.
- **Fertilizers:** 15-20 t/ha of FYM plus 60-90:60:40 kg/ha NPK.
- **Weed control:** Weeds like *Chenopodium album, Lathyrus* spp., *Meliolotus indica, Cirsium arvense* can be controlled easily with the application Nitrogen or Isoproteuron @ 1.5 kg a.i./ha.
- **Yield:** The average yield of rapeseed and mustard is 500-800 kg/ha; sarson 800-1,000 kg; and rai 1,000-1,200 kg/ha.

Sesamum / Sesame / Til / Gingerly (*Sesamum indicum*)

It is, originated in Africa, an important and ancient oilseed crop having oil content of 46-52%, and 20% protein. Cake is a rich source of Protein, Carbohydrates and Mineral nutrients, such as Calcium and Phosphorus. India ranks first, both in the area and production of sesame in the world. Now it is cultivated in Uttar Pradesh., Rajasthan, Madhya Pradesh., Andhra Pradesh, Orissa, Gujarat, Tamil Nadu. and Karnataka. It is a warm season crop grown in three seasons, *viz. kharif* (70%), semi-*rabi* (20%) and summer (10%).

- **Varieties**: Type 12, Type 13, Punjab til 1, Pratap, No. 122, Gwalior-5, Gwalior 35, N-32, Patan-64, Patan 65, Gauri, Madhvi, T-85, Phule til no. 1, TMV 2, TMV 3, Vinaya, B-9, B-14, B 67.
- **Seed rate and spacing:** 3-5 kg/ha with the spacing of 25-35 × 10-20 cm.
- **Fertilizers:** 25-30:20-30:0-20 kg/ha NPK.
- **Pests**: Leaf-eating caterpillar (*Antigastra catalaulmlis*) and Gall-fly (*Asphon dylia-sesalili*) can be controlled with the application of Carbaryl 0.2% as spray.

- **Diseases**: Stem and root-rot (*Macrophominia phaseoli*), Phyllody (mycoplasma), Bacterial leaf-spot (*Pseudomonas sesami*) and Leaf-curl (virus) can be controlled by seed treatment with Captan @ 3-9/kg of seed; Agrimycin @ 01-100 ppm at 15-day intervals for bacterial leaf spot; Phyllody and leaf-curl with Phosphamidon 0.05% or Dimethoate 0.05% or Dichlorovas 0.05% as spray.
- **Yeild**: *Kharif* 800-1000 kg/ha.

Linseed or Flax (*Linum ugitatissimum*)

Linseed seeds are rich in oil (33-47%) used for paint and varnishes, oilcloth, waterproof fabrics and linoleum manufacturing. The cake contains 36% Protein. It is cultivated in Madhya Pradesh, Uttar Pradesh, Maharashtra, Bihar, Rajasthan, Karnataka and West Bengal. Madhya Pradesh and Uttar Pradesh together contributing 70% of total linseed production of India. It is grown in *rabi* season on deep clayey black and loam soil. The crop is grown at 20 × 30 cm spacing with the seed-rate of 30-40 kg/ha.

- **Varieties:** Neelam, Hira, Mukta, T-397, K-2, Himalini, R-17, B-67, L.C. 54, Gaurav, Chambal, Lock 8528, etc.
- Linseed requires 30:15:00 kg/ha NPK for rainfed and 60:30:00 kg/ha NPK for irrigated condition.
- **Pests**: Linseed gall midge (*Dasyneura lini*) is the most serious pest; 5% Aldrin or Chlordane @ 25 to 30 kg/ha is used for the management of both the pests by mixing them in soil.
- **Yield**: 2.1-4.5 q/ha (rainfed) and 12-15 q/ha (irrigated).

Castor (*Ricinus communis*)

Castor originated in Ethopia, is an important industrial oilseed crop having 35-58 per cent oil. Its deep root system makes it drought resistant. India ranks first in area (0.049 Mha) second in production (0.014 MT), Brazil being the, first in the world. In India, Andhra Pradesh (67.2%), Gujarat (12.7%) Karnataka (7.1%) and Orissa (5.8%) account for over 90% of the area and production. The seed is sown either in the plough furrow or with a seed-drill or by handdibbling.

- **Varieties:** Aruna, Bhagya, Saubhagya, Dwarf Mutant, H.C. 6, Rosy, Girja, C.H. 1, S.A. 2, GCH-3, J-44, GAUC-1, Type-3, Tarai-4, Punjab Castor-1, W.B. 1.
- **Seedrate:** 18-20 kg/ha (behind plough), 8-10 kg/ha (hand-dibbling) with spacing of 90-120 × 45-60 cm.
- **Require:** 60:40:40 kg/ha NPK.

- **Pests**: Castor semi-looper (*Achow janaga*) and the Capsule-borer (*Dicitocrocis punctiferalis*) are most serious pests and can be controlled by dusting 10% BHC or 0.1% Carbaryl.
- **Diseases**: Seedling blight (*Phytopiathora colocasii*) and Alternaria blight (*Alternaria ricini*) are important pests and can be managed by seed treatment with Thiram at the rate of 3 g/kg of seed.
- **Yield**: Rainfed 10-20 q/ha; irrigated 25-28 kg/ha.

Safflower (*Carthamus tinctorius*)

According to N.I. Vavilov it is the indigenous to India. In India, it is grown in Maharashtra, Karnataka and Andhra Pradesh. Safflower is grown mostly as a mix crop with Wheat, Barley, Gram and *rabi* Jowar. Seeds contain 20-36% oil, used for manufacture of paints, varnishes, and linoleum.

- **Varieties:** Nag-7, Tara, A-1, A-300, Manjira, N-7, T-65, E.B.-7, NP-30, NP 18, K-1, C 438.
- **Seed rate:** 15-20 kg/ha.
- **Insect pests:** The safflower aphid (*Dactynotus carthami*), thrips (*Franklinieya sulphurea*) and the Flower bud fly (*Acanihiphilus helianthi*) are the serious pests of the crop. Spraying with Fenithion (0.1%), Dimethoate (0.03%) and Endosulfan (0.07%) for controlling aphids, thrips and bud fly, respectively is used.
- **Diseases:** Rust (*Puccinia carthami*), Leaf-spot (*Alternaria carthami*) and Root-rot (*Phytophthora drechsleri*) are the important diseases of safflower, and can be managed by resistant varieties.
- **Yield:** Rainfed: 6-8 q/ha, Irrigated: 15-20 q/ha, Mixed crop: 2-3 q/ha.

Sunflower (*Helianthus annus*)

It is a native of Southern United States and Mexico and popularly called '*Surajmukhi*'. It was introduced in India in 1969. Seeds contain 45-50% oil. The crop is sown in first week of July (*Kharif*), October (*Rabi*), and March (*Zaid*). Edible oil of sunflower is of superior quality because of anti cholestrol and non-cholestrol contents. Its oil is used for making vanaspati, soap, margarine; husk is used for preparation of ethyl alcohol.

- **Varieties:** Peredovik, Armavirskij, BSH-1, Modern Dwarf, Sunrise selection, Pant 209, Pant 1234, Pant 406, Pant 639, K 75, L 9-12, Pusa 4, Pusa 6, Type 8, MSFH 8, PSFH-67, GKSFH-2002, Jwalamukhi, Mega-363 and NSFH-592.
- **Seed rate:** 8-10 kg/ha.

- Pendimethylin (STOMP @ 2.51/ha) is used as pre-emergence for effective weed control of weeds.
- **Pests:** For Cutworm (*Agrotis* spp.) apply 5 litrers of Dursban/ Radar 20 EC (Chlorpyriphos). For Tobacco caterpillar (*Spodoptera litura*), Cabbage Semi-looper (*Plusia orichalcea*), Bihar hairy caterpillar (*Spilosoma obliqua*), spray 1.125 l/ha Folithion/ Sumithion 50 EC (fenotrothin) or 1.225 l/ha Thiodan 35 EC (endosulfan) or 500 ml Nuvan 100 EC (dichlorvos) in 250 litres of water per hectare. Head borer (*Helicoverpa armigera*) is controlled by spraying 2.5 kg of Sevin 50 WP (Carbaryl) or 2.0 litres of Asataf 75 SP (Acephate) or 2.125 litres Folothion 50 EC (Fenitrothion) or 2.5 litres of Dursban 20 EC (Chlorpyriphos) or Thiodan 35 EC (Endosulfan) or 1.25 litre of Nuvacron 30 SI (Monocrotophous) in 375 litres of water per hectare.
- **Yield:** 20 q/ha.

Niger (*Guizotia abyssinica*)

India is the chief Niger-producing country in the world. It is cultivated in M.P., Bihar, Maharashtra, Orissa and Tamil Nadu. Oil percentage in Niger is about 37 to 43 per cent of the seed weight, which is used for culinary purposes, anointing the body, manufacturing paints and soft soaps, lighting and lubrication, and manufacturing cosmetics. Niger is grown as a *kharif* crop under rainfed conditions.

❑❑❑

16

Cash Crops

Sugarcane and sugarbeet are two main crops that contribute approximately 70 and 30 per cent of crystal sugar, respectively.

Sugarcane (*Saccharum officinarum*) $2n=80$, *S. barberi* : $2n = 82$

It is the tropical crop and main source of sugar in India. U.P. has the largest acreage under sugarcane (51%) and accounts for 47 per cent of the annual production in terms of raw sugar. But the production per hectare (productivity) is highest in Tamil Nadu, followed by Karnataka, Maharashtra and Andhra Pradesh. The average productivity during 2003-2004 has been 67.4 t/ha in South India and 55.3 t/ha in North India. India ranks second in the world with 20.4% area and 18.6% production.

- Sugarcane is cultivated from stem cuttings since ancient times. Leading producers of sugarcane today include Brazil and India. Sugarcane is also grown in Brazil as a source of alcohol for automobiles. The crushed cane, called **bagasse**, is used as forage and fuel. In tropical areas such as Brazil, Hawaii, and Cuba, cane has a growth period ranging from one year to 18 months and harvested from January to August. The small spikelets are sometimes borne in panicles (inflorescence) and are surrounded by long, silky fibres, called **arrow**.
- Planting of autumn, spring and adsali sugarcane is done in October, February-March and July, respectively. 1/3rd top portion is best for sowing.
- Earthing in sugarcane is done in the month of June-July after giving final top dressing of nitrogen.
- There are three methods of planting, *viz.* flat planting, furrow planting and trench planting.

1. **Flat planting:** In this method, shallow furrows are made with the spacing of 80-100 cm and setts are placed in such a way that ends of setts join to form a line. The setts are covered with 5-7 cm of soil.
2. **Furrow planting:** Furrows are made about 10 to 20 cm deep, and setts are put as above covering only 5-7 cm, leaving the upper portion of the furrow unfilled. Immediately after sowing irrigation is given.

3. **Trench planting:** Trenches are made with the depth of 20-25 cm following rectangular or trapezoidal pattern. The setts are placed end-to-end or otherwise in the furrows and covered, as in the case of flat planting. After sowing trenches are irrigated.

- Crop should be harvested when the refractometer reading is 17 to 18. Average yield in North India is 400-500 q/ha.

Sugarbeet (*Beta vulgaris*) Chenopodiaceae, $2n = 90$

It is originated in Mediterranean region. The crop is important as the source of about two-fifths of the world supply of crystal sugar. Sugar-beet flourishes on a rich, deep, loamy soil having pH even up to 9.5, in a climate with a mean temperature of about 21°C during the growing season. Sugarbeet being temperate and cold climate crop is cultivated in USA, France, Germany, Italy, Poland and Turkey also.

- Sugarbeet is one of the most efficient converter of solar energy to stored energy. It is 6-7 months crop yielding sugar equal to 12-month sugarcane crop.
- German chemist Marrggraf in 1746 reported the quality of crystal sugar from sugarbeet as equal to the crystal sugar from sugarcane. Kranz Karl Achard for the first time practically proven it, and reciprocated that white skinned and fleshy type beet varieties have sweetest juice.
- The seed is sown at 15 cm high ridges planted with a depth of 2.5 cm. Crop require 7-9 irrigations at an interval of 25 days depending upon the season.

Tobacco (*Nicotiana* spp.) $2n = 48$

The name tobacco has arisen from *Tobago* (a tubelike structure) through which the Arawak people of the Caribbean used to smoke tobacco, as observed by Christopher Columbus in 1492. It is a common name applied to plants cultivated for their leaves, which after curing, are used for smoking, chewing, and as snuffing.

- Tobacco produces 10-20 broad leaves that branch alternately from a central stalk are used to produce cigarettes, cigars, and chewing tobacco. There are four species of *Nicotiana, viz. N. tabacum* (the most widely cultivated species), *N. rustica, N. gossei* and *N. ingulba*, of these, the former two are cultivated in India.
- *N. tobaccum* can attain a height up to 150-550 cm with large and narrow leaf base and fine texture. The nicotine content varies from 0.5-5.5% and is mostly used for smoking and chewing purposes. *N. rustica* has the plant height from 90-120 cm, contains 3.5-8% nicotine and used for Hookah, Chewing and Snuffing proposes.
- China is the largest tobacco producer, followed by the United States, India, and Brazil.

- Tobacco also **contains certain alkaloids**, including nicotine, which is a mild stimulant and is considered an addictive drug. The amount of nicotine in tobacco depends on the species, the crop, and the growing conditions.
- **Topping:** It is the removal of flower heads either alone or with few upper leaves in order to improve the quality of leaves. This technique is **not needed for crop meant for wrapping** purposes. It is done to divert energy from top to the leaves.
- **De-suckering:** After topping lateral buds form the bulk of leaves; the thinning of these axillary buds is called de-suckering.
- **Curing:** The curing of tobacco is a slow process carefully monitored to produce tobacco leaves with specific colours, wilts, and degrees of dryness. Three different methods of curing, *viz.* air curing, fire curing, and flue (heat) curing, impart distinctive flavours to the tobacco leaves.
- A cigar is made from cigar-filler leaf (85%), cigar-binder leaf (15%), and a final enveloping with cigar-wrapper leaf (5%) is done. Only the **most expensive cigars are rolled by hand.**
- **Chewing tobacco is the most inferior tobacco** and is often blended with flavourings, such as honey or liquorices.

Cotton (*Gossypium* spp.)

Gossypium arboreum , $2n = 26$, and *G. herbaceum* $2n = 26$ are called Desi Cotton; *G. hirsutum* $2n = 52$ and *G. barbadence* (Egyptian cotton) $2n = 52$ are called commonly, **American Cotton**. Cotton originated in India as natural vegetable fibre of great economic importance as raw material for cloth. The cotton plant is a shrub. The immature flower bud (called **square**), blooms and develops into an oval fruit called a **boll** that splits open at maturity, revealing a mass of long white hairs, called **lint**, that cover the numerous brown or black seeds. It is grown at the large scale in Maharashtra, Gujarat, Karnataka, M.P., Punjab, Rajasthan, etc. Black cotton soils having pH between 5.5-8.5 are most suitable for the crop.

- Cotton produces sweet nectar that attracts a variety of destructive insect pests including the boll weevil, bollworm, armyworm, and the red spider. The bollworm is a native to India. It is one of the most destructive insect pests affecting the cotton plant. It damages cotton plants by burrowing into the cotton bolls and eating the seeds.
- The **cotton gin** is used to separate raw cotton fibres from seeds and other foreign materials before baling (1 cotton bale = 170 kg) and marketing. Eli Whitney invented the cotton gin in 1793.
- Application of plant modification such as Planofix (α NAA) and Cycocel (CCC) @ 10 ppm near flowering helps in more bud retention capacity, and induce sympodial branching in plants.

- $\text{Ginning percentage} = \frac{\text{Weight of lint}}{\text{Weight seed cotton taken for ginning}} \times 100$
- Ginning percentage varies between 24-43 per cent in different cotton varieties.
- **Seed cotton** is common term for both seed and lint together; however, the term **Cotton seed** is applied for seed after removing lint.
- $\text{Lint index} = \frac{\text{Weight of 100 seed} \times \text{ginning percentage}}{\text{100 - Ginning percentage}} \times 100$

Jute (*Corchorus spp.*) 2n = 14

Jute, called **Jew's mallow**, is a bushy herb, producing small yellow flowers, which grow singly or in pairs, giving rise to capsular fruits. The fibres of the inner vascular tissue, called *bast* fibres or phloem fibres, are glossy and tenacious but are brittle and easily injured by moisture. Most cultivated jute is grown in alluvial soils of the river valleys of India. **India is the second largest producer of jute after Bangladesh.**

There are two species of jute grown in India, *viz. C. capsularis* and *C. olitarius*.

- *C. capsularis* is a hardy plant tolerating waterlogging. It is popular for its white fibre therefore it is sometimes called **'white jute'**. Bitter taste of species is due to **cochorin** known as 'Tita pat'. *C. olitorius* is known as **'Tossa'** for its fine fibre which is short, stronger, lustrous, yellow to red in colour. The leaves are tasteless, hence it is called **'Metha pat'**.
- **Varieties:** Maribo Marcopoly, Maribo Magnapoly, Maribo Resitapoly, Hh Monitor 212, US-75, Pant composite 1, 2, 3, Pant S 1, 2, 3, and 10, IISR comp 1, VSH 6, 8 and 9, UH 35, UH 36, MSH 102, BGW 674, JRO 632, JRO 878, JRO 7835, JRC 212, JRC 321, D-154.
- One jute bale (a unit of measurement) is equal to 180 kg jute.

Sunnhemp (*Crotalaria juncea*) 2*n* = 16

It is a warm season crop grown both in *kharif* (North India) and *rabi* (South India) on well-drained loamy soil.

- It is composed of 2-4% fibre of its weight of green stem and 8-10% of its dry weight. The yield obtained varies from 8-10 q/ha.
- **Retting:** It is a process for loosening and separating fibre from the woody stalk. It involves the immersion of stalk bundles in to 30-60 cm deep running water for 3-4 days in straight position. After this period when bottom (root side) of the bundles get half rotten then the bundles are fully immersed in water for a week. After this period bundles are washed and fibre extracted. Best retting requires 34 °C temperature.

Package and Practices

Crop and duration(day)	Season	Seed rate (kg/ha)	Fertilizer N:P:K (kg/ha)	Spacing (cm)	Special features and varieties
Sugarcane 12-18 months	Sep.-Oct., Feb.-Mar., June-July	75 q two budded, 188 q single budded	275:100:80 (South) 120:80:60 (North)	75-90 cm between rows	Co 1148, Co 1158, Co 62399, Co. S 767, Bo 91 (early maturity), Co 6907, Co 975 (good for jaggery), Bo.54 (wilt resistant), Co.7704 (smut resistant); **Yield:** 400-500 q/ha.
Sugarbeet	Oct.-May	8-10 cm	120:80:90	40 × 20	Pant Composite 1, 2, 3, Pant S 1, 2, 3, and 10, IISR comp 1, VSH 6, 8 and 9, UH 35, UH 36, MSH 102, BGW 674; **Yield:** 500-700 q/ha.
Tobacco 90-120	Oct.- Mar.	50-60 g/ha	25:50:50 (Cigarette) 125:50:50 (Others)	Chew/Cigar 75 × 50-75 Cheroot 60 × 45 Hookah 45 × 25	**Wrapper:** S-5, Dixie shade, Rangpur Sumatra; **Filler:** Olor 10, KV-1, VV-2, Havana; Cheroot: OK 1, Bhavani Special, DR 1; Hookah and **Chewing:** DD 413, 141, 415, 417, HD 65, DD 437, R 12. **Chewing:** Bhagyalaxmi, Vairam, DP-401; **Bidi:** K-20, Anand-3, Anand 23, S-20.

Crop and duration(day)	Season	Seed rate (kg/ha)	Fertilizer N:P:K (kg/ha)	Spacing (cm)	Special features and varieties
Cotton 140-160	*Kharif* *Rabi*	Desi-15, American 3.75	Desi80:40:40 American 120:60:60	Desi 75 × 30, American 120 × 60	Sujata-first Egyptian cotton released in India; Savita, Varalaxmi. **Rainfed:** MCU 10, LRA 5166, K9, 10, 11. **Rice fallow:** MCU-7, LRA 611. **Yield:** 15-20 q/ha.
Jute 120-150	Mar.-April April-May	6-8 kg (White) 4-5 kg (Tossa)	40:20:20 20:20:20	20 × 5 cm 30 × 5 cm	**White:** Sonali (JRC-321), Sabujsona (JRC 4444; **Tossa:** Baisakhi (JRO 632), 212), Shyamli (JRC 7447), UPC 94, JRC Chaitali (JRO 878), Basudev (JRO 7835), Navin ((JRO 524).**Yield:** 20-27 q/ha fibre; 3-5 q/ha seed

17

Genetics

Genetics is the "study of the way in which genes operate and the way in which they are transmitted (heredity) from parents to offspring".

Gregor John Mendel
(July 20, 1822 to Jan., 6 1884)

Gregor John Mendel the 'father of modern genetics' published his work on garden pea (*Pisum sativum*) in the proceedings of the local society of naturalists in Brunn, Austria (now Brno, Czechoslovakia), in 1866. His methods differed in two essential respects from those of his predecessors:

1. Instead of trying to describe the appearance of whole plants with all their characteristics, Mendel followed the inheritance of single, easily visible and distinguishable traits, such as round versus wrinkled seed, yellow versus green seed, purple versus white flowers, etc.
2. He made exact counts of the numbers of plants bearing this or that trait; it was from such quantitative data that he postulated the rules governing inheritance, *viz.* Law of segregations and Law of independent assortment.

- Mendel died in 1884.
- **Rediscovery of Mendel's work:** Hugo de Vries in Holland, Carl Erich Correns in Germany, and Erich Tschermak von Seysenegg in Austria, rediscovered Mendel's work independently in 1900.
- The British biologist William Bateson coined the term Genetics in 1905.
- In 1908 an English mathematician and a German physician formulated **Hardy-Weinberg principle**, which provided the foundation for population genetics.

- A German physician, August Weismann, showed that reproductive cells (germplasm) are independent of other body cells (somatoplasm).
- Two French Nobel Prize winners, Francois Jacob and Jacques Monod, discovered the mechanism by which hereditary information is transferred from genes to the site of protein synthesis. Their work resulted in the **discovery of the genetic code** by H.G. Khurana. George W. Beadle and Edward L. Tatum working with the mould *Neurospora* proved that the function of most of the genes is to direct the synthesis of enzymes.
- Robert Brown discovered **nucleus** in 1833. Benda discovered **mitochondria** in 1897. Bateson and Punnett gave the term of **mutation**. Johnson proposed the **concept of pure line theory** in 1903. J.H. Muller, a U.S. geneticist, induced mutations in the fruit fly with X-rays (roentgen in the unit of X-ray) in 1927.
- Barbara McClintock received a Nobel Prize in 1983 for studies of jumping genes in maize.

Mendel's Law of Segregation

Mendel's first law illustrates that genes are transmitted in a particular ratios. Let *R* (Dominant) stand for the gene conferring purple flowers and *r* (recessive) gene for white flowers. Since the gene *R*, is dominant over *r*, the F_1 generation hybrids will have purple flowers They are phenotypically purple, but their genotype contains both *R* and *r* genes, and these alternative (alleles) genes do not blend or contaminate each other and the allelic genes segregate and pass to different gametes. If the gametes unite at random, then the F_2 generation would contain ¼ white-flowered and ¾ purple-flowered plants making it to the ratio of 3:1 (Constituting 1 *RR*, 2 *Rr* and 1 *rr* genotypes).

Mendel's Law of Independent Assortment

Mendel crossed yellow round seeded variety of pea with a green wrinkled seeded variety; the F_1 generation hybrids produced yellow round seeds. Yellow (*A*) and round (*B*) traits were dominanted over green (*a*) and wrinkled (*b*). By allowing the F_1 plants (genotype *AaBb*) to self-pollinate, Mendel obtained an F_2 generation of 315 yellow round 101 yellow wrinkled, 108 green round, and 32 green wrinkled seed (a ratio approximately 9:3:3:1). The important point here is that the segregation of the colour (*Aa*) is independent to the trait of seed surface

(*Bb*). This is expected if the F_1 generation produces equal numbers of four kinds of gametes, carrying the four possible combinations of the parental genes: *AB*, *Ab*, *aB*, and *ab*. The random union of these gametes gives rise to four phenotypes in the ratio of 9:3:3:1 (9 dominant-dominant:3 recessive-dominant:3 dominant-recessive:1 recessive-recessive).

Important Ratios in F_2 Generation after Different Gene Actions

- Typical dihybrid gene action : 9:3:3:1
- Duplicate gene action : 15:1
- Complementary gene action : 9:7
- Supplementary gene action : 9:3:4
- Inhibitory gene action : 13:3
- Masking gene action : 12:3:1
- Polymeric gene action : 9:6:1

CELL DIVISION

It is the process of development of new cell(s) from the pre-existing cells (parent cells). It occurs in following two stages, *viz*. Cytokinesis and Karyokinesis. Cytokinesis is the division of cytoplasm and Karyokinesis is the division of nucleus. Cell division occurs both in somatic cells (mitosis) and reproductive cells (meiosis), otherwise it is called **somatic division** and **reproductive division** respectively.

The Mitosis (Greek *Mito* = thread)

Walter Flemming used the term Mitosis for the first time for somatic division in 1878. It is the somatic division creating two cells from one cell without recombination. It completes in four phases, *viz*. Prophase, Metaphase, Anaphase and Telophase. At the end of every cycle, there is a rest known as Interphase, which again complete in three states the G_1, *S*, and G_2 stages.

(*i*) **Prophase:** It is a preliminary stage where chromosomes become shorter and thicker.

(*ii*) **Metaphase:** The middle stage in which chromosomes are arranged in equatorial plate.

(*iii*) **Anaphase:** During this stage chromatids (parts of chromosomes) move towards the centromere (at both the poles) through spindle fibres.

(iv) Telophase: During this stage chromosomes reach to the opposite poles.

(v) **Interphase:** It is the stage of DNA synthesis. The G_1 phase is called pre DNA replication phase. *S* phase is the DNA replication phase. G_2 phase the post DNA replication phase.

Meiosis (Greek *Meioum*=to reduce)

It is also called **reduction division** where each germ cell divides into four cells (or gametes) involving two fissions of the nucleus, each possessing half the number of chromosomes of the original cell (the *meiocytes* having $2n$). The cells formed by meiosis are *haploid* (n).

- The name meiosis was first given by J.B. Farmer in 1905.
- Crossing over and recombination occur during meiosis.
- Meiotic division includes two nuclear divisions *viz.* Heterotypic or First Meiotic division or reduction division and Homotypic or Second Meiotic division or equational division.

First meiotic division: This division completes in four phases, *viz.* Prophase first, Metaphase first, Anaphase first, Telophase first.

1. **First prophase:** Chromosom starts movement. The Nucleus grows in size due to excess hydrogen. The phase is again divided into (excluding *Proleptotene*: Similar to interphase of mitosis it is rest period for chromosome synthesis) following sub-stages:

(i) **Leptotene:** In this stage chromosomes are coiled forming a thread, like structure. Each chromosome has ball-like (due to chromomeres) structures arranged in series giving beaded appearance of chromosome. Size of nucleus increases.

(ii) **Zygotene:** Pairing (*synapsis*) homologous chromosome takes place. Paired chromosomes are called *bivalent*. Since, each chromosome is made up of two chromatids, therefore, a pair of homologous chromosomes consist of four chromatids called *tetrad*. The synapsis is either *proterminal* (pairing starts from terminal end of homologous chromosome) or *Procentric* (pairing from centre) or *Random* (random pairing).

(iii) **Pachytene:** It is the longest sub-phase. Paired chromosomes become coiled. The crossing over takes place between non-sister chromatids.

(*iv*) **Diplotene:** Chromosome starts to uncoil and separating each other due to loss of synaptic force of attraction. During separation last part, which remain attached to each other called *chiasmata*. Nuclear membrane disappears in last of this stage.

2. **First metaphase:** Spindle formation takes place. Chromosome moves towards equator through centromere.
3. **First anaphase:** Tetrad separates into two daughters. Chromatids assume the shape of 'V'. The process of separation of chromatids called *disjunction*.
4. **First telophase:** Stage starts when haploid group reach to the poles. Chromosomes become thin and elongated. The nuclear membrane is formed around each haploid group of chromosomes. Nucleus reappears.

- **Cytokinesis:** During this stage the cytoplasm and various cell organelles of parent cell divide to form two daughter cells.
- **Interphase:** Two above daughter cells pass through a resting period.

Second meiotic division: It is similar to mitotic division where each haploid cell turns to two haploid cells leading four haploid cells from two daughter cells (from first meiotic division). Division completes in Prophase, Metaphase, Anaphase and Telophase similar to meiotic division.

PHYSICAL BASIS OF HEREDITY

Chromosome is the microscopic, thread-like part of the cell that carries hereditary information in the form of genes serves as the physical basis of heredity. They vary in size and shape and usually occur in pairs. The members of each pair, called **homologues** (are phenotypically similar but genetically different from each other), closely resemble each other.

Thomas Hunt Morgan and his associates based on their theory of heredity, using *Drosophila*, found that chromosomes were passed from parent to offspring in characteristic way as described by Mendel. They proposed that genes occupy specific physical locations on chromosomes.

- When two gametes ($n \times n$) unite in fertilization, the resulting cell, called the zygote, contains the full, double set ($2n$) of chromosomes. Half of these chromosomes come from one parent and half from the other.

- The evidence that DNA acts as the carrier of the genetic information was first demonstrated by the U.S. geneticist Oswald T. Avery and his co-workers in 1944.

Nucleic Acids

In 1869 a substance containing nitrogen and phosphorus was extracted from cell nuclei. It was originally called *nuclein*, but is now commonly called **nucleic acid** for both DNA and RNA.

Nucleic acids are long chain-like molecules consist of repeated sequences of phosphate and sugar linkages (ribose sugar in RNA and deoxyribose sugars in DNA). Attached to the sugar links in the backbone there are two kinds of nitrogenous bases: purines and pyrimidines. The purines are adenine (*A*) and guanine (*G*) in both DNA and RNA; the pyrimidines are cytosine (*C*) and thymine (*T*) in DNA and cytosine (*C*) and uracil (*U*) in RNA.

- A single purine or a pyrimidine is attached to each sugar, and the entire phosphate-sugar-base subunit is called a **nucleotide**.
- The ratios of Adenine (*A*) to Thymine (*T*), and Guanne (*G*) to Cytosine (*C*) are always equal.
- **Double helix model of DNA:** In 1953 James Watson and Francis Crick proposed double helix model of DNA, which shows that DNA is composed of two spirally wound (*i.e.,* helical) chains. They based their model largely on X-ray crystallography.
- DNA replication takes place with the help of an enzyme, DNA polymerase. DNA replication occurs in the cytoplasm (at the site of ribosome). This enzyme can be extracted from *E. coli.*
- **Semi-conservative nature of DNA:** Matthew Meselson and Franklin Stahl working with *E. coli* in 1958 suggested that DNA replicates semi-conservatively to form two helices, each with one old and one new strand. The old strand acting as a template for the formation of a new strand.
- **Modification in central dogma:** The replication of DNA was hitherto believed as to occur as the theory of **central dogma** (DNA RNA Protein). The central dogma has since been modified to accommodate the discovery of retroviruses. When retroviruses enter into a host cell, they produce an enzyme called reverse transcriptase. This enzyme permits the transcription of the viral RNA into DNA, which then may become incorporated into the genetic material of the host cell.

- Termination of the synthesis of a polypeptide chain is signaled by three different RNA codons that do not specify an amino acid: UAA, UAG and UGA.
- Garrod is known as the father of chemical genetics.

One Gene One Enzyme Hypothesis

George W. Beadle and Edward L. Tatum studied biochemical reactions in the bread mould *Neurospora crassa,* resulted in the formulation of the "one gene-one enzyme" hypothesis. It illustrates that one gene is necessary to take responsibility of one enzyme. They were awarded Nobel Prize for Physiology or Medicine in 1958. Now it has been modified to "one gene-one polypeptide" (similarly gene is responsible for even up to polypeptide level) hypothesis or even more accurately to the "one structural gene-one polypeptide" principle.

SEX LINKAGE AND SEX LINKED CHARACTERS

The male of many animals has one chromosome pair, the sex chromosomes, consisting of unequal members called *X* and *Y*. At meiosis the *X* and *Y* chromosomes first pair, then disjoin and pass to different cells. One-half of the gametes formed (spermatozoa) contain the *X* and the other half the *Y* chromosome. The female has two *X* chromosomes, and all egg cells normally carry a single X. The eggs fertilized by *X*-bearing spermatozoa give females (*XX*), and those fertilized by Y-bearing spermatozoa give males (*XY*). The genes located in the X chromosomes exhibit what is known as sex-linkage or crisscross inheritance.

Important Sex-linked Characters

Colour blindness is an inability to distinguish between red and green colour and sometimes between blue and yellow, which is caused by a defect in one of the three colour-sensitive cells in the retina. Colour blindness affects approximately one person in thirty. **Red-Green Colour Blindness Test** is the standard image test for colour blindness. Individuals with normal colour vision used to see the number 57, whereas those with red-green deficiencies read the number 75.

- **Haemophilia** is the sex-linked disease is caused by recessive gene (*h*).

ALLELIC INTERACTIONS

Dominance relationships: The operation of Mendelian inheritance is frequently more complex than in the case of the traits recorded by Mendel. For example, when red and white-flowered varieties of four-o'clock (*Mirabilis jalapa*) plants or **snapdragons** are crossed, the F_1 hybrids produce flowers of intermediate pink or rose colour, a situation that seems more complex by the blending of genes than by Mendelian concepts.

Codominance: Codominance is a form of dominance in which the heterozygote displays the phenotypic characteristics of both alleles. For example, in *MN* blood group system of human beings, *MN* blood type is governed by two alleles: *M* and *N*. Individuals those are homozygous for the *M* allele has a surface molecule (called the *M* antigen) on their red blood cells. Similarly, those homozygous for the *N* allele have the *N* antigen on the red blood cells. Heterozygotes carry both antigens.

Multiple alleles: Many genes are sometimes represented by multiple alleles within a population. As in case of human *ABO* blood groups system, the gene governing *ABO* blood types has three alleles: I^A, I^B, and I^O. I^A and I^B are codominant, but I^O is recessive. Because of the multiple allelic action and various dominance relationships, there are four phenotypic *ABO* blood types: type *A* (genotypes I^AI^A and I^AI^O), type *B* (genotypes I^BI^B and I^BI^O), type *AB* (genotype I^AI^B), and type *O* (genotype I^OI^O).

GENE INTERACTIONS

Many individual traits are affected by more than one gene.

Epistasis: Some genes mask the expression of other genes just as a fully dominant allele masks the expression of its recessive counterparts. The gene that masks the phenotypic effect of another gene is called the epistatic gene (subordinates gene is called hypostatic gene) and phenomenon is called Epistasis, *e.g.* the gene for albinism (lack of pigment) in humans is an epistatic gene.

Complementation: The phenomenon of complementation is a form of interaction between non-allelic genes. For example, there are mutant genes that in the homozygous state produce profound deafness in humans. One would expect that the children of two persons suffering from such hereditary deafness would all be deaf. This is frequently not the case, because different genes often cause the parents' deafness. Since the mutant genes are not alleles, the child becomes heterozygous for the two genes and hears normally. In other words, the two mutant genes complement each other in the child. Complementation thus becomes a test for allelism. In the case of congenital deafness illustrated above, if all the children had been deaf, one could assume that the deafness in each of the parents was due to mutant genes that were alleles.

Polygenic inheritance: Traits that are expressed as variations in quantity or extent, such as weight, height, and pigmentation, usually depend on more than two genes (polygenes) as well as on environmental influences. Effect of different genes often becomes additive as each gene seems to produce a small increment or decrement, independent of the other genes.

CHROMOSOMAL ABERRATIONS

The chromosomal aberrations or abnormalities occur are categorized, *viz.* numerical and structural changes.

1. **Numerical aberrations:** These result from non-disjunction from the failure of a pair of homologous chromosomes or a pair of sister chromatids to separate during cell division. When non-disjunction occurs during meiosis two types of germ cells are formed, those with an extra chromosome and others with a missing chromosome. If extra chromosome cell combines with a normal germ cell, the new fertilized egg and all the cells of the individual it produces will have an extra chromosome (**trisomy**). If missing chromosome cell combines with a normal germ cell, the fertilized egg will lack a chromosome (**monosomy**). If non-disjunction occurs after fertilization, the resulting individual will be a mosaic and will have two or more populations of cells differing in chromosomal number.
2. **Structural aberrations:** Such aberrations result from chromosome breakages, they may break spontaneously, or broken by such environmental agents as radiation, viruses, and toxic chemicals. If a chromosomal segment breaks off and is not rejoined, it may be lost entirely in the gametes or somatic cells that derive, respectively, from meiosis or mitosis. Such a loss is called a **deletion**. In other instances, the broken-off segment may rejoin its chromosome but with its position inverted 180°; such **inversions** can alter the sequence of genetic information along the chromosome. In other cases, the segment may become **translocated**; that is, it may become attached to a different chromosome. When such a rearrangement occurs between two non-homologous chromosomes without net loss or gain of chromosomal material, it is called a balanced, or reciprocal, translocation, and the individual is not phenotypically affected.

Noble Prize Winners in Genetics

Thomas H. Morgan (1933) : Chromosomes and genes.

Edward A. Doisy ; Henrik Dam (1943) : Discovery of vitamin K.

Sir Alexander Flemming (1945): Discovery of Penicillin antibiotics.

Beadle; Edward L. Tatum (1959) : Discovered of genes and hereditary characteristics.

Robert W. Holly, Har Gobind Khorana: Deciphering of genetic code.

Max Salvador Luria ; Alfred Hershey (1969): Sexual reproduction (*genetics of bacteria*).

D. Baltimore, R. Dulbecco ; H.M. Temin (1975) : Discoveries related to interaction between tumour viruses and the genetic material (*of the cells*).

Arber ; Martis ; Davis (1978) : Discovery of restriction enzymes.

Cech and Altmann (1989) : Nobel Prize in chemistry for the discovery of RNA (*acting as catalytic enzyme*) and the monopoly of enzyme to be protein is changed. (*Ribozyme and RNase-P are non-protein exzymes*).

Murray and Thomas (1990) : Discovery of medicine for organ and cell transplantation. Dr. Murray made first human kidney transplant in identical twins.

Roberts and Sharp (1993) : Deciphering gene structure in eukaryotes. Discovery of spilt genes in eykaryotes.

Lewis Christain, Eric. Wieschaus (1955) : Awarded Nobel prize in medicine for "How do genes control development in Womb" ?

18

Plant Breeding

Plant Breeding is the practical application of genetic principles to the development of improved strains of agricultural and horticultural crops. Initial advances were made in the field of plant breeding by the American horticulturist **Luther Burbank** using technique of selection.

- **Selection** is a method used for crop improvement in which plant breeders choose plants with desirable traits for further propagation, and discard plants that are inferior for those traits.
- **Clone**: Clone is group of plants, produced from a single plant through asexual reproduction. Asexually propagated plants are mostly perennials, *e.g.* Sugarcane, Citrus, Apple, and Grape.

Aims of Plant Breeding

1. To improve the quality of lysine content in cereals; methionine and tryptophan contents in pulses; lecithin content in perishable crops.
2. To develop disease and insect resistant varieties; changing the maturity duration of varieties; develop photo and thermo insensitive varieties; develop synchronous maturity, *e.g.* in Mung bean; develop determinate growth varieties in pulses and cotton; develop varieties for new season, areas etc.; develop salt and moisture stress tolerant varieties.
3. To eliminate toxic substances, *viz.* neurotoxin b-N-Oxalyl amine alanine (BOAA) found in Grass pea (*Lathyrus sativus*) which causes paralysis in human beings; reduce erucic acid and Glucosinolate from *Brassica* spp. which causes harmful effects in human beings.

Important Achievements

1. **Production of semi-dwarf cereal varieties:** Incorporation of dwarfing gene from Japanese variety NORIN-10 into Indian wheat varieties by Norman Earnest Borlaug in CIMMYT, Mexico; and incorporation of dwarfing gene from 'Dee-geo-woo-gen' variety of Japonica rice from Taiwan into Indian rice varieties, are the classic examples of green revolution.

2. **Nobilization in sugarcane:** Development of lodging in sugarcane through crossing the *Saccharum barberi* × *Saccharum officinarum* by C.A. Barber and T.S. Venkatraman at SBI, Coimbatore.

3. **Development of hybrids:**

- **Maize varieties: Hybrids** like Ganga-1, Ganga-101, and composites, Manjari, Vikram, Sona, Vijay, Kisan, Co-1, NLD, Renuka, Kanchan, Diara have been developed through breeding programmes. Ganga-1, Ganga-101, Deccan, Ranjit, are first four hybrids leased in 1961.
- **Jowar hybrids**: CSH-1, CSH-2, CSH-3, CSH-4, CSH-5, CSH-6, CSH-9, CSH-10, CSH-11.
- **Bajra hybrids**: PHB-10, PHB-14, BJ-104, BK-560.
- **Cotton hybrids**: The first hybrid H-4 (*Gossypium hirsutum* × *G. barbadence*) was developed from intra-varietal cross at GAU in 1970. JKHY-1, Godavari, Suguna, H-6, ACK 468 from intra-specific cross (*G. hirsutum*); Varalaxmi, Jayalaxmi, Savitri, CBS-156 from interspecific cross (*G. hirsutum* × *G. barbadence*) have been developed.

Main Centres of Origin by Nikolay Ivanovich Vavilov

Centres of origins are the area showing great diversity from the crop plants evolved:

S.No.	Centre of origin	Belonging crops
1.	The China Centre	Common millets (*Panicum miliaceum*), Naked oat (*Avena nuda*), Bunda (*Colocasia antiquorum*), Radish, Brinjal, Onion, Pear, Peach, Plum, Apricot, Opium etc.
2.	Hindustan centre including South East Asia and India	Rice, Red gram, Mung bean, Cow pea, Brinjal, Cucumber, Hemp, Cotton, Pepper, Turmeric, Mango, Coconut, Banana, etc.
3.	The central Asia/ Afghanistan Centre	Wheat, Peas, Broadbean, Linseed, Sesame, Safflower, Hemp, Cotton, Garlic, Carrot, Apple, Almond, Grape, etc.
4.	The Asia Minor/ The Near East/ The Persian Centre	Wheat, Alfalfa, Carrot, Cabbage, Almond, Pomegranate, Grape, Fig, etc.

5.	The Mediterranean Centre	Wheat, Barley, Chickpea, Pea, Broadbean, Clover, Artichoke, Asparagus etc.
6.	The Abyssinian Centre, including Ethiopia, Eritrea	Sorghum, Cucumber, Grass pea, Castor, Linseed, Sesame, Safflower, Onion, Okra, Coffee, etc.
7.	American/Mexican Centre	Maize, Rajma (*Phaseolus vulgaris*), Lima bean, American cotton (*Gossypium hirsutum*), Sweet potato, Chillies, Pumpkin, Papaya, Guava, Avacado, etc.
8.	The South American Centre (Brazil, Peru, Bolvia, Colombia, Ecuador, Paraguay)	Maize, Groundnut, Tomato, Tobacco, Tapioca, Potato, Egyptian cotton (*Gossypium barbadence*), Pineapple, Guava, Quinine, Rubber, Cashew etc.

The Flower

1. **Bisexual/Perfect/Hermaphrodite**: Such type of flower has both stamen and pistil.
2. **Unisexual**: Flowers of unisexual in nature have only either pistil or stamen. Unisexual Flowers divided into two type:

(*i*) **Monoecious flowers**: In such flowers stamen and pistil are found on the same plant, *e.g.* Maize, Colocasia, Castor, Coconut.

(*ii*) **Dioecious flowers**: This of group of flowers characterized as the stamen and pistil are found on different plants, *e.g.* Papaya, Date- palm, Pistachio nut, Hemp, Asparagus, Spinach, Nutmeg.

Pollination

Pollination is the transfer of pollen from the stamen to stigma of flower. It is mainly of two kinds, *viz.* Self pollination and Cross pollination.

1. **Self-pollination (autogamy):** In self-pollination the pollen is transferred from the stamen to the stigma of the same flower, Rice, Wheat, Oat, Barley, Legumes, Solanaceous vegetables, Linseed, Apricot and Citrus.
2. **Cross-pollination (allogamy):** In cross-pollination, pollen is transferred from one flower to another on the same plant (**geitonogamy**) or another plant of the same species (**xenogamy**). Cross-pollinated crops are Maize, Bajra, Rye, Alfalfa, Clovers, Umblifers, Crucifers, Cucurbits, Sugarcane, Sunflower, Castor, Fruit trees, etc.
3. **Often-cross-pollinated** crops are those where cross-pollination occurs up to 30 per cent, these include Sorghum, Cotton, Tobacco, Red gram, Safflower, Triticale.

- Self-pollinated crops are homozygous whereas cross-pollinated crops are heterozygous in nature.
- Many plants avoid self-pollination by producing certain chemicals that prevent pollen from growing on the stigma of the same flower, or from developing pollen tubes in the style. Other plants, such as Date-palms, some orchard trees, and stinging nettles, have become **dioecious**, producing only male (**staminate**) flowers on some plants and female (**pistillate**) flowers on others. Some plants are **dichogamous** (the pistil ripens before or after the stigma in the same flower becomes receptive).

Mechanism of Pollination Control

There are two kinds of mechanisms involved in control of pollination:

1. **Self-in-compatibility:** In such kind of mechanism, pollination does not occur because of:

(*i*) **Heteromorphic system/ heterostyly:** In heterostyly both stamen and pistil have different size of styles, *e.g.* Distyly found in Primula and Tristyly in Lythrum and Brinjal.

(*ii*) **Homomorphic system:** In this system gametes or pollen are suppressed from growth, e.g. Gametophytic control occurs in *Nicotiana sander*, Tomato, Brinjal etc and Sporophytic control is found in Cauliflower.

2. **Male sterility:** The male serility is characterized by non-function of pollen grains, whereas female gametes function normally. It is further classified as:

(*i*) **Genetic male sterility (GMS):** Genetic male sterility is governed by single recessive gene 'ms'. Such kind of male sterility is maintained by crossing with heterozygous male fertile plants. It is utilized for hybrid seed production. So far in Red gram and Castor, Genetic male sterility has been exploited.

(*ii*) **Cytoplasmic male sterility (CMS):** CMS is determined by cytoplasm that decides sterility/fertility of plants. The nuclear gene is non-restorer. CMS can be transferred to a given species by using that strain as a recurrent parent in backcross programme. CMS is utilized in ornamental plants or species where vegetative part is used for propagation.

(*iii*) **Cytoplasmic genetic male sterility (CGMS):** It is known in Maize, Jowar, Rice, Sunflower, Bajra, Wheat, etc.

Chemicals Used for Induction of Male Sterility

Chemicals used for induction of male sterility are known as **Gametocides** or Pollen suppressant or Chemical hybridizing agents, which upon application inhibit the production of pollen grains. These chemicals are classified into two categories:

1. **General gametocides:** These are used to kill pollen of any species, *e.g.* $CaSO_4$ @ 2,000 ppm, and Ethrel @ 6,000-8,000 ppm.
2. **Selective gametocides:** They are selective for crops, *e.g.* FW-450 for Cotton; Colchicines for Sorghum; Maleic Hydrazide (MH) for Onion; and Ethrel for Wheat and Rice, etc.

HYBRID, SYNTHETIC AND COMPOSITE VARIETIES

Hybrids: Hybrids are the first generation offspring (F_1) from crosses between two pure lines (self-pollinated crops), inbreds (cross-pollinated crops), open-pollinated variety and other genetically dissimilar populations. Hybrids can be produced following:

(*i*) **Single Cross:** It is a cross between two inbreds or pure lines, *e.g.* ($A \times B$).

(*ii*) **Double Cross:** A cross between the outcomes of two single, *e.g.* ($A \times B$) × ($C \times D$).

(*iii*) **Three way cross:** It is the cross made between an inbreds achieved through single cross and then crossed with another inbred, *e.g.* ($A \times B$) × C).

(*iv*) **Top-cross or inbred variety cross:** Inbred crossed with an open pollinated variety. It is done to test general combining ability (GCA) of a variety.

- **Inbreds:** Inbreds are nearly homozygous lines obtained through a continuous inbreeding in a cross-pollinated species.
- **Test cross:** Test cross is made to assess the combining ability. This cross is made within inbreds (to test specific combining ability), hybrids, synthetic or open-pollinated variety (to test general combining ability).

Step Involved in Hybrid Production

(*i*) Development of inbred lines from open-pollinated variety, synthetic variety, single/double cross variety etc.

(*ii*) Evaluation of inbred lines for their ability through combining ability both general and specific.

(*iii*) Hybrid seed production through different methods using, CGMS, CMS, GMS (exploited in Maize, Bajra, Jowar, Onion, Cotton and Sugar beet); and self-incompatibility (*Brassica* spp.).

(*iv*) **Emasculation** is the physical removal of pollen grains from flowers, *e.g.* Maize, Tomato, Cotton, etc.

Types of Hybridization

1. **Intravarietal/intraspecific hybridization:** It is the cross between two individuals of same species.
2. **Distant/Interspecific hybridization:** It involves the crossing between individuals of different species of the same genus or different genera.

Synthetic Varieties (Hays and Garbar, 1919)

Synthetic varieties are produced by crossing individuals in all possible combinations. They are maintained by open pollination in isolation. Inbreds used for synthetic varieties are **always tested for combining ability** (through top cross; poly cross is used to evaluate storage crops), *e.g.* Forage crops and clonal crops like Cocoa, Alfalfa, Clovers.

Composite Varieties

Open pollination is encouraged to produce crosses in all combinations among mixed lines. The variety used for production of composite variety, are **rarely tested for their combining ability,** therefore yield cannot be predicted.

- **Recent composites is maize:** Co-1 (resistant to downy mildew).
- **Opaque-2-gene consisting composites** in maize are rich in lysine and tryptophan, *e.g.* Ratan, Shakti, Protina.

Comparison of Hybrid, Composite and Synthetic Varieties

Basis of comparison	Hybrids	Composites	Synthetics
Base population	Inbreds	Variety or other heterozygous source	Inbreds or clones
Number of parents used	Two	Two- Four	Four-Ten
Pollination	Controlled	Open pollination	At random
GCA	Tested	Usually not tested	Tested
Heterosis	More	Less than hybrid	Less than hybrid
Seed used	F_1	$F_1 - F_4$	$F_1 - F_4$
Seed cost	More	Less	Less than both
Varietal maintenance	Difficult	Easy	Easier than composite

HETEROSIS AND INBREEDING DEPRESSION

Heterosis: Shull used the term heterosis in 1914. It is a superiority or inferiority of F_1 over the parents. It may be with following degrees:

1. **Average heterosis:** If the F_1 is equal to the average of both the parents.
2. **Heterobeltosis:** It is the superiority of F_1 over the superior parent.
3. **Hybrid vigour:** It is the only superiority of F_1 over the parents, not inferiority. Koelreuter, 1673 reported such type of vigour for the first time in *Nicotiana* spp.

Inbreeding Depression

It is a loss of vigour due to mating between closely related homozygous individuals. East (1908) and Shull (1909) independently studied inbreeding depression in maize.

MUTATION IN CROP IMPROVEMENT

Mutation is a sudden heritable change in the characteristics of an organism. **Hugo de Vries** in 1900 used the term mutation. **Muller** (1927) induced mutation for the first time artificially using X-rays.

Types of Mutation

1. **Macro mutation:** It is the broader change created due to mutation, and can be easily identified.
2. **Micro-mutation:** Such mutation produces small changes and it is measured in terms of mean and variance.
3. **Gene/point mutation:** Mutation was produced in the base sequence of genes due to base pair transition or transversion, deletion, duplication, or inversion, etc.
4. **Chromosomal mutation** changes were produced in the number of chromosomes or structure of chromosome.
5. **Cytoplasmic mutation:** If mutation occurs in extra cytoplasmic genetic material.
6. **Bud/somatic mutation:** Mutation occurs in buds or somatic tissues, e.g. clonal crops
7. **Spontaneous mutation:** It is a kind of mutation occurring spontaneously in the natural population. It always occurs at very slow rate (10^{-6}).
8. **Induced mutation:** If the mutation is created by using artificial mutagens, it is called induced mutation, *e.g.* X-ray. While inducing such mutation in an individual some characteristic occurs giving a special genotype, *e.g.* **Chimera**.

- **First Gamma garden** was established at Bose Research Institute, Calcutta in 1959, followed by IARI, and Bhabha Atomic Research Centre (BARC). **Gamma Garden** is an area where mutation is induced using gmama radiation.
- **Chemicals used as mutagens** include **EMS** (Ethyl Methyl Sulphonate), **MMS** (Methyl Methane Sulphonate), Ethidium Bromide, Sodium Azide, Nitrous Acid, etc.

Varieties Developed through Mutation

Regina-II was the first variety of mustard developed through mutation. Other varieties include BGM 408, BGM 413 (Chickpea); Hans (Pea); Trombay Vishaka-1 (Pigeon pea); Sarbati Sonora (Wheat); Jagannath, Prabhavati (Rice); MCU-7, MCU-10 (Cotton); BSR-1 (Turmeric); Jayshri, Bhavya (Tobacco).

POLYPLOIDY IN PLANT BREEDING

Polyploid: Polyploid is an individual with more than two identical or distinct genomes.

Diploid: An organism having two copies of a single genome.

Haploid: An individual carrying *n* (haploid) number of chromosomes. Such individuals are also called Hemizygous.

Heteroploid: An individual with a chromosome number other than the normal diploid (2*n*).

Ploidy may be classified into two different categories:

1. **Aneuploidy:** It is the state in which an individual possess one or few chromosome extra or missing from 2*n* (somatic numbers) numbers.
2. **Euploidy:** This is the situation with an individual possess more than two genomes. It is further classified as:

(*a*) **Monoploid:** An individual with basic × number of chromosomes, *i.e.* with one set of genomes.

(*b*) **Autopolyploid:** An individual with two or more identical genomes.

(*c*) **Allopolyploid:** An individual with two or more distinct genomes.

- **Amphidiploid:** Amphidiploid is a situation having an individual of allopolyploid character with two copies of each genome present in it. The individual behaves like diploid during meiosis.
- **Segmented allopolyploid:** An individual containing two or more genomes, which are identical with each other, except for some minor differences.

- **Lutz** in 1907 reported for the first time variation in chromosome numbers in *Oenothera* spp.
- **Blakeslee and Nebal** in 1937 demonstrated chromosome doubling using Colchicine.
- **Colchicine** ($C_{22}H_{25}S_6N$) is isolated from seeds @ 0.2-0.8 per cent, bulbs @ 0.1-0.5% of *Colchicum autumnale*. It blocks the spindle fibres formation thereby restricting the movement of sister chromatids to the opposite poles. It is applied through seed treatment @ 0.2% or directly @ 0.5-1.0%.
- **Triploid:** Tea cultivar TV-29 produces more biomass and larger shoot.
- ***Trifolium alexandrium*** var. ***Pusa giant***, a variety of berseem was the first polypolid released for cultivation, which produces 20-30% more yield.
- Most of the cultivated crops are allopolyploids, *e.g.* Wheat, Rye, Rape, Barley, Cotton, Cabbage, Tobacco, Sugarcane, Clovers, etc.

Terms Used in Ploidy

Term	Symbol	Type of change
Aneuploid	$2n \pm$ few	One or few chromosomes extra or missing.
1. Disomic or Normal	$2n$	Normal somatic chromosome number.
2. Nullisomic	$2n - 2$	One pair of chromosome missing.
3. Monosomic	$2n - 1$	One chromosome missing.
(*a*) Double monosomic	$2n - 1 - 1$	Two chromosomes of different pairs are missing.
4. Trisomic	$2n + 1$	One chromosome extra.
5. Double trisomic	$2n + 1 + 1$	One chromosome extra in different pairs.
6. Tetrasomic	$2n + 2$	One pair of chromosome extra.
Euploid		
7. Monoploid	x	One genome or one set of basic chromosome.
8. Diploid	$2x$	Two set of genomes.
9. Autotriploid	$3x$	Three set of genomes of same kind, *e.g.* Banana, Sugarbeet, Tea, Watermelon, Spinach.
10. Auto tetraploid	$4x$	Four set of genomes of same kind, *e.g.* Coffee, Groundnut, alfalfa, Berseem.
11. Allopolyploid	$2x_n$	Distinct set of genomes, *e.g.* Raphanobrassica, Triticale.
12. Allotetraploid	$2x_1 + 2x_2$	Two distinct set of genomes.
13. Allohexaploid	$2x_1 + 2x_2 + 2x_3$	Three distinct set of genomes.

Evolution of Bread Wheat (*Triticum aestivum*)

In the development of bread wheat various diploid species contributed three genomes namely *A*, *B*, and *D* for *Triticum aestivum*. Genome *A* has come from *Triticum monococcum* ($2n = 14$); *B* from *Aegilops speltoids* ($2n = 14$) and *D* from *Aegilops squarrosa* ($2n = 14$).

- Natural cross between *Triticum monococcum* and *Aegilops speltoids* led to *AB* genome in F_1, upon spontaneous chromosome doubling it led to *AA*, *BB* genome set. *AA*, *BB* the tetraploid emmer wheat, naturally crossed with *Aegilops squarrosa* producing *ABD* (sterile) progeny, which upon spontaneous chromosome doubling become *AABBDD* set of genomes (amphidiploid) led the development of bread wheat.

Evolution of *Nicotiana tabaccum* ($2n = 48$)

Natural mating between *Nicotiana sylvestris* ($2n = 24$) and *N. tomentosa* ($2n = 24$) led to the development of *Nicotian tobaccum*.

Evolution of *Gossypium hirsutum* ($2n = 52$)

Natural mating between *Gossypium barbadence* (Asiatic cotton, $2n = 26$) and *Gossypium thurberi* (wild American cotton, $2n = 26$) led to the development of sterile cotton, which upon chromosome doubling created *Gossypium hirsutum*.

Single Zero (0) and Double Zero (00) Varieties in Mustard

Varieties of mustard having erucic acid less than 2 per cent and less than 30 micromoles of glucosinolate are said to be **double zero varieties**, and those having either less than 2 per cent erucic acid (pronounced zero erucic) or less than 30 micromoles of glucosinolate (pronounce zero glucosinolate) are commonly called **single zero varieties**.

Rapeseed-mustard is the second most important edible oilseed crop in India after groundnut and accounts for nearly 30% of the total oilseeds produced in the country. When compared to other edible oils, the rapeseed mustard oil has the lowest amount of harmful saturated fatty acids and its oil contains adequate amounts of the two essential fatty acids, linoleic and linolenic acids, which are not present in many of the other edible oils.

- Mustard oil contains high amount of erucic acid (which may cause cardiac problems) and glucosinolates (sulphur compounds present in oil cake which are harmful to animals as feed).

- "Canola" quality, oil must have less than 2% erucic acid in the seed oil and less than 30 micromoles of glucosinolate for every gram of oil free cake. Therefore Indian rapeseed mustard varieties have limited export market, as they do not match with the requisite international standards.
- Multiple recessive genes having multiple alleles govern erucic acid and glucosinolate contents.
- **Examples of single zero (zero erucic) varieties**: M21-INGR 98001 (*B-juncea*), R 03-INGR 98002 (*B-napus*), R 09-INGR 98005 (*B-napus*).
- **Examples of Double zero varieties**: Unnat, R985-INGR 99008, R986-INGR 99007 (*B.napus*).

Evolution of *Brassica* spp.

Based on U's triangle proposed by N.U. (1935)

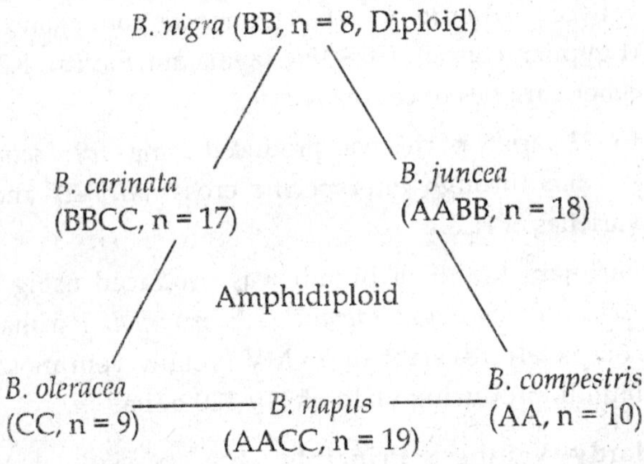

- **Bridging species:** Some amphidiploids serve as bridging species to transfer some character from one species to another related species, *e.g. Nicotiana digluta* is used to transfer TMV resistance from *N. sylvestris* to *N. tobaccum*.

Development of Triticale

Triticale was synthesized by mating between *Triticum turgidum* (*AABB*, High yielding, and Superior grain quality) and *Secale cereale* (RR, Rye, Hardiness). F_1 produced having *ABR* genomes was sterile, but upon chromosome doubling with Colchicine treatment, produced a fertile progeny having *AABBRR* genome. It is a classic example of the Allohexaploid and Amphidiploid created by man (Rimpau, 1980), hence it is also called **Manmade cereal**. **DT** series of variety released belongs to Triticale.

Development of Raphanobrassica

Raphanobrassica was created from a cross between *Brassica oleracea* and *Raphanus sativus*. Raphanobrassica was trailed for production of both Curd of Cauliflower at the top and Radish as root from same plant.

Development of Variety through Distant Hybridization

- **First distant** hybrid was produced by **Thomas Fair Child** in 1717.
- **Varalaxmi** of cotton was created by an interspecific cross between *Gossypium hirsutum* (American cotton) and *G. barbadence* (Egyptian cotton). CBS-156, Jayalaxmi, Savitri, K2HC, etc. are other varieties of cotton.
- **Co-31** variety of **rice** was produced using *Oryza sativa* and *Oryza perennis* through interspecific cross. ADT-27 and Co-30 are varieties of rice.
- **Parbhani kranti** of bhindi was produced using *Abelmoschus esculentus* cv. *Pusa sawani* × *A. manihot*. Parbhani kranti is completely resistant to YVMV (yellow vein mosaic virus) of bhindi, producing yield of 110-120 q/ha.

The Hardy-Weinberg Principle

In 1908, Godfrey Harold Hardy and Wilhelm Weinberg independently formulated a theorem that became the foundation of population genetics. According to the **Hardy-Weinberg** principle, two or more gene alleles will have the same frequency in the gene pool generation after generation, until some agent acts to change that frequency.

Breeding Methods at a Glance

Breeding method	Procedure	Application/ Achievements
A. Methods used for non-segregating generations		
Mass selection: Similar phenotype of large number are selected and their seeds are mixed together to constitute a new variety.	Based on appearance of phenotype, homozygous plant are selected and mixed to lead the variety.	• Purifies existing pure lines. • Variability cannot be generated • Dharwad, a cotton variety was isolated from *G. hirsutum.*
Pure line selection: Pure line is a progeny of single, homozygous, self-pollinated plants.	Individual plant selected and selected progenies released as new variety. Variation is due to environment and it is non-heritable.	• Improves old/local varieties, *e.g.* Shyama from Kalimooch-64, a rice variety. • Helps in seed certification.
B. Methods Used for Segregating Generations		
Pedigree method: Pedigree is the description of the ancestors of an individual.	The selected plants are hybridized and superior progenies are selected. Transgressive segregants may be recovered.	• Weaknesses in the existing varieties can be recovered. • Rice variety Jaya, Padma, Cauvery, Krishna, Ratna, Sabarmati, released. • Laxmi in cotton, Pusa early dwarf in tomato released.
Bulk / Mass / Population methods: F_2 and subsequent generations are harvested in mass to raise next generation.	Natural selection followed; take longer time, up to 30 years, to develop a variety. Singl eseed Descent method is applied and single seed from each of 1000-2000 F_2 plant bulked to raise F_3 progenies.	• In mustard Narendra rai developed.

Back cross method: A cross between a hybrid (F_1) and its either of parents. It is the only method for interspecific gene and cytoplasm transfer.	Recurrent/recipient parent to which genes are transferred from donor parent. Character to be transferred must have high heritability.	• Any character can be transferred. Isogenic line can be produced. • Cotton wilt RVs: Digvijay, Vijay, Vijpala, Kalyan, BD-8, released.
C. Other Approaches		
Multiline varieties: Mixture of several pure lines of similar height, flowering, maturity, agronomic characteristics, seed colour and having different genes for single character.	N.E. Borlaug in 1954 introduced the concept and techniques. He used resistant lines for development of multilines.	• Wheat multilines-KSML-3, MKLS-11, KML-7406 and Bajra variety-MS-521 developed.

❑❑❑

19

Biotechnology in Crop Improvement

The term biotechnology composed of two Greek words, *bios*-means life and *technologia* means systematic treatment. It is the controlled use of biological agents, such as microorganisms (or) cellular components, for beneficial use.

Biotechnology aims to improve genetic make up, phenotypic performance, and multiplication rates of economic plants; and exploit plant cells for useful product or services.

The inception of biotechnology dates back to French chemist Louis Pasteur who showed that fermentation was promoted by microbes. During World War I the chemist (and later first President of Israel) Chaim Weizmann showed that propanone could be produced by the bacterium *Clostridium acetobutylicum*. Another major episode in the emergence of biotechnology was the commercial production of penicillin from the mould *Penicillium notatum* by Howard Florey and colleagues in Oxford during World War II.

Biotechnology uses basic techniques of plant tissue culture and genetic engineering to a new horizon.

SCOPE AND IMPORTANCE OF BIOTECHNOLOGY

Biotechnology is not a single branch of science but an interdisciplinary science involving an integrated approach with other branches such as plant breeding, genetics, biochemistry, pathology, entomology, dairy, microbiology, biophysics and fermentation technology etc. It has great influenced from various aspects in our daily life. Figure 1.1 shows various fields of biotechnology.

Biotechnology is making important contributions to agriculture development. It holds promise for increasing the yield, quality, genetic processing and utilization of products, for decreasing reliance an agrochemicals. Biotechnology may be defined as "any technique that uses living organisms to make or modify a product, to improve plants or to develop micro-organisms for specific uses." The development and application of modern biotechnology based on new enabling techniques of recombinant DNA technology, often called as "Genetic engineering." The techniques of biotechnology offer the potential of moving any cloned gene from any organism into any other organism and confer much greater precision and speed in achieving results than conventional techniques. The use of intellectual property rights in industrialized countries suggest that the application of biotechnology will hold the key to competitiveness and comparative advantage in various fields.

TISSUE CULTURE

It is the cultivation of plant organs, tissue or cells in test-tubes on artificial media, also called *in-vitro* techniques. It reduces more than half of the time taken in conventional breeding programmes. Tissue culture is purely based on the totipotency of cells. **Haberlandt** first demonstrated the totipotency of cells in 1902.

- **Totipotency** is the ability of a plant cell to perform all the function of development, which is a characteristic of zygote.
- Braun regenerated the first plant from mature plant cell in 1959, whereas from embryo culture Laibach regenerated whole plant in 1925.
- **Guha** and **Maheswari** in 1964 produced haploid plant of *Datura* from pollen grains.

Tissue Culture Techniques

1. **Surface sterilization**: The explant (the plant or plant part excised for the *in-vitro* cultivation) is surface sterilized to eliminate contaminants using sodium hyporchlorite @ 1-2% or mercuric chloride @ 0.1% solution.
2. **Nutrient medium**: It is a medium containing salts, trace elements, vitamins, carbon sources, growth regulators etc. on which plants are cultured. As growth regulators 2, 4-D @ 0.5-2.0 mg/L is commonly used. **Organic supplements** like coconut water, casein hydrolysate, yeast extract are used. **Solidifying agent** such as agar-agar is used.
   - Generally B-5 medium (Gamborg *et al.*) or MS medium (Murashige and Skoog) are used.
3. **Sub culturing**: Transferring of tissue to fresh media after a stipulated time. Usually sub-culturing is done after every 4-6 weeks. However, the suspension cultures are sub-cultured after every 3-14 days.

4. **Plant regeneration and transfer to soil:** First the transfer of cultured plant is done in small pots and then to greenhouse and finally in soil. Transfer is done when roots and shoots appears (the process is known as regeneration and **organogenesis**).

Classification of Tissue Culture Techniques

Based on the plant parts used, such techniques are divided into embryo culture, meristem culture, anther/pollen culture, and Tissue and cell culture techniques.

1. **Embryo culture**: Young embryo is removed from developing seeds and planted on a suitable nutrient medium to obtain seedlings. In **Iris** and **Orchids** embryo from mature plant is used. Globular stage embryo is used in barley.

Application of Embryo Culture

(*i*) **Recovery of distant hybrids**: Embryo culture is applied when there is an inability of pollen grains to grow or failure to germinate or degeneration of endosperm. In these conditions embryo culture is used to recover hybrids, e.g. Hybrids from *Hordeum vulgare* × *Secale cereale, Triticum aestivum* × *Agropyron repens* have been recovered through embryo culture.

(*ii*) **High recovery of hybrids:** High recovery is observed in the embryo from 10-14 days old caryopsis. In conventional breeding progenies of *Triticum aestivum* × *Hordeum vulgare* are not obtained, whereas through embryo culture it is successful.

(*iii*) **Propagation of orchids**: Orchid seed lack stored food material; therefore, natural development is negligible. But through embryo culture callus formation is possible in orchids.

(*iv*) **Shortening the breeding cycles**: Breeding time is reduced drastically using embryo culture technique.

(*v*) **Overcoming dormancy**: When we used embryo culture technique, there is no dormancy check, *e.g. Prunus* spp. and *Taxus* spp.

2. **Meristem culture**: Meristem culture is a cultivation of axillary or apical meristem. It involves the development of existing shoot apical meristem and regeneration of adventitious roots. Approximately 5-10 mm shoot apices with leaf primordial are used. Due to higher concentration of cytokinin in the medium, the apices develop axillary branching. Each axillary branch is excised and transferred to a fresh medium. The technique is

used for quick vegetative propagation. This technique is widely used for development of virus free ex-plants.

Applications of Meristem Culture

(*i*) **Vegetative propagation**: Meristem culture is used to obtain clones termed as mericlones (clones developed through meristem). The technique is useful for vegetatively propagated plants, *e.g.* Ginger, Turmeric, Fruits, Timber trees, Teak, Sandal wood, Sugarcane, Banana and Tapioca etc.

(*ii*) **Recovery of virus free stocks**: The apices do not contain viruses, in general. Use of 'meristem' makes possible to obtain virus free seedlings or clones, *e.g.* Potato, Sugarcane, Tapioca. This technique is extensively used over the conventional chemotherapy for obtaining virus free seedling.

- **Virus indexing** is a technique, which detects the presence of virus in the explants or seedlings.
- The chemicals like Virazole (ribavirin), Cycloheximide, actinomycin-D are used for eradication of viruses in medium. Virazole eradicate Potato virus X and its elimination improves yield by 20-30%.

(*iii*) **Germplasm conservation**: Germplasm conservation is an art to conserve species for long time. It is possible by meristem culture, which is stored in liquid nitrogen (at –196°C, also called **cryopreservation**).

3. **Anther or pollen culture**: Guha and Maheswari (1964) applied this technique for the first time in *Datura innoxia*. In this technique haploid plants are obtained from pollen grains by placing anther or pollens into a suitable medium. This technique is used to obtain haploid plants.

4. **Tissue and cell culture**: In this technique cell or a group of cells (tissue) are obtained and cultured into a suitable medium. The whole plant is regenerated through tissues or cells of somatic in nature. Technique is used for clonal propagation, somaclonal variation, mutant isolation, biochemical production and bio-transformation.

Somatic Hybridization

In this technique fusion of protoplasts (cells without cell wall) of two different plant species/varieties carried out to produce hybrid plants. The hybrids produced through this technique are known as Somatic hybrids. Technique completes is four steps *viz.*

(*i*) **Protoplast isolation**: Treat the cells or tissues with cell wall degrading enzymes (*e.g.* pectinage or macerozyme, @ 0.1-1.0% and Cellulase @ 1-2%).

(*ii*) **Fusion of desired species of protoplasts**: The pre-isolated protoplasts are fused in medium containing PEG (Poly Ethylene Glycol). Wash the protoplast to remove PEG in alkaline solution having 9-10 pH.

(*iii*) **Selection of somatic hybrid cells**: Heterokaryotic protoplast fused together are selected, which occurs only 0.5-10% of total protoplast, used for fusion.

(*iv*) **Regeneration of hybrid plants**: Heterokaryotic hybrids are regenerated into a whole plant as the technique suggested earlier for propagation.

- **Achievements:** Using somatic hybridization, hybrid varieties from *Solanum tuberosum* × *Lycopersicon esculentum*, *Atropa belladonna* × *Nicotiana chinensis* and *Datura innoxia* × *Atropa belladonna* have been developed.

Cybrids or Cytoplasmic Hybrids

Hybrids produced using nucleus of one parent cell and cytoplasm of both the cells are called **cybrids**. It involves the fusion of a normal protoplast of one species with protoplast having inactivated nucleus of another species.

(*i*) Inactivation of nucleus is done using either chemicals or irradiation (gamma rays or X-rays).

(*ii*) Transfer plasma genes of one species to the nuclear background of other species, in a single generation.

Genetic Engineering

Genetic engineering is the artificial manipulation, modification, and recombination of DNA or other nucleic acid molecules in order to modify an organism or population of organisms. Genetic engineering was pioneered in 1973 by the American biochemists Stanley N. Cohen and Herbert W. Boyer, who were among the first to cut DNA into fragments, rejoin different fragments, and insert the new genes into *E. coli* bacteria, which then reproduced. Genetic engineering works through recombinant DNA technology.

Recombinant DNA Technology

The term recombinant DNA literally means the joining or recombining of two pieces of DNA from two different species. The techniques allow an investigator to biologically purify (clone) a gene from one species by inserting it into the DNA of another species, where it is replicated along with the host DNA. The technique involves:

(*i*) Cleaving DNA by microbial enzymes called **restriction endonucleases or biological scissors**; each of these enzymes cleaves DNA at a specific site defined by the sequence of four or more nucleotides.

- Once the desired DNA fragment has been removed from the donor cell, it must somehow be inserted into the bacterial cell. Usually it is done by first inserting the donor DNA into a plasmid or bacteriophages. Plasmids are used as vectors to carry the foreign gene into bacteria. Bacteriophages are sometimes used as vectors to carry the foreign DNA into the bacteria through transduction.

(*ii*) Recombining fragments of DNA, inserting eukaryotic DNA into bacteria so that large quantities of the foreign genetic material can be produced.

(*iii*) Determining the nucleotide sequence of a segment of DNA (or chemically synthesizing DNA).

Plasmids

Plasmid is an independent, circular, self-replicating autonomous molecule of DNA, existing in cells as extrachromosomal genomes. Some plasmids can be inserted into a bacterial chromosome, where they become a permanent part of the bacterial genome, which leads to the importance of the plasmids in molecular science. Plasmids are easy to manipulate and can be easily integrated into genomes. They are the basis of recombinant DNA technology. There are two categories of plasmids, **Stringent plasmids**, which replicate only when the chromosome replicates and **Relaxed plasmids**, replicate on their own.

- There are some minimum requirements for plasmids that are useful for recombination techniques, which include Origin of replication (ORI), Selectable marker and Restriction enzyme sites in non-essential regions.

Restriction Enzymes

Werner Arber, the Swiss microbiologist, discovered restriction enzymes in 1968. Type II restriction enzymes, were identified by American molecular biologist Hamilton O. Smith in 1969. They are essential tools for recombinant DNA technology. The enzyme scans a DNA molecule with a particular sequence, usually of four to six nucleotides. Once it finds this recognition sequence, it stops and cuts the strands. This is known as enzyme **digestion**. On double stranded DNA the recognition sequence is on both strands, but runs in opposite directions. This allows the enzyme to cut both strands. Sometimes the cut is blunt; sometimes the cut is uneven with dangling nucleotides on one of the two strands. The uneven cut by these enzymes is known as **sticky ends.**

Examples of Endonucleases

Name of enzyme	Organism from which derived
Ava I	*Anabaena variabilis*
Bam HI	*Bacillus amyloliquefaciens*
Bgl II	*Bacillus globigii*
Eco RI	*Escherichia coli* RY 13
Eco RII	*Escherichia coli* R 245
Hae III	*Haemophilus aegyptius*
Hha I	*Haemophilus haemolyticus*
Hind III	*Haemophilus inflenzae* Rd
Hpa I	*Haemophilus parainflenzae*
Kpn I	*Klebsiella pneumoniae*
Mbo I	*Moraxella bovis*
Mbo I	*Moraxella bovis*
Pst I	*Providencia stuartii*
Sma I	*Serratia marcescens*
SstI	*Streptomyces stanford*
Sal I	*Streptomyces albus* G
Taq I	*Thermophilus aquaticus*
Xma I	*Xanthamonas malvacearum*

Achievements through Biotechnology

- **Transgenics** are genetically modified plants, which have been created by mobilizing genes of interest from one species to another species.
- **Opaque-2** gene of maize is responsible for lysine content in maize. Using recombinant DNA technology this has been transferred to maize genotype, which produces high amount of lysine. Ratan, Shakti, Protina varieties developed using this gene.

- **Flavr-savr tomato**: Enzyme ACC synthase is involved in production of ethylene. Therefore, antisense of ACC synthase regulates ripening of tomato thereby increasing the shelf life of tomato by decreasing quick ripening.
- **Bruise resistance in tomato**: The enzyme polygalacturanase (PG) attack on pectin and degrade the same causing soft rotting in tomato. The antisense of PG prevents pectin degradation in tomato, thus, tomato remain fresh and hard for long time.
- **Herbicide resistance**: Herbicides normally affect the photosynthesis or biosynthesis of essential elements. Transgenic plant **Proteina** has been developed by modification of the target protein against glyphosat (herbicide).
- **Insect resistance**: Bt gene possessed by bacteria (*Bacillus thurigiensis*) produces a toxin called **endotoxin**. When it binds with the receptors of mid-gut of lepidopteron insects causing or perforation in mid-gut and promote leaching of essential elements necessary for insects, thus insect dies due to deficiency of such elements. So far this gene has been transferred in Cotton, Tomato and Tobacco.
- **Resistance against pathogens**: Acetyle tranferase gene has been used to develop transgenic tobacco against *Pseudomonas syringae*, wildfire disease of tobacco. The prevention of crown gall disease formation is achieved by spraying young plants or seeds with avirulent species of *Agrobacterium radiobactor* var. *radiobactor* K-84. In maize, somaclonal variation has induced resistance to race T of southern corn leaf blight. In sugarcane, resistance to Fiji disease and downy mildew, have been recovered.
- **Barnase Barn-star system**: The system was used by Mariani *et al.* (1992) to develop male sterile lines. In this system a ribonuclease (Barnase gene) gene is isolated from Bacteria (*Bacillus amyloliquifaciens*) and hooked with TA 29 promoter from Tobacco. Promoter then transferred to *Brassica napus*. The progenies of *B. napus* are male sterile (due to inhibition of mRNA, thereby preventing meiosis). Now Barnase gene which is male sterile crossed with Barn-star gene (isolated from same bacteria and hooked with TA 29). The progenies out of this cross-become fertile as Barn-star gene kills the activity of Barnase gene, producing a chimeric ribonuclease system or genetically engineered male sterility.

- **Production of pathogen-free plants**: Plants traditionally being vegetatively propagated are systemically infected with viruses and other pathogens, which greatly reduce yield and quality as well. For instance, potato leaf roll virus (PLRV) or potato virus Y (PVY) can cause up to 95% reductions in the tuber yield.
- **Genes identified for disease resistance:** So far disease resistant genes have been identified for Garlic mosaic virus; Cabbage black ring spot virus; Turnip mosaic virus, Cauliflower mosaic virus chlorotic mottle, Green Flower, stunt vein mottle, virus B; Dahlia mosaic virus, vein mottle by virus B; Soya bean mosaic virus, Feathery mottle, Hanmon Mosaic; Cucumber mosaic virus; African cassava mosaic; Tobacco mosaic virus; and Potato virus.
- **Finding virus-free plants:** In some cases meristem-tip culture do not provide the virus-free plants, because viruses (like TMV, potato virus X, cucumber mosaic virus) invade the growing tip. In such cases virus free plants are obtained by combining meristem-tip culture with high temperature treatments.
- **Improvement of nutritional quality**: The cereals and legumes are major sources of storage seed proteins; deficient in certain amino acids essential for human beings. Majority of cereals are deficient in lysine and legumes in sulphur amino acids. Approaches are made to rich the cereals with amino acids and legumes with sulphur containing amino acids.
- **Selection for salt and draught tolerance**: Salt tolerance has been incorporated into rice lines with improved plant type. Some of the improved rice cultivars, *viz.* IR 42, IR 43 and IR 52 are salt tolerant.
- Tolerance to draught is a polygenic trait, which involves highly complex osmo-regulatory functions. Draught tolerances have been achieved in transgenics developed in media incorporated with non-penetrating osmotic solutes such as PEG (polyethylene glycol) and dextrans.
- **Molecular farming:** The synthesis of certain chemicals through transgenic plants is known as molecular farming. The genes confirming quality characters are being transferred to get increased synthesis of some chemicals, *viz.* Mannital dehydrogenage gene from *Escherichia coli* is transferred to

tobacco for increased production of mannital.

- In 1973, Cohen and Boyer transferred a gene from one organism into another. In 1982, the first biotech plant, an antibiotic resistant tobacco, was developed. In January 1983, at a meeting of genetic researchers in Miami, three different teams reported success in using *Agrobacterium tumefaciens*, a bacterium, to carry new genes into plant cells, heralding the dawn of modern agricultural biotechnology. The **bacterium is known as "natural genetic engineer"**, as it splices its own genes into host plant cells.
- **Genetically Engineered Organisms (GEOs):** Field tests for Genetically Engineered (GE) crops resistant to pests and pathogens were first conducted in the US, in 1985. A co-coordinated framework for the regulation of GEOs was established and the first GE tobacco was released, in 1986.
- In India, the Genetic Engineering Approval Committee (GEAC), has approvej GE varieties for commercialization.

Achievements in Cotton

- **Genes for insect resistance,** *e.g.* Toxin genes from *Bacillus thuringiensis*; and Protease inhibitor genes from plants and the hornworm (*Protoparce sexta*, and *P. quinquemaculata*); Cholesterol oxidase genes; *Heliothis* stunt virus genes against *Heliothis* spp have been identified.
- **Genes used for herbicide resistance,** *e.g.* Nitrilase gene *Klebsielia* spp. (a bacteria) for Bromoxynil resistance; Mono-oxygenase gene from a bacteria *Alcaligenes eutrophus* for 2, 4-D resistance, identified.
- **Genes used to improve fibre qualities,** *e.g.* Polyhydroxybutyrate and polyhydroxyacetate from bacteria have been identified for the expression of indigo pigment in fibres.
- **Commercial varieties of cotton:** Bollworm resistant transgenics, NUCOTN 33M and NUCOTN 35B. Herbicide (Bromoxynil) resistant transgenics, BXN 57 and BXN 53 have been released

Production of Disease-free Plants

Important use of tissue culture technique is isolation of disease-free tissues from a species and its regeneration into whole plant. Thus tissue culture can help in reviving some of the varieties of crop plants which have become obsolete due to their susceptibility to a particular disease. Mosaic virus is a serious problem in pulse crops like green gram, black gram, soyabean and other crops like papaya and okra. Tissue culture can help in isolation of mosaic free lines in these crops.

Under normal conditions plants are infected by a range of pathogens including bacteria, fungi, viruses, viroids, nematodes, and insects. Most of the perennial plants and those propagated by vegetative means are systemically infected with one or more pathogens, which affect yield, vigour and quality of the plant. If explants for micropropagation are derived from an infected plant, the pathogens can multiply and spread to a large number of plants. It is therefore, highly advisable to use disease free stocks to initiate cultures for micropropagation. Eradication of viruses and other pathogens is also desirable from the point of view of international exchange of plant materials.

While bacteria and fungi present on the surface of the plant material can be easily eliminated by treatment with surface sterilizing agents, there is no entrely effective treatment against viruses. Viruses can multiply with the shoots *in vitro* without visible symptoms. Traditionally, thermotherapy has been used for virus elimination but is not effective against all viruses. Moreover, heat treatment may adversely affect the plant tissue.

For some reasons viruses are unable to enter or survive in the apical meristems. Therefore, even infected plants the apical meristems are generally free of viruses. Taking advantage of this observation, Morel and Martin (1952) developed the technique of shoot tip culture to raise virus free plants from infected individuals. Since then it has become the most popular method of virus elimination. It involves excision of 0·5–1 mm long shoot tips, comprising apical meristem and one or two leaf primordia, and their cultivation on a suitable medium to regenerate whole plants. Sometimes combining chemotherapy or thermotherapy with shoot tip culture has enhanced the efficiency of the latter for virus eradication. However, the plants regenerated from shoot tips must be thoroughly tested for the suspected viruses before declaring them virus free. Using this approach, several countries grow *in vitro* cultured virus-free seedlings of several crops, *viz.*, potato, cassava, sugarcane.

Development of Biotechnology in India

- The Government of India established National Biotechnologic Board in 1982 under the DST, Govt. of India.
- In 1986 a separate Department of Biotechnology (DBT) w created under the Ministry of Science and Technolog Government of India.
- United Nations established International Centre for Gene Engineering and Biotechnology (ICGEB) H.Q. at Triesta (Ital and a centre in New Delhi in 1987.
- Lal Bahadur Shastri Centre for Advanced Research Biotechnology, IARI, New Delhi was established in 1988 (4 October).

20

Seed Technology

The first symbolic importance of seed started after the report of amine Commission (1881). First private seed company **'Sutton and ons'** came into existence in 1912 in Kolkata. Presently ICAR has 54 reeder seed Production units producing 3,700 tonnes of Breeder seed; JAS, Dharwad is at the top in producing breeder seed. There are 103 eed testing laboratories in India.

The term **seed** is applied to the ripened ovule of a seed plant before ermination. Seed has three main parts, *viz.* the embryo (consists of he cells that will develop into the structures of the adult plant such s root, bud, stalk, and leaf); the cotyledons (the organs of absorption) nd the seed coat. Cotyledons in monocots are called the endosperm vhereas in gymnosperms it is called **megagametophyte**. The otyledons themselves serve as storage tissue in dicots.

- During the process of fertilization, the pollen tube enters the ovule through a small opening known as the micropyle. One of the two sperm nuclei in the pollen tube unites with the egg cell in the ovule to form a zygote, which develops into the embryo.
- In flowering plants the other sperm nucleus unites with two polar nuclei present in the embryo sac to form an endosperm nucleus, which later produces the nutritive endosperm tissue surrounding the embryo in the seed (the cotyledons).
- In gymnosperms, the endosperm is formed from the tissue of the embryo sac itself.
- The nucellus (megasporangium) is a tissue composing main part of ovule.
- **Seed coat** is derived from the integument (outer layer) of the ovule and known as the **testa**. In flowering plants a second seed coat occurs within the testa; this second coat is thin, membranous known as **tegmen**.
- **Aleurone layer:** A prominent layer of rectangular cells, which contain protein lies next to the seed cents.

- **The endosperm**: The entire mass of tissue below the aleurone layer is made up of cells, which contain plenty of starch grains forming endosperm.
- **The embryo**: The scutellum has an upper free part which has a flesh projection known as **'ventral scale'**. Below this upper ventral scale and almost at the middle of the free part there is another outgrowth, which can be called as the **'inner ventral scale'**. The inner ventral scale is peculiar in rice embryos only.
- On the surface of the embryo this outgrowth along with the epiblast forms a continuous covering around the plumule. The structure between the scutellum and the plumule is called **mesocotyl.**
- Coloured varieties of rice have thicker aleurone layer than the white rice varieties. The coarse rice generally has a larger aleurone layer than the finer rice. It has also been found that in poor soils, the aleurone layer is thin and improves in thickness with the fertility of the soil and manure.
- **Public hybrid:** The hybrids developed by Government. agencies or Govt. Institutions and Agricultural Universities are called public hybrids.
- **F_1 hybrid:** The resultant seed obtained from crossing of two genetically dissimilar parents is called **F_1 hybrids.**

Characteristics of Good Seed

Seed is a mature embryo having good viability, genetic purity, physical purity, vigour, moisture content, health, size and uniformity to produce same individual.

- **Genetic purity** means the seed is coming from an authentic source and it has no adulteration of other same genera or species. To produce genetically pure seed proper isolation distance is maintained. It is tested by field plot test.
- **Physical purity** means, there is no inert matter (sand, pebbles, soil particles, straw), weed seeds, and other crop seeds included in the lot of seed. Such contamination is permitted up to some extent, *e.g.* maize (1.0%) and carrot (5%).
- **Germination percentage** indicates the potential of seeds for developing and establishing into seedlings. It is calculated based on pure live seed (PLS).

- $$PLS = \frac{\text{Number of seeds germinated (healthy seedlings)}}{\text{Total Number of seeds tested for germination}} \times 100$$
- Standards of germination for seed certification: Maize (90%), Cotton (60%), Rice (80%), Chillies (60%), Wheat (85%), and Carrot (60%).
- **Vigour** is the ability of seed to emerge in varying environments of fields. Generally, high germination percentage is associated with high vigour.
- **Seed moisture** varies from crop to crop in ranges from 9-12%.
- **Seed health** refers that the seed is free from any kind of disease propagule (spore, mycelium, etc.), either active or latent.

Seed Dormancy

Dormancy is the resultant of the slowing down effect of the metabolic process during seed maturation.

Seeds from most plants are ready to germinate when they ripen. Many of the woody perennials have some type of dormancy, however, which must be broken before planting. If the dormancy is of the embryo type (embryo itself must go through a period of dormancy or maturing), the seed is stored in cold conditions (0° to 10°C) in containers with abundant moisture. The process, called **stratification**, lasts for 30 to 120 days, depending on the species. If the dormancy is seed-coat type (coat is tough and must be softened before germination can take place), the seed may be placed in a cement mixer with limestone chips or treated with concentrated sulphuric acid; this process is called **scarification**.

- **Breaking seed dormancy** : Among the several methods available the most suitable method to break seed dormancy at farmers level is nitric acid treatment. Soaking the seed in 0.1 N nitric acid @ 6.3 ml/litre of water for 12 to 24 hours effectively breaks the seed dormancy.
- **International seed testing association** was organized on 10 th July, 1924, is involved in the work of standard seed testing throughout world.
- Rice varieties Masoorie, I.R. –50, have no seed dormancy and in periods of wet weather at harvest time, the seed may germinate on the panicle itself.

Classes of Quality Seed

International Crop Improvement Association (ICIA) in 1946 classified seed into different categories, like breeder seed, foundation seed, certified seed, and fixed the standard for the same.

- **Breeder seed:** It is 100 per cent pure seed directly controlled by seed producing agencies, breeders, and institutions. **Plant breeder supervises** the seed production.
- **Foundation seed:** It is the progeny of breeder seed whose origin can be traced to breeder seed. Its production is **supervised by seed certification agency**. The foundation seed produced from breeder seed is designated as **foundation seed stage first** and further produced from stage first is designated as **foundation seed stage second**. It serves the source for certified seed.
- **Certified seed:** As mentioned, it is the progeny of foundation seed.

Other Classes of Seeds

- **Nucleus or basic seed:** It refers to the initial handful of seeds produced by the original breeder himself for development of the particular cultivar/genotype.
- **Registered seed:** It is the progeny of foundation seed and source of certified seed. This class is absent in Indian seed industry.
- **Truthfully labelled seed:** It is the seed offered for sale after testing germination percentage and physical purity etc. It is **not a certified seed,** as there is no inspection carried out by the certified person.

Methods of Seed Production

As per the Seed Act, 1966, the seed is produced with methods deciphered in act.

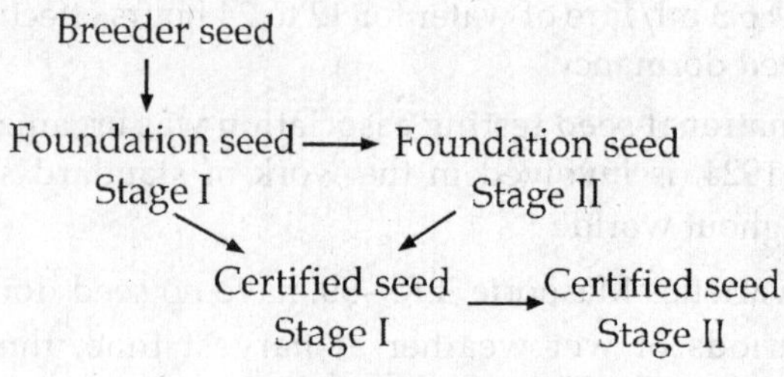

Fig. 1: *Stages of seed production*

Rogue: It is the variation from standard type of variety or strain. The **Roguing is the removal of undesirable individuals from a varietal mixture in the field by hand pulling.**

Isolation Distance

Isolation distance is a separation distance of pure and healthy plants from that of contaminated plants. It is maintained to avoid the contamination or cross-pollination.

Isolation Distance of Different Crops

Crop	Distance for foundation seed (m)	Distance for certified seed (m)
Self-pollinated crops	3	3
General including Rice, Wheat, Ragi, Groundnut		
Greengram, Cow-pea, Tomato	50	25
Cross-pollinated crops		
Maize, Mustard, Greens	400	200
Pearl millet	1,000	25
Lucerne	400	100
Sunhemp	200	100
Castor	300	150
Sunflower	1,000	500
Carrot	1,000	800
Onion	1,000	400
Cucumber	800	400
Often cross-pollinated crops		
Cotton	50	30
Pigeon-pea	100	50
Sorghum	200	100
Chilli, Bhindi	400	200
Brinjal	200	100

Permitted moisture contents for safe storage of seed:

Wheat, Sorghum, Rice	12%
Oat, Barley, Maize	13%
Soya bean	11%

Seed Testing

Seed testing consists of series of tests designed to determine the quality of seed. The quality of seed is generally determined by purity, germination or viability and moisture contents in the seed.

- The sampling is done on random basis, the sample collected are called **primary samples.** Primary samples are mixed together and from this mixture a **composite sample** is taken, which is quite little in amount. Then composite samples are again mixed following above procedure and a random **'working sample'** is taken. Each working sample contains approximately 25 g of seeds.
- **Purity test** denotes the real percentage of desirable seed from a lot of seed with several impurities (seeds of other varieties, other crop, defective seeds, weed seeds, inert matter, sand, straw, stones, pebbles, soil particles, etc.).
- $\text{Purity percentage} \frac{\text{Weight of pure seed}}{\text{Total weight of the working sample}} \times 100$
- The impurity percentage in known as **dockage.**
- **Real value of seed:** It is the value of seed sample in comparison to another pure germinating seed percentage. It is calculated as:
- $\text{Real value of seed} = \frac{\text{Purity percentage} \times \text{Germination percentage}}{100}$
- **Test weight and seed index:** Test weight is the weight of 1,000 normally developed seeds, whereas seed index is the weight of 100 normally developed seeds.

Tests Conducted at Seed Testing Laboratory

- **KOH bleach test for sorghum:** In this, test seeds are immersed in a 1:5 wt./vol. Solution of potassium hydroxide (KOH) and fresh household bleach (5.25% NaCl) for 10 (for brown seeds) or 5 (for white seeds) minutes. Mixed stirred gently. Seeds are rinsed with tap water; air-dried and observed for the presence of dark pigmented tannic acid and light pigmented testa.
- **NaOH test for wheat:** The test is conducted to examine whether presence of fungicide or any other chemical in the red and white coloured grains. The seeds are immersed in 5% sodium

hydroxide (NaOH) solution and observed for 60 minutes. The red seeds become bright yellow, just after immersion, then turn to dark orange within 15 minutes and finally become orange in 60 minutes. But white seeds become bright yellow on immersion; the colour fades to straw colour in 10 minutes and it lasts for longer period.

- **Seed viability** is the percentage of live seeds, which produce seedlings. The viability of seed can be tested either by germination test or viability test.

- $$\text{Germination percentage} = \frac{\text{Total number of germinated seeds}}{\text{Total number of planted seeds}} \times 100$$

- **Tetrazolium test for viability:** In this test 2, 3, 5-tetrazolium chloride is used, which is colourless but develops intense red colour upon reduction with live cells. The seeds are soaked in tap water for overnight and split open longitudinally with the help of a scalpel in such a way that half of the embryo is attached to each part. Then the seeds are put in aqueous solution of tetrazolium for 4 hours and then washed with tap water. The numbers of seeds stained with red colour are counted. These coloured seeds are viable seeds. Their percentage can be calculated as:

$$\text{Viable seeds percentage} = \frac{\text{No. of half seeds stained red}}{\text{Total No. of half seeds in seed sample}} \times 100$$

- **Germination tests:** It is the testing of seeds through germination, it can be carried out by any following methods,

1. **Top paper (TP) germination:** The seeds are germinated on the top of one or more layers of paper, which are placed in transparent Petridishes in growth chamber.
2. **Sand germination:** Seeds are planted in uniform layers of moist sand and then covered to depth of 1-2 cm with sand. **Substrates** for germination are moistened with 0.2% KNO_3 solution.

Important Seed Hardening Chemicals

Crop seed	Chemical and procedure for hardening
Black gram	Soak the seeds in 20 ppm Succinic acid solution (one litre solution for 3 kg seed) for 4 hours.
Chick-pea	Soaking of seeds in 1 per cent solution (one litre solution for 3 kg seed) of potassium dihydrogen phosphate (KH_2PO_4) for 4 hours.
Cotton	Soaking of seed in 1,000-ppm Chlorochlorine chlorides (CCC) solution for 6 hours. Seed then can be treated with fungicides or bio-fertilizers.
Green gram	Soak the seeds in 100-ppm Manganese sulphate solution (one litre solution for 3 kg seed) for 4 hours.
Groundnut	Soaking of seed in 0.5 per cent Calcium chloride solution (one litre solution for 3 kg seed) for 6 hours. Seeds are then air dried and process repeated 2-3 times for 2 hours each.
Red gram	Soaking of seed in,1000-ppm solution (one litre solution for 3 kg seed) of Zinc sulphate for 4 hours. Treatment with fungicides or bio-fertilizers is possible after seed hardening.
Sorghum	Soaking of seed in 0.5 per cent solution (one litre for one kg seed) of Potassium dihydrogen phosphate (KH_2PO_4) for 10 hours. After hardening, seed may be treated with pesticides or bio-fertilizers.
Sunflower	Soak the seed in 0.5 per cent solution of Disodium Hydrogen phosphate (Na_2HPO_4, one litre solution for one kg seed) for 6 hours. Seed after drying to original moisture content can be treated with fungicides, etc.

Seed Technology in India

National Seed Corporation (NSC) was founded in 1963. Tarai Development Corporation (TDC) came into existence in 1969. Uttar Pradesh Tarai Development Corporation was formed in 1978.

- First seed testing laboratory was established at IARI in 1961. Division of Seed Science and Technology, IARI, founded Indian Society of Seed Technology in 1971.

❏❏❏

21

Biochemistry

Biochemistry (term derived from Greek two words, *bios* means 'life' and *logos* means study) is the biochemical process held in the body of an entity. The beginning of Biochemistry started from the work of Robert Boyle during 1650 to 1780 and culminating into that of Antoine Laurent Lavoisier, the father of modern chemistry.

- John Mayow observed the fundamental analogy between the respiration in animals and oxidation of organic matter in air.
- The photosynthesis is the essential procedure to counteract respiration, was demonstrated by Joseph Priestley, Jan Ingenhousz, and Jean Senebier, which became the milestone in the development of biochemical thoughts.
- Justus von Liebig and Louis Pasteur were particularly responsible for the successful application of chemistry in the study of biology, called modern biochemistry.
- Justus von Liebig is called the **Father of Agricultural Chemistry**.
- In1929 adenosine triphosphate (ATP) was isolated from muscle cells. In 1940 F.A. Lipmann proposed that ATP is the common form of energy exchange in many cells.
- R. Schoenheimer and D. Rittenberg initiated the use of radioactive isotopes of chemical elements to trace the pathway of substances in the animal body in 1935.

Chemical Composition of Living Matter

Every living cell is composed of water, minerals, organic compounds (protein, carbohydrate and fat, etc.). Fats constitute a heterogeneous group of organic chemicals. The conversion of carbohydrate to fat occurs continuously in the body. **The liver is the main site of fat metabolism**. High level of fat in the blood is associated with occurrence of **arteriosclerosis** ("hardening" of the arteries).

Carbohydrates

Carbohydrates are the organic compounds with a general formula of $(CH_2OH)^n$. These are classified into three different groups, *viz.* Monosaccharides, Oligosaccharides and Polysaccharides.

1. **Monosaccharides** are found in grapes, other fruits, and honey and contain three to nine carbon atoms. Glucose (also called dextrose, grape sugar, and corn sugar), Fructose (fruit sugar), and Galactose, being monosaccharides have the same molecular formula: $(C_6H_{12}O_6)$, but, because their atoms have different structural arrangements, the sugars act differently. The generic nomenclature ending for the monosaccharides is *'ose'*. For example, sugar with five carbon, called pentose; six carbon, hexose, etc.
2. **Oligosaccharides**, consist of two to six monosaccharide units, are found in natural sources. Depending upon the number of monosaccharides presence, these may be classified into three categories: **Disaccharides** (two monosaccharides) *e.g.* Sucrose, Maltose, Lactose, Cellobiose; **Trisaccharide** (three monosaccharides), *e.g.* Raffinose; and **Tetrasaccharide**, (four monosaccharides), *e.g.* Stachyose.

- **Sucrose** is the outcome from á 1, 2-glycosidic linkage between á-glucose and â-fructose. It is a non-reducing sugar.
- **Maltose** consists of two units of glucose linked together with α **1, 4-linkage** having the property of reducing sugar **found largely in germinating seeds.**
- **Cellobiose** consists of two units of glucose linked together with β **1, 4-linkage**. It is a reducing sugar.
- **Lactose** consists of one molecule each of β, D-glucose and β, D-galactose linked together with β 1, 4-glycosidic linkage.
- **Stachyose** is a tetrasaccharide consisting of one molecule of glucose and fructose each and two molecules of galactose.

Trioses are simple sugars derived from hydrolysis of oligopolysaccharides having 'C' atom ranging from 3-9. Trioses are two types:

(*a*) **Aldoses** are sugars with terminal CHO aldehyde group aldotriose-glyceraldehyde, *e.g.* Aldotetrose (Erythropse, Trehalose); Aldopentose (Arabinose, Ribose, Deoxyribose); Aldohexose (Glucose, Galactose, Mannose).

(*b*) **Ketoses** are with >C=O group *e.g.* Ketotriose (Dihydroxy acetone, the simplest keto sugar); Ketohexose (Fructose, the simplest among all the sugars).

3. **Polysaccharides:** Polysaccharides consist of as many as 10,000 monosaccharide units linked together, representing most of the structural and energy-reserve carbohydrates found in nature. These are present as:

(*a*) **Storage polysaccharides: Amylose** (unbranched chain of glucose units joined together by α 1, 4 glycosidic linkage, into non-linear helical chain), **Amylopectin** (highly branched chain joined together with an α 1, 4 linkage and at ends with α 1,6 linkage) are the examples of storage polysaccharides.

(*b*) **Glycogen:** It is present in the animal cells, just like starch in plants. It is heavily branched, compact and contains both α 1, 4 linkage and α 1, 6 linkage.

- The term Starch has been derived from the old English word *stercan* meaning "to stiffen".

(*c*) **Structural Polysaccharides** include:

1. **Cellulose:** The polymer of glucose joined together by β 1, 4-linkage.
2. **Hemicelluloses:** Polymer of L-arabinose, D-glucose, D-galactose, D-xylose, along with uronic acid (galacturonic acid).
3. **Pectin:** It is a polymer of galacturonic acid normally present in cell wall as calcium pectate.

Proteins

Berzelius suggested name protein. The term protein has been derived from Greek word *Proteios* that means primary. Proteins are polymer of amino acids. Each amino acid is linked together with another by peptide – C = O – NH bond. Proteins are two types:

1. **Simple proteins:** Such proteins contain only amino acids.
2. **Conjugated proteins:** Proteins that contain non amino acid components also in addition to amino acids. These additional factors are called **prosthetic groups**.

Structural Levels of Protein

Proteins with primary structure have linear arrangement of amino acids. The secondary structures are sometimes being produced by interaction between neighbouring amino acids of same chain.

- **Quaternary structures** are produced by association of more than one polypeptide, *e.g.* **Collagen** (muscle protein); **Keratin** (hair and wool protein); **Fibroin** (silk protein); and **Elastin** (protein from insect wings).

Enzymes

Enzymes are polymers of amino acids, that act as catalysts to regulate the speed of the many chemical reactions involved in the metabolism of living organisms. Term enzyme has been derived from the Greek phrase *en zyme,* meaning "in leaven". Enzymes are classified into several broad categories, such as hydrolytic, oxidizing, and reducing, depending on the reaction they catalyze:

1. **Hydrolytic enzymes**: These enzymes upon reacting with water molecule accelerate reactions to break the substance into simpler compounds.
2. **Oxidizing enzymes (oxidases)**: Accelerate oxidation upon reaction with oxygen.

- The term enzyme was coined in 1867 by the German physiologist Wilhelm Kuhne. Zymase was the first enzyme discovered in yeast.
- Individual enzyme is named by adding suffix '***ase***' to the name of the substrate they react. Some enzymes, such as the trypsin and pepsin, retain their original names as they were discovered.
- Pepsin, and trypsin possess the peculiar property known as autocatalysis, which permits them to cause their own formation from an inert precursor called **zymogen**. As a consequence, these enzymes may be reproduced *in vitro*.

Terminology Regarding Enzymes

- **Holoenzyme:** It consists of an apoenzyme plus prosthetic group.
- **Apoenzyme:** It is the enzyme without prosthetic group.
- **Active site**: The site responsible for catalysis of molecule.
- **Regulatory site**: It is the site other than catalytic site.

Some Special Classes of Enzymes

- **Allosteric enzymes:** They are the regulatory enzymes, which have more than one polypeptide. Such enzymes have a well-developed regulatory mechanism, and produce a sigmoid curve (instead of classical parabolic curve).

- **Isozymes:** They are different enzymes, which catalyze the same reaction in different tissues. They are different in molecular weight.
- **Ribozymes**: They are catalyzing RNA with enzymatic activity. They are **only non-protein enzymes** found in whole molecular world.

AMINO ACIDS

Amino acids are the important class of organic compounds that contain (except Proline) both the amino (-NH_2) and carboxyl

(-COOH) groups. Twenty amino acids serve as the building blocks of proteins, known as the standard, or á amino acids, comprising Alanine, Arginine, Asparagine, Aspartic acid, Cysteine, Glutamic Acid, Glutamine, Glycine, Histidine, Isoleucine, Leucine, Lysine, Methionine, Phenylalanine, Proline, Serine, Threonine, Tryptophan, Tyrosine, and Valine. These may be grouped into following classes,

1. **Amino acids with aliphatic R-groups:** Glycine, Alanine, Valine, Leucine, Isoleucine;
2. **Non-aromatic amino acids with hydroxyl R-groups:** Serine, Threonine;
3. **Amino acids with sulfur-containing R-groups:** Cysteine, Methionine;
4. **Acidic amino acids and their amides:** Aspartic Acid, Asparagine, Glutamic Acid, Glutamine;
5. **Basic amino acids:** Arginine, Lysine, Histidine;
6. **Amino acids with aromatic rings:** Phenylalanine, Tyrosine, Tryptophan;
7. **Imino acids:** Proline.

Essential amino acids: Such amino acids are not synthesized from precursors in the body, therefore, they must be provided in the diet. There are 10 essential amino acids, which include, Lysine, Tryptophan, Valine, Histidine, Leucine, Isoleucine, Phenylalanine, Threonine, Methionine, and Arginine. They are found in adequate amounts in protein-rich foods from animal sources or in combinations of plant proteins.

VITAMINS

Funk introduced the term vitamin for the first time. Vitamins are organic compounds required by the body in small amounts for metabolism, to protect health, and for proper growth children in particular. Vitamins also assist in the formation of hormones, blood cells, nervous-system chemicals, and genetic material. They generally act as catalysts. Thirteen well-identified vitamins may be classified based on their solubility:

1. **Water-soluble**: These cannot be stored and must be consumed frequently, preferably every day *e.g.* Vitamin B complex (B_1, B_2, B_{12}), C, Niacin (Nicotinic acid).
2. **Fat-soluble:** These are generally consumed along with fat-containing foods *e.g.* Vitamins A, D, E, K.

Vitamins Their Function and Deficiency Symptoms

A (Retinal): It is a pale yellow primary alcohol derived from carotene. It affects the formation and maintenance of skin, mucous membranes, bones, and teeth; vision; and reproduction. Found in Carrots, Broccoli, Squash, Spinach, Kale, and Sweet potatoes; Milk, Butter, cheese, Egg yolk, liver, and Fish-liver oil. The deficiency causes Xerophthalmia or Xerosis and night blindness.

B_1 (Thiamine): Thiamine is a colourless, crystalline substance, acts as a catalyst in carbohydrate metabolism, enabling pyruvic acid to be metabolized enabling carbohydrates to release their energy. Thiamine also plays a role in the synthesis of nerve-regulating substances. Deficiency of thiamine causes **beriberi**, which is characterized by muscular weakness, swelling of the heart, and leg cramps and may, in severe cases, lead to heart failure and death. Foods rich in thiamine are Pork, Organ meats (Liver, Heart and Kidney), Eggs, Leafy green vegetables, Whole or Enriched cereals, Wheat germ, Berries, Nuts, and Legumes.

B_2 (Riboflavin): Riboflavin like thiamine, serves as a coenzyme in the metabolism of carbohydrates, fats, and, especially, in respiratory proteins. Riboflavin deficiencies are skin lesions, especially around the nose and lips, and sensitivity to light, blurred vision, cracks on skin at angle of mouth. The best sources of riboflavin are Liver, Milk, Meat, Dark green vegetables, Whole grain and Enriched cereals, Pasta, Bread, and Mushrooms.

B_3 (Niacin): Niacin works as a coenzyme in the release of energy from nutrients. A deficiency of niacin causes **pellagra**, the first symptom of which is sunburn like eruption that breaks out where the skin is exposed to sunlight. Later symptoms are a red and swollen tongue, diarrhoea, mental confusion, irritability, and, when the central nervous system is affected, depression and mental disturbances. The best sources of niacin are Liver, Poultry, Meat, Whole grain and Enriched cereals, Dried beans and Peas, and Nuts.

B_6 (Pyridoxine): Pyridoxine is necessary for the absorption and netabolism of amino acids. It plays roles in the use of fats in the body and in the formation of red blood cells. The deficiency causes skin lisorders, cracks at the mouth corners, smooth tongue, convulsions, lizziness, nausea, anaemia, and kidney stones. The best sources are Whole grains, cereals, Bread, Liver, Avocadoes, Spinach, Green beans, and Bananas.

B_{12} (Cynocobalamin): Cobalamin is one of the most recently solated vitamins, necessary for the formation of nucleoproteins, proteins, and red blood cells, and functioning of the nervous system. The deficiency causes **Pernicious anaemia** (due to ineffective production of red blood cells, faulty myelin synthesis, and loss of epithelium of the intestinal tract). It is obtained only from animal ources like Liver, Kidneys, Meat, Fish, Eggs and Milk.

B Complex (Folic acid): Folic acid, or folacin, is a coenzyme needed or forming body protein and haemoglobin. Folic acid is effective in he treatment of anaemia. Dietary sources are Organ meats, Leafy green egetables, Legumes, Nuts, and Whole grains.

B Complex (Pantothenic acid): Pantothenic acid plays a role in he metabolism of proteins, carbohydrates, and fats. It is abundant in nany foods and is manufactured by intestinal bacteria as well.

B Complex (Biotin): Biotin is also synthesized by intestinal bacteria nd widespread in foods, plays a role in the formation of fatty acids nd the release of energy from carbohydrates.

Vitamin C (Ascorbic acid): It is important in the formation and naintenance of collagen. **Scurvy** is the classic manifestation of severe scorbic acid deficiency. It is found in citrus Fruits, Fresh Strawberries, ineapple and Guava; Broccoli, Brussels sprouts, Tomatoes, Spinach, Green peppers, Cabbage and Turnips.

Vitamin D (Calciferol): Also called "sunshine vitamin", is ecessary for normal bone formation and for retention of calcium and hosphorus in the body. It is found in Egg yolk, Liver, and vitamin-D ortified milk; also manufactured in the body with sterols. **Rickets** ccurs due to failure of the body to absorb calcium and phosphorus.

Vitamin E (Alpha Tocopherol): The vitamin plays some role in rming red blood cells and muscle and other tissues and in preventing e oxidation of vitamin A and fats. It is found in Vegetable oils, Wheat germ, Liver and Leafy green vegetables. Deficiency of vitamin auses Sterility.

Vitamin K: Vitamin K is necessary for the coagulation of blood as it helps forming prothrombin, an enzyme needed to produce fibrin for blood clotting. The richest sources of vitamin K are alfalfa and fish livers; Leafy green vegetables, Egg yolks, Soya bean oil, and Liver. Deficiency may create problem in blood clotting.

BLOOD

Haemoglobin is confined within the red blood corpuscles and carries oxygen from the lungs to the tissues. Oxygen concentration in lungs is relatively high; the haemoglobin combines with oxygen in the lungs and releases the oxygen in the tissues (where the oxygen concentration is low).

- The gamma-globulin fraction of the plasma proteins contains the antibodies of the blood and is of practical value as an immunizing agent.

NUCLEIC ACIDS

Nucleic acid was discovered by Swiss Biochemist (Friedrich Miescher) is 1869.

These naturally occurring complex phosphorus compounds are acidic in character, and capable of being broken down chemically to yield phosphoric acid, sugars, and a mixture of organic bases, purines (Adenine, Guanine) and pyrimidines (Thymine, Cytocine and Uracil).

- Nucleic acids are long chain of polynucleotides consisting of repeating structural units called **nucleotides**. The nucleotide contains a pentose (or five-carbon) sugar, a purine or pyrimidine base, and a phosphate residue. The pentose sugar is ribose in RNA and 2-deoxyribose in DNA.
- There are two **classes of nucleic acids**: ribonucleic acids (RNA) and deoxyribonucleic acids (DNA).
- There are three types of RNA are involved in protein synthesis, *viz.* messenger RNA (mRNA) serves as the template for protein synthesis; transfer RNA (tRNA) attaches to a specific amino acid and pairs it to the appropriate codon (three adjacent nucleotides) on the mRNA molecule; and ribosomal RNA (rRNA), which, with proteins, makes up the ribosome, the site at which protein synthesis occurs.

LIPIDS

Lipids are biological molecules that are insoluble in aqueous solutions and soluble in organic solvents, are classified as lipids. The lipids of physiological importance for humans have four major functions:

1. They serve as structural components of biological membranes.
2. They provide energy reserves in the form of triacylglycerols.
3. Both lipids and lipid derivatives serve as vitamins and hormones.
4. Lipophilic bile acids aid in lipid solubilization.

FATTY ACIDS

Fatty acids are long-chain hydrocarbon molecules containing a carboxylic acid moiety at one end. The numbering of carbons in fatty acids begins with the carbon of the carboxylate group. At physiological pH, the carboxyl group is readily ionized, rendering a negative charge to the fatty acids. There are following fatty acids, Myristic acid, Palmitic acid, Palmitoleic acid, Stearic acid, Oleic acid, Linoleic acid, Linolenic acid, and Arachidonic acid.

- **Saturated fatty acids:** Fatty acids that contain no double bonds in carbon are termed saturated fatty acids. Those contain double bonds are called **Unsaturated fatty acids.** The presence of double bonds in fatty acids significantly lowers the melting point relative to a saturated fatty acid.
- Saturated fatty acids of less than eight carbon atoms are liquid at physiological temperature, whereas those containing more than ten are solids in nature.
- **Essential fatty acids: Linoleic, linolenic** and **arachidonic** fatty acids cannot be synthesized from precursors in the body, and are thus considered the **essential fatty acids**; essential in the sense that they must be provided in the diet.

METHODS IN BIOCHEMISTRY

- Quantitative colour spectrum analysis is done using spectrophotometer.
- Respiratory quotient is measured using **Gasometric techniques** from oxygen and carbon dioxide. Respiratory quotient is the ratio of carbon dioxide produced against oxygen used.
- **Centrifugation**: It is the technique in which rapid spinning imposes high centrifugal forces on suspended particles or molecules in solution, and causes separations of such matter on the basis of differences in weight.
- Proteins are separated by ultracentrifugation (very high speed spinning).

- **Electrophoresis:** It is the technique based on positive and negative charge, which adopt different rates of migration of molecules toward positively (anode) or negatively (cathode) charged poles and permit separation. Such separations can be carried out in solutions or when the proteins saturate a stationary medium such as cellulose, starch, or acrylamide gels.
- **Chromatography:** It is also a technique based on same principle of electrophoresis, but it is done on filter paper. Through the chromatography even small amounts of substances can be separated on filter paper and identified by appropriate colour reactions. **Column chromatography** is based on the relative rates of penetration of molecules into beads of a complex carbohydrate according to size of the molecules. Larger molecules are excluded relative to smaller molecules and emerge first from a column of such beads. This technique not only permits separation of biological substances but also provides estimates of molecular weights.
- **Isotopes** (heavy or radioactive elements) have been employed in labelling biological compounds and tracing their fate in metabolism. Measurement is done based on labelled probe.

❑❑❑

22

Crop Physiology

Physiology is the study of the physical and chemical processes taking place in living organisms during the performance of life functions. It is concerned with reproduction, growth, metabolism, respiration, excitation, and contraction as they are carried out within the cells, tissues, organs, and organ systems of the body.

Respiration

The term Respiration has dual meaning in biology involving two different processes: first, the physical process by which living organisms take oxygen and emit waste carbon dioxide; and secondly, the chemical process by which fuel molecules such as sugars and fats are broken down within a cell to liberate energy for cellular life processes. Respiration in plants consists of Glycolysis and Krebs cycle (or Citric acid or TCA, tricoboxylic acid) and ETC (Electron Transport Chain).

- Glycolysis occurs in the cytoplasm: Krebs cycle and Electron Transport Chain in mitochondria. Glycolysis occurs in anaerobic condition. Final product of glycolysis is pyrubic acid. TCA cycle starts with acetyl coenzyme A and oxaloacetate. ETC is present in the cristae of mitochondria where ATP synthesized during respiration.
- Total ATP synthesis, as a net gain, from one molecule of glucose in respiration is 38 ATP whereas gross production is 40 ATP.
- Products of anaerobic respiration are ethanol and lactic acid.
- CO_2 molecules are released from the mitochondria during respiration.

- Oxidative phosphorylation of ADP with inorganic phosphate synthesizes high-energy compounds.
- Cytochromes are electron carriers in the respiratory ETC.
- One molecule of glucose yields 686 kcal energy.
- One molecule of ATP yields 7.6 kcal energy.
- One molecule of $NADH_2$ yields 52 kcal energy.

Photosynthesis is the process by which chlorophyll containing organisms (green plants, algae, etc.) capture energy in the form of Sunlight and convert it to chemical energy.

- Normal photosynthetic reaction is $6CO_2 + 2H_2O \xrightarrow[\text{Light}]{\text{Chlorophyll}} C_6H_{12}O_6 + H_2O + O_2$.
- CO_2 concentration in atmosphere is 350 ppm.
- Photosynthesis occurs at 400-700 nm active radiations.
- Major photosynthesis active pigments of higher plants are chlorophyll *a* and chlorophyll *b*. Important accessory pigments in plants are carotenoids like carotenes and xanthophylls.
- Photosynthesis completes in two different phases, *i.e.* light reaction or hill reaction which takes place in the graina of chloroplast and dark reaction or Calvin cycle takes place in stroma of chloroplast. The products of light reaction are ATP and $NADPH_2$.

Mechanisms of Photosynthesis

C_3 pathway or reductive pentose pathway or Blackman reaction or Calvin cycle takes place in Rice, Wheat, Pea, and Soybean. First product is 3 PGA.

C_4 pathway or Hatch and Slack pathway or Dicarboxylic acid pathway or Bicarboxylation cycle or cooperative photosynthesis occurs in Sorghum, Maize, and Sugarcane. C_4 plants have two types of photosynthetic cells with Kranz leaf anatomy, *viz.* mesophyll cell and bundle sheath cells, causing higher Photosynthetic rate. The first product is oxaloacetic acid in C_4 plants.

CAM (Crassulacean Acid Metabolism) pathway is found in Pineapple and *Opuntia*.

- The most important enzyme involved in photosynthetic CO_2 fixation is Rubisco (Ribulose-bi-phosphate carboxylase). This is most abundant protein found in the world.
- First enzyme in the CO_2 fixation in C_3 plant is **Rubisco** whereas in C_4 is PEP carboxylase.
- Order of water use efficiency CAM > C_4 > C_3.
- Harvest index in cereals ranges from 0.4 to 0.5 whereas in pulses it is 0.2 to 0.3.
- Formation of ATP in chloroplast with the help of light is called as photophosphorylation.
- One $NADH_2$ produces 3 ATP molecules whereas one molecule of $FADH_2$ produces 2 ATP molecules.

Mineral Nutrition

Some 40 elements are obtained in the analysis of plant body but 16 elements are considered essential for plants. The criteria of essentiality of an element for plant life are as follows:

1. It takes part in the physiological functions.
2. In its absence normal functioning hampers and the deficiency is exhibited in the form of certain sign and symptoms.
3. The deficiency so caused can only be corrected by the application of specific element only.

Some sources now claim that there are 21 essential elements, adding Na, Ve, Co, Si and Ni to the list. Nickel along with Cobalt has been found useful in legumes.

These elements are sometimes considered, as beneficial because of their essentiality *in toto*, however, could not be established hitherto.

Nutrients, Functions, Deficiencies and Their Management

Nutrient	Functions of element	Symptoms of deficiency	Management
Nitrogen	Present in most substances of cells.	Plants grow poorly and are light green in colour. Lower leaves turn yellow or light brown and stems are short and slender.	Besides balance NPK foliar spray of 2% urea.
Phosphorus	Present in DNA/ RNA, Phospholipids (Membranes), ADP, and ATP etc.	Plants grow poorly and leaves are bluish green with purple tints. Lower leaves sometimes turn light bronze with purple or brown spots. Shoots are short and thin, upright and spindly.	Apply phosphatic fertilizers in the basal dressing; Foliar spray is phytotoxic to most plants.
Potassium	Acts as a catalyst or many reactions.	Plants have thin shoots, which in severe cases show dieback. Older leaves show chlorosis with browning of tips, scorching of margins, and many brown spots usually near the margins. Fleshy tissue shows end necrosis.	Apply potash fertilizers in the basal dressing. Fiolior spray is phytotoxic.
Magnesium	Present in chlorophyll and is part of many enzymes.	First older, then younger leaves become mottled and chlorotic, then reddish. Sometimes necrotic spots appear. Tips and margins of leaves may turn upward and leaves appear cupped. Leaves may drop off.	Spray with Epsom salts @ 2%. Apply Mg limestone (9-11%), Epsom salt (10%), Kieserite (16%), Kainite (3%) in basal dressing.

Nutrient	Functions of element	Symptoms of deficiency	Management
Calcium	Regulates permeability of membrane. Forms salts with pectin. Affects activity of many enzymes.	Young leaves become distorted with tip hooked back and margins curled. Leaves may be irregular in shape and ragged with brown scorching or spotting. Terminal buds finally die. Plants have poor and bare root system. Cause blossom end rot of many fruits. Increase fruit decay in storage. Responsible for tip burns in mature detached lettuce heads at high (24-35°C) temperature.	Soil application of lime or gypsum and superphosphate. Spray with calcium nitrate or calcium chloride @ 800 kg in 1,000 lit/ha
Boron	Affects translocation of sugars and utilization of calcium	Bases of young leaves or terminal buds become light green and finally break down. Stem and leaves become distorted. Plants become stunted. Fruit, fleshy roots or stems, etc. may crack on the surface and /or rot in the centre.	Apply borax @ 2 kg/ha in the basal dressing
Sulphur	Present in amino acids and coenzymes	Young leaves are pale green or light yellow without any spots. Symptoms resemble those of nitrogen deficiency.	Soil application of lime or gypsum and sulphur, and super phosphate.
Iron	Acts as a catalyst of chlorophyll synthesis. Part of many enzymes	Young leaves become severely chlorotic, but main veins remain characteristically green. Sometimes brown spots develop. Part or entire leaves may dry. Leaves may be shed.	Soil application of iron chelate like EDDHA; Foliar spray with Fe EDTA @ 0.05%.

Nutrient	Functions of element	Symptoms of deficiency	Management
Zinc	Is a part of enzymes involved in auxin synthesis and oxidation of sugars	Leaves show interveinal chlorosis. In due course of time they show necrotic and purple pigmentation. Leaves are few and small, internodes are short and shoots form rosette, and fruit production is low. Leaves are shed progressively from base to tip.	Spraying with Zinc sulphate (5 kg) and Urea (20 kg) or lime (2.5 kg) in 1000 lit/ha.
Copper	Part of many oxidative enzyme.	Tips of young leaves wither and their margins become chlorotic. Leaves may fail to unroll and tend to appear wilted. Heading is reduced and heads are dwarfed and distorted. Citrus, pome, and stone fruits show dieback or twigs in the summer, burning of leaf margins, chlorosis, rosetting etc.	Soil application of copper sulphate @ 60 kg/ha.
Manganese	Part of enzymes of respiration, photosynthesis and nitrogen utilization.	Leaves become chlorotic but smallest veins remain green and produce a checked effect. Necrotic spots may appear scattered on leaf. Severely affected leaves turn brown and wither.	Foliar application of manganese sulphate @ 9 kg/ha.
Molybdenum	Is an essential component of nitrate reductase enzyme.	Melons, and some other plants show severe yellowing and stunting and fail to set fruits.	Foliar application of sodium molybdate or ammonium molybdate @ 300 g/ha.

Symptoms Caused by Some Air Pollutants

Pollutants	Source	Symptoms
Ozone (O_3)	NO_2 released from internal combustion engine combines with O_2 in sunlight forms O_3.	• Stippling, mottling and chlorosis of upper leaf surface of leaves. Spots are small to large, bleached white to tan, brown or black. Premature defoliation and stunting occurs in plants. • Normally enters through stomata
Peroxyacyl nitrate (PAN)	Gasoline released from internal combustion engine combines with O_3 + NO in sunlight forms PAN.	• Causes silver leaf on plants, *i.e.* white bleached to bronze spots on lower surface of leaves. • In severe condition resembles with ozone injury. • Spinach, petunia, tomato, lettuce and dahlia are sensitive.
Sulphur dioxide (SO_2)	From factory stacking and internal combustion engine.	• General chlorosis at low concentration whereas high concentration cause bleaching of interveinal tissue of leaves. • Toxic at 0.3 to 0.5 ppm.
Nitrous oxide (NO_2)	From oxygen and nitrogen in nature and furnace, internal combustion engine.	• At low concentration it suppresses growth. • At high concentration it resembles with SO_2 symptoms. • Bean and tomato are sensitive. • Toxic at 2-3 ppm.

Pollutants	Source	Symptoms
Hydrogen fluoride (HF)	Stacks of factories processing ore or oil.	• Leaf margins of dicots and leaf tips of monocots turn tan to dark brown, die and sometimes fall from plants. • Toxic at 100 to 200 ppm.
Chlorine (Cl) and Hydrogen chloride (HCl)	Refineries, glass factories.	• Leaves show bleached necrotic areas between veins. Leaf margins often appear scorched. Leaves may drop prematurely. • Toxic at 0.1 ppm.
Ethylene (CH_2CH_2)	Automobile exausts, burning of gas, fuel oilfrom ripening fruits.	• Stunting and abnormal leaf fall. Few blossoms are produced. • Apple is sensitive which show scald like symptoms. • Toxic at 0.05 ppm.
Dust	From roads, cement factories, ores, burning of coal, etc.	• Crusty layer on plant surface. Plant become chlorotic, grows poorly sometimes die. • May cause burning of leaves after reaction with rainwater.

□□□

23

Plant Pathology

Plant pathology is the study of Maladies in plants. Malady is a common term applied for both diseases and disorders. The term **Pathology** has been derived from the two Greek words *pathos* (suffering, disease) and *logos* (study). Disease may be defined as "*Any harmful deviation in the normal functioning of physiological processes due to continuous irritation*".

- **Anton de Bary** is called the Father of Plant Pathology whereas E.J. Butler is called Father of Modern Plant Pathology in India.
- The term **Disease** is restricted to malfunctions caused by pathogenic organisms or viruses, whereas those caused by other factors (including nutritional imbalance) are termed as **Disorders**.

Pathology involves the determination of the cause (etiology) of the disease, the understanding of the mechanisms of its development (pathogenesis), the structural changes associated with the disease process. **Pathogenesis** completes in three fairly distinct stages:

1. **Inoculation**: Transfer of the pathogen to the infection court, or area in which invasion of the plant occurs, *e.g.* stomata, hydathodes, or lenticels etc.
2. **Incubation**: It is the period between the arrival of the pathogen in the infection court and the appearance of symptoms.
3. **Infection**: Establishment of pathogen inside the host and appearance of disease symptoms.

Important Enzymes and Toxins Involved in Pathogenesis

1. **Cutinase enzyme** degrades the cutin layer.
2. **Suberin-degrading enzyme** degrades suberin.
3. **Pectic enzymes:** There are two kinds of enzymes which act upon respective pectic substances, as

(*a*) **Pectin methylesterase**, which act upon pectinic acid (pectin) that have uronic acid molecule containing up to 75% methoxy group. It converts pectin into polygalacturanic acid.

(*b*) **Polygalacturanases** act upon pectic acid (polygalacturanic acid) that have uronic acid molecule containing more than 75% methoxy group. There are two types of polygalacturanases:

(*i*) **Exopolygalacturanase** cleaves polygalacturanic acid in terminal manner, *i.e.* release only monomeric galacturonic acid.

(*ii*) **Endopolygalacturanase** cleaves polygalacturanic acid in random manner, *i.e.* release oligogalacturonic acid.

(*c*) **Pectinmethylgalacturonases** act like polygalacturanases but prefer to act upon the pectin instead on polygalacturanic acid in both exo and endo manner of cleavage.

4. **Hemicellulases** degrade different molecules of hemicelluloses.

5. **Cellulases** act upon cellulose in a series manner. These are further classified into:

(*a*) **C_1 enzyme** acts on the cellulose at the crystalline areas.

(*b*) **C_2 enzyme** converts cellulose fibre into insoluble short fibres.

(*c*) **C_X enzyme** converts loosened cellulose fibrils into soluble sugars like cellobiose.

(*d*) **b-glucosidase (cellobiase):** This enzyme converts cellobiose into glucose.

Environmental Factors Affecting Disease Development

1. **Temperature:** Each pathogen has an optimum temperature for growth. The development of disease is dependent on temperature in certain diseases, *e.g.* blue mould of tobacco (*Peronospora tabacina*), downy mildews of vine crops (*Pseudoperonospora cubensis*) and lima beans (*Phytophthora phaseoli*), late blight of potato and tomato (*Phytophthora infestans*), leaf spot of sugar beets (*Cercospora beticola*), and leaf rust of wheat (*Puccinia recondita tritici*).

2. **Relative humidity:** Relative humidity is very critical in fungal spore germination and the development of storage rots. If relative humidity is maintained at 85 to 90 per cent diseases like soft rot of sweet potato does. Germination of powdery mildew spores occurs at 90 to 95 per cent relative humidity.

3. **Soil moisture:** High or low soil moisture may be a limiting factor in the development of certain root rot diseases. High soil-moisture level favours the development of destructive water moulds, *e.g.* *Aphanomyces*, *Pythium*, and *Phytophthora*. Some

diseases are more most severe under low soil-moisture levels, *e.g.* take all of cereals (*Gaemmanomyces = Ophiobolus graminis*); charcoal rot of Maize, Sorghum, and Soya bean (*Macrophomina phaseolina*); common scab of Potato (*Streptomyces scabies*); and Onion white rot (*Sclerotium cepivorum*).

4. **Soil pH:** Soil pH drastically influences the development of a few diseases, *e.g.* common scab of Potato and Clubroot of crucifers (*Plasmodiophora brassicae*). Growth of the Potato scab organism is suppressed at a pH of 5.2. It is advisable to add sulphur in the soil to keep the pH about 5.0 for controlling potato scab and add lime (to make pH 7.2) to control clubroot of crucifers.
5. **Soil type:** Most of pathogens thrive better on loam soils followed by clay soils. Some fungal pathogens, *e.g. Phymatotrichum* causing root rot in cotton, are more serious in black alkaline soils (with pH 7.3 or above with low organic matter). *Fusarium* wilt disease is more common in lighter and higher (topographically) soils. Nematodes are also most damaging in lighter soils that warm up quickly.
6. **Soil fertility:** Certain nutrients required by plants frequently influence the development of some infectious diseases. Some diseases (like fire blight of Apple and Pear (*Erwinia amylovora*), stalk rots (*Macrophomina phaseolina*) of Maize and Sorghum, *Botrytis* blights, *Septoria* diseases, powdery mildew of wheat, and northern leaf blight of maize are more destructive at excessive amounts of nitrogen fertilizer. Addition of adequate amounts of potash often counteracts this condition.

mportant Pathogens

There are several pathogen, either living (biotic) or non-living abiotic) in nature.

Fungi (singular Fungus) studied under Mycology: The term fungus s derived from Latin word '*Mykes*' meaning 'mushroom'. The fungi are eukaryotic microorganisms, devoid of chlorophyll. The body of ungus is called **thallus** (no distinction between roots and shoots) consists of microscopic branching threadlike filaments of various engths, called **hyphae** (singular hypha). The hyphae are arranged nto a network called a **mycelium**. Fungi reproduce asexually (binary ission, budding, fragmentation, etc.) and sexually (gametangial contact and gametangial copulation) producing variety of spores, *viz.* Conidiospores, Chlamydospores, Oospores.

Bacteria (singular Bacterium) studied under Bacteriology: Bacter are prokaryotic microorganisms having single-cell and one circul chromosome. The principal genera of plant pathogenic bacteria incluc *Agrobacterium, Clavibacter, Erwinia, Pseudomonas, Xanthomona Streptomyces*, and *Xylella*. With the exception of *Streptomyces* specie all are small, single, rod-shaped cells approximately 0.5 to 1.0 μm width and 1.0 to 3.5 μm in length. *Streptomyces* develop branche aerial mycelia with curled chains of spores on the tips of the myceli

- Bacterial pathogens enter into plants through wounds (*X. oryz* pv. *oryzae*), Hydathodes (*X. axonopodis* pv. *compestris*), Flor nectaries (*Erwinia amylovora*), Lenticels (*Streptomyces scabies*) an stomata (*Pseudomonas tabaci* and *Xanthomonas malvacearum*).

Viruses studied under Virology: Virus is an infectious agent small size and simple composition that can multiply only in livin cells. Beijerinck gave the name virus for the liquid he called *contagiu vivum fluidum*. First disease known was tobacco mosaic virus (TMV

- Most disease-causing viruses are carried and transmitted b insects and mites called **vectors**, *e.g.* aphids (transmit mosai viruses), leafhoppers (transmit yellows-type viruses), whitefli (Leaf curl viruses), thrips, mealybugs, planthopper grasshoppers, scales, and beetles etc.
- A small number of plant viruses are soil borne. Viruses causin grapevine fan leaf, tobacco rattle, and tobacco and tomato rin spots, are spread by nematodes. A few soil borne viruses (*e.g* big vein of lettuce, wheat mosaic, tobacco necrosis) are sprea by the swimming spores of *Olpidium* spp. and *Polymyxa* sp of fungi.

PLANT DISEASE CONTROL

Effective disease control measures are aimed at breaking 'diseas triangle' (comprising of environment, pathogen and host and thei interactions).

Breaching of disease triangle can be done as:

1. **A virulent pathogen** can be eradicated by reducing inoculum and exclusion (quarantine measures).
2. **Susceptible host** can be managed by providing nutrition to th host; bringing out resistance; and through protection of host.
3. **Environment** can be altered by crop management; soi management; and water management practices.

Generations in Fungicides

Fungicides (from *caedo* means 'to kill') are the chemicals used to kill the fungi. The first fungicide discovered was Bordeaux mixture in 1982 by P.M.A. Millardet considered as landmark in the history of chemicals in disease control.

1. **First generation:** Bordeaux mixture and other inorganic fungicides (sulphur, mercury).
2. **Second generation:** Started from 1934 in which development of organic chemicals *i.e.* dithiocarbamates, *viz.* dialkyl and monoalkyl, quinone, chloro, PCNB belongs to this generation. These chemicals cannot penetrate the host hence considered as surface protectants.
3. **Third generation:** Also in this generation chemicals were of organic in nature but they had capability to enter the host system and control the established pathogens, *e.g.* Benzimedazole, carboximides (vitavax and plantvax), phenyl amino compounds (fosetyl AL, Azole) and morpholines etc.
4. **Fourth generation (the present generation):** Consists of compounds *in vitro* non-toxic still control plant disease in the natural conditions. These chemicals upon application interfere with the host physiology and enhance the resistance in the plants, *e.g.* **Trcyclazole** leads malfunctioning of appressoria and **Propiconazole** triggers defense mechanism in plants.

Systemic Fungicides and Their Groups

Chemicals those are systemic or mobile within the plant from the site of application to different parts of the plants are called systemic in nature. These chemicals follow either/and **Apolastic movement** (movement through Xylem tissue) or **Symplastic movement** (downward movement through phloem tissue. Important groups of fungicides are:

1. **Benzimedazoles:**

(*i*) **Benomyl** (C_{16} H_{18} N_4 O_3): It was developed by du Pont de Nemours Co. (USA). It is marketed with trade names of Benlate and Benlate 50 WP. It is insoluble in water or soil but slightly soluble in water, but it is soluble in chloroform. When it come in contact with water hydrolyzes to MBC (Methyl Benzimedazole- yl-carbamate) + butyl amine + CO_2). It moves in plants through xylem tissues having toxicity of 9,500 mg/kg of body weight LD^{50}. In plants it disrupts the reproductive ability of the fungi, *i.e.* affect biosynthesis of DNA at the time of mitosis.

(*ii*) **Carbendazim** ($C_9 H_9 N_3 O_2$): It is a grey powder, resembling to Benlate. Most soluble in acetic acid and diethyl formalin. Available as Bavistin-50 WP (BASF), Derosal 50 WP (Hoechst India) and Carbendazim or MBC 50% (Moti Lal Pesticides).

(*iii*) **Thiabendazole (TBZ)** used to control post harvest diseases of fruits and vegetables. It interferes with the biosysnthesis of DNA and Mitosis.

2. **Thiophanate group:** There are three fungicides in this group based on chemical thiourea. It is available in the market as Topsin, Topsin M and Cercobin. When thiophanate comes in contact with water gets metabolise in MBC, hence sometimes called Benzimedazole.
3. **Oxanthin group:** Von Schemelling and Kulka discovered Fungicides of this group in 1966. **Corboxin** comes in the name of *Vitavax* used against smuts in wheat. **Oxycorboxin** comes in the name of *Plantvax* for the control of rusts of wheat and other crops.
4. **Phenyl amide group:** The important fungicide of this group is **Metalaxyl** that comes in the name of Redomyl-50 WP, Apron and Redomyl 35 WP. Metalaxyl is the first fungicide effective against Downy Mildews produced by CIBA Geigy.
5. **Triazoles** are most important fungicide consisting of **tebuconazole**, which comes in the name of Raxyl for the control of smuts and *Macrophomina phaseolina.* Other chemicals of this group are Propiconazole, Aconazole, Bitarlazole, Etaconazole, Difenconazole, Flusilazole, Hexaconazole, Imzalil, Penconazole, Tetraconazole, Tridemefon, Trcyclazole, Trifumizole.
6. **Morpholines:** In this group there are two fungicides, *viz.* Triademorph (calixin) and dodimorph (meltatox). Morpholines are effective against powdery mildews of wheat, vegetable, fruits especially mango and all cucumbers.
7. **Alcyl phosphate:** The important fungicide of this group is Fosetyl-AL. It moves through phloem tissues.
8. **Imidazole group:** Important fungicide is piperazin which comes in the name of Cela W 524.

LD_{50} Doses of Some Selected Fungicides

Name of fungicide	LD_{50} dose/kg of body weight
Sulphur fungicides	>17,000 mg
Thirum	780 mg
Alkylbisdithiocarbamate	8,000 mg
Mercurial fungicides	30-200 mg
Mercuric chloride	1,000-5,000 mg
Captan	9,000 mg
Dithane M-45	8,000 mg
Dithane Z-78	5,200 mg
PCNB	1,700 mg
Vitavax	2,000 mg
Metalaxyl	669 mg
Carbendazim	6,400 mg
Maneb	6,750 mg

QUARANTINE

In the 14th century the growth of maritime trade and the recognition or plague was introduced. The ships returning from the Levant led to the adoption of quarantine in Venice. It was decreed that ships were to be isolated for a limited period to allow for the manifestation of the disease and to dissipate the infection brought by persons and goods. Originally the period was 30 days, *trentina,* but this was later extended to 40 days, *quarantina.*

- In 1423 Venice set up its first lazaretto (quarantine station), on an island near the city. The Venetian system became the model for other European countries and the basis for quarantine control for several centuries.

Mechanism of Biological Control of Plant Diseases

Mechanisms of biological control is classified as:

1. **Induced Resistance**: Induced resistance is a plant response created *de novo* showing resistance against microorganisms or abiotic agents or pathogens, normally susceptible plants.
2. **Hypovirulence**: Hypovirulence is a term used to describe reduced virulence found in some strains of pathogens. The phenomenon was first observed in *Cryphonectria parasitica* (chestnut blight fungus) on *Castanea sativa* in Italy. These slower growing hypovirulent strains contain a single cytoplasmic element of double-stranded RNA (ds RNA) similar to that found

in mycoviruses. Hypovirulence has also been reported in *Rhizoctonia solani, Gaeumannomyces gramini* var. *tritici, Ophiostoma ulmi.*

Important Microbial Biocides Used for Disease Management

Trade name	Origin of biocide	Targeted against
Gliogard	*Gliocladium virens*	Damping off
F-Stop	*Trichoderma herzianum*	Damping off and seedling blights due to *Rhizoctonia solani/Sclerotium* spp.
Bioderma	*T. herzianum*	Wilts of different crops
BINAB-T	*T. polysporum*	Wood decay
Aspire	*Candida aleophila*	*Monilia fructicola*
Gallex/Galltrol	*Agrobacterium radiobacor K-84*	Crown gall of stone fruits
Nogall	*A. radiobacor K-1026*	Crown gall of stone fruits
Dagger-G	*Pseudomonas fluorescens*	*Rhizoctonia solani/ Pythium* spp./ *Sclerotium* spp.
Kodiak	*Bacillus subtilis*	Damping off and soft rots
Biosave	*Pseudomonas syringae*	Post harvest decay in citrus/ apple/pear due to *Monilia fructicola*
Frostban	*Pseudomonas syringae strain F-105*	Frost injury
Metaquino/ Metabiol	*Metarrhizium anisopliae*	Sugarcane insect pests
Bio 1020	*Metarrhizium anisopliae*	Sugarcane insect pests
Boverin	*Beauveria bassiana*	Forest trees pests
Thuricide/ Biotrol	*Bacillus thuringiensis*	Lepidopteron insects, mites and mosquitoes
Collego	*Colletotrichum gloeosporiodes f.sp. aeschynomene*	*Aeschynomene virginica* in rice and soya bean
Biocon	*Paecillomyces lilacinus*	*Meloidogyne* spp.

- IARI has signed a MoU with M/s Cadilla Pharmaceuticals Limited for production of Kalisena SD and Kalisena SL. For the same technology has been provided by IARI, New Delhi (produced by Binita Sen, Division of Plant Pathology).

nportant Outbreaks Due to Diseases

- Late blight of potato in Ireland in 1845-60 (called **Irish famine**) caused death of one million persons of starvation and 1.5 million persons emigration.
- Downy mildews of grape in France (1851 and 1878).
- Coffee rust in Ceylon (1870).
- Southern bacterial wilt of tobacco (1900).
- Sigatoka leaf spot and Panama disease of banana in Central America (1900-65).
- Black stem rust of wheat (1916 1935, 1953-54).
- Southern Maize leaf blight (1970).

mportant Disorders (Caused by Non-Parasitic Causes)

- **Due to physical/ water stresses in soil,** *e.g.* Blossom end rot of tomato; Internal decline of lemon; Tirak leak of cotton; and Die back of coffee.
- **Due to high water/oxygen stress/Fe^{++}, Mn^{++} stress,** *e.g.* Pansukh disease of rice (=tip burn of rice). Splitting and water injury of citrus (due Ice nucleation bacteria, the *Pseudomonas syringae*).
- **Due to combination of high temperature (above 90°F), low oxygen concentration, bad ventilation,** *e.g.* Black heart of potato; Brown heart of apple; and Cracking of litchi (due to high temperature).
- **Due to unfavourable oxygen relation,** *e.g.* Black heart of potato.

Deficiency Disorders

1. **Phosphorus:** Weak root system becomes susceptible to rotting fungi, *e.g.* tip burn and marginal necrosis of mango.
2. **Potassium:** Poor root growth leaves lack luster, *e.g.* Tip drying of onion; and Marginal chlorosis of plum leaves.
3. **Calcium:** Young leaves and shoot tip affected, *e.g.* Blossom end rot of tomato; Blossom end rot of grape berries (Calcium Nitrate @ 1% controls the disease); Black heart of celery; Cavity spot of carrot; Wither tip of flax.
4. **Zinc:** Khaira disease of rice; Little leaf of Cashewnut; and Folliocellosis or mottling of citrus.
5. **Manganese:** Phala blight of sugarcane; Marsh spot of garden pea; Grey speck of oat; and Speckle yellow of beet.

6. **Boron:** Browning and hardening of head of Cauliflower; Blac tip of mango/tip necrosis of mango; Water por of cauliflower; Heart rot/brown rot/internal black spot of bee and Internal necrosis of aonla (apply borax @ 0.6%).
7. **Molybdenum (coupled with nitrate supply):** Enrolling, cuppin and internal rotting, *e.g.* Whiptail of cauliflowers.
8. **Copper:** Chlorosis and withering of leaves, *e.g.* Reclamatio disease of cereals; and Exanthema of citrus.

Disorder's Due to Left Crop Residue in the Field

Crop residue left in field produces some of toxic chemicals thereb causing maladies in crops:

- Akiochi leaf of rice occurs due to H_2S toxicity.
- Physiological complex of rice.
- Eti-etti disease: due to cadmium toxicity.
- Freckle of sugarcane: due to silicon deficiency.
- Minimata disease of rice: due to Hg toxicity.
- Linear stripe of maize: due to fluoride (HF) toxicity.

Diseases Due to Genetic Defect

Corky stunt of tomato: It is due to presence of single recessive gene (Stevenson, 1976).

Disorders Due to Malnutrition

Cauliflower:

- **Buttoning** is the check in the growth of vegetative seedlings caused by temperature, nitrogen supply, root injury by insects or by some diseases (*Rhizoctonia*) and over aged seedlings contribute improper curding.
- **Raciness:** Premature initiation of floral buds is the cause of this malady, which is due to higher temperature/lower temperature than the normal.

Tomato:

- **Cat face:** Blossom end of fruits have ridge, furrows and blotches that looks like cat face.
- **Puffiness:** Fruits remain light in weight, the condition is due to high or low temperature/moisture.

- **Sunscald:** Tissue of fruit has blistered water soaked appearance due to extreme heat.
- **Cracking:** The condition of cracking occurs due to high temperature in dry spell of rainy season.

Carrot:

- **Cavity spot:** Cavity in the cortex, epidermis collapses to form a pitted lesion. The condition is due to accumulation of potassium and decreased accumulation of calcium.
- **Carrot splitting:** Simple cracking of roots due high ammonium concentration in soil.

Lettuce:

- **Tip burn of lateral margin of the inner leaves:** Due to high temperature, light, maturity duration, excess N_2, Ca and Bo deficiency, high Mn content.
- **Crushing/brushing/rosette spotting/brown stain:** Due to excess CO_2.

Mango:

- **Leaf scorch:** Scorching of older leaves at the tip and margin. The condition is **due to excess amount of chloride ions,** which render potash deficiency (generally in saline soil/blackish water used for irrigation/MOP used most).
- **Spongy tissue:** Spongy development in flesh, which leaves fruit bad odour (common in Alphanso), occurs due to Calcium involvement.

Grape:

- **Internal chlorosis:** Yellowing of interveinal spaces noticed. The condition is due to Mg, Zn and Fe deficiency.
- **Bud flower and berry drop:** Due to improper application of N_2, improper fertilization of berries, heavy crop head, uneven ripening, auxin deficiency.
- **Bud killing:** Formation of limited number of buds (specially in Thompson seedless variety) due to excessive N_2 application.

Pineapple:

- **Sunscald:** Due to high sunlight, can be controlled by covering with dry straw during May-April.
- **Fasciation and multiple crowning:** Due to genetical/ soil/ environmental complex.

Important Disorders of Fruits and Plantation Crops

Disorders	Fruit crop(s)
Gummosis	Almond
Stoning	Custard apple
Fruit necrosis	Aonla
Bitter pit, water core, Jonathan spot and Russeting	Apple
Dry neck and Die back	Avocado
Fruit cracking	Cherry, Citrus, Litchi, Pomegranate
Little leaf, Exanthema, Granulation, Suscald and Sun burn.	Citrus
Witches broom	Cocoa
Crown choking and button shedding	Coconut
Hen and chicken	Grape
Spongy tissue	Mango
Cock's comb	Sapota

Important Perfect/Imperfect Stages

Imperfect state/Anamorph	Perfect state/ Telomorph
Colletotrichum/Gloeosporium	Glomerella
Septoria/ Cercospora	Mycosphaerella
Oideum	Erysiphe
Oidiopsis	Leveillula
Ovulariopsis	Phyllactinia
Aspergillus	Eurotium/Emericella/Sartoya
Pencillium	Talaromyces/Eupenicilium/ Carpectilis
Pyricularia	Magnaporthe
Fusarium	Gibberella/Nectria
Sphaeropsis	Physalospora
Botrytis	Sclerospora
Trichoderma/Gleocladium	Hyporcrea
Graphium	Ceratocystis
Rhizoctonia	Thanatophorus
Sclerotium	Aethalia/ Cortium
Alternaria/ Stemphyllium	*Pleospora*

24

Microbiology

Microbiology is the study of microorganisms including protozoa, algae, moulds, bacteria, viruses, viroids, virusoids, and prions.

Microbes those have a primitive and dispersed kind of nuclear material are called **prokaryotes** (*Pro* = primitive + *karyon* = nucleus), *e.g.* the blue-green algae, bacteria, and rickettsiae; those with true nucleus bounded by a membrane, *e.g.* small algae other than the blue-greens, yeasts and moulds, and protozoans, are called eukaryotes (*Eu* = true + *karyon* = nucleus).

- Antonie van Leeuwenhoek, a Dutch draper (woolen cloth maker) whose hobby was lens grinding and microscope making, was the first to provide proper descriptions for protozoans from the guts of animals and bacteria from teeth scrapings. He conveyed microorganisms as 'animalcules' in his findings to the British Royal Society in 1676.
- Robert Koch, a German physician, defined the procedures for proving cause of a specific disease. These procedure later became the rule of Koch are commonly called "Koch Postulates".
- The students of Pasteur and Koch in Europe securely laid the foundation of microbiology during 1880 to 1900 studying in Pasteur Institute, Paris.

Bacteriology (Study of Bacteria)

- F.J. Cohn, German botanist, between 1853 and 1892 gave the modern account of bacteria. Cohn's classification of bacteria was published in 1872.
- Robert Koch introduced bacteriological techniques in 1882 and isolated the organism of Asiatic cholera, diphtheria (1883) and tetanus (1885).
- In 1878, the U.S. botanist T.J. Burrill discovered the bacterial cause of fire blight in apple and pears.

Protozoology (Study of Protozoa)

The name Protozoa has been taken from Greek word meaning "first animal". Leeuwenhoek first observed protozoa in the 17th century.

Phycology (Study of Algae)

Algae are the heterogeneous group of primitive organisms capable of carrying photosynthesis for their livelihood.

Virology (Study of Viruses)

Viruses are the link between living and non-living, as they are comprised of nucleic acid encapsidated (enclosed) with protein coat. The Russian bacteriologist D. Ivanovski in 1892 found that a filtrate of sap from tobacco plants infected with mosaic disease could be used to transfer infection to healthy plants. Dutch microbiologist M.W. Beirjerinck in 1898 confirmed the work, as it was filterable through bacterial filter, he named this filtrate as *Contagium vivum fluidum* and later he named this filterable agent as Virus.

Viroids

Viroids are the tiny infectious particle that causes disease in higher plants. These are less than one-tenth the size of the smallest known viruses. Unlike viruses, which can contain either RNA or DNA, viroids consist solely of RNA. Viroids are further separated from viruses by their lack of a capsid (protein coat). Stricken plants show stunted growth and discoloration and may eventually die, e.g. Potato spindle tuber viroid.

Rickettsiae

In 1910, Howard Taylor Ricketts and his associate described the organism of typhus fever, *Rickettsia prowazekii* in 1916, in honour of Ricketts and Stanislas von Prowazek, both of whom died of the disease.

Prions

Prions are an infectious agent, which does not contain any nucleic acid but rather an abnormal form of a glycoprotein. These are simpler in the form than viruses. Prions cause diseases in human beings and animals, the best known being bovine spongiform encephalopathy (BSE), Creutzfeldt-Jakob disease (CJD), and scrapie. Before the identification of prions, these diseases were known collectively as the spongiform encephalopathies (degradation of brain) only linked by their similar symptoms.

Whittaker's Five Kingdom Classification

Whittaker's five-kingdom classification based on intake of food, laid the foundation of modern microbiology in which whole living world was categorized to five following kingdoms:

1. **Monera** includes all Prokaryotes.
2. **Protista**– unicellular Eukaryotes.
3. **Plantae**– multicellular plants and higher algae that normally carry out photosynthesis for nutrition.
4. **Fungi**– multicellular higher fungi, which take nutrition by absorption.
5. **Animalia** includes all animals, which takes their food as ingestion.

Bergey's manual of systematic bacteriology (formerly, *Bergey's manual of determinative bacteriology*) is the standard manual for taxonomy of protozoa, fungi, bacteria, actinomycetes, and BGA, having 4 volumes and 31 sections.

Average Size of Microbes

- Bacteria 0.5-3.0 µm
- Fungi 1.5-10 µm
- Protozoa 2-200 µm
- Algae 0.1 µm (BGA) to several feet (higher algae)
- MLOs 0.1-0.3 µm

Important Antibiotics and Their Mode of Action

Antibiotic	Produced by	Mode of action	Target Microbes
B-Lactam			
Penicillin	*P. chrysogenum / P. notatum*	β 1, 4-linkage in cell wall	Prokaryotes
Cephalosporin	*Cephalosporium* spp.	Cross linkages	Prokaryotes
Macrolides			
Erythromycin	*Streptomyces erythreus*	Inhibits function of 50S ribosome	Prokaryotes
Carbomycin	*S. halstedii*	Inhibits function of 50S ribosome	Prokaryotes

Aminoglycosides			
Streptomycin	*S. griseus*	Inhibits function of 30S ribosome	Prokaryotes
Neomycin	*S. fradiae*	Inhibits function of 30S ribosome	Prokaryotes
Kasugamycin	*S. kasugaensis*	Inhibits function of 16S ribosome and tRNA	Prokaryotes
Tetracyclines			
Oxyteracycline	*S. nimosus*	Inhibits function of 16S ribosome and tRNA.	Prokaryotes
Polypeptides			
Polymixin G	*Bacillus polymyxa*	Destroys cytoplasmic membrane	Prokaryotes
Bacitracin	*Bacillus subtilis*	Murein biosynthesis	Prokaryotes
Bulbiformin	*Bacillus subtilis*	Murein biosynthesis	Prokaryotes
Polyene			
Chloram-phenical	*S. venezualae*	Inhibits translation of 70S ribosome	Eukaryotes
Amphotericin	*S. nodosus*	Sterol inhibition	Eukaryotes
Nystatin	*S. nouresii*	Sterol inhibition	Eukaryotes
Filipin	*S. filipinensis*	Sterol inhibition	Eukaryotes
Aureofungin	*S. cinnamomius-tericola*	Sterol inhibition	Eukaryotes
Miscellaneous			
Cycloheximide	*S. griseus*	Inhibits transfer of amino acid to the 80S ribosome from peptidyle tRNA to in coming N-acetyle tRNA	Eukaryotes
Grisiofulvin	*Penicillium griseofulvum*	Inhibits cell division	Eukaryotes
Helenine	*P. funiculosum*	Protein synthesis	Virus
Statolon	*P. stoloniferum*	Protein synthesis	Virus

- Alexander Fleming discovered penicillin, the first antibiotic, in 1929. S.A. Wakesman discovered streptomycin in 1943 and used for the first time against *Mycobacterium tuberculosis,* the cause of Tuberculosis. Vasudeva *et al.*, 1958 reported Bulbiformin. Thirumalachar *et al.*, 1964 discovered aureofungin, the antibiotic against fungi.

METHODS IN MICROBIOLOGY

Microscopy

Leeuwenhoek had seen microbes with convex lens for the first time. Robert Hooke, the **Father of the Cell Theory**, observed filamentous fungi (1667) through a compound microscope.

Types of Microscopy

1. **Bright field**: In this the background is brightly lighted, the objects studied are dark, and the power of magnification is about 1,000.
2. **Dark field**: On dark background, light objects are seen.
3. **Phase contrast**: Controlled illumination is obtained by the use of special equipment that enables the refraction, or bending, of light. These equipments separate the cells, which become visible.
4. **Fluorescence microscopy**: It utilizes the ultraviolet microscope. A chemical substance is used which absorb ultraviolet waves and emit visible light in the mixture of microorganisms thus allow to distinguish the microbes.
5. **Electron microscopy**: In this microscopy the waves of electrons (negatively charged particles) and magnetic fields are used to see the image.

Cultivation of Microorganisms

Microbes growing on a nutrient medium are referred to as a **culture**. Early experiments (1776) by Spallanzani, laid the foundation for the technique of sterile culture.

- In 1853 it was discovered that flasks should not be sealed after boiling but could be closed with a plug of cotton then can be sterilized in autoclave at 15lb/psi (per square inch) pressure (which virtually is equal to 121.6°C) for 15 or 20 minutes.
- Robert Koch added a solidifying agent, gelatin to a nutrient medium. But in 1883, Frau Hesse, replaced gelatin with agar-agar (extracted from sea weed *Gelidium subcostatum* and *Gelidium amensii*).

Sterilization

Sterilization is the complete removal of all microbes through heat, chemicals, filters and ionization.

Sterilization through Heat

(*i*) **Direct flaming**: The object to be sterilized are passed through flame of spirit lamp, *e.g.* slide sterilization.

(*ii*) **Hot air sterilization:** Objects like vessels are sterilized in hot air oven at 160 to 180°C for two hours.

(*iii*) **Moist heat without pressure (Tyndelization)**: In this method material is sterilized by heating at 100°C for 30-60 minutes for three consecutive days. The idea behind this practice is that if a propagule on first day is left for killing, it germinates on next day, which upon heating gets killed.

(*iv*) **Moist heat with pressure (Autoclaving)**: In this method material is sterilized in an instrument called autoclave at 15 lb/psi (per square inch) pressure (which almost equals to 121.6°C) for 15 minutes.

Sterilization by Filtration

(*i*) **Porcelain filters, chamberland filters, kaolin, China clay, or quartz filter:** Such filters come in different grades ranging from L_1 (the big holes) to L_{13} (the smallest holes).

(*ii*) **Berfeld (from Germany) / Mandler (from USA) filters:** These filters are made up of diatomaceous clay. They also come in different grades like *W* (dense), *N* (normal) and *V* (coarse).

(*iii*) **Sintered glass filters:** They are available in different grades as required for filtration. *EL* (Extra Large), *C* (Coarse), *M* (Medium), *F* (Fine), *UF* (Ultra Fine) are the different grades of such filters.

(*iv*) Asbestos filters/seitz filters

Sterilization through Ionization and Radiation

It is a process by which electrically neutral atoms or molecules are converted to electrically charged ions, which sterilize the object.

Sterilization through Chemicals

A suitable chemical agent for sterilization is usually called 'sanitizer' is used to reduce the number of microbes. Sanitizers are commonly used to sterile equipments of laboratory. Propylene oxide @ 5 ml/10 ml of culture is used for sterilizing the microbes.

Sterilization through Ultrafiltration

Ultrafiltration is carried out using celodion membrane filters. Celodion filters are made up of porcelain and glacial base acetic acid, used for the purpose of sterilization.

Disinfection: Disinfection destroys pathogenic microorganism. Sodium hypochlorite or mercuric chloride is used for surface disinfection of disease sample from which the pathogenic organism is to be isolated.

Culture Collection Centres

These are the centres from where the required cultures of microbes can be obtained.

- First centre was established as Kral Collection in Prague (1900).
- American Type Culture Collection (ATCC), Rockville, Maryland.
- Japanese Type Culture Collection (JTCC), Tokyo.
- British National Collection of Type Cultures, London.
- Indian Type Culture Collection (ITCC), IARI, New Delhi.

Staining Techniques

Gram's stain: A Danish physician, Hans Christian Gram, devised gram-staining technique for identification and characterization of bacteria in 1884. In the technique of Gram's staining of bacteria is done with following procedure:

1. A slide containing heat-fixed smear of bacterial cells, is treated with crystal-violet stain (a basic dye), during which the cells turn purple.
2. The slide is then flushed with Gram's iodine solution.
3. Then an organic solvent acetone is used for decolourizing the bacteria. At this stage gram-positive bacteria remain purple because they have a single thick cell wall that is not easily penetrated by the acetone alcohol whereas gram-negative bacteria are decolourized as they have cell walls with much thinner layers that allow easy penetration.
4. In a final step, a counterstain (safranin) is used to distinguish bacteria into gram positive (purple coloured) and gram negative (pink coloured).

The Nitrogen Cycle

Nitrogen is an important component of proteins, enzymes, chlorophylls nucleic acids etc. Like carbon, nitrogen has its own biogeochemical cycle, circulating through the atmosphere, lithosphere, and hydrosphere. It is the predominant atmospheric gas, making up about 79 per cent of the volume of the atmosphere. Plants cannot use nitrogen in its gaseous form and they are able to assimilate it only after it has been converted to ammonia (NH_3) and nitrates (NO_3^-). Nitrogen transformation (cycling) occurs into following stages, *viz.* nitrogen fixation, nitrogen assimilation, ammonification, nitrification, and denitrification (for details refer chapter 7, Manures and Fertilizers).

The Carbon Cycle

Life is built on the conversion of carbon dioxide into the carbon-based organic compounds in living organisms. Short-term cycling of carbon occurs in the continual physical exchange of carbon dioxide

(CO_2) between the atmosphere and hydrosphere. Carbon dioxide from the atmosphere becomes dissolved in water (H_2O), reacting to form carbonic acid (H_2CO_3) This carbonic acid dissociates into hydrogen ions (H^+) and bicarbonate ions (HCO_3^-), which further dissociates into hydrogen and carbonate ions (CO_3).

In terrestrial communities, plants convert atmospheric carbon dioxide to carbon-based compounds through photosynthesis. In terrestrial environments, forests are the largest carbon reservoirs.

The Sulphur Cycle

Sulphur is found in all living organisms as a constituent of some proteins, vitamins, and hormones. It has major reservoirs in both the atmosphere and the lithosphere.

In the weathering process sulphur is released from the rock coming in contact with air, converted into sulphate (SO_4), which is taken up by plants and microorganisms and then converted into organic forms Animals acquire organic forms of sulphur from plants in their foods

When organisms die and decompose, some of the sulphur enters the tissues of microorganisms and other is released again as sulphate Sulphur re-enters the atmosphere naturally in three major ways:

1. Sea spray releases large amounts of the element from the ocean into the atmosphere,
2. Anaerobic respiration by sulfate-reducing bacteria causes the release of hydrogen sulphide (H_2S) gas especially from marshes tidal flats, and similar environments in which anaerobic microorganisms thrive and
3. Volcanic activity releases additional but much smaller amounts of sulphur gas into the atmosphere.

Phosphorus Cycle

The cycle operates as follows: Compounds such a calcium phosphate, sodium phosphate, etc. are leached from the rocks into the soil and water, they are taken up by plant roots. The plants are subsequently consumed by herbivores, which is turn are eaten by carnivore. On the death of either herbivores or carnivores decomposition takes place and the compounds are returned to the soil through the action of water-hence sedimentary cycle.

In the sea there is a similar cycle in which phosphate compounds from sediments pass through the aquatic food chain, some fish being eaten by sea birds, whose droppings (gauno) are rich in these compounds, and recycling eventually takes place.

□□□

25

Plant Disease Management

Diseases of Cereals

1. Powdery mildew of wheat: *Erysiphe graminis f. sp. tritici*: Superficial, white to greyish reddish brown, powdery growth appears on upper surface of leaves. Plants become stunted. The leaves become wrinkled, twisted and deformed. Use resistant varieties (RVs) like CPAN 1922, CPAN 1676, VL 401 and HD 2074; seed treatment with Bayleton @ 1.5 g/kg of seed; spraying with a mixture @ 2 kg/ ha in 800-1,000 litre of water of fungicides: 16 parts Dithane M-45, 4 parts Karathane 25 WP.
2. **Loose smut of wheat**: *Ustilago segetum* var. *tritici* (internally seed borne): Infected plants produce early head than normal. In Sonalika (RR-21) variety, yellow chlorotic streaks develop on the flag leaves before emergence of ears. Infected spikelets are transformed into a black powdery mass of olive-green teliospores. Use RVs like NP 710, 718, 761, Bansi 224, MPO 117, 125, 137; seed treatment with hot water at 56°C for 10 minutes or with Vitavax or Bavistin @ 2.5-3.0 g/kg of seed. Solar treatment (Luthra, 1934) of seeds (soaked in ordinary water from 8:00 AM to 12:00 Noon; and then spread seeds as thin layer and dry in bright sunlight from 12:00 Noon to 4:00 PM).
3. **Karnal bunt of wheat**: *Neovossia indica* (Mitra *et al.*, 1931, from Karnal; airborne disease) Some grains are partially or wholly converted into black colour looks like as roasted. Affected grains smell like rotten fish due to production of trimethylamine. Fumigate the soil with Methyl bromide @ 570 kg/ha and Metham @ 100 lit/ha for wet and dry soils, respectively. Use RVs like UP 270, UP 368, HD 2222, HD 2227, HD 2235, WL 1562, Sonalika, PBW 120, TL 1210; treat the seed with Vitavax @ 2.5 g/kg of seed followed by spraying with Bavistin + Dithane M-45.

4. **Brown/orange/leaf rust:** *Puccinia recondita;* occurred as Epidemic in 1972-73; heteroecious fungus; *Thallictrum* spp. alternate host: In North India it appears in the last week of November when crop is 5-6 weeks old. Minute round, orange, sori develop on the leaves. Plant, mature early, produce shriveled grains due to poorly developed root system.
5. **Yellow/stripe rust:** *Puccinia striformis tritici:* This rust is limited to the Northern and Eastern part of India appearing in the month of January-February. This is more destructive and appears earlier than black rust. Pustules (sori) appear as bright yellow chiefly on the leaves giving faded streaky appearance.
6. **Black stem rust:** *Puccinia graminis* var. *tritici:* In South India disease appears during November-December, causing severe losses. Rust appears in the form of flecking on stem and leaf sheath. In severe infections plants are stunted, produce small spike and produce no grains, if produced they are shriveled.

- **Management of wheat rusts:** Seed dressing with Plantvax @ 2 g/kg of seed; spraying with sulphur dust 400 Mesh @ 15 kg/ ha or Plantvax @ 8 l/ha; use of RVs like S 227, S 307, S 308, S 331 (for all rusts), HD 2278, HW 741, WL 614 (for stem rust) and WL 359, C 306 (for leaf and stripe rust).

7. **Smut of Bajra:** *Tolyposporium penicillarriae:* Ovaries are exclusively attacked, but not all the grains in an ear are infected. Sori are greenish to chocolate brown when young and almost black at maturity. Intercropping with mung bean; seed treatment with a mixture of Thiram and Agrosan GN in the ratio of 2 g and 1 g per kg of seed; spraying with Vitavax @ 1.2 kg / ha at the boot leaf stage; use of resistant bajra lines like SSC PS-252-S-4 and ICI 7517-S-1, controls disease.
8. **Green ear or downy mildew of bajra:** *Sclerospora graminicola:* **Downy mildew symptoms:** Affected leaves show chlorotic streaks on the upper surface, corresponding to every streak lower surface show downy growth of the fungus. **Green ear symptoms:** The ear head become abnormal in all the tillers, which are replaced, by a bunch of leafy structure. Bristles of the spikelets become hypertrophied; stamen becomes leaf like. Use of RVs like ICMH 451, Pusa 23, ICMH 88088, NHB-10, HB-5; seed treatment with hot water at 55°C for 10 minutes or 1.0 g Agrosan GN plus 4 g thiram(75% a.i.) /kg of seed, followed by seed dressing with Apron SD-35 @ 8 g/kg of seed and foliar spray with Ridomil MZ-72 WP or Ridomil ZM-28 FW is successful in controlling disease.

9. **Ergot of bajra:** *Claviceps fujiformis* (=*C. microcephala*): In 1967 and 1968 appeared in epidemic form on HB 1 (the first hybrid of bajra released). Ergot sclerotia contain toxic alkaloids like agroclavine, elymoclavine, chanoclavine, penniclavine and setoclavine. Symptoms appear as viscous, turbid, cream coloured, fluid (honeydew) oozing out as small droplets from florets turning to pink or brown in colour. Adjustment of sowing dates near to 15 July; intercropping with mung bean reduces disease; use of hyperparasite like *Fusarium sambusinum / F. setectum* var. *majus* which attack both honeydew and sclerotia; spraying with a mixture of copper oxychloride and Zineb (1:2).
10. **Stripe disease of barley:** *Drechslera graminea* with Telophase *Pyrenophora graminea,* soil borne: Small yellow spots appear on old leaf blade and sheath. Spots elongate as long streaks parallel to each other. Seed treatment by soaking the seed in copper sulphate solution @ 0.3% or zinc sulphate @ 0.5% or Agrosan GN/Ceresan @ 0.2%; use of RVs like K 12, CN 292, K 40, K 69, KN 30, K 125, K 129, K 131, K 133 is useful.
11. **Covered smut of barley:** *Ustilago hordei,* externally seed borne: Symptoms appear as blackened ears emerging from the leaf sheath. Every spikelet attacked becomes converted into black mass of teliospores. This powder remains held up with ovary wall and the glumes (due to white silvery membrane). Seed treatment with Agrosan GN @ 2.5 g/kg of seed or Vitavax or Benlate @ 2.0 g/kg of seed and use of RVs like BHS 4, BM 23, LB 873, EB 4032, HBL 7, K 24, NP 109 is useful.
12. **Grain smut of jowar:** *Sphaecelotheca sorghi,* externally seed borne: Disease becomes apparent at the time of grain formation. Every ovary is transformed into a dirty grey spore sac (sorus). Size of sori varies with the variety but generally they are larger than the normal grain. Seed treatment with 0.5% formalin or in 0.5-3.0% copper sulphate followed by drying; seed dressing with Vitavax/ Bavistin @ 2.0 g /kg of seed, or sulphur @ 5.0 g/kg of seed or thiram slurry @ 1 g/kg of seed; RVs like CSH 9, SPV 104, SPV 102, SPV 115, SDM 9, CSH 5.
13. **Blast of rice:** *Pyricularia grisea* with Telophase *Magnaporthe grisea*: Small, bluish, water soaked flecks of spindle shape appear on leaves, leaf sheath and rachis. Centre of the spot is pale green or dull green. The neck of the panicle is infected (black neck or neck blast) and panicle hangs down towards earth. Use of RVs Co 4, TKM-1, Co 29, IR 579, A 200, A 249, A 90, T 141; seed treatment with Thiram @ 2.5 g/kg of seed followed by spraying with or Benlate (1 g/

l) or Bavistin (1 g/l) or Blasticidin-S or Kasugamycin (kasumin) @ 20 ppm at the interval of 10 days.

14. **Khaira disease of rice**: *Zinc* deficiency (Common in Tarai areas of U.P.): Disease usually appears after 10-15 days after transplanting. Small bronze coloured spots appear on the lamina and base of the leaves showing chlorotic appearance. Plants become stunted. Root growth is restricted, main root turn brown and finer root destroyed. Spraying of a mixture of zinc sulphate (5 kg) and lime (2.5 kg) or urea (20 kg) in 1000 litres of water after 10 days of sowing in the nursery, controls the disease.

Diseases of Pulses

15. **Wilt of pigeon pea**: *Fusarium udum*: E.J. Butler in India first reported the disease in 1906. Disease appears in early stage of plant growth, *i.e.* 4-6 week old crop. Typical symptoms appear as gradual or sudden withering and drying of green plants appearing as suffering from drought. Crop rotation of 3-4 years; use of RVs like NP (WR) 15, DDN-1; amend the soil with neem or castor oil cakes, rice husk or sawdust; apply Bavistin (2,000 ppm) as soil drench 10 days before disease appearance.

16. **Wilt of chick pea:** *Fusarium oxysporum* var. *ciceri*: Leaves in the initial stage become pale yellow and ultimately dry up. Roots decompose at the severity of disease. Use of RVs G-24, C-214; seed treatment with Benlate @ 2 g/k g of seed; adjusting sowing date during 2nd week of October.

17. **Powdery mildew of pea:** *Erysiphe polygoni*: Formation of white powdery patches on both the surfaces of leaves including tendril, stems and pods. Use of RVs T-10, T-56, P-185, P-388; spraying with Karathane @ 0.2% controls the disease.

18. **Powdery mildew of urd**: *Erysiphe polygoni*: Production of white, powdery growth on the leaves. In case of severe infection, defoliation occurs and pods fail to develop. Dusting with sulphur @ 25 kg/ha or spraying with wettable sulphur @ 3 kg/ha, 2 to 5 times or Karathane (1 ml per litre of water), or with Bavistin (0.5 g per litre of water) twice at 15-day interval manages disease.

19. **Yellow-mosaic of urd**: *MYMV* white fly transmits the disease: The symptoms appear on young leaves as mild scattered yellow specks. The diseased plants usually mature later and bear relatively few flowers and pods. Use of RVs like Pusa 1, Mash 1-1, Mash 48, UPU 1, UPU 2, 4-5-2, UG 117 and Pant U 26; application of 0.07% Endosulfan or 0.05% Malathion or 0.03% Methyl Demeton + 2% Orchard oil controls the disease.

20. **Bean-mosaic of urd:** *Urd bean mosaic virus*: The first symptoms appear on the young leaves in the form of irregular chlorotic areas followed by mosaic, vein banding, puckering and distortion of leaves. Use of RVs like D 6-7, Gwalior 18, Khargone 3 and N 212, is recommended.

Diseases of Oilseeds

21. **Rust of linseed:** *Melampsora lini*: Disease occurs in crops sown during October-November and harvested during March-April. In North India disease appears in November. Characteristic bright orange coloured, minute, round rust pustules are produced first on leaves and then on stem, which are irregular and elongated in shape. Use of RVs like NP (RR) 9, 10, 56, 95, 218, 368, 387, 389, 415, LC-216, LC-255 and LC-256; spraying with Dithane Z-78 @ 2 g/litre of water, or dusting with Sulphur dust @ 15-20 kg/ha, or Borax @ 60 kg/ha controls the disease completely.
22. **Leaf spot or Tikka disease of groundnut:** *Cercospora arachidicola* (Early symptoms), telophase *Mycosphaerella arachidis*. *Cercospora personata* (Late symptoms), Telophase *Mycosphaerella berkeleyii*: Seed treatment with 0.5% copper sulphate followed by seed dressing with Agrosan GN @ 2 g/kg of seed and foliar spray with Bordeaux mixture (1%) / Dithane Z-78 (0.2%)/ Fycol 8E/ Cosan three times starting from 40th day of sowing controls disease.

Symptoms produced by *C. arachidicola*	Symptoms produced by *C. personata*
Symptoms are sub-circular to irregular one to 10 mm in diameter.	Symptoms are usually circular and smaller 1 to 6 mm in diameter.
Lesions are commonly dark reddish brown to black on the upper surface whereas light brown on the lower surface of leaf.	Spots are dark gray or black on the lower leaf surface.
Conidial production is limited to the upper surface.	Conidial production is limited to the lower surface of leaf.

23. **Alternaria blight of mustard:** *Alternaria brassicae*: Brown circular spots appear on all the parts of the plant, with sooty black concentric rings. Spraying with Dithane M-45 @ 1.5 kg/ha immediately after the appearance of the disease.

24. **White rust /white blisters of crucifers:** *Albugo candida* (obligate parasite): **White rust symptoms:** Such symptoms appear on the under surface of leaves in the form of shining white or cream-yellow pustules. **Symptom of hypertrophy:** Leaves become thick fleshy and reduced in size, followed by twisting of stem, deformation of flower, swelling and gall formation. Spraying with Bordeaux mixture @ 0.8%/Blitox-50 @ 0.3%/Difolatan @ 0.3%/Daconil @ 0.1%/Dithane M-45 @ 0.2%/Dithane Z-78 @ 0.2%/Ridomil @ 0.1% at the interval of 8-10 days.

Diseases of Fruits

25. **Panama wilt of banana**: *Fusarium oxysporum f. sp. cubense*: Infected plant shows a characteristic yellowing of leaves, which develops as a band along the margin and spreads towards the mid rib. Infected plants are stunted. Field fallowing and long rotation; Vapam 850 g in 100 litre of water as a soil drench; preplanting treatment of suckers and drenching of soil with Bavistin (0.1%) controls disease.
26. **Leaf spot/Sigatoka of banana**: *Mycospherella musicola*: Early symptoms are small, yellow linear marking on leaves parallel to the veins. Spots upon enlargement become brown in colour. Affected leaves turn yellow and die. Spraying with Bavistin (0.1%) or Topsin-M (0.1%) or Daconil (0.2%) gives good control.
27. **Banana bunchy top:** *Banana bunchy top virus*: The first symptom appears as irregular, dark green streaks on the underside of the leaf. In badly attacked plants, leaves are small, erect and bunched together at the apex. Planting with virus-free suckers, control of insect vector using thiodemeton, dimethoate and phorate @ 25 g/plant is useful.
28. **Downy mildew of grape:** *Plasmopara viticola*: Leaves, shoots, tendrils, flowers and fruits of the vine are affected. Light green to olive yellow translucent spots appears on the upper surface of leaves. Burn infected leaves and prune infected twigs; spraying with Bordeaux mixture 5:5:50 or Difolatan (0.2%) or Ridomil (0.1%) controls disease.
29. **Wilt of guava:** *Fusarium oxysporum f. sp. psidii/ Macrophomina phaseolina*: First sign is the yellowing of leaves from tip downwards. The disease is severe at the time of fruit bearing. Dying branches destroyed; uprooting and burning severely affected trees; treating the soil with lime and gypsum (4 lb/ tree) to prevent further spread or soil drenching with Bavistin (0.1%).

30. **Fruit rot of guava::** *Pestalotia psidii*: Dark brown, water soaked, circular spots appear at the blossom end of the immature green fruits. Disease is serious during rainy weather. Spraying with Ridomil (0.1%) or Aliette (0.2%) or Dithane Z/78 (0.2%) or Aureofungin @ 10 ppm controls disease.

31. **Leaf spot of sapota:** *Phavophleospori indica*: Conspicuous dark brown, circular spots appear on the leaves and result in defoliation. The disease is serious during rainy season. Dithane Z-78 (0.2%) is effective during May to February.

32. **Powdery mildew of mango:** *Oideum mangiferae*: White powdery growth appears on the leaves, tender stems, inflorescence and young fruits during February to June. Fruits shed as diseases advances. Dustings twice with Sulfex (0.2%) or Wettasul (0.2%) or Thiovit or Bavistin (0.1%) or Calixin (0.1%) at fortnightly interval are effective.

33. **Mango Malformation:** *Fusarium maniliformae* var. *subglutinans*: It is abnormal development of inflorescence where flowers are malformed and appear in clusters. When shoot is malformed giving witches broom appearance it is called bunchy top or vegetative malformation. The malformed parts do not bear fruits. Application of Captan (0.2%) or Benlate (0.1%) and naphthalene acetic acid (NAA) 200 ppm during first week of October followed by deblossoming spray in January-February is effective.

34. **Mango anthracnose:** *Colletotrichum gloeosprioides*: Brown spots appear on the leaves and inflorescences. Twigs show die-back symptoms. Flowers shed when inflorescence is infected. Black spots appear on fruits. Spray Topsin-M (0.1%) or Bavistin (0.1%) before flowers open and again during fruit formation. Dip fruits in Benlate (500 ppm) or TBZ (1,000 ppm) or Bavistin (500 ppm) during storage.

35. **Koeli/Black Tip/Tip Necrosis of Mango:** *Physiological / boron deficiency*: Six to eight week old fruits are prone to disorder. Development of small-etiolated area at the distal end of the fruit. The tip is flattened with the outer skin turning hard and sunken. The inner portion of the tip is soft and yields a dark brown liquid due to rotting induced by bacteria. Brick kiln release gaseous smoke, which causes disturbance in boron metabolism leading to disorder. Spraying of borax @ 6.5 g/litre of water starting before flowering, second during flowering and third during fruit set.

36. **Foot and stem rot of papaya:** *Pythium aphanidermatum*: Water soaked lesions appear on the bark just above the ground level. Simultaneously terminal leaves become yellow, drop and fall off. Fruits shrivel and drop. Roots deteriorate and decay. Stem is girdled at the base. Removal of diseased plants; drenching with Emissan (0.2%) or Ridomil (0.1%) or Calixin (0.1%) or Daconil (0.2%) control disease.
37. **Papaya leaf curl:** ***Papaya leaf curl** Virus*: Severe curling, crinkling and distortion of leaves accompanied by vein clearing and reduction of leaf size. Inverted cups are formed due to inward and downward curling of leaves. Controlling collateral hosts (tomato, tobacco, Cape gooseberry and Zinnia); spraying with insecticides for virus vectors, control disease.
38. **Papaya mosaic:** *Papaya mosaic virus*: Profuse mottling, puckering, chlorosis and malformation of leaves with increased number of lobes and constrictions. Water soaked areas on stem and petioles even on fruits. Use *Carica cauliflora* rootstock or seed.
39. **Fruit canker of ber**: *Colletotrichum* spp.: It produces numerous circular to raised dark coloured corky cankerous growths on the fruits. Spraying with Dithane Z-78 (0.2%) or Difolatan (0.2%) at monthly intervals during July to October give good control.
40. **Citrus gummosis**: *Phytophthora palmivora/parasitica/citrophthora*: Profuse oozing of gum on the affected bark. Affected bark gradually turns dark brown and develops longitudinal cracks. When scrapped, the affected portions of the bark appear brown. Infected trees die due to girdling after complete rotting of bark. Application of Bordeaux paste control disease.
41. **Citrus canker:** *Xanthomonas axonopodis pv. citri*: Small, water soaked spots with raised convex surface appear on leaves, fruits, and stem. The spots on leaves are surrounded by chlorotic halo. Spraying of neem cake @ 20 kg/ham or Streptomycin sulphate (0.05%), Copper oxychloride (0.5%) or Bordeaux mixture (1%) control disease.
42. **Citrus tristeza:** *Citrus tristeza virus*: **On acid lime:** Vein flecking, vein clearing, stem and root pitting, stunting and yellowing of plants. Leaves are twisted and brittle. Bark becomes abnormally thick and wood remains thin. Plants flower heavily and bear large number of small fruits before showing decline symptoms. **On mandarins/sweet oranges:** Complete suppression of new flush of growth and appearance of various types of deficiency

symptoms. Periodic sprays of insecticides reduce the secondary spread of tristeza within the orchards as it controls the vector.

43. **Citrus greening:** *Lyperobacterium africana, L. asiatica*: Leaves show interveinal chlorosis or complete chlorosis of leaf lamina, reduced size of leaves, early defoliation. Application of antibiotics like penicillin and Oxytetracycline hydrochloride, control disease.

44. **Leaf spot of pomegranate:** *Colletotrichum gloeosporiodes*: The disease starts as minute, dull violet black or black spots. Soon the region surrounding the spot turns yellow. The spot enlarges and turns from black to dull purplish-black. The fruits show dark brown to black depressed spots, which enlarge and coalesce covering the large portion of fruit. Spraying with Bavistin @ 0.1 per cent at 20 days intervals control disease.

Diseases of Vegetables

45. **Buck eye rot of tomato fruits:** *Phytophthora parasitica* var. *parasitica*: Brownish spots on mature and young green fruits appear bearing concentric rings, resembling slightly the markings on a buckeye nut. Seed treatment with Captan (0.2%); spraying with Difolatan (0.2%) or Blitox-50-50 (0.4%) at 10 days interval, control disease.

46. **Early blight of tomato and potato:** *Alternaria solani*: Circular, brown concentric ringed leaf spots appear on leaves. Infection on fruits appears as brown to black depressed spots. Seeds carrying the infection are usually black. Seed treatment with 0.2% Captan or Thiram followed by spraying with Dithane Z-78 (0.2%); **RVs of Potato** Kufri Naveen, K. Sinduri and K. Jeevan; 4-5 sprays with 2.5 kg Dithane M-45 or Difolatan 80 WP or Dithane Z-78 or Blitox-50 or Fytolon in 1,000 litres of water at the interval of 7-10 days, control disease.

47. **Late blight of potato and tomato**: *Phytophthora infestans*: Infection appears on all the above ground plant parts. Water soaked spots on leaves and dark olivaceous spots on fruits. Spraying with Bordeaux mixture (4:4:50) or Blitox-50 (0.4%) or Dithane Z-78 (0.2%); pre-treatment of tubers in 1% of Bordeaux mixture; spraying with Ridomil @ 7 kg/ha in combination with Dithane M-45; use of RVs (Potato) Kufri Naveen, K. Jeevan, K. Alankar, K. Badshah, K. Swarna, K. Khasi Garo, K. Moti and K. Mutu, control disease.

48. **Tomato mosaic:** *Tobacco mosaic virus*: Dark green mottling appears on leaves, accompanied by wilting of young leaves in

sunny days. The leaflets are usually distorted, puckered and small. Seed treatment with trisodium phosphate @ 90 g/lit for 15 min and washing of tools in 3% trisodium phosphate solution before use, is helpful in controlling disease.

49. **Tomato spotted wilt:** *Tospo virus*: Sudden browning of leaves followed by cessation of growth of the plants. Leaves show bronze colouring and necrosis. Fruits from infected plants exhibit concentric circular markings. Seed treatment with furadon or Disyston @ 1 kg a.i./ha at sowing and repeating the same with 1.5 kg a.i./ha at the time of transplanting, followed by 2-3 foliar sprays of either Dimethoate (0.05%) or Monocrotophos (0.05%) or Metasystox (0.02%) at 10 days intervals, control disease.

50. **Tomato leaf curl:** *Tomato leaf curl Gemini virus*: Leaf curl causes stunting, downward curling and crinkling of the leaves. Older leaves become leathery and brittle. Control is same as tomato spotted wilt.

51. **Tomato big bud:** *Tomato big bud virus*: The first indication of infection appears at the tip of the actively growing shoots, which assume an upright position. There is a proliferation of axillary buds and thickening of the stem. Terminal buds completely ceases to grow. Control is same as tomato spotted wilt.

52. **Bacterial wilt of tomato and potato:** *Pseudomonas solanacearum*: Rapid and complete wilting of normal grown up plants. Pathogen is mostly confined in vascular region. Infected plant parts when cut and immersed in clear water, a white streak (ooze) comes out from cut end. Use of resistant Line CRA-00 Sel A, Dingras Multiple Purple, Sinampro; application of bleaching powder @ 15 kg/ha before planting, control disease.

53. **Mosaics of potato**: *Potato virus PVS, PVY, PVM, PVA, PVF/G* (acuba mosaic): The term covers vide range of symptoms ranging from semilatent to transient and typical mosaic to general chlorosis accompanied by various type discoloration and deformation, as

- **Mild mosaic or mottle:** Irregular intermixing of normal green and chlorotic areas on leaves.
- **Yellow mosaic:** Small light yellow spots on lower leaves with no effect on vigour but necrotic brown blotches in the flesh of tubers.
- **Veinal mosaic:** Chlorosis along the main veins, irregular shape of chlorosis and their distribution, which extends over the

adjacent interveinal regions to form irregular pattern distinct from mosaic or mottle.

- **Leaf drop streak:** General chlorosis with leaf margins turning downward. Necrosis of underside veins and petioles leading to leaf drop. Necrotic spots on tubers also. In severe disease condition puckering of leaves is noticed.
- **Rugose mosaic or common severe mosaic:** Interveinal puckering of leaves with or without veinal necrosis. Greatly reduced in vigour.
- Spraying with Metasystox or Rogor @ 600-750 ml in 500-600 liter of water, or Dimecron @ 200 ml/ha in 750 litres of water, at the interval of 10-15 days, or application of Thimet 10 G @ 15-20 kg/ha with fertilizers at the time of planting reduce aphid population thereby reducing incidence.

54. **Common and yellow mosaic of beans:** Common symptoms are the development of a pattern of light and dark green area, yellowing of veins. Plants affected show mottling, yellowing and malformation of leaves and pods. Use of RVs like **Urd-**pant U84, UPU2 for MBYMV; spraying with disyston @ 40-100 kg/ha or Aldicarb @ 11.2 kg/ha reduces aphid population thereby reducing disease incidence.

Beans	Disease	Virus
Soya bean	Soya bean mosaic	Soya bean mosaic virus (SMV)
	Soya bean yellow mosaic	Bean yellow mosaic virus (BYMV)
	Mung bean yellow mosaic	Mung bean yellow virus (MBYV)
Mungbean	Mung bean mosaic	Bean common mosaic virus (BCMV)
	Mung bean yellow mosaic	Mung bean yellow mosaic virus (MBYMV)
Urd bean	Urd bean mosaic	BCMV
	Urd bean yellow mosaic	MBYMV
French bean	Common bean mosaic	BCMV
	Bean yellow mosaic	BYMV
Lima bean	Lima bean mosaic	BCMV
Broad bean	Broad bean mosaic	BYMV

55. **Little leaf of brinjal:** *Phytoplasma like organism*: Plant produces very small leaves of yellowish colour touching to stem. Internodes are very short. Plant usually do not flower and remain always green. Pathogen survives on *Datura alba* during offseason and transmitted by *Hishimonus phycitis,* and *Amrasca bigutella bigutella.* Use of RVs like BB-7, BWR-12, Pant Rituraj and H-8; dipping of nursery roots in the 1,000 ppm solution of tetracyclin followed by spraying with Ledermycin @ 500 ppm.

56. **Chilli anthracnose:** *Colletotrichum capsici*: Disease appears as dark, round, sunken spots on fruits and seed. Infected fruits drop off prematurely. Seed treatment with Thiram (0.2%) or Brassico (0.2%) followed by spraying with Difolatan (0.2%) or Dithane M-45 (0.2%) or Blue Copper/Blitox (0.4%) at 15 days interval, control disease effectively.

57. **Powdery mildew of chilli**: *Leivillula taurica* anaphase *Oidiopsis taurica*: White talcum powder like growth on the leaf. It can be controlled by Spraying Sulfex (0.2%) at 10 days interval

58. **Leaf spot of chilli:** *Cercospora capsici*: Oval or oblong spots with light grey centres on leaves, stalks and stem. Infected leaves drop off prematurely. Seed treatment with Bavistin (0.2%) or Dithane M-45 (0.2%) followed by spraying with Bavistin (0.1%) or Difolatan (0.2%) or Dithane Z-78 (0.2%) at 15 days interval, is effective.

59. **Powdery mildew of bhindi:** *Erysiphe cichoracearum*: White powdery growth on both the sides of the leaf. Diseased leaves drop off prematurely. Spraying with Sulfex (0.2%) or Karathane (0.05%) at 10 days interval, control the disease.

60. **Yellow vein mosaic:** *Yellow vein mosaic virus*: Homogenous interwoven network of yellow veins enclosing green part of leaf is noticed. Infected plants remain stunted and bear very few deformed and small fruits. Since, virus is transmitted by White fly (*Bemisia tabaci*), application of Furatox-10G @ 15 kg/ha followed by four foliar spray with Metasystox 25EC @0.03% at the interval of 15 days and application of Thimet 10G @ 20 kg/ha in furrows at is recommended.

61. **Anthracnose of cucurbits:** *Colletotrichum laginarium*: The spots on the leaves are irregular, angular to circular water soaked, yellowish brown and finally become brown in colour. The spots on the fruits are circular, water soaked-depressed and dark brown. Seed treatment with Bavistin (0.1%) or Benlate (0.1%) followed by spraying with Difolatan (0.2%) or Dithane M-45

(0.2%) or Topsin (0.1%) or Captan (0.2%) at 8 days interval manages disease.

62. **Sclerotium wilt of cucurbits**: *Sclerotium rolfsii*: Sudden wilting and dehydration of leaves is noticed. In Frosty white mycelial growth, mustard shaped brown coloured sclerotia are found on the stem at the ground level. Infected seeds are chalky white. Application of Brassicol (0.2%) and Dithane M-45 (0.3%) in soil is helpful.

63. **Charcoal rot of fruit of cucurbits:** *Macrophomina phaseolina:* Symptoms on fruit are slightly sunken; the surface of the fruit becomes black, encrusted with sclerotia. The flesh becomes black and densely impregnated with sclerotia. Seed treatment with Bavistin (0.2%) or Vitavax (0.2%), control disease.

64. **Pumpkin mosaic:** *Watermelon mosaic virus-1*: Vein clearing of the leaves followed by severe mosaic mottling, blistering and distortion occurs. Eradication of infected plants; application of Furadon @ 1.5 kg ai. / ha at the time of sowing followed spraying with Dimecron (0.05%) or Dimethoate (0.05%) or Metasystox (0.02%) at 10 days interval, control the disease.

65. **Cucumber mosaic:** *Cucumber mosaic virus*: The symptoms of the diseases are mosaic, mottling, stunting and distortion of leaves. Spraying of Dimecron (0.05%) or Metasystox (0.02%) at 10 days interval, control disease.

Coffee Diseases

66. **Coffee leaf rust:** *Hemileia vastatrix*: Small pale-yellow spots appear on lower surface of leaves, with leads to defoliation and die back. Applications of 0.5% Bordeaux mixture is useful.

67. **Black rot:** *Corticium koleraga*: Blackening and rotting of affected leaves, young twigs and berries. Affected leaves get detached and hang down by means of slimy fungal strands. Application of 1% Bordeaux mixture is helpful.

68. **Anthracnose:** *Colletotrichum coffeanum*: **Radcliff symptoms** appear as yellowing of one or more functional leaves, necrosis of nodes, leaf-fall, die back of twigs and death of many branches. **Stalk rot symptoms** appear as necrosis of nodes and internodes from the junction of brown wood and green wood towards apex followed by berry drop and defoliation due to decaying of stalk portion. **Brown blight symptoms** appear as round spots first brown, and then turn grey making the leaf look blighted. Maintenance of good drainage to remove excess water from the

root zone followed by spraying with 0.5% Bordeaux mixture to prevent defoliation.

69. **Berry blotch**: *Cercospora coffeicola*: Neurotic spots appear on the exposed surface of green berries. Fruit skin shrivels and sticks fast. Spraying with 1% Bordeaux mixture during June and late August, control disease.

Cash Crops Diseases

70. **Red rot of sugarcane:** *Colletotrichum falcatum* with Telophase *Glomerella tucumanensis* (=*Physalospora tucumanensis*). Epidemic occurred during 1939-40 and 1946-47 in Bihar and U.P. Symptoms of red rot appear as discoloration of young leaves. Red elongated lesions are produced on the midrib of leaf blade. Reddish patches on the leaf sheath during rainy season. When the internodal portion of cane is split open tissue appears as dull red, interrupted by transverse white patches. Tissue smells of vinegar odour. Use of RVs like Co 449, Co 527, Co 658, Co 1148, Co 1158, CoL 9, CoC 671; treatment of setts with hot water at 52°C for 18 minutes or hot air treatment of setts at 54°C for 8 hours, or Dipping of setts in 0.25% solution of Agallol or Aretan for 5 minutes followed by foliar spray with Blitox-50/ Dithane Z-78/ Carbendazim @ 1 kg/ha.

71. **Tobacco mosaic:** *Tobacco mosaic virus* (ssRNA virus, rod shaped): Disease appears as chlorosis, curling, mottling, dwarfing, distortion and blistering of leaves. Use RVs like TMVRR-2, TMVRR 2a, TMVRR-3; followed by spray with tanic acid @ 6 kg/ha at the interval of 10 days, control the disease.

26

Weed Management

Jethrotull used term Weed for the first time for unwanted and undesirable herbaceous or woody plants grown in cultivated lands. Selective control of broad-leaved weeds in fields of cereal crops was discovered in France in the late 1800s. Sinox, the first major organic chemical herbicide, was developed in France in 1896. 2,4-D, 2, 4, 5-T and IPC were introduced in 1945.

- Weeds are basically classified into monocots (*Phalaris minor*) and dicots (*e.g. Cleone*). They are further divided based on their habitat into terrestrial and aquatic categories. Based on duration they again divided into annuals, biennials and perennials.
- **Annual** weeds live and produce their seeds in a single growing season, *e.g. Phyllanthus niruri* (*Kharif*), *Chenopodium album* (*Rabi*), *Solanum nigrum* (Summer).
- **Biennials** need two growing seasons: in one season they pass through their vegetative phase followed by reproductive stage in ensuing season. The multiplication of both the annuals and the biennials are through seed, *e.g. Zingiber casumunar.*
- **Perennials** live indefinitely and are propagated mostly vegetatively through underground structures, such as rhizomes, stolon, bulbs and tubers. Perennials are of two types: the simple and the creeping. Simples multiply only through seeds. Creeping perennials are spread by creeping roots, stolon, and rhizomes, *e.g. Ipomoea cornea* (simple), *Allium vineale* (Bulbous), *Cynodon dactylon, Imperata cylindrica, Sorghum halepens* (creeping).
- Some weeds propagate themselves by means of tubers which are modified rhizomes adapted for the storage of food, *e.g. Cyperus rotundus, Inula indica. Oxalis repens, Colocasia antignourum, Pistia stratiotes* have rhizomes but not meant for storage.

Classification of Weeds Based on Origin

(*i*) **Exotic weeds**: Exotic weeds are those, which have been introduced in India from other countries, *e.g. Eichhornia* spp. Introduced in India as Ornamental plant in 1986 from Brazil.

(*ii*) **Indigenous weeds**: Such weeds have originated in India itself include *Acalypha* spp.

Crop Weed Competition

Weeds under many conditions are better competitors than crop plants for light, water, nutrients and soil space.

1. **For water:** The transpiration coefficients for *Cynodon dactylon* (813), *Tephrosia pupurea* (1, 108) is quite more than *Sorghum vulgare* (430), which illustrate the competition of weeds with crops.
2. **For nutrients,** *e.g.* Maize weeds and Groundnut weeds take over 64:64:83% and 30:86:82% of total NPK in field. Wild mustard (*Brassica sinensis*) requires twice NPK as of wheat.
3. **For light:** Weeds reduce photon influx density, *e.g. Amaranthus hybridus* reduce 90% in cotton and *Sorghum halepens* 56-63% in maize.

- Some crops like Sudan Grass, Sorghum and Cow pea are good competitors while Linseed, Groundnut and Lentil are poor competitors. The raising of highly competitive crops called **smother cropping.**

Principles of Weed Management

Annual weeds may be destructed before flowering by any of the following technique, *e.g.* Stale seed bed technique or pre-crop emergence herbicide or post-crop emergence selective herbicide.

- Biennial weeds may be destructed by translocated herbicides or digging or flooding.
- Perennial weeds are reduced by destruction of aerial shoots through digging and flooding or using translocated herbicides or fallowing.
- Flooding the field could control *Cyperus rotundus; Echinochloa* through complete destruction; and *Trianthenca* by complete drying.

Weed Management

Preventive methods: Avoid feeds with weed seeds; avoid OM with weed seeds; avoid mulch with weed seeds; avoid livestock that carries weed seed to healthy field; avoid shifting soil that carries weed seed to healthy field; avoid irrigation water that carries weed seed to healthy field, etc.

Cultural Methods

1. **Crop rotation:** Through crop rotation weed-like *Cyperus rotundus* in rice field could be controlled.
2. **Planting of high leaved variety:** Short, erect variety allow more weeds, whereas broad leaves suffocate the weeds.
3. **Planting method:** Transplanting must be preferred to avoid overcrowding of weeds.
4. **Transplanting density:** High-density crop suffocates the weeds.
5. **Fertilizer application:** Crops respond fast to N_2 than the weeds like *Cynodon* and *Cyperus.*
6. **Irrigation and drainage:** Frequent irrigation and weed in initial stage produce more weeds. Standing water in field reduce weeds.

- **Mechanical/Physical control of weeds** include Tillage, Hand weeding, Hand hoeing, Digging, Mowing, Cutting, Dredging and Chaining, Mulching, Burning and Flooding. Burning of weeds is called flame cultivation.

Biological Control through Insects

1. *Lantana camara*	*Agromyza lantanae, Crocidosema lantana* from Hawai
2. *Opuntial inermis*	*Cactoblastis cactorum* from Australia; *Dactylopins opuntiae* –USA; *D. indicus, D. tomentosus*-India
3. *Hypericum perforatum*	*Chrysolinus hyperici* – Australia
4. *Cuscuta* spp.	*Melanagromyza cuscutae*
5. *Imperata cylindrica*	*Orseoliella javanica*
6. *Cyperus rotundus*	*Bactra vermosana*

Bio-control in Vogue India

7. *Lantana camara*	*Teleonemia scrupulosa* from Australia
8. *Opuntia vulgaris*	*Dactylopius indicus* from Brazil
9. *Opuntia delleni*	*Dactylopius opuntiae* from Sri Lanka
10. *Eupatorium adenophorum*	*Procecidochares utilis* from New Zealand
11. *Cyperus rotundus*	*Bactra vermosana*
12. *Parthenium hysterophyllus*	*Diacrisia oblique*
13. *Loranthus* spp.	*Delias hyparete*
14. *Orobanche* spp.	*Phytomyza* spp.

- Grass carp (*Ctenopharyngodon idella*) controls effectively the submerged water vegetation comprising *Najasminor, Hydrilla, Verticillata, Ceratophylum demersum, Lemna minor* etc.
- Basket grass controls *kans* grass (*Saccharum spontaneum*) by excreting some substances inhibitory to *kans*.

Selectivity of Herbicides

1. **Differential absorption:** It is noticed in:

(*i*) **Foliage active herbicides:** Dicotyledonous weed leaves are wide, flat with small depression retaining more herbicide, *e.g. Setaria viridis* retain 7-8 times Propanil than Wheat. In contrast monocots crop leaves are narrow, erect, waxy, retaining less or no herbicide, hence, crops escapes from herbicides.

(*ii*) **Soil active herbicides (top 2-3 cm of soil):** Weeds normally have roots in upper topsoil as comparison to crops. Upon application of herbicide weeds get killed but crops escape as their roots are 4-5 cm deep, *e.g.* **Molinate against *Echinochloa* in rice**: crown roots of rice are usually found below the toxic layer; **Trifluralin against green foxtail in wheat**: coleoptiles nodes are deeper in soil; **Trialallate against *Avena fatua* in wheat**: wheat has no mesocotyl and it reaches in the topsoil area when meristem is covered by leaf base.

(*iii*) **Induced selectivity:** Selectivity is modified by the use of absorbents and antidotes. **Absorbents** are materials with capacity to adsorb herbicides. They are placed near crop seeds so that they adsorb the herbicides, *e.g.* **activated charcoal** for 2,4-D; 2, 4, 5-T; EPTC; Butachlor; Propachlor; Trifluralin; nitralin; diuron; neburon; simazine; chloroben. **Antidotes** are used in addition as non-specific measures to counteract the effects of chemical poison, *e.g.* **NA** against Butylate; **R-25788** against Alachlor, Metachlor. Antidotes are applied as seed dressing material.

2. **Differential translocation:** Such herbicides are given to target weeds grown in combination, *e.g.* 2, 4-D against beans in sugarcane and terbutryn against weeds in dwarf wheat.
3. **Differential protoplasmic resistance:** In crop plants there is some mechanism of resistance through which they resist against herbicides, *e.g.* Dalapan resistant plants show pantothenic acid deficiency; Tolerance in mustard to trifluralin is due to

protoplasmic resistance; Tolerance in rice to molinate is due to protoplasmic tolerance.

4. **Differential rate of deactivation:** Some herbicides when reach in crop plants become non-toxic for them, but remain toxic to weeds. It may be due to:

- **Metabolic deactivation:** Breakdown of herbicide to non-toxic chemicals, *e.g.* Terbacil against morning glory in peppermint. Peppermint breaks down terbacil quickly whereas morning glory breaks down terbacil slowly hence inhibition of photosynthesis. Simazine is harmful to all other plants except maize, as maize converts the simazine into non-toxic hydroxy-simazine through special mechanism.
- **Reverse metabolism:** 2, 4-D and MCPB are not phytotoxic as such, but metabolites of these compounds are toxic to plants. The metabolism is enzymatic. Most of the **plants having no such enzyme to cause metabolism** are naturally tolerant to herbicidal action.
- **Conjugation:** It is the coupling of intact herbicide molecules with some cell constituents. Conjugation takes the toxic herbicide concentration out of the mainstream activity of plants, *e.g.* Soya bean is tolerant to chloramben because chloramben conjugate with glucose and changes to N-glucosy chloramben.

Classification of Herbicides

A) **Selective herbicides:** Such herbicides affect specific plant species.

(*a*) **Foliage applications** include herbicides, which are applied on leaves of growing plants, in the form of sprays or dust.

(*i*) **Contact herbicides:** Contact herbicides kill only the plant or the portions of the plant that actually come into contact with the chemical, *e.g.* Dicryl, Potassium cynate, Carrot oil, Sodium arsenate, Propanil and Sulphuric acid.

(*ii*) **Translocated herbicides:** Translocated herbicides move within the plant. The property makes them effective in destroying the roots of perennial weeds, *e.g.* 2, 4-DB; MCPB; 2, 4-5-T; 2, 4, 5-TP.

(*b*) **Soil applications:** Both fumigants and sterilants are used:

(*i*) **Soil fumigants:** Fumigants function as a vapour that diffuses throughout the layer of soil, *e.g.* Carbon disulphide, Chloropicrin, Vapam, Methylbromide and Cyanamide, etc.

(*ii*) **Soil sterilants:** These chemicals make the soil sterile for varying length of time, depending upon the chemical and amount used, *e.g.* inorganic chemicals like borates and chlorates; organic compounds like Simazine and Atrazine; urea herbicides like Diuron, Monuron, Fenuron, Linuron, Neburon; and Uracils (Bromacil, Terbacil) are used as soil sterilants.

B) **Non-selective herbicides:** Higher/excessive doses of herbicides may act as non-selective. H_2SO_4 is considered all times non-selective herbicide. Atrazine is non-selective when it is applied @ 10 kg/ha and selective when applied at 1 kg/ha.

Herbicide Formulation

Formulation refers to the way in which the basic weed-killing chemicals are prepared for practical use. Herbicides are formulated to apply as solutions in water or oil, emulsions, wet table powders, granules and dusts.

- **Solutions of water or oils:** The salts of most herbicides are soluble in water. They are dissolved in convenient amounts of water and then sprayed, *e.g.* sodium and amine salts of 2, 4-D, 2, 4, 5-T, MCPA, amine salts of DNBP, sodium salts of Pentachlorophenol, TCA and Dalapon.
- **Emulsions:** An emulsion is a liquid in which one liquid is dispersed in another liquid, each maintaining its original identity. The two liquids are prevented from reacting with each other by the addition of an emulsifying agent, *e.g.* Ester formulations of 2, 4-D are oil-like and form emulsions. Emulsions are milky in appearance.
- **Wettable powders:** It is a type of formulation in which herbicide is absorbed generally on an inert carrier, together with an added surface-acting agent, and finely ground so that it will form a suspension when agitated with water. Simazine, Atrazine, Monuron, Diuron and Neburon are wettable powders.
- **Granular herbicides:** In these formulations the herbicide is absorbed on, mixing with, or impregnated into, a generally inert carrier in such a way that the final product consists of granular particles, *e.g.* clay, sand vermiculite and finely ground plant parts (ground corn cobs, tobacco leaf trash) are used as inert carrier.
- **Dusts:** Insecticides and fungicides are very often made in the form of dusts.

Calculation of the Dosage Levels

The active ingredient is that part of a chemical formulation which is directly responsible for the herbicidal effects. The strength of the herbicides is expressed in terms of the active ingredient (a.i.).

A formula for calculating the dosage is given below:

$$\text{Quantity of product} = \frac{\text{Dose of herbicide required}}{\text{Percentage contents of active ingredient}} \times 100$$

Mode of Action of Herbicides

1. **Inhibition of photosynthesis:** Herbicides like Triazines, Urea and Carbamates **deactivate water-splitting enzymes** in hill reaction whereas Uracils, Anilides **interfere electron carrier** in ETC, hence inhibit photosynthesis.
2. **Inhibition of respiration:** Herbicides of group dinitrophenols, dinitroanilines and anilides uncouple oxidative phosphorylation and energy released during oxidation is not used for phosphorylation hence they inhibit respiration.
3. **Inhibition of protein synthesis**: Herbicides like triafluralin inhibits RNA synthesis by binding to chromatin whereas paraquat inhibits thymidine incorporation in *Vicia faba* hence they inhibit protein synthesis.
4. **Inhibition of lipid synthesis**: Herbicides like thicarbamates inhibits wax production.
5. **Inhibition of vitamin synthesis**: Herbicides like dalapan inhibits the synthesis of panthothenic acid.
6. **Inhibition of cell division**: Carbamates like trifluralin, and dinitroanilines inhibit cell division.
7. **Inhibition of germination**: Alachlor and propachlor inhibit gibberellic acid production.
8. **Abnormal tissue development**: 2, 4-D, 24-DB, MCPA, MCPB, Chloramben, Picloram produce uncontrolled growth of tissue by mitigating carbon metabolism.

Herbicidal Residue: Carry over of toxic effect of herbicide to the next following seasons, *e.g.* Atrazine leaves effect on Wheat, Soya bean, Cotton, Cow pea; Simazine on Green gram; Trifluralin to Wheat; Diuran to Wheat, Sorghum and Bengal gram.

Selected	Herbicides
Designation	**Chemical name**
Amitrole (Weedazol)	3-amino-1, 2, 4-triazole
Aqualin	Acrolein or acryladehyde
Atrazine	Acrolein or acryladehyde 2-chloro-4 ethylamino-6-isopropylamino; 1, 3, 5-triazine
Bromacil (Weedazol)	5-bromo-6-methyl-3-5-butyluracil
Carbyne(Barban)	4-chloro-2-butynyl N (3-chlorophenyl) carbamate
CDAA (Allidochloro)	2-chloro-NN-diallylacetamide
CIPC (Chloropropham)	Isopropyl N-(3-chlorophenyl) carbamate
CMMPP (Mecoprop)	4-chloro-2-methylphenoxypropionic acid
Dalapon (Dowpon)	2, 2-dichloropropionic acid (sodium salt)
Desmetryne (Weedazol)	2-methylmercapto-4-isopropylamino-6-methylamino 5-triazine
Dichlone	2, 3-dichloro-1, 4-naphthaquinone
Dicryl (chloranocnyl)	N-(3, 4-dichlorophenyl) methacrylamide
Diphenamid	N, N-dimethyl-LL-diphenylacetamide
Diquat (Reglone)	1, 1-ethylene-2, 2-dipyridylium dibromide
Diuron	3-(3, 4-dichlorophenyl) 1, 1-dimethylurea
Endothil	3, 6-endoxohydrophthalic acid
EPTC (Eptam)	Ethyl N, N-dipropylthiocarbamate
IPC (Propham)	Isopropyl N-phenylcarbamate
Lasso (Alachlor)	a-chloro-2, 6-diethyl-N (methoxymethyl) acetanilide
Linuron (Afalon)	3, 4-dichlorophenyl-N-methoxy-N-methylurea
Machete (Butachlor)	2-chloro-2, 6-diethyl-N-(butoxymethyl) acetanilide
MCPB	2-methyl, 4-chlorophenoxybutyric acid
Methabenzothiazuron (Tribunil)	1, 3-dimethyl-3-(2-benzothioazolyl) urea
Molinate (Ordram)	5-ethyl NN-hexamethylenethiocarbamate
Monuron	3-(p-chlorophenyl) 1, 1-dimethylurea
MSMA	Monosodiummethanearsonate

Nitrofen (TOK-E25)	2, 4-dichlorophenyl p-nitrophenylether
PCP	Pentachlorophenol
Paraquat (Gramaxone)	1, 1-dimethyl-4, 4-bipyridylium dichloride
Picolinic acid (Picloram)	4-amino-3, 5, 6-trichloropicolinic acid
Prometryne (Caparol)	2, 4-bis (isopropylamino)-6-(methylthio)-5-triazine
Propanil (Stam F-34; Rogue)	3-4-dichloropropionanilide
Propazine	2-chloro-4, 6-bisisopropylamino-1, 3, 5-triazine
Pyrazone (Pyranin)	5-amino-4-chloro-2-phenyl-3-pyridazinone
Simazine (Tafazine)	2-chloro-4, 6-bisethylamino-1, 3-5-triazine
2, 4-D	2, 4-dichlorophenoxyacetic acid
2, 4-DB	2, 4-dichlorophenoxybutyric acid
2, 4-DES (Crag herbicide)	2, 4-dichlorophenoxyethyesulphate
2, 4, 5-T	2, 4, 5-trichlorophenoxyacetic acid
TCA	Trichloroacetic acid

Common Weeds and their Management

Weed	Recommended herbicides
Justicia quinquangularis	**Rice**: MCPA or MCPB @ 5 kg ha plus urea 3%; **Cotton**: CMU pre-emergence @ 0.5-1.0 kg/ha; **Maize and sugarcane**: Atrazine or Simazine pre-emergence @ 1 kg/ha.
Amaranthus spinosus (Kataili Chaulai) *A. viridis*	**Rice**: MCPA or MCPB @ 0.5 kg/ha + urea 2%; **Cotton**: CMU pre-emergence @ 0.5-1.0 kg/ha.
Calotropis gigantean	2, 4-D amine 1-2 litre/ha in 900 litres of water before flowering.
Cannabis sativa (bhang)	2, 4-D ester or a mixture of 2, 4-D + 2, 4, 5-T @ 1.0-2.0/ha during flowering or earlier.
Chenopodium album (Lamb's-quarter or Bathua)	2, 4-D amine @ 0.5 kg/ha plus urea 3%; **Peas and linseed**: MCPB @ 0.84 l/ha; **Potato and carrot**: Linuron @ 0.5 kg/ha pre-emergence; **Sugarbeet**: pre-emergence Pyrazon 2-3 kg/ha.

Carthamus oxyacantha (Wild safflower); *Sonchus oleraceus* (Doodhi); *Ageratum conyzoides* (Mahakua); *Cnicus arvensis* (Kantaili) *Parthenium hysterophorus* (Congress grass)	Linuron @ 0.5 kg/ha pre-emergence; MCPB, 2, 4-D, aminotriazole, Paraquate Banvel D and MSMA at 2-4 litres/ha.
Convolvulus arvensis (Field Bindweed or Hirankhuri); *Ipomoea reptans* (Aquatic weed); *Evolvulus alsinoides* (Vishnu Krantha); *Cuscuta* spp. (Dodders)	**Binweed and ipomoea**: 2, 4-D amine 1.0 litre/ha + urea 3 % in 900 litres of water before flowering of the weed. **Dodder**: 2 kg/ha granulated CIPC.
Brassica sinensis (Wild Mustard), *Nasturtium indicum and Cyperus rotundus* (Nutgrass or Motha)	**Peas and potato**: Linuron @ 0.5 kg/ha pre-emergence; **Wheat**: 2, 4-D 2-4 litres/ha + urea 3%; **Linseed**: MCPB @ 0.84 l /ha. 2-4 ploughing during May and June; spraying with a mixture of 2, 4-D + Dalapon 2 kg/ha of each; **Maize**: atrazine pre-emergence @ 1 kg/ha.
Euphorbia prostrata (Milkweed); *E. hirta* (Dudhi); *Phyllanthus niruri* (Hazardana)	2, 4-D, or MCPA or MCPB at 1 kg/ha in 700 litres of water.
Echinochloa crusgalli (Barnyard grass); *E. colonum* (Samaghas); *Cynodon dactylon* (Bermuda grass or Doob grass); *Saccharum spontaneum* (kans); *Sorghum halepense* (Johnson grass or baru); *Avena fatua* (Wild oats); *Phalaris minor* (Mimicry weed)	**Rice**: Propanil 2 l/ha post-emergence; **Cotton**: Treflan 2 l/ha or Diuron or Cotoran 0.5-1.0 kg/ha pre-emergence; **Maize and sugarcane**: Atrazine or Simazine pre-emergence @ 1 kg/ha; **Wild oats**: Carbyne @ 0.5 l/ha or Avadex at 2 l/ha; **Phalaris**: pre-emergence Tribunil @ 2 kg/ha in 900 litres of water.

Melilotus indica (Senji); *Vicia sativa* (Common vetch); *Tephrosia purpurea*. *Prosopis juliflora* (Mesquite); *Alhagi camelorum* (Camelthorn or javasa); *Mimosa pudica* (Touch-me-not or Lajjavanti)	2, 4-D in cereals at 1 kg/ha kill the annual legumes. For perennials, a mixture of 2, 4-D and 2, 4, 5-T at 1-2 l/ha before flowering.
Orobanche cernua/ indica (Broomrape)	Spraying with 1-2 l/ha 2, 4-D amine or 2, 4-DES @ 6 kg/ha or amyl alcohol (0.1-0.2%) .
Argemone nexicana (Prickly poppy or Satyanasi)	**Monocot crops**: 2, 4-D amine @ 0.5 kg/ha plus urea 3%; **Mustard**: nitrofen pre-emergence 1-2 l/ha.
Striga asiatica (Witch weed)	**Monocot crops**: 2, 4-D amine @ 1 kg/ha or fence @ 3 kg/ha.
Solanum xanthocarpum (Kateli) *Solanum elaeagnifolium* (White Horse Nettle);	2,4,5-T @ 1 kg/ha or 2, 4-D amine @ 2 l/ha.
Lantana camara (Tantani)	A mixture of 2, 4-D + 2, 4, 5T @ 1-2 kg in 1,000 litres of water at pre-bloom stage.

Management of Aquatic Weeds

Aquatic weeds are classified into three types, *viz.* submerged (*e.g. Hydrilla*), immersed (*e.g. Typha*) and floating (*e.g. Eichhornia*). Submerged aquatics are anchored to the bottom of the habitats, e.g. a ditch, and grow entirely beneath the surface of the water. Immersed once have their roots beneath the surface of the water, but the leaves and stems are above the water line. Floating weeds or surface aquatics either float freely on the water or float only in a limited area.

- A number of chemicals are used for controlling some submerged aquatic weeds by dissolving or emulsifying them in water in canals, ditches, ponds and lakes, *e.g.* Aqualin, Aromatic solvents, Chlorinated benzenes, Copper sulphate, Endothal, Fenac, Sodium arsenite and 2, 4-D, etc.

Management of Important Aquatic Weeds

Weed	Management
Water hyacinth (*Eicchornia crassips*)	2, 4-D @ 4 kg/ha, or Paraquat (0. 5 kg/ha), or Diquat (1.0-1.5 kg/ha), Amitrol-T(0.5-1.5 kg/ha), Ametryn (3-4 kg/ha).
Cattails (*Typha angustata*)	Dalapon @ 25-30 kg/ ha, Amitrol-T(8 kg/ha), Paraquat (1.2-1.6 kg/ha).
Hydrilla (*H. verticillata*)	2, 4-D @ 2.5 ppmw, Diuron @ 0.5 ppmw, Paraquat @ 1 ppmw, $CuSO_4$ @ 4 ppmw.
Water lettuce (*Pistia stratiotes*)	Diquat (1-1.5 kg/ha), Paraquat (1.5-1.75 kg/ha).
Salvinia (*Salvinia molesta*)	2, 4-D @ 4 kg/ha, or Paraquat (1.0 kg/ha)
Swamp morning glory (*Ipomea aquatica*)	2, 4-D @ 4 kg/ha, or Paraquat (0. 5 kg/ha).

Noxious Weeds

Such weeds are troublesome and undesirable. They are difficult to be controlled, *e.g. Cynodon dactylon, Cyperus rotundus, Sorghum halepense.*

□□□

27

Insect Pest Management

Entomology is a branch of zoology dealing with the scientific study of insects. The Greek word *entomon,* meaning, "notched", refers to the segmented body plan of the insects. It emerged as a distinct field of study in the early 19th century, with the publication of *British Entomology* (1824-39) in 8 volumes by John Curtis, and with the foundation of entomological societies in Paris and London.

- **Aristotle** in 4th century BC provided descriptions of insect anatomy and led the groundwork for modern entomology.
- The Italian naturalist Ulisse Aldrovandi published a major treatise, *De Animalibus insectis* ("Insects of Animals") in 1602.
- Modern insect classification began in the 18th century. The French biologist Rene-Antoine Ferchault de Reaumur published the first of six volumes of *Memoires pour servira l histoire des insectes* (Memoirs Serving as a History of Insects) in 1734.
- Carolus Linnaeus, in *Systema Naturalis* (10th ed., 1758), applied his system of binomial nomenclature to organize the classification of insect species.
- **Insects** belong to class Insecta (formerly Hexapoda), the largest class of the phylum Arthropoda being largest among the animal phyla. Insects are distinguished from other arthropods by their body, which is divided into three major regions: (1) the **head,** which bears the mouthparts, eyes, and a pair of antennae; (2) the **thorax,** has three pairs of legs and usually one or two pairs of wings; and (3) many-segmented **abdomen** contains the digestive, excretory, and reproductive organs of insect.
- The orders Coleoptera (beetles), Lepidoptera (butterflies and moths), Hymenoptera (ants, bees, wasps), and Diptera (true flies) comprise the greatest numbers of insect species.
- Roughly 2,500 insects are found in one yard^2 of moist land in the North Temperate Zone.

- The most important domesticated insects are the silkworm (Lepidoptera) and the Honeybees (Hymenoptera).
- The desert locust (*Schistocerca gregaria*) and the migratory locust (*Locusta migratoria*) swarm and destroy crop drastically.
- The protozoan *Plasmodium*, which spends most part of its developmental cycle in *Anopheles* mosquitoes, causes malaria.
- Sleeping sickness in man and a group of cattle caused by protozoan *trypanosomes*, and transmitted by tsetse flies (Glossina).
- In early 1940s the production of DDT was started, which is still a highly toxic to most insects.
- Larvae, which vary considerably in shape, are classified in five forms: eruciform (caterpillar-like), scarabaeiform (grub-like), campodeiform (elongated, flattened, and active), elateriform (wireworm-like), and vermiform (maggot-like).
- **Pupae** are mostly three types, *viz.* **obtect** with appendages more or less glued to the body; **exarate** with the appendages free and not glued to the body; and **coarctate** essentially exarate but remaining covered by the cast skins (exuviae) of the next to the last larval instar (name given to the form of an insect between moults).
- A hormone from neurosecretory cells in the brain called **ecdysone** initiates moulting.
- During summer months in temperate latitudes, aphids occur only as parthenogenetic females in which embryos develop within the mother (**vivipary**).
- **Tactile hairs** found around the body of insect serve to inform the insect about its surroundings and its body position (a phenomenon known as **proprioception**). Exceedingly sensitive organs in insects is called **sensilla** are concentrated on bushy antennae of the male mosquitoes. Moths with these sensitive organs can perceive the high-pitched sounds emitted by bats (bats hunt by echolocation).
- The insect is covered by the **cuticle** which consists mainly of chitin, or polyacetylglucosamine, and sclerotin, a hard substance composed of protein tanned by quinones. In insects with hard bodies, the cuticle is made up of hardened areas called sclerites.

Pheromone

Pheromones are endogenous chemicals secreted in minute amounts by the insects in order to elicit a particular reaction. Pheromones are used as attractants in reproduction where organisms of complementary reproductive cell types grow or move toward each other. Pheromones can be used to control insects using as attractants.

Pesticides in India

- Number of pesticides registered in India are 155 (as on 31 Dec, 1999).
- 66 technical grade pesticides are being manufactured in India.
- Insecticides Act, 1968 was promulgated on the recommendations of Thakur committee. Insecticides rules were formed in 1971.
- Per hectare consumption of pesticides is 480-500 g/ha. Total consumption of pesticides is maximum in Andhra Pradesh, whereas per hectare consumption is maximum in Tamil Nadu. Mostly consumed pesticides include Carbaryl, Chlorpyriphos, Monocrotophos and Endosulfan.
- Cypermethrin followed by endosulfan, aluminium phosphide and lindane are mainly exported from India.

Classification of Insecticides

1. **Inorganic chemicals,** *e.g.* Arsenicals, Fluosilicates, etc.
2. **Organic chemicals of plant origin,** Nicotine sulphate, Pyrethrins, Rotenone, Ryania, etc.
3. **Synthetic organic chemicals,** *viz.*

(*i*) **Chlorinated hydrocarbons,** *e.g.* Aldrin, DDT, Endrin, Dieldrin, Chlordane, Methoxychlor, Endosulfan, etc.

(*ii*) **Organophosphates,** *e.g.* Parathion, Malathion, Phosphamidon, Dimethoate, Monocrotophos, Disulfoton Phorate, Dichlorvos, etc.

(*iii*) **Carbamates,** *e.g.* Carbaryl, Isolan, Dimetilan, Carbofuran, etc.

(*iv*) **Miscellaneous groups,** *e.g.* DNOC, Lethane, Thanite, etc.

INSECT PEST MANAGEMENT

Pests of Sugarcane

1. **Shoot borer** or early shoot borer: *Chilo infuscatellus*: Rotten portion of straw-coloured called dead heart emits offensive odour. If it is pulled, it comes easily. It can be **controlled** by earthing during early stage; trash mulching; by applying *Trichogramma chilonis*, egg parasite; soil application of Gamma HCH emulsion @ 1.0 kg a.i./ ha over the cane setts at the time of planting and by applying Granulosis virus.

2. **Top borer**: *Scirpophaga excerptalis:* Mid-rib tunnelling is shot (holes on axial bud growth leaves dead heart and can be pulled out easily). Aerial root formation is observed, which leaves in bushy appearance. It is controlled by avoiding frequent irrigation; applying carbofuran @ 1.0 kg a.i./ ha which synchronizes brood emergence; pre-pupal parasitoid *Isotima javensis;* and by using resistant cultivars like CoJ 67 and Co 1007.
3. **Internodes borer**: *Chilo sacchaviphagus indicus*: Attach starts from 4th month onwards. Internodes constrict and shortened with many bore holes (holes with wet frass), stunted growth and hardening of internodes. It is controlled by detrashing at 5th, 7th and 9th months and by applying *Trichogramma chilonis* @ 3.5 cc/ha at the interval of 15 days from 4th month to one month before of harvesting.
4. **Gurdaspur borer**: *Acigone steniellea*: Two phases: (*i*) Gegarious phase feed on first internode and larvae inters into and carve through single hole; (*ii*) Solitary phase dispersed to other canes by silken treads.
5. **White grub**: *Holotrichia consanguinea, H. serrata, Anomal bengalensis*: Drying of crops, yellowing and nibbling of leaves, cutting of roots is seen. It is controlled by puddling and crop rotation and by applying *Metarrhizium anisopliae.*
6. **Termites**: *Odentotermes* spp. and *Microtermes obesi:* Older leaves dry up first and cane falls down if disturbed. Filled with moist soil inside the papery rind.
7. **Sugarcane scale**: *Melanaspis glomerata:* Greyish black appearance of stem. Reduced yield, juice quality and Jaggery production. It is controlled by detrashing and trash burning.
8. **Leaf hopper**: *Pyrilla perpusilia*: Yellowish white spots on leaves, sooty mould on later stages. It is controlled by external parasitoid, *Epiricarlia melanoleuca* and applying green muscardine fungus (*Metarrhizium anisopliae*).

Pests of Cotton

9. **Aphid:** *Aphis gossypii*: Nymphs and adults suck the sap from the leaves and shoot resulting in crinkling and curling of leaves. Seed treatment with Imidacloprid 70 WS (5 g/kg) or Thiamethoxam 70 WS (4 g/kg) or Carbosulfan 25 SP (50 g/kg); apply carbofuran @ 12-14 kg/acre or Phorate @ 4-5 kg/acre.

cause damage to the stem, which result into 'dead heart' and 'white head'. They eat growing parts of plant from the base, leading to drying of plant parts (dead heart) and at the time of flowering drying of flower (white head). Application of Furadon 3 G @ 33 kg/ha or Thimet 10 G @ 10 kg/ha manages the pests.

28. **Paddy gall fly:** *Pachdiplosis oryzae*: Maggots attack the base of the growing-point and produce long, tubular silvery galls (silver shoots); plant growth is adversely affected; active during May to September-November. Spraying with 0.03% Phosphamidon or Dimethoate, 4 times during the vegetative phase of the crop manage the pest.

29. **Rice hispa** : *Dicladispa armigera*: Adults are responsible for causing losses by scrapping on upper surface of leaf blade, leaving lower epidermis. Damaged area shows white streaks parallel to mid rib. Grubs make long winding tunnels into leaves. Spraying of Dimecron 10 EC @ 400 ml/800 litre of water/ha or Fenitrothion 50 EC @ 1 ml/litre of water.

30. **Swarming caterpillar:** *Spodoptera mauritia*: Caterpillars cause heavy losses, specially when cold weather is suddenly followed by a spell of warmth or drought (30-40 days) and heavy rains during July-August. Flooding the field and spraying with 0.03% Diehlorvos or Endosulfan is helpful.

31. **Armyworms**: *Mythimna unipuncta, M. albistigma*: Caterpillars voraciously feed on foliage, which appear after heavy rains or early floods. Spraying with 0.05% Endosulfan in early stage controls caterpillars.

32. **Paddy jassids**: *Nephotettix apicalis, N. impicticeps*: Nymphs and adults suck plant sap. Affected plants turn yellow. Spraying with 0.04% Phosphamindon, Dimethoate, Monocrotophos or Diazinon or application of Phorate 10 G, 3 and 6 weeks after transplanting.

33. **Paddy mealy bug:** *Ripersia oryzae*: Mealy bug infest succulent paddy stems by sucking cell sap leading stunted growth of plants. Spraying with 0.04% Phosphamindon, Diamethoate, Diazinon or Monocrotophes.

34. **Rice root aphid**: *Tetraneura hirsute*: Nymphs and adults suck sap from roots just below soil surface. Affected plants become pale and wither. Applications of Phorate 10 G or Disulfoton 5 G near the base of the plants control the pests.

35. **Hoppers**: *Hieroglyphus banian, H. Nigrorepletus, H. furcifer H. oryzaevorus, Acrida exultata, A. turrita, Aelopus tamulus Aularaches miliaris, Oxya bidentata, O. multidentata, O. velox.* White backed plant hopper and brown plant hopper are two types of hoppers found in rice. White backed mostly found during July August. Brown plant hopper occurs during October-November Both the hoppers cause damage by sucking sap resulting 'hopper burn'. Application of Furadon 3 G @ 33 kg/ha or Thimet 10 G @ 10 kg/ha or Sevidol 4.4 G @ 12 kg/ha manages the pest.

36. **Paddy leaf-roller:** *Cnaphalocrocis medinalis*: Caterpillars roll the leaf tips and feed inside. Dusting with Malathion.

37. **Paddy skippers:** *Pelopides mathias*: Caterpillar feeds on leaves and cause damage. Dusting with 4% Carbaryl or spraying with 0.05% Endosulfan manage the pests.

38. **Paddy root weevil**: *Echinocnemus oryzae*: Grubs attack paddy roots and affects the growth of plants. Application of Aldrin 5% or Chlordane 5% in soil before sowing controls the pest.

Pests of Maize

39. **Aphid**: *Rhopalosiphum maidis*: Aphids suck sap from plants and cause yellowing and mottling. Honeydew excreted by aphids favours the development of sooty moulds. One spray of systemic insecticides like dimethioate or monocrotophos at 0.1% will control the aphids.

40. **Pink borer**: *Sesamia inferens*: Newly hatched larvae begin chewing on the stem and epidermal layer of the sheath. Seed treatment with Carbofuran (40 F) @ 2.5 g / kg of seed.

41. **Shoot bug**: *Peregrinus maidis*: Adults and nymphs suck sap, resulting in unhealthy, stunted and yellow plants. Leaves wither from top downwards and plants die in severe conditions. 15 days after sowing spray 0.1% Endosulfan. After 30 days spray 4% granules endosulfan @ 15 kg.

42. **Shoot fly**: *Atherigona soccata, A. naqui*: The attack is more in the seedling stage. The tiny maggots creep down under the leaf sheaths and cut the growing point or central shoot, which results in the formation of characteristic dead hearts. Application of 10% Phorate granules @ 15 kg/ha in the furrows before sowing; following by spraying with 0.01% Metasystox one week after the germination.

43. **Stem borer:** *Chilo partellus*: The young larvae first feed on the leaves, making a few shot holes and then bore their way downwards through the central whorl as it opens. Effective control schedule may be as 1st foliar application of Endosulfan 0.1% at 15 days after sowing followed by 2nd application of 4% granules a 15 kg/ha a fortnight later against *C. partellus*.

Pests of Jowar

44. **Aphids**: *Phopalosiphum maidis, Aphis sacchari*: Nymphs and adults suck the sap from the leaves and shoots, exclude honeydew, on which a sooty mould grows, giving the leaves a black appearance. Spraying with 0.02% Phosphamindon, 0.04% Diazinon, Methyldemeton or Dimethoate control the pest.
45. **Shoot fly:** *Atherigona soccata*: Larvae cut the growing points to seedlings, causing dead-hearts. Adjusting the sowing date, increasing the seed-rate; application of 3% Carbofuran, 5% Disulfoton or 10% Phorate granules manage the shoot fly.
46. **Sorghum midge:** *Contarinia sorghicola*: Adult fly lay eggs inside the glumes and the larvae feed on the ovaries preventing seed formation. Application of 0.05% Endosulfan, 0.1% Carbaryl or 0.05% Lindane as sprays or dusts.
47. **Sorghum shoot bug:** *Peregrinus maidis*: Nymphs and adult suck the sap from the leaves and whorls turning them pale green. Spraying with 0.02% Phosphamindon, 0.04% Diazinon, Methyldemeton or Dimethoate.
48. **Stem borers**: *Chilo zonellus, Sesamia inferens*: Caterpillars feed on foliage and bore into the stems, causing dead-hearts, tunnel the stem and bore into earheads. Application of 4% Endosulfan or Carbaryl granules or spraying with 0.05% Lindane.

Pests of Bajra

49. **Leaf roller**: *Marasmia trapezalis*: Caterpillars fold and roll the leaves near the tips and feed on the chlorophyll. Dusting with Malathion controls the leaf roller.
50. **Shoot fly:** *Atherigone approximata*: Adult flies cut the growing points, causing dead-hearts during the seedling stage. In the later stage they feed on earheads and cut down peduncles. Spraying with 0.04% Endosulfan or 0.1% Carbaryl for control.

Pests of Crucifers

51. **Cabbage head borer:** *Hellula undalis*: Caterpillars initially mine the leaves and make it white papery. Afterwards they bore into

stems, close entrance hole with silk and excreta. Spraying wit monocrotophos is effective.

52. **Diamond back month:** *Plutella xylostella*: Caterpillars feed o leaves and bores into pods. Spraying with triazophos i effective.

53. **Leaf webber:** *Crocidolomia binotalls*: Newly hatched larvae fee initially on young leaves followed by older leaves, buds an pods, and make webbings over them. Carbaryl o monocrotophos sprays are effective.

54. **Mustard aphid**: *Lipaphis erysimi*: Both the nymphs and th adults suck the plant sap from the tender portion of the plar from December to February. Application of Malathion 5% du @ 25 kg/ha or Carbaryl 10% dust @ 25 kg/ha or Fenetrothio 5% dust @ 20 kg/ha.

55. **Mustard Saw Fly:** *Athalia proxima*: Its activity is generall confined to the period of October to March. The larval stag damages the crop by voraciously feeding on the young cro The plants become dry or remain stunted. Hand picking grubs and 0.1% spray of Brestnol 45 WP as protectant fro pest is effective; dusting with Malathion 5% dust @ 25 kg/h or Thiodan 4% dust @ 30 kgs/ha or Carbaryl 5% dust @ 25 kg ha; spraying with Dimecron 100 EC @ 0.250 lit/ha or Thioda 55 EC @ 1.0 lit/ha or Nuvan 100 EC @ 0.250 lit/ha.

56. **Painted bug:** *Bargrada cruciferarum*: The nymph and adult cau the damage. They suck the sap from the leaves, stems an tender parts of the plants. Irrigating field with 5 kg of crude o emulsion/ha; dusting with Malathion 5% dust @ 25 kg/ha Carbaryl 10% dust @ 25 kg /ha; spraying with Malathion 5 EC @ 1.25 lit/ha or Dimecron 100 EC @ 0.250 lit/ha or Rog 30 EC @ 1.00 lit/ha.

Pests of Pulses

57. **Aphids**: *Aphis craccivora, A. cardui*: Nymphs and adults infe the tender growing shoots, flowers and young pods and suc the sap. Infested parts dry and no pod or seed formation tal place. Spraying with 0.03% Monocrotophos, Phosphamido Dimethoate or Methyl-demeton.

58. **Cow pea stem fly:** *Melangromyza phaseoli*: Maggots mine t leaves and stem. Dusting with 4% Carbaryl + 5% LDT spraying with 0.05% Monocrotophos or Dimethoate.

59. **Cutworm:** *Agrotis ypsilon, A. flammatra, A. biconica, A. segetum, A. spinifera*: A characteristic feature of the damage is that the caterpillars drag the cut parts into soil for feeding. Cutworms can be controlled by dusting aldrin (5%) at 20 to 25 kg/ha.

60. **Galerucid beetle**: *Madurasia obscurella*. Adult beetles feed on foliage and make small circular holes in the leaves. These are active during July-October. Application of Phorate 10 G or Disulfotan 5 G @ 1.5 kg/ha at the time of sowing, control the disease.

61. **Gram pod fly**: *Agromyza obtuse*: Maggots bore into the pods and feed on the seeds. Dusting with 4% Carbaryl + 5% LDT or spraying with 0.05% Monocrotophos or Dimethoate.

62. **Hairy caterpillars**: *Amsacta moorei, A. albistriga, Diacrisia oblique*: Caterpillars feed gregariously and voraciously on foliage. Spraying with 0.05% Dichlorvos (DDVP).

63. **Jassid:** *Empoasca herri*: Nymphs and adults suck the sap of leaves, which turn brown in colour. Spraying with 0.03% Monocrotophos, Phosphamidon, Dimethoate or Methyl-demeton.

64. **Leaf caterpillars:** *Azazia rubicans*: Caterpillars feed on leaves and tender plant parts. Dusting with 4% Carbaryl.

65. **Plume moth borer**: *Exelastis atomosa*: Caterpillars feed on flowers and later on bore into pods to feed on the developing seeds. Dusting with 4% Carbaryl + 5% DDT or spraying with 0.04% Monocrotophos or 0.05% Endosulfan.

66. **Pod borer:** *Helicoverpa armigera*: Damage is caused on pods by the strain of *H. armigera* Hb. It is manage by sowing trap crops like marigold at 50 plants/acre; release of *Trichogramma* parasites @ (20,000/acre); applying NPV 200 LE + ½ kg Jaggery + 200 ml Sandovit (or) Teepal.

67. **White fly:** *Bemisia tabaci*: The flies suck the sap from leaves and tender growing parts, which dry and wither. Spray twice 0.03% Monocrotophos, Phosphamidon, Dimethoate or Methyl-demeton.

Integrated Pest Management (IPM)in Pulses

- **Cultural Method:** Early sowing; wider spacing of 45 cm rows; intercropping with mustard, wheat, barley, linseed, safflower and sorghum; deep summer ploughing; use of resistant varieties like G 130 and C 124.

- **Mechanical method:** Use of pheromone trap; use of light traps; use of neem seed kernel extract (5%).
- **Biological method**: Use of *Apanteles* for gram cutworm caterpillars and *Trichogramma minutum* for eggs of *Heliothis armigera; Bacillus thuringiensis* bacterium for *Plucea orichalcea* (Gram semi-looper); use of NPV 250 LE/ha against *Heliothis armigera;* use of *Trichogramma chilonis* for pod borer.
- **Chemical Method:** Presowing treatment of soil with chlorphyriphos (20 EC) 3 litre or lindane (20 EC) 4 litre/ha with 10 kg of sand in cutworm prone areas; spraying of 0.07% endosulfan 35 EC against *Heliothis armigera* and gram semi-looper.
- **Antifeedants:** Use of Triphenyl tin hydroxide (TTH) and Triphenyl tin acetate (TTA) against caterpillars of *Heliothis armigera* and Brestan against larvae of cutworms.

Pests of Groundnut

68. **Aphids**: *Aphis craccivora*: Adults and nymphs feed mostly on growing tips and young foliage resulting in the chlorosis and leaf curl. Dusting with Endosulfan 4% @ 1 kg a.i./ha or release of predators like *Cocciilella sezptumpunctata, Menochiles sexmaculata* manage the aphids.
69. **White grub:** *Lachnosterna consanquinea, L. serrata, L. insularis*: The 'C' shaped white, robust grubs feed on rootlets and nodules. Soil application of quinolphos or Isofenphos @ 1.5 kg a.i./ha; spraying with Folithion/Sumithion 50 WP or Fenitrothion 50 EC in 100 litres of water; seed treatment with Chlopyriphos (Dursban 20 EC) @ 12.5 ml/kg seed or Isofenphos 40 SD.
70. **Red hairy caterpillar**: *Amsacta albistriga, A. mooreii, Diacrisia oblique*: Dusting of Carbaryl or Parathion @ 25-30 kg/ha; use of 200 ml Dichlorovos 100 EC in 400 litres of water/ha for the control of grown up caterpillars.
71. **Tobacco caterpillar:** ***Spodoptera litura***: Larvae are polyphagus and appear on groundnut crop both in vegetative phase and at the time of pod formation after December. Spray Chlorpyriphos 3 ml/l of water or Quinolphos 2 ml/l of water or Acephate 1g/ l of water are recommended.

Pests of Sesame

72. **Gall fly**: *Asphondylia sesami*: Maggots feed inside the flower and produce galls. The damaged flower does not produce capsule. Spraying with 0.03% Phophomidon @ 750 litres/ha.

73. **Hawk moth**: *Acherontia styx*: Caterpillars feed voraciously on the leaves. Spraying with 0.25% Carbaryl @ 600 litres/ha when the pest starts appearing.

74. **Leaf roller and capsule borer**: *Antigastra catalunalis*: Caterpillars web and feed on the tender leaves in the early stage and feed inside voraciously on the leaves. Spraying with 0.25% Carbaryl @ 600 litres/ha when the pest starts appearing.

Pests of Linseed

75. **Cutwarm caterpillar:** *Laphygma exigua*: Caterpillars cut the plants near the roots under the soil. Application of Aldrin 5% to the soil.

76. **Linseed caterpillar:** *Laphygma exigua*: The moth lays eggs on the under side of the leaf. The newly hatched larva feed on kernels. The handpicking of caterpillars; ploughing the fields after harvesting the crop to destroy pupae.

77. **Linseed fly (gall midge)**: *Dasyneura lini*: The orange coloured fly destroys the flower bud while laying eggs in folds of the calyx. Growing of resistant and early-maturing varieties is recommended.

Pests of Vegetables

78. **Aphids**: *Aphis gossypii* and *Myzus persicae*: Both Nymphs and adults suck the sap from the leaves and shoot resulting in crinkling and curling of leaves. Seed treatment with Imidacloprid 70 WS (5 g/kg) or Thiamethoxam 70 WS (4g/kg) or Carbosulfan 25 SP (50 g/kg); application of carbofuran @ 12-14 kg/acre or Phorate @ 4-5 kg/acre.

79. **Gram caterpillar**: *Helicoverpa armigera*: Active during October to March. The larva damages by boring into squares, flowers and bolls and feeds on inner contents. Release of *Trichograma pretiosum* eggs parasite @ (20,000/acre); NPV @ 200 LE + ½ kg Jaggery + 200 ml Sandovit (or) Teepal.

80. **Mite**: *Polyphagotarsonimus latus*: Nymphs and adults suck sap from leaves. Affected leaves curl downward along the margins of the leaf and attain an inverted boat shape. Spraying with Phosolone 3 ml/litre or Wettable sulphur 3 g/l of water or Dicofal 5 ml/lit of water.

81. **Pink bollworm**: *Pectinophora gossypiella*: Larvae enter the fruit and remain inside feeding on immature seed. Economic threshold level is 5-10% incidence. Soaking of seeds solution of Monocrotophos or Dichlorovas.

82. **Red spider mite**: *Tetranychus telarius*: Mites puncture the leaves from under surface and feed on the sap. Later, the upper surface of the leaves turn red and finally the leaves wither and shed. Economic threshold level is 10 mites/m^2. Dusting sulphur @ 20 kg/ha; spraying 0.05% Methyl parathion @ 700-900 l/ha or dicofal @ 2 ml/litre of water.

83. **Root grub**: *Holotrichia consanguinea*: Grubs eat away the nodules, fine rootlets girdle the main root, ultimately killing the plants. Before sowing (July-August) use 20 kg 2% Folidol dust; seed treatment with Phorate 10 G 50 g a.i/kg of seed or quinolphos 5 G 50 g a.i/kg of seed; spraying with Isofenphos 5 G 25 kg/ha. or Quinolphos 25 E.C 0.02%; dusting with mustard seed powder @ 60 kg/acre or neem seed powder @ 80 kg/acre.

84. **Shoot and fruit borer**: *Earias vittella, E. insulana*: Larvae bore into tender shoots and tunnel downwards. Spraying with Endosulphan (2 ml/l) or Chlorpyriphos (2 ml/l) or Carbaryl (3 g/l); release of egg parasite @ 20,000/ha.

85. **Spotted bollworm**: *Earias vittella, Earias insulana*: Larva bores into flower buds and terminal shoots leading to death of the shoots and subsequent development of lateral shoots and branches. Economic threshold limit is 5-10% incidence. Spraying with Endosulphan (2 ml/l) or Chlorpyriphos (2 ml/l) or Carbaryl (3 g/l).

86. **Thrips**: *Scirtothrips dorsalis:* Thirps appears in Nursery (July-August) and main field (November). Both adults and nymphs damage the crop, lacerate the leaf tissue, and suck the sap. Spraying with Carboryl or Phosolone 3 g/l of water or Methyl demton 0.05% (2 ml/litre) or Acephate 1 g/litre or Triazophos 1 ml or Fipronil 2 ml or Monocrotophos 1.5 ml/lit of water.

87. **Tobacco caterpillar**: *Spotoptera litura*: Freshly hatched larvae feed by scraping the leaves from ventral side in night on the foliage. Control mentioned earlier.

88. **White Fly**: *Bemisia tabaci*: Nymphs and adults suck the sap usually from the under surface of the leaves and excrete honeydew causing leaf curl. Economic threshold is 8-10 adults or 20 nymphs/leaf. Use of tolerant varieties Kanchana, LK 861, NA 1280; spraying with Trizophos 2.5 ml/l or Prophanophos 2 ml/l.

Pests of Fruit Crops

89. **Almond beetle:** *Mimastra cyanura*: Adult beetles appear in swarms during May, defoliate the trees, causing huge losses. Peak activity reaches during July-August.
90. **Apple blossom thrips**: *Taenniothrips rhopalantennalis*. Nymphs and adults scrape tissues from flower buds, therefore no fruit setting. Spraying with 0.03% Phosphamindom, Dimethoate, Monocrotophos or Methyl demeton before opening of flowers.
91. **Apple leaf rollers**: *Cacoecia sarcosttega, C. ecicyota, C. pomivora, C. termias, C. subsidiaria*: Larvae feed on the leaves, buds and flowers; after rolling or webbing them together, they feed within on soft tissues. Spraying with 0.05% Fenitrothion or 0.03% Endosulfan or Phosphamindon in the month of April.
92. **Hairy caterpillars**: *Euproctis signata* (common on Apple), *E. fraternal, E. flava*: Caterpillars feed voraciously and defoliate trees. Dusting with Malathion.
93. **Leaf-defoliating and fruit-eating beetles**: *Adoretus duvauceli, A. versutus, Anomala lineatopennis*: Grubs feed on vegetation under ground till next summer, when comes out in June feed on foliage and attack on tender fruits usually during night. Spraying with 0.2% Carbaryl twice at 7-day intervals starting as soon as adults appear or application of 5% Aldrin dust in soil around the trees.
94. **San Jose scale**: *Quadraspidiotus perniciosus*: Insects infest leaves, twigs, and fruits and suck the sap. Active from March to December. Spraying with 3% Miscible oil @ 6-8 litres per tree; use of 0.04% Diazinon as summer spray.
95. **Weevils**: *Myllocerus laetivirens, Mylocerus undecimpustulatus, M. discolor, Amblyrrhinus poricollis*: Young weevils feed on roots and adults feed on the foliage. Initially they cut irregular holes and gradually eat up entire leaves leaving only the mid ribs. Dusting with Malathion.
96. **Woolly aphid:** *Eriosoma lanigerum*: A cosmopolitan sucking insect infest on twigs and main roots below ground. Remain active from March to December, but severe during July-August. Use of RVs, *e.g.* Merton-778, 779, Malling type III; spraying with 0.03% Dimethoate, Phosphamindon or Monocrotophos during spring (March-April) and again during summer (June-July).

STORAGE INSECT PESTS AND THEIR MANAGEMENT

There are 16 insect pests involved in storage; of them nine are very important infesting about 10-12% loss in the storage. The warm season and the high moisture content after the rain are highly conducive factors for the development and rapid multiplication of insects' pests in storage. At the time of storage grains are dried up to the moisture level goes to 9% (preferably 6-7%). Important insects pests are included here:

1. **Almond or Fig moth:** *Ephestia cetella*: Moth has primary status in infestation and causes losses in Dry fruits, Fig, Dried Mango, Garlic Bulbs, various cereal grains, etc.
2. **Angoumois grain moth:** *Sitotrogus cerealella*: Moth has primary status and causes infestation in Maize, Wheat, Oat, Barley, and Sorghum. The larvae cause damage by feeding on grain kernels. The bored grains when broken, releases pellets of moth excreta.
3. **Indian meal moth:** *Plodia interpuntella*: It has primary status in infestation and causes losses in different cereal Grains, Cooked meals, Breakfast food, Soya bean, Dry fruits, Fignut. Active crawling caterpillars completely web the surface of grains with silicon threads. Adults are responsible to spread infestation. Larvae are active from March to October.
4. **Khapra beetle:** *Trogoderma granarium*: Beetle has primary status in infestation and causes losses in Cereal including Wheat, Pulses including Gram, Dry fruits including Walnut, etc. Grubs cause greater damage, which prefers to eat on grains near the embryo or other weak points and remain, confined to upper 50 cm layer of grains in a heap.
5. **Lesser grain borer:** *Rhizopertha dominic.*: Borer has primary status in infestation and causes losses in Cereal grains, Dried potatoes, Beans, Pumpkin seeds, Tamarind seeds, Millets, etc. Both adults and grubs cause damage by making a regular holes and feeding inside the grains.
6. **Pulse beetle:** *Colosibruchus chinensis*: Beetle has primary status in infestation and causes losses in Gram, Moong, Peas, Cow pea, Lentil, Pigeon pea, etc. Larvae soon after hatching bore into the grain and make a cavity by feeding on the grain content. The damage is at the peak during June-July to September-October.
7. **Rice moth:** *Corcyra cephalonica*: Moth has secondary status and causes infestation Rice, Gram, Maize, Cotton, Sorghum, Groundnut, etc. Larval stage is the damaging stage; it pollutes the food grains with moults and dense webbing. Larvae prefer partially damaged grains.

8. **Rice weevil:** *Citphilus oryzae, S. granaries*: Weevil has primary status in infestation and causes losses in Rice, Wheat, Maize including small millets, etc. Both adults and grubs cause damage soon after hatching. Larvae directly bore into the grain and feed upon the grain contents.
9. **Rust red flour beetle:** *Tribolium catenium*: Beetle has secondary status in infestation and causes losses in Wheat flour, Dry fruits, Pulses, Cooked cereal foods, etc. Both adults and larvae cause damage. In case of severe infestation the flour turns greyish and releases foul odour.

Management of Storage Pests

1. **Surface treatment** of godowns is necessary before storage. It can be done by spraying 0.5% Malathion @ 3 litres/25 m^2. But some insects like *Tribolium* and *Sitosphilous* have become resistant to this insecticide. Such insects can be controlled by DDVP, Bromophos, Phenitothion, Chlorpyriphos @ 0.3-0.5%.
2. **Seed dressing** before storage can be done with 5% Malathion @ 2.5 g/ kg of seed.
3. **Use of edible oils:** Coconut, Groundnut or Mustard oil @ 0.25-0.5% is effective against pulse beetles.
4. **Prophylactic treatments:** Insecticides like Malathion 50 EC or Perimiphos methyl 50 EC or Pyrethrum 2 EC @ 3 liters/25 m^2 are used for protective measures.
5. Fumigants:

- Ethylene Di Bromide (EDB) is one the most effective chemical for insects of storage @ 3 ml ample/q of grains.
- **EDB Plus** is the mixture of EDB and Carbendazim in the ratio of 1:8 w/w basis. It is used @ 11 ml/q of wheat grains and 15 ml/q of paddy grains.
- Ethylene Dichloride and Carbon Tetrachloride (EDCT) is also a mixture of Ethylene Dichloride and Carbon Tetrachloride in ratio of 3:1 v/v basis. It is used @ 15 ml/q of grains.
- **Aluminum phosphide** is available in the form of tablets of 3 g each. Active ingredient in Aluminum phophide is phosphine gas. It is used @ 2-3 tablets/t of grains or 25 tablets/100 m^3 of space.
- **Methyl bromide** is also used @ 3.5 kg/100 m^3 space.

Important Receptacles in Storage

- **Pits:** Wheat, Paddy, Sorghum, Fingermillet, etc., can be stored underground for a period of 2 years. These structures are simple underground dig-outs up to a depth of 5 m varying in sizes to hold from a small quantity up to 50 tonnes. The pits are lined with brick or concrete so that moisture from walls and bottom does not damage the grain. At the time of filling a layer of straw is placed on all sides. After the pit is filled, straw is spread over the grain and then topped with a layer of soil. Insect infestation is less in the under-ground storage.

Several types of above ground storage structures mentioned below are also in use in our country:

Mud bins: The mud bins are made of unburnt clay mixed with straw with 1 to 3 inch thick wall and oval, rectangular or circular. A small hole is provided at the base. Both the inlet and outlet holes are plugged while grains are stored.

Straw bins: For storing paddy in humid zones dried plants are used for making temporary structures, which after being filled with grain are further reinforced from outside by winding paddy straw ropes around the whole structure. Each structure holds 2-6 quintal grains.

Bukhari bins: This is a cylindrical structure and is made of mud and split bamboo's. The bin is always placed on a wooden or a masonry platform to prevent its contact with the ground. The capacity may vary from 3 to 10 tonnes.

Kothar: This type bins are very much similar to that of timber box placed on a raised platform, which is generally supported on pillars. Both the floor and walls are made of wooden planks, where the tiled or thatched roof is placed over it as a protection against sun and rains. The capacity may vary from 9 to 35 tonnes.

Metal bins: Bins made of steel, aluminium, R.C.C., are used for storage of grains outside the house. These bins are fire and moisture proof. The bins have long durability and produced on commercial scale. The capacity ranges from 1 to 10 tonnes. Silos are huge bins made with steel, alluminium or concrete. Usually steel and alluminium bins are circular in shape. The capacity of silo ranges from 500 to 4,000 tonnes. A silo has facilities for loading and unloading grains.

Institutions Involved

- Indian Grain Storage Institute (IGSI), Hapur with its branch at Ludhiana and Hyderabad have developed several metal bins of different capacities for scientific storage of grain in rural areas.
- National Centre for Insect Pest Management (NCIPM), IARI, New Delhi.

□□□

28

Nematode Management

The term Nematode has been derived from a Greek word *Nemata* for which the literal meaning is thread. Sometimes they are called eelworms because of their resemblance to the eel fish and the round body (Transverse Section) of worms. Nematodes are soft body heterotrophic, hermaphrodite, exhibiting a serpentine motion through the lateral creeping side.

A plant disease with which association of a nematode could be noticed was first reported by Nedham is England in 1743.

- During 1950 over 90% of 22 million plants of black pepper were destroyed by yellow diseases, which were later diagnosed to be caused by *Radopholus similis* nematode. The extensive losses to the potato crop were noticed which were caused by *Globodera roastochienensis* (Golden Nematode) in U.K., which laid the development of plant Nematology.
- Barbour reported root knot nematode on tea plant in South India. It was the first report of plant parasitic nematode from India.

1913 -1919 Butler reported for the first time **'ufra disease of rice'** from West Bengal, which was caused by *Dytelenchus angustus*.

1936 Dastur reported 'white tip disease of rice', which was caused by *Aphelenchoides besseyi*.

1959 Vasudeva reported Cereals Cyst Nematode (*Heterodera avenae*) from Rajasthan.

1961 Johns reported Golden Nematode.

1966 Nayer, Das and Menon reported burrowing nematode *Radopholus similes* from banana plantation.

1969 Nematological Society of India was established at division of nematology IARI (New Delhi). The society first started its Journal "Indian Journal of Nematology" in 1971.

Sexual Dimorphism

Sexual dimorphism in certain nematode species play an important role in the characteristic shape of the females to attain pear shape (*Meloidogyne* spp.) whereas lemon shaped female are seen in *Heterodera* spp. In the *Globodera* spp. females are round in shape whereas kidney shaped females are found in *Rotylenchus renyformis*. The females of *Anguina* spp. are swollen with increase in body width, whereas the females of *Tylechulus* have long neck.

Size of Nematodes

The size of plant parasitic nematode ranges between 200-800 micron and seldom goes beyond one mm of size. The smallest plant parasitic nematode is reported from *Pratylenchus* spp., which has the length of 150-180 micron whereas the largest plant parasitic nematode belongs to genus *Paralongidorus,* having size of 8-10 millimetre.

- In non-plant parasitic category of nematodes, the *Graffiola* spp. has the smallest size of 100-150 micron and the largest being *Placentonema gigantisima* measuring 8 m in length, which is a parasite of whale sperm.

Morphology of Nematodes

The body of nematode is composed of two different tubes, the outer body wall and inner body tube. **Outer Body Wall** is composed of three different layers, *viz.* cuticle, hypodermis and musculature. **Cuticle** is the outermost covering of the body of the nematode, which is delicate flexible, transparent and semi-permeable in nature. Cuticle is composed of three different layers, *i.e.* cortex, matrix and basal lamella. **Hypodermis** is the layer in the outer body tube beneath the cuticle. It is thicker than the cuticle, which provides the stream to the nematode body. **Musculature** is present below the hypodermal layer in the interchordal region, representing muscles of the nematode.

Classification of Important Nematodes

Phylum: Nematoda
Suborder: Tylenchida
Super-family (A): Tylenchoidea
Family:

1. Anguinidae:
   Genera: 1. *Anguina*: Wheat or seed gall nematode
   2. *Ditylenchus*: Stem or bulb nematode
2. Belonolaimidae:
   Genus: 1. *Belonolaimus*: Sting nematode of cereal, legume and cucurbits
2. *Tylenchorhynchus*: Stunt nematode
3. Pratylenchidae:
   Genus: *Pratylenchus:* Lesion nematode
4. Hoplolaimidae:
   Genus: 1. *Hoplolaimus:* Lance nematode of Maize, Sugarcane, Cotton
   2. *Rotylenchus*: Spiral nematode
5. Heteroderidae:
   Genus: 1. *Globodera:* Round cyst nematode of Potato
   2. *Heterodera:* Cyst nematode of Tobacco
   3. *Meloidogyne*: Root knot nematode

Super-family (B): Crinconematodea

Family 1 Crinconematodae:
Genus: *Crinconemella*: Ring nematode of wood plants.
Family 2. Paratylenchidae:
Genus *Paratylenchus:* Pin nematode.
Super order: Aphelenchina
Family: 1. Aphelenchoididae:
Genus: *Aphlenchoides*: Foliar nematode of almost all crops.
Sub-order: Dorylaimida.
Family: 1. Longidoridae:
Genera 1. *Longidorus*: Needle nematode.
2. *Xiphinema*: Dagger nematode.
Family 2. Trichodoridae:
Genera 1. *Paratrichodorus:* Stubby root nematode of vegetables.
2. *Trichodorus*: Stubby nematode of potato.

Important Diseases Caused by Nematodes

Disease	Responsible nematode
Ufra disease of rice	*Ditylenchus angustus*
Potato tuber rot	*Ditylenchus destructor*
Wheat ear cockle	*Auguina tritici*
Potato cyst nematode	*Globodera rostochinensis*
Root knot nematode of cucumber and tomato	*Meloidogyne incognita*
Root knot nematode of tobacco, sugarcane, banana and vegetables	*Meloidogyne javanica*
Molya disease of wheat and barley	*Heterodera avenae*
Rice white tip nematode	*Aphelenchoides besseyi*
Citrus slow decline nematode	*Tylenchulus semi-penetrans*
Banana rhizome rot, pepper slow wilt	*Radopholus similis*
Reniform nematode in cotton, maize, cow pea, black gram and banana	*Rotylenchus reniformis*
Root lesion of coffee	*Pratylenchus coffeae*

Important Nematodes Transmitting Viruses

Name of nematode	Virus transmitted
Longidorus macrosoma	Prunus necrotic ring spot virus
Xiphinema americanum	Tobacco ring spot virus
Paratrichadorus teres	Pea early browning virus
Trichodorus similis	Tobacco rattle virus

Nematode Management

1. **Crop rotation:** *Heterodera, Globodera* and *Meloidogyne* do not survive in soil for long time and they can be controlled by adopting proper crop rotation.
2. **Clean seed:** *Anguina tritici* galls are found mixed with wheat seed therefore, cleaning of seed controls nematode.
3. **Cleaning of farm implements:** Nematodes do not move more than a few inches in a year of their own; rather they are transmitted by some agency. The infested soil sticking to farm implements should be cleaned before taking them to new field.
4. **Selection of healthy propagating material:** Banana rhizome ro nematode spreads through suckers. Hence healthy suckers alone should be used.
5. **Organic manures:** Organic manures enhance nematophagous (fungi attacking on nematodes) fungi and antagonistic bacteria hence amendment of soil with organic manures reduces the nematode infestation.
6. **Enemy plants:** Root exudates of some plants are inhibitory to nematodes, *e.g. Tagetes erecta* reduces *Pratylenchus* infestation Asparagus reduces *Paratrichodorus; Christiei crotolaria* reduces *Meloidogyne;* white mustard reduces potato cyst nematode Intercropping with enemy plants provides beneficial results.
7. **Trap cropping:** Oats is an efficient trap crop for *Heterodera avenae* which attacks wheat and barley.
8. **Biological control:** Many nematophagous fungi; *Pseudomonas* bacteria; virus infection in *Meloidogyne incognita;* amoeboid organisms attacking larvae of potato cyst nematode are responsible to control nematode biologically.
9. **Physical methods:** Passing the steam into the soil through perforated pipes kills potato cyst nematodes. Hot water treatment is useful to control cyst nematodes in potato tubers. Rice white tip nematode can be eliminated by hot water treatment.
10. **Chemical control:** Many fumigants are available to control nematodes, *e.g.* Methyl bromide (Dowfume MC-2) @ 400-900 kg/ha, dichloropropene (Telone) at 500-900 kg/ha, dibromochloro propane (Nemagon) at 120 kg/ha, and metham- sodium (vapam) Some of the insecticide granules also reduce nematode population *e.g.* Aldicarb (Temik) at 11 kg/ha and Oxamyl (vydate) @ 11 kg/ha Carbofuran @ 075-1.0 kg/ha.
11. **Quarantine:** Potato cyst nematode can be controlled through quarantine; strict quarantine prevents the movement of the nematode from one country to another as well as one state to other state in India.

□□□

29

Plant Protection Appliances

Pest: Pest is any organism that causes economic loss in terms of some human resources. Under the category of pest, weeds, insects, fungi, bacteria, viruses, nematodes, rodents, and birds are included.

- Pest cause heavy **losses**, Weeds (33%), Diseases (26%), Insects (20%), Rodents (6-8%), Birds (1-2%) and others (1-3%), of total production. Despite all the control efforts used, pests annually destroy about 35 per cent of all crops worldwide.

Pest management is done on the principle of prevention, suppression, and eradication.

Existing Practices of Management of Pests

Method of management	Practices used
Physical control	Physical removal, barriers, traps and environmental manipulation, etc.
Cultural control	Crop rotation, cropping systems, crop spacing, trap crops, tillage, etc.
Plant resistance	Immunity, resistance, tolerance, etc.
Biological control	Parasites, predators, viruses, bacteria, fungi, protozoa, nematodes, etc.
Genetic control	Male sterile technique, hybrid sterility, chromosomal translocation, etc.
Chemical control	Pesticides, insect hormones, and pheromones.
Integrated control	Rational use of all the above pest control methods, rather solely depending upon any one.

PESTICIDE FORMULATIONS

The formulations used in pest management are the mixture of active ingredients (a.i.) and inert matter in certain proportions to kill insects at the level best. These formulations may be either solid or liquid:

Solids

- **Dusts (D):** Free flowing powder contains active ingredient or technical material in the range of 2-10% and inert matter.
- **Granules (G)**: Granules contain active ingredient in the range of 3-10% and granule base.
- **Water dispersible (wettable) powders (WP):** Free flowing powder contains technical material (a.i.) in the range of 25-75% and wetting, dispersing agent, and carrier.
- **Water-soluble powders (WSP):** Similar to water dispersible powders but active ingredient is soluble in water.

Liquids

- **Water-soluble liquids (SL):** Liquid formulations based on technical material, which are soluble in water, contain 36-85% active ingredient and solvent.
- **Emulsifiable concentrate (EC):** Liquid formulations based on technical material, which are not soluble in water, contain 25-80% active ingredient solvent and emulsifier.
- **Fumigants:** Formulations used for grain storage.
- **Flowable concentrates:** Thick slurry like, formulations mixable in water.
- **Aerosols:** Liquid under pressure filled in cans, which upon release give a misty spray.
- **Ultra low volume (ULV) formulations:** Such formulations are suitable for ultra low volume applications.

Types Of Appliances Used In Plant Protection

		Manual		**Power operated (through gasoline engine, PTO tractor, electricity, etc.)**	
		Portable	**Movable**	**Portable**	**Movable**
Sprayers	**Energy base**				
Used for soluble powder, wettable powder, emulsifiable concentrate, liquid and flowable	* Hydraulic	Lever operated knapsack	Foot operated	Piston pump operated	Piston type
		Shoulder hanged knapsack	Rocker		Diaphragm type
		sliding	Stirrup	Diaphragm	Roller type
	Gaseous			Mist blower	Blower type

concentrates.	Centri-fugal	Knapsack type	Traction type	Spinning disc type	Spinning disc type Wire gauze with disc and blade
Dusters Used for dust-based formulations	Plunger type Bellower type Bellower type Rotary	Hand held Belly mounted Knapsack type Hand held Shoulder mounted Knapsack type Belly mounted		Mist bellower type	Bellower Rotary type
Spreaders Used for spreading granules	Bellower or rotary type	Knapsack type belly mounted	Traction type	Mist bellower type	Spreader type

*Droplets produced by hydraulic nozzle are not uniform in size.

NOZZLE

It atomizes liquid into droplets; disperses the droplets in a specific pattern and provide hydraulic momentum. Nozzles may be with strainer or without strainer. Nozzles based on their tip patterns are grouped into three, *viz.* hollow cone pattern, flood jet pattern, and flat fan pattern:

1. **Hollow cone pattern:** It produces finer droplets. Spray penetrates better into the foliage. In such pattern the spray angle is narrow to medium (>45° but <110°). It is suitable for **insecticide** spray.
2. **Flood jet pattern:** It produces course droplets giving wider coverage. Spray angle is wide (>110°). Suitable for **herbicide** spray.
3. **Flat fan pattern:** It produces medium sized droplets giving even and uniform coverage. The spray angle is narrow to medium (>45° but <110°). It is suitable for **herbicide** spray.

Nozzles are two types, *viz.* adjustable nozzle and double swirl spray nozzle.

1. **Adjustable nozzle:** It is most suitable for targets which are not within the reach of a man, as it gives wide angle hollow cone to a straight solid stream forming a jet to a cone type of spray pattern.
2. **Double swirl spray nozzle:** It is used for simultaneous spraying in two different directions. Two different nozzles with different nozzle tips are fitted (like hollow cone, solid cone or flat fan) together to cover different directions simultaneously. It is suitable for high volume application of pesticides.

- **Angle and swath of nozzle tip orifice:** The shape and size of 'nozzle tip orifice' controls the spray angle, discharge rate and spray pattern. Finer the tip orifice (or lesser the angle) form narrow swath, whereas wider tip orifice form wider swath. Flood jet pattern has wider swath and hollow cone or flat fan pattern has narrow swath.

PRESSURE IN SPRAY

Spraying is done at either low (10 pound per square inch) or high (40 lb PSI).

- **Low pressure:** In the low pressure, there is low flow rate, coarser droplets and smaller fan angle.
- **High pressure:** It is characterized by the higher flow rate, finer droplets and bigger fan angle.
- **Droplet size** (diameter of droplet) and **Droplet density** (number of droplets per unit area of target) are two important factors for effective spraying.
- **Droplet diameter** is measured as median of either volume or number of droplets.
- Volume of droplet is a cubical (inclusive of length, breath and height) relation whereas; area of spray is a square (only length and breath) relation. If the droplet size is reduced from 2 μm^3 to 1 μm^3, number of droplets produced will increase by 8 times from the same volume.

Required Droplet Size

Target pests	Droplet sizes (Microns)
Flying insects	10-50
Insects on foliage	30-50
Foliage spray	40-100
Soil application	250-500

Spray and Droplet size

Name of spray	Droplet size	Amount required	Remark
High volume	0.5-3.0 mm	700 litres/ha for ground spray 1,120 litres/ha-foliar spray	Suitable for insecticides, fungicides, herbicides; Knapsack sprayer or tractor-mounted sprayers are used.
Low volume	15-40 μm	225-400 litre/ha for ground spray350-800 litres/ha-foliar spray	Suitable for insecticides, and fungicide; motorized Knapsack sprayers are used.
Ultra low volume	35-70 μm	20 litres/ha for ground spray 56 litres/ha for foliar spray	Suitable for insecticides; High RPM spinning disc, motorized knapsack sprayers fitted with special spinning disc are used.

Number of Droplets Required Per Unit Area (General Consideration)

Pesticides types	Number of droplets per unit area
Translocated herbicides	5-10 droplets/cm^2
Insecticides and systemic fungicides	20 droplets/cm^2
Non-systemic fungicides	50-70 droplets/cm^2

$$\text{Spraying efficiency (\%)} = \frac{\text{Minimum spray volume required}}{\text{Actual spray volume applied}} \times 100$$

Care and Maintenance of Pesticide Appliances

Before spraying

- Cleaning of all components particularly filling and suction strainer, spray tank, cut off device and nozzles.
- Replacement of sworn out parts like 'O' rings, seal, gasket, worn out nozzle tips, hose clamps and valves.
- Checking the nozzle spray pattern and discharge rate.
- Calibration of sprayer, settings of sprayer speed and nozzle swath by adjusting spray height and nozzle spacing.
- Ensuring the availability of soap, towel, and water for concerns with spraying.

During spraying

- Take only that much of amount of pesticide which is to be used.
- Make sure pesticides are mixed in correct quantities
- Wear appropriate clothing.
- Do not spray in high wind, temperature and rain.
- Avoid drift by choosing proper direction.
- Do not drink, eat, and smoke while spraying.
- Never blow clogged nozzles with mouth.
- Follow correct technique and pressure.
- Never allow children during mixing.
- Never leave pesticide unattended in field.
- Never spray if wind is blowing toward pastureland

After spraying

- Left pesticide should be disposed off in pits dug on wasteland.
- Never empty the tank into irrigation canals or ponds. Always clean equipment properly.
- Do not use empty pesticide containers for any purpose. Crush and burry the containers in dump.
- Clean buckets, jars, etc. used in spraying.
- Remove and wash clothing and footwear.
- Keep an accurate record of pesticide usage.
- Prevent persons from entering treated areas.
- Mark the sprayed plots with a flag.

Abbreviations

VMD: Volume Median Diameter

NMD: Narrow Median Diameter

Institution Involved

Control Plant Protection Training Institute Hyderabad (A.P)

❑❑❑

30

Fundamentals of Horticulture

The word horticulture has been derived from two Latin words, *hortus*, "garden," and *colere*, "to cultivate".

Pomology deals with fruit and nut crops; **Olericulture** with herbaceous plants for vegetables; **Floriculture** for production of flowers and ornamentals including cut flowers, pot plants, and greeneries; **Ornamental and Landscaping** is a little broad category that includes plants for the landscape, including lawn turf, shrubs, trees, and climbers.

Nutrition in fruits: Fruits have several vitamins, proteins, and minerals therefore they are rightly called **protective foods.**

Vitamins and Their Sources in Fruits/Nuts

Vitamin(s)	Source
Vitamin A	Mango, apricot fresh, raspberry, papaya, loquat, dates, jackfruit
Vitamin B_1	Cashewnut, Walnut, Almond, Apricot, Banana, Apple and Plum etc.
Vitamin B_2	Bael, Litchi, Papaya, Pineapple, Pomegranate, etc.
Vitamin B_3	Apricot dried, Bael, Custard Apple, Mango, etc.
Vitamin B_6	Avocadoes, Peach, Grapes, Guava, Plum and Bananas
Vitamin B_{12}	Avocadoes, Peach, Grapes, Guava, Plum and Bananas
Vitamin C	Cherry, Aonla, Guava, Orange, Lemon, Lime, Grape, Strawberry, Gooseberry, Pineapple

- **Proteins** are necessary for the formation and maintenance of body tissue, which can be availed from Cherry, Avacado, Custard apple, Banana, Guava, Apricot, Grape, Palm, Peach, Cashewnut, Almond and Pistachio-nut.

- **Carbohydrates** are found in Dates (75.8%), Custard apple (23.6%), Jackfruit (19.8%), Sapota (25.8%), Bael (31.8%), Grapes (19.2%), Mango (16.2%), Apple and Pear (14.9%), Litchi (14.6%).
- **Fats** are mostly found in Walnut (64.5%), Coconut dried (62.3%), Almond (58.9%), Pistachio (53.5%), Cashewnut (46.9%), Avacado (24.0%).
- **Minerals** like **Calcium** from Fig, Citrus, Guava, Dates, Sapota, Grapes, Custard apple, Apricot dried, Cherry; **Phosphorus** from Bael, Raspberry, Avacado, Apricot dried, Dates, Lasora, Pomegrnate etc.; **Iron** from Karonda, Cherry, Dates, Guava, Grapes, Apricot, Avocado, Custard apple, Sapota and Plum.

Horticultural Zones

- **Temperate zones:** Temperate zones are characterized where frost in winter occurs either regularly or rarely. It is never classified based on latitude and/or longitude.
- **Tropical zones**: There is no sharp line of demarcation between the tropics and the subtropics; only the elevation is a determining factor for such zone.

Fruit Growing Zones of India

	Zone	States under zone
1.	Temperate zone	Jammu and Kashmir, Himachal Pradesh, Parts of Uttar Pradesh, and Parts of Nagaland, Arunanchal, Niligiris and Palni hills.
2.	North western sub-tropical zone	Rajasthan, Punjab, Haryana, Parts of Uttar Pradesh and Parts of Madhya Pradesh.
3.	North eastern sub-tropical zone	Bihar, Assam, Meghalaya, Tripura, Parts of Arunanchal and Parts of West Bengal.
4.	Central tropical zone	Parts of Madhya Pradesh, Parts of Maharashtra, Gujarat, Parts of Orissa, Parts of West Bengal, Parts of Andhra Pradesh, Parts of Karnataka.
5.	Southern tropical zone	Parts of Karnataka, Parts of Andhra Pradesh, Parts of Tamil Nadu, Parts of Kerala.
6.	Coastal tropical humid zone	Coastal Maharashtra, Kerala, Andhra Pradesh, Tamil Nadu, Orissa, West Bengal., Tripura, Mizoram, Parts of Gujarat.

Systems of Planting Fruit Plants

There are different systems used for transplanting saplings.

1. **Square system:** In this system whole field is divided into squares and saplings are transplanted at each corner of square.
2. **Rectangular system:** In this system field is divided into rectangles and trees are planted at each corner in the straight row running at the right angles. It allows more trees for planting in the row.
3. **Triangular system:** In this system field is divided into triangles and trees are planted on a corner of.each angle.
4. **Hexagonal system:** In this system, a tree is planted at each corner of an equilateral triangle. In this way six trees form a hexagon with the seventh tree in the centre. This system is preferred if land is costly or more productive.
5. **Quincunx system:** In this system, one tree is planted in the centre of the square of permanent trees. This tree is short spanned and called **filler**. In the place of filler fruits like Banana, Papaya, Pomegranate, and Phalsa can be planted. This filler tree is removed when main crop develop with its full canopy.
6. **Contour system:** In this system, contours are drawn according to slope. Planting is done at the every contour for uniform distribution of irrigation water.

PROPAGATION

Propagation can be achieved sexually by seeds or asexually by specialized vegetative structures of the plant or employing such techniques as cutting, layering, grafting, and tissue culture.

Types of Propagation

1. **Seed propagation:** It is most common in self-pollinated plants. In the seed propagation seed dormancy is the limiting factor.
2. **Vegetative propagation**: Asexual or vegetative propagation is based on the ability of plants to regenerate tissues and parts. It is accomplished by use of (1) apomictic seed; (2) specialized vegetative structures such as runners, bulbs, corms, rhizomes, offshoots, tubers, stems, and roots; (3) layers and cuttings; (4) grafting and budding; and (5) tissue culture.

Vegetative Structures

Many plants produce specialized vegetative structure such as tubers that enable the plant to survive adverse conditions or organs adapted for natural propagation, *e.g.* runners or rhizomes.

- **Bulbs** commonly grow at ground level, though bulb like structures (**bulbils**) may form on aerial stems, as in lilies or in association with flower parts, as in the onion.
- **Buds** in the axils (angle between leaf and stem) of the fleshy leaves may form miniature bulbs (**bulblets**) that when grown to full size are known as **offsets**.
- **Offsets or offshoots** are the lateral shoots, which upon rooting serve to propagate vegetatively, *e.g.* ratoons, or slips.
- **Corms** are short, fleshy, underground stems without fleshy leaves. Corms are used to propagate **Gladiolus and Crocus**.
- **Slips** arise from the fruiting stem and crown on top of the fruits, *e.g.* Pineapple.
- **Rhizomes** are horizontal, underground stems that are compressed (*e.g. Iris*), or slender (*e.g.* turf grasses).
- **Runners** are specialized aerial stems, a natural agent of increase and spread of plants, *e.g.* strawberry, gernanium.
- **Tubers** are fleshy enlarged portions of underground stem. The edible portion of the potato is, the tuber, is also used as a means of propagation.
- **Roots** may also be structurally modified as propagative and food-storage organs. These tuberous roots, fleshy swollen structures, readily form shoots (called adventitious, because they do not form from nodes), *e.g.* sweet potato and dahlia.
- **Suckers** are shoots that rise adventitiously from roots. Red raspberry is propagated by suckers.

3. **Apomixis:** Apomixis is the development of asexual seed in a form of vegetative propagation for some horticultural crops including mango and citrus.

Methods of Propagation

1. **Layering and cutting**: When the regenerated part is still attached to the plants the process is called **layerage, or layering** whereas, if the regenerating portion is detached from the plantd the process is called **cuttage** or **cutting**.

- Layering often occurs naturally as in black raspberry, the drooping stems tend to root upon contact with the soil.

2. **Marcottage or air layering:** This process is successful with certain hard-to-root species. A branch tip is girdled (a ring of bark is removed from around the branch). The area surrounding the girdle is then packed with moist sphagnum moss and wrapped in plastic. Eventually, a pronounced callus (thick new tissue) forms at the upper side of the girdle, and roots appear. These roots grow into the sphagnum moss, *e.g.* **Crotons** are propagated using this method.
3. **Grafting:** Grafting involves the joining of the **rootstocks** and **scions** together. However, if more than two parts are involved, the middle piece is called the **interstock**. Stock cambium and scion cambium forms callus tissue to fill the injured portion in both rootstock and scion. Grafting may be classified into different types, Inarch grafting, Tongue grafting, Saddle grafting, Cleft grafting, Veneer grafting (most common for Mango), Crown grafting, Side grafting, Bridge grafting, Buttress grafting.

- Success in grafting depends upon the warm temperature (80-85 °F), which increases callus formation and improves "take" in grafting.

Important Rootstocks of Fruit Crops

Crop	Rootstock	Remarks
Apple	M 9	Suited for high density planting; resistant to woolly aphid.
	M 27 (M 13 × M 9)	Suited for high density planting.
Wood apple	*Aegle fraeglegaboensis*	
Jujube	*Zizyphus nummularia, Z. rotundifolia*	For dwarfing.
Cherry	*Prunus puddum, P. erasoides,P. mehlab, P. aviaum*	For vigorous and wild trees.
Citrus	Citranges	Tolerant to gummosis and tristeza
	Citrus unshitu	Tolerant to freezing temperatures
	Cleopatra mandarin	Tolerant to tristeza and nematodes
	Flying dragon	For dwarfing.
	Karna Khatta	Suitable for heavy soils of U.P.
	Rangpur lime	Suitable for heavy and deep soils;

		tolerant to tristeza.
	Severnia bouxifolia	Resistant to salts.
	Soh sarkar	For kinnow.
	Sour orange	Suitable for sandy loam soil.
Citrus	Trifoliate orange	Resistant to Phytophthora, tristeza and nematodes; suitable for shallow and high rainfall areas.
Custard apple	*Annona glabra*	
Fig	*Ficus glomerata*	Resistant to nematodes
Grape	Dogride	Resistant to pierce's disease and Phylloxera.
Guava	*Psidium friedrichsthalianum* var. *lucidum*	Dwarfing and wilt resistance.
	P. pumilum	For dwarfing.
Mango	Kurrukan	Resistant to salts; polyembryonic.
	Moovandan and Nekkare	Tolerant to salts.
	Olour	Vigorous crop.
	Rumani	Dwarfing.
	Vellaikolamban	Dwarfing and alloploid.

4. **Budding:** In budding a bud is removed from its stem along with a shield of bark and is inserted into a T-shaped cut at the base of the stock plant. The site is then wrapped with a grafting rubber band. After the bud has taken up, the rootstock is removed. Budding is classified into Sheild budding, Patch budding, Forkert budding, and Ring budding.

Training/Pruning

There are several methods of training and pruning which involve, Bower system, Cordon, Dwarf pyramid, Espalier, Head system, Head row plantation, Meadow, Palmate, Spindle bush, Tatura trellis system, Trellis system and Kniffin system.

Cold Frames

Cold frames are 'low enclosed beds' covered with a removable sash of glass or plastic, used to start the plants before the normal growing season. In cold frames radiant energy passes through the transparent top and warms the soil directly.

PLANT GROWTH REGULATORS

Certain substances affect the growth of plants miraculously, are referred as hormones. The term hormone has been derived from a Greek word for which the literal meaning in English is to urge or to stimulate. Hormones of plants are referred as phyto-hormones.

Important Growth Regulators

Name growth regulators	Example
Auxins	Indole acetic acid (IAA), Indole butyric acid (IBA), NPA, NAA, 2, 4-D, etc.
Gibberellins	Gibberellic acid (GA)
Cytokinins	Kinetin, Zeatin
Ethylene	Ethylene
Dormins	Abscisic acid (ABA), Phaseic Acid
Flowering hormones	Florigin, Anthesin, Vernalin
Phenolic substances	Coumarin
Miscellaneous natural substances	Vitamins, Phytochrome Tranmatic Substances
Synthetic growth retardants	CCC, Amo 1618, Phosphin (D, Morphactin, Malformis)
Miscellaneous synthetic substances	Synthetic auxins, Synthetic Cytokinins

Functions of Auxins

Auxins are characterized for causing polar translocation (the apical development); root initiation; delay in abscission; differentiation of xylem elements; stimulation of apical bud formation; inhibition of lateral bud formation; cell division and shoot elongation; increase in RNA contents; role in reproductive phase of flowering, etc.

Applications of Auxins

- **Germination**: IAA, IBA, NPA, 2, 4-D are mostly used to promote germination. Seeds are soaked at low concentrations.
- **Root**: NAA, 10% induces 100% rooting in mango (Dashehari, Langra). IBA with Sugar application leads to greater number of root-structures and changed vascular bundles.

- **Flowering**: IAA promotes formation of female flowers. Increases spikelet numbers, leaf numbers, weight, and number of grains in wheat. NAA and IAA increase boll-set in cotton (*G. hirsutum*).
- **Parthenocarpy**: IBA, NAA induce seedless fruiting.
- **Fruit setting**: By using 2, 4, 5-T fruit setting and yield of ber fruit increases. IAA, IBA, and NAA induce high percentage fruit set. Prevention of pre-mature drop of fruits is brought out by 2, 4, D, IAA, IBA, 2, 4, 5-T particularly, in sweet oranges (@ 100-500 ppm).
- **Tissue and organ culture**: IAA and Kinetin.
- **Auxins as inhibitors**: High concentration of auxins inhibits the growth and exerts toxic effect on plants. In normal case, self-produced auxins inhibit the growth and development of lateral buds, and as a result apical buds, remains dormant.

Gibberellins

Second most important category of growth hormones includes more than 60 types of gibberellins named as GA_1, GA_2 up to GA_{60}. About 51 types are found in higher plants. These are characterized for its apical bud dormancy; role in sub-apical meristem; cell elongation; fruit growth; flowering; and metabolic activities of food in seed storage cells.

- **Mechanism of Gibberellins actions**: GA exerts its physiological effect on altering the auxin status of tissue. It acts at the gene level to cause suppression of specific genes. The activated genes by producing new enzymes bring about observed morphological changes.

Applications of Gibberellins

- **Germination**: Increases length of hypocotyls and cotyledonary leaf area.
- **Root growth**: Gibberellins inhibit root growth.
- **Leaf expansion**: Leaves become broader and enlarged (Cabbage, Sweet corn) upon application of gibberellins.
- **Hyponasty of leaves**: GA treated leaves of chrysanthemum plants hold their leaves more erect.

- **Flowering**: GA induces flowering in long day plants and promotes formation of male flowers.
- **Parthenocarpy**: Induces parthenocarpy (*e.g.* Brinjal, Guava).
- **Fruit setting**: Increases fruit setting (Phalsa, Sweet lime, Grapes).
- **Stem elongation**: Increases number of internodes in *Chorchorus capsularis* and extension of stems.
- **Breaking dormancy**: In temperate fruits, buds become dormant in later summer and do not sprout even when exposed to sufficient moisture, temperature and oxygen. GA overcomes this dormancy and enhances cell elongation.
- **Other uses**: Sprayed on fruits to prevent rind disorders. Thomson seedless grape bunches if sprayed with GA, also causes elongation of bunch.

Cytokinins

Cytokinins are characterized by the initiation of cell division; delaying senescence; callus development; and counteract apical dominance (apical bud development). In tissue culture high auxin and low cytokinin give rise to root development; low auxin and high cytokinin encourage shoot development.

Application of Cytokinins

- **Mobility**: Immobile; obstructs moment of amino acids, phosphate and various other substances.
- **Nucleic acid metabolism**: Quickly increases the amount of RNA and decreases DNA.
- **Protein synthesis**: Increases DNA and rate of protein synthesis.
- **Flowering**: Induce flowering in short day plants.

Abscisic Acid (ABA)

Induces bud dormancy; promotes senescence; accelerates leaf abscission (in cotton plant); and counteracts GA.

Ethylene

Ethylene is a hydrocarbon compound, which acts as a plant hormone to stimulate fruit ripening as well as rooting and flowering of some plants. An ethylene-releasing compound, 2-chloroethylphosphonic acid, has most promising work of uniform ripening of tomatoes and the stimulation of latex flow in rubber.

Role of Ethylene

- **Abscission**: Principle accelerator of abscission and capable of promoting changes associated with pre-abscission and aging of leaves, petioles, flowers and fruits.
- Auxins increase ethylene level in plants, resulting into increase percentage of female flowers, apical bud dominance and leaf epinasty.
- De-greening occurs after ethylene treated (5-10 ppm) parts are exposed to air, which accelerate maturity and induces uniform ripening (Pineapple).

Florigen

It is responsible for flower initiation in plants. It is synthesized in older leaves and then transferred to growing regions, where it initiates floral buds.

Morphactins

They are synthetic growth regulators, *e.g.* Phenoxyalkancarboxylic acid (synthetic auxin); substituted benzoic acid; maleic acid hydrazide; Flurene (carboxylic acid and their derivatives); Chlorflurenol; Chlorfluron; Flurenol; Methyle benzilate; and Dichlorflurenol etc. The growth inhibitor maleic hydrazide has been effective in preventing the sprouting of onions and potatoes.

Role of Morphactins

- **Seed germination:** Inhibits seed germination.
- **Growth of seedlings**: Inhibits growth of both roots and shoots; this property of morphactins is similar to cytokinin.
- **Stem elongation:** Morphactins cause dwarfing effects.
- **Apical dominance and branching**: Increase tillering and stimulates lateral shoot growth in cereals and grasses.
- **Flowering**: Morphactins prevent, flowering in short day plants, sequence of flowering, position and number of flowers and parthenocarpy, etc.

Traumatic Acid

Traumatic acid increases activity in response to wound or injury, therefore it is also called **wound hormone**. It stimulates meristmatic cork cambium to cover wounded or injured portions.

Some Other Growth Regulators

- **Triacontanol**: Saturated primary alcohol isolated from shoots of alfalfa, increases growth in Rice and Maize.
- **Brassins**: Steroid growth promoters isolated from pollen grains of rapeseed. It has distinct growth promoting activity.
- **Xanthoxin**: Potent growth inhibitor, which is converted metabolically to ABA.
- **Batasins**: Isolated from yam, causes dormancy in bulb crops.

Institutions and Societies Involved in Horticulture

- Indian Institute of Horticultural Research, Bangalore, Karnataka
- Indian Institute of vegetable Research, Varanasi, Uttar Pradesh
- Central Institute for Sub-Tropical Horticulture, Lucknow
- Central Plantation Crops Research Institute, Kasargod, Kerala
- Central Institute for Temperate Horticulture, Srinagar, Jammu and Kashmir
- Central Potato Research Institute, Shimla, Himachal Pradesh
- NRC for Cashew, Puttur, Karnataka
- NRC for Citrus, Nagpur, Maharashtra
- NRC for Oilpalm, Pedavegi, Andhra Pradesh
- NRC for Orchids, Pakyang, Sikkim
- NRC for Grapes, Pune, Maharashtra
- NRC for Litchi, Muzaffarpur, Bihar.
- NRC for Onion and Garlic, Rajgurunagar, Pune, Maharashtra
- NRC for Banana, Trichi, Tamil Nadu
- NRC on Seed Spices, Tabiji, Ajmer, Rajasthan
- NRC on Cashew, Puttur, Karnataka

Horticultural Societies

- The first society devoted to horticulture originated in 1804 as Royal Horticultural Society, England.

- The American Pomological Society was formed in 1848.
- The American Horticultural Society, established in 1945.
- The American Society for Horticultural Science was established in 1903.
- The International Society for Horticultural Science, formed in 1959 with permanent headquarters in The Hague.
- The scientific and technical horticultural literature since 1930 is abstracted in *Horticultural Abstracts*, prepared by the Commonwealth Bureau of Horticulture and Plantation Crops, East Malling, Kent, England.

❑❑❑

31

Fruit Production

Fruit is the mature ovary in flowering plants, together with all inseparably connected parts of the flower. The term "fruit" is often restricted to succulent, edible fruits of woody plants including melons, and strawberries.

Classification of fruits

Dry fruits	Examples
Dehiscent / capsular	
Legume	All legumes like pea, bean
Follicle	Calotropis
Siliqua	Mustard
Silicula	Capsella
Capsule	Okra, Datura, Cotton, Poppy
Indehiscent/achenial	
Achene	*Clamatis, Narvelia*
Caryopsis	Members of Graminae
Cypsella	Members of Compositae
Nut	Cashew nut, Litchi, Oak, Trapa
Samara	*Holoptelea indica* (Chilbil)
Schizocarpic or splitting fruits	
Lomentum	*Mimosa pudica,* Groundnut, Indian Laburnum, *Acacia, Tamarindus*
Cremocarp	Carrot, Coriender
Regma	Geranium, Castor
Carcerulus	*Ocimum,* Hollyhoek, *Abutilon*
Double samara	*Acer* spp.

Aggregate fruits

Etaerio of berries	Custard apple
Etaerio of drupe	Strawberry, Raspberry

Composite fruits

Sorosis	Pineapple, Jackfruit, Mulberry
Syconus	*Ficus* spp.
Succulent or Fleshy	
Drupe	Mango, Peach, Plum, Ber.
Berry	Guava, Grape, Banana, Papaya.
Pome	Watermelon, Muskmelon.
Hesperidium	All citrus fruits.
Balausta	Pomegranate.

TROPICAL AND SUB-TROPICAL FRUITS

Banana (*Musa paradisiaca*) × = 7, 9, 10, 11

India is the leading producer of Banana. It is cultivated mainly in Tamil Nadu, West Bengal, Kerala, Maharashtra, Gujarat, Karnataka, Assam, Andhra Pradesh and Bihar and commonly called **Adam's fig**. Inflorescence of banana is called **spadix**. Edible banana is developed by parthenogenesis.

- *Musa balbisiana* is a rich gene pool consisting of genes for resistance to various biotic and abiotic stresses.
- Application of cement kiln flue dust (0.5 kg/plant) and 30,000 litres of distillery effluent/acre with 60% K leads to 25% increase in bunch weight in both plant and Ratoon crops of Ney Poovan.
- **Radiotracers:** Radiotracers are used for nutrient feeding of banana from the distal end. This novel technique which, feed banana bunches through distal end for increased bunch weight, was developed by IIHR Bangalore.
- **Varieties:** Poovan, Champa, Amrit Sagar, Basrai, Safed Velchi, Lal Velchi, Rajeli Champa Mortaman, Rastali, Sirumalai, Chakkarekeli, Ney Poovan, Kadali, Pacha Nadan, Basrai (Mauritius, Vamankeli, Cavendish, Governor, Harichal), Robusta, Nendran bananas, Monthan, Myndoli and Pacha Montha Bathis; **Cultivars** Lady finger (Australia) and Grand Nain MS (France) are resistant to bunchy top of banana; **Hybrids:** Co 1, H 1, H 2, FHIA 1 (Sigatoka resistant).

- **Propagation and planting:** Propagated by sward suckers @ 2.5-3 kg/ha, planted in small pits of 2 m × 2 m (dwarf) and 4 m × 4 m (tall) size.
- **Manuring:** 20-25 kg FYM plus 150:150:300 g/plant NPK.
- **Irrigation:** Requires heavy irrigation with intervals of 7-10 days.
- **Harvesting:** Harvest after seven months of planting; fruits require three more months to ripen. **Yield** 26-55 t/ha.
- **Curing and Marketing:** The ripening of banana is done in several ways, *e.g.* exposing bunches to the sun, placing them over a hearth, wrapping them in closed godowns or through smoking. The application of Vaseline (a layer of clay or coal-tar) to the cut-ends of the stalks prevents rotting during ripening and storage.

Mango (*Mangifera indica*) amphidiploid, $2n = 4\times = 40$, Anacardiaceae

It is originated in Indo-Burma region. India is the largest producer f Mango. Vellaicollamban is the only octoploid ($2n = 8\times = 80$) variety. indhu is a seedless variety of mango. Rosica is the only mutant ultivar in mango.

- Five sprays of Micnelf along with 300 g Borocal (a micronutrient preparation) and 60% of recommended fertilizers could result in maximum fruit yield for Dashehri.
- **Varieties: Early;** *viz.* Bombay yellow, Alphonso, Gopal Bhog, Zafran; **Mid-late:** Langra, Desheri, Safeda Lucknow, Safeda Malihabad, Fajrizafrani; **Late:** Fajri, Same Bihisht, Chausa, Taimura **U.P.:** Bombai, Alphonso, Hemsagar, Krishna Bhog, Aman Dashehri, Gulab Khas, Langra, Aman Abbasi, Khasul-Khas, Sinduri, Sukal, Taimuria. **Polyembryonic:** Cambodina, Neeleshwar dwarf; **Hybrids:** Sindhu (Ratna × Alphonso), Ratna (Neelum × Alphonso), Arka Neelkiran (Neelum × Alphonso), Arka Anmol (Alphonso × Janardhan Prasad), Arka Puneet (Alphonso × Banganpalli), Arka Aruna Rumani (Rumani × Neelum) and Manjira (Rumani × Neelum) are some promising cultivars of mango.
- **Varieties suitable for Northern India**: Dashehri, Langra, Chausa, Bombay green; **Southern India:** Banglora, Neelum, Swaranrekha, Banganpalli, Alphonsho;p **Eastern India**: Himsagar, Langra, Fazli, Zardalu, Kishanbhog, Gulabkhas **Western India:** Alphonso, Rajapuri, Malkurad and Jamadar.

- Dashehri-51 is a regular bearing clone of Dashehri, which resistant to mango malformation. Bombay green is the be pollinators for Dashehri. Mango Bangalora is the heavy fruite (380 g) variety. Mango, EC 95.862, Ambika, H 1591, H 16 and H-533, are suitable for processing purpose.
- **Propagation and Planting:** Propagated by inarching or buddir *in situ*. Veneer grafting has been found to be the best method mango propagation. Planting is done in pits pre-filled wi FYM (45 kg) plus 225:45:225 g of NPK having a distance 15-17 m. The graft-joint should be at least 15 cm above th ground.
- **Manures and fertilizers:** 45-70 kg of FYM plus 500-700:70 1000:1200-1500 g NPK/tree. Nitrogen application at 450-5 g/tree during spring season provides regular bearing in tre and application of Ethrel (200 ppm) from September onwar induces flowering.
- There are several disorders in mango that include fruit dr (apply 2, 4-D @ 10 ppm): Spongy tissue (most common Alphonso), Black tip (Borax @ 0.8%); Clustering (or Jhoomk due; to improper pollination), Leaf scorch (due to chlori toxicity); and Internal necrosis (Boron deficiency).
- **Harvesting and yield:** The fruits mature in five to six month A grafted tree yields about 300-500 fruits in the tenth yea about 1,000 in the 15th year and 2,000 to 5,000 from the 20 year onwards.

Harvesting of fruits:

February to March	Malabar region
April to May	Western India
May to June	Deccan region
April to July	Coastal Andhra Pradesh
May to August	Mysore and Rayalaseema
June to August	Northern India

Citrus (*Citrus* spp.) $2n = 2x = 18$, $2n = 4x = 36$

Total area under citrus is over 67,650 hectares belonging primari to M.P., Tamilnadu and Maharashtra.

- Paclobutrazol @ 18 g/plant is effective in inducing floweri even in problematic high clay soils.

- Chlormequat chloroide (CCC) @ 2,000 ppm induces *hasta* flowering in October. Ledermycin (600 ppm) along with $ZnSO_4$ and $FeSO_4$ @ 200 g each per plant reduces citrus greening disease drastically.
- A hybrid between King × Willow leaf is called **Kinnow**, is the most successful introduction for commercial cultivation grown mainly in Nagpur district of Maharashtra.
- *Bahar* is the method of controlling irrigation for regularizing flowering in citrus.

Grapefruit (*Citrus paradisi*)

The name grapefruit has been derived from the habit of bearing the fruit in clusters like grapes. It is mostly cultivated in Punjab, western U.P. and in Poona (Maharashtra).

- **Varieties:** Marsh Seedless, Foster (pink-fleshed), Red Blush, Triumph, Saharanpur special, Thompson and Duncan (yellow-fleshed).
- **Propagation and planting:** It is propagated by budding or *in situ*. Mostly used rootstocks *kharna khatta*, the *Citrus karna* (Northern India) Jamburi (south India and Bombay-Deccan) and Rabab tenga (Assam).
- The harvesting can be done from January to March in the North and from September to November in the South India.

Lemon (*Citrus lemon*)

Lemon requires a comparatively cool climate for regular bearing. Propagated by seed. Baramasi, Assam Lemon, Gandhraj, Serville, Nepali, Oblong are important **cultivars.**

Acid lime (*Citrus aurantiifolia*)

India is the largest producer of acid lime. Andhra Pradesh is the leading state. Rangpur lime is used as rootstock for acid lime. Lime includes both sour (*kaghzi nimboo*) and sweet (*mitha nimboo*). Sour lime is propagated mainly from seed. Budding, layering, or morcotting are also practised. The tree is susceptible to frost. It flowers twice in a year in February-March and again in August. The main crop is obtained in August from the first flowering. The second crop is ready in the following February. Sweet lime is propagated through mature woodcuttings.

Mandarin Orange (*Citrus reticulata*)

It grows successfully in all tropical and sub-tropical parts of the country. It is cultivated under rainfed conditions in Coorg, Wynad tract, Palni Hills and the Nilgiris. In Assam, the main centres of production are the Khasi, Jaintia and Lushai Hills. The region around Nagpur produces a superior quality of Mandarins grown under irrigated conditions.

- **Varieties:** Nagpur orange, Khasi orange, the Coorg orange, Desi Emperor and the Sikkim orange.
- **Propagation:** The propagation of Mandarin orange is largely through seed, except the Nagpur and Emperor varieties, which are propagated by budding. The variety Emperor is budded on the *kharna khatta* rootstock. The *santra* orange is usually budded on rough lemon (jambhiri, Soh-myndong or *jatti khatti*) rootstock. Rangpur lime, Kodakthuli and Troyer citrage are good rootstocks for Mandarin.
- **Planting:** Trees are usually transplanted during the monsoon with a distance of 4.5-6 m.
- **Manuring:** 20-25 kg FYM plus 90 g each of NPK/tree for first year.
- **Harvesting:** Seeded trees bear fruits in 8-10 years whereas Budded trees start bearing from the fourth year onwards.

Sweet Orange (*Citrus sinensis*)

It is grown both under sub-tropical and tropical conditions. Dry season with distinct summer and winter having low rainfall are most favourable conditions.

- **Varieties:** Blood Red, Pineapple, Hamlin, Jaffa and Valencia Late (North India); Mosambi (Western India); Sathgudi and Batavian orange (South India).
- **Propagation and planting:** Propagated by budding. The most suitable rootstock is Jamberi or *jatti khatti*. The trees are planted 6 to 7.5 m apart each way in January or August-September in the North and in July-August in the South India. **Root Exposure** in the Bombay-Deccan region is given to bring them into flowering at a particular time of the year.
- **Manuring:** 20-25 kg FYM plus 90 g NPK/tree for first year.
- **Harvesting.** Bearing starts from the fourth year onwards. The main harvesting season is December to February in North and October to March in south India. In the Bombay-Deccan region, there are two main seasons, November to January for *ambe bahar*, and March to May for *mrig bahar*

Pummelo (*C. grandis*)

It is monoembryonic citrus species. Granulation is prominent disorder found in pummelo. Chakotara and Gargar are important varieties of pummelo.

Grape (*Vitis vinifera*) $2n = 38$

It is originated from Afghanistan and now it is cultivated in sub-tropical areas having well dry climates with short sharp winter. The grape grows best on light loamy soils with free drainage.

- **Varieties:** Black Prince, Bedana, Kandhari Dakh, Muscat of Alexandria, Perlette (Northern India); Thomson Seedless, Sultana, Kishmish White (Dry and temperate areas); Bangalore Blue, Pachadraksha, Anab-e-Shahi, Gulabi, Black Champa, Thompson Seedless (South India); and Cheema Sahebi, Anab-e-Shahi, Thompson Seedless (west).
- Grape Centennial Seedless is suitable for raisin, while Concord and Country Bangalore for juice making.
  Embryo rescue technique has been standardized in Thompson Seedless grape.
- Quality of Sharad Seedless grape can be improved with the use of GA_3 @ 50 ppm and BA @ 10 ppm. The sources of seedlessness, are Queen of vineyard and Pusa seedless.
- **Hybrids:** Arkavati (Black Champa × Thompson Seedless), Arka Kanchan (Anab-e-Shahi × Queen of Vineyard), Arka Hans (Bangalore Blue × Anab-e-Shahi), Arka Shyam (Bangalore Blue × Black Champa), Arka Neelmani (Black Champa × Thompson Seedless), Arka Sweta (Anab-e-Shahi × Thompson Seedless), Arka Majestic (Anab-e-Shahi × Black Champa), Arka Chitra (Angoor Kalan × Anab-e- Shahi), Arka Soma (Anab-e-Shahi × Queen of vineyard), Arka Trishna (Bangalore Blue × Convent Large Black), Arka Krishna (Black Champa × Queen of vineyard), Pusa Urvashi (Hur × Beauty Seedless) and Pusa Navrang (Madeleine Angavine × Ruby red).
- **Propagation and Planting**: Propagated by cuttings during October and February (North India) and transplanted in January-February at 2.5 m × 3.0 m (if vines are trained on the head system) and 6 m × 6 m (for the overhead pergola). Dogridge is a drought tolerant rootstock. It has become very popular in Maharashtra, Andhra Pradesh and northern Karnataka. Use of Dogridge helps mitigate twin problems of salinity and drought.

- **Manuring:** 25-30 kg FYM plus 70-90:540-570:135-180 g NPK/ vine.
- **Training and pruning:** It is important practice required for grape cultivation and is done in following ways:

1. **Head system**. The vines are trained in the form of a dwarf bush. They are allowed to grow into an upright stem having 3-4 lateral branches with the support and the developing shoot is cut off at a height of 1 to 1.25 m in July. The first pruning is done in February where lateral branches are shortened to spurs with one to two buds each.
2. **Cane system**: This system is suitable for training on a two-wire trellis. The trunk is headed back, as in the head system; four arms, two on each side of the trunk, are allowed to develop and are pruned to a 30-m length after a year. Fruit canes, each carrying 10 to 20 buds, develop on each arm, which is tied to the trellis wire.
3. **Cordon system**: When vine has reached a height of 0.5 to 1 m, the stem trained along the single-wire trellis. On each arm that develops from the trunk, short fruiting spurs, each carrying two to four buds, are allowed to remain at the time of pruning. The replacing spurs are also provided close to the base of the fruiting spurs.
4. **Pergola system**: It is also called **arbour** or **bower system**. In this method the vine is allowed to develop into two or three branches up to 1 m from the ground. The branches are fastened to the horizontal wires of the pergola and allowed to grow and spread on the roof. The branches that grow on the arms are pruned each year according to the mode of bearing of the variety planted.

Guava (*Psidium guajava*) 2*n* = 22 or 2*n* = 33

The total area under guava in the country is about 30,000 hectares, of which U.P. has the largest area (9,840 hectares), followed by Bihar (4,800 hectares). Guava fruits are rich in vitamin C (35 to 100 mg per 100 g) content.

- Allahabad Safeda and Sardar guavas produces maximum fruit yield in guava.
- Flowering is regulated (*Bahar*) by NAA @ 400-800 ppm or Ethepon @ 1,000-1,500 ppm or Urea @ 15-20% in May.
- **Varieties:** Lucknow-49 (wilt resistant), Allahabad Safeda, Seedless, Arka Mridula, Safed Jam (Allahabad Safeda × Kohir), Arka Amulya (Allahabad safeda × Seedless) and Hybrid 16-1.

- **Propagation and planting:** Propagated through seeds or inarching or layering including air layering planted at 5.5- 6m.

Papaya (*Carica papaya*) 2*n* = 18

Ranchi 1 variety produces maximum fruit yield, whereas maximum TSS is produced by Washington variety. Coorg Honey Dew (without male flowers) variety has either female or hermaphrodite flowers and produces fruits. Washington, Honey Dew (Madhubindu), Singapore, Pant Papaya 1, Pant Papaya 2, Pant Papaya 3, Pusa Dwarf, Pusa Giant, Pusa Majesty, Pusa Delicious, Co 1, Co 2, Co 3 Co 4, Co 5 (high content of papain), Co 6 and Ceylon are other important varieties. Pusa Nanha is a dwarf variety developed through gamma radiation.

- **Propagation:** Propagated through seeds.
- **Harvesting:** Fruits are ready for harvesting in ten months. Yield varies from 30 to 150 fruits per tree.

Pineapple (*Ananas comusus*) 2*n* = 50

It is originated from Brazil, primarily grown in humid tropical condition in Assam, W.B., Tripura, U.P., A.P., Kerala and Karnataka on 12,000 hectares of land.

- **Varieties:** Queen, Mauritius, Kew (for Canning), Cayenne and Singapore Spanish.
- **Propagation and planting:** Propagated from suckers or slips at 30 × 60 cm distance covering 43,000 plants/ha in rainy season.
- **Manures and fertilizers:** 25-50 tonnes of FYM/ha in two doses in the 6th and 12th month after planting plus 16:2.5:00 g NPK/ plant. Foliar application of 4% urea is beneficial.
- **Induction of flowering:** Uniform flowering can be obtained by the application of NNA (Planofix), calcium carbide or Ethrel (100 ppm) at the 4-5 leaf stage.
- **Harvesting:** Fruits are ready from July to September. The yield is 12 to 17 tonnes per hectare for Queen and Mauritius varieties whereas 25-30 tonnes/ha for Kew in the first year.

Sapota (*Achras zapota*)

Sapota is popularly known as *chiku* in western and central India. It is an evergreen plant, growing and flowering almost throughout the year in alluvial or sandy-loam soils having good drainage.

- **Varieties:** Cricket Ball (round), Dwaropudi (round), Bangalora, Vavila Valasa (both oval), Jonnavalasa (round), Kirtabarati and Pot (dwarf trees), Kalipatti, Co 1, Co 2, PKM 1, PKM 2, PKM 3, DSH 1 and DSH 2 (Kalipatti × Cricket ball), and Chatri (both oval).
- **Propagation and Planting:** Propagated by layering, *gootees* (air-layering) or inarching. Rootstocks used are rayan or manikara (*Manilkara hexandra*) or mohwa (*Bassia latifolia* and *B. longifolia*) at distance of 4.5-6 m (North) and 9-12 m (South).
- **Harvesting:** Fruiting starts from the fourth to fifth year. The fruit takes four months to mature in three seasons, *viz*. March-April and August-September (Northern India); February-June and September-October (Southern India) and January-February and May-June (Western India).
- Sapota can be artificially ripened by the application of Ethrel @ 500 ppm and 10 g NaOH pellets.
- **Yield:** Varies from 200 to 300 fruits in the fourth year, from 700 to 800 in the seventh year, from 1,500 to 2,000 between the tenth and 15th year, and from 2,500 to 3,000 from the 20th to 30th year.

Pomegranate (*Punica granatum*)

In cold season tree is deciduous whereas in the plains it is evergreen.

A hot, dry summer produces the best quality fruits. Pomegranate is sub-tropical fruit. The deep loamy and alluvial soils are ideal for its cultivation. Mainly cultivated in Maharashtra on 500 hectares of land.

- **Varieties**: Ganesh, Alandi, Dholka, Kandhari, Muskat, Nabha, Jyoti, G-132, G-107, G-137, P-13, P-16, P-26, Mridula, Ruby, etc.
- Jalore seedless is early ripening pomegranate variety.
- **Fruit cracking** is prominent disorder, which can be managed by application of 0.4% boron. Mrig bahar (season) is most prone to cracking. Bedana, Bosec and Kohg varieties are resistant to cracking.
- **Propagation:** Propagated from cuttings of 8-10 cm long; also by air layering or *gootee*. Application of IBA @ 10,000 ppm in lanolin as carrier is found to improve rooting. Planted in pits of 60 × 60 × 60 cm having a distance of 6 × 6 m, pre-filled with 22-25 kg FYM.
- **Manuring and fertilization:** 250:125:125 g/plant NPK for first year, 500:125:125 g/plant NPK for third year onwards.

- There are three crop seasons, *viz.* June-July (***Mrig bahar***), Feb.-March (***Ambe bahar***) and Sept.-Octo. (***Hasth bahar***).
- **Harvesting**: Fruits become ready for harvesting in 5-7 months after blossom producing an average yield of 200-250 fruits/ tree.

Wood Apple or Bael (*Aegle marmelos*)$2n = 4x = 36$

It is originated from India. It is the richest source of Riboflavin; **propagated** by patch budding in July.

- Mirazapuri, Rampuri, Azamati, Khamaria, Etawah, Kagzi, Sewan Large and Deoria are local cultivars; NB 1, NB 5, NB 7, NB 9 are promising **varieties**.

Avocado (*Persea americana*)

The avocado fruit is rich in **protein** and **fat**. The fruit is neither sweet nor juicy. It is cultivated mostly in Maharashtra.

- **Varieties:** Fucshina, Lula, Hass, Pollock, Yulia, Paradeniya Purple Hybrid and Feurte (Callinson × Winslowson) are grown in the foot of the Nilgiris.
- It is propagated through seeds at the distance of 7-9 m.
- **Harvesting:** The trees generally flower between February and April and the harvesting of the fruits is done in August to September.

Cashew nut (*Anacardium occidentale*) $2n = 2x = 42$

The Portuguese originally introduced cashew into India during the 16th century. The shells contain high quality oil known as cashew nut shell liquid (CNSL), has wide industrial uses. Cashew is grown mainly for nuts and secondly for cashew apple (fruit). Cashew apple is eaten fresh or mixed in fruit salads and a drink is prepared from the juice. Cashew can be distilled to produce alcoholic drinks (Fenny). It is the unique combination of fat (47%), protein (21%) carbohydrates (22%) and vitamins.

- **Varieties:** Ullal 1, 2, 3, BPP 3, 4, 5, Bapatla 1, 2, 3, Madakkathara, Pryanka and Dhana. **Hybrids**: BPP 1, BPP 2, Vengurla 3, 4, 5, 6.
- **Propagation and planting:** Propagated through seeds *in situ* at a distance of 6 m in lateritic and rocky soils to 12 m in deep loamy soils.
- **Harvesting:** First bearing occurs normally in three years. The fruits ripen from March to May yielding 110-220 kg nuts/ha.

Jackfruit (*Artocarpus heterophyllus*)

Jackfruit is grown in humid climate. Warmer plains are suitable, provided there is adequate soil moisture.

- **Propagation and Planting:** Propagated through seedlings or inarching planted at a spacing of about 12 m.
- **Harvesting and yield:** Singapore variety produces fruits in 18-36 months after planting whereas normal bearing comes after 7-8 years from March to June. **Yields** 250 fruits/tree.

Loquat (*Eriobotrya japonica*)

Loquat is grown mainly in Punjab and U.P., Delhi, Assam, Maharashtra and hills of Southern India.

- **Varieties**: Golden Yellow, Pale Yellow, California Advance, and Tanaka.
- **Propagation and planting:** Propagated through seed or inarching in July-August and planted at a distance of 6.5 m × 6.5 m in square system to accommodate 225 plants/ha in pits of 1 × 1 × 1 m size.
- **Manuring and fertilizers:** 10-20 kg FYM plus 300-500:200-500:150-400 g/tree NPK up to three years.

Litchi (*Litchi chinensis*)

Litchi is originated from Southern China and now grown extensively in northern Bihar, western U.P. and in Punjab. It grows well in sandy and clayey loams containing large quantities of lime.

- Litchi rose scented variety produces highest qualitative yield when planted in double hedgerow system.
- **Fruit cracking** is the prominent disorder. It can be managed by the application of boron @ 0.4%. Dehradun is resistant cultivar to fruit cracking.
- **Varieties: Bihar**: China, Purbi, Deshi, Bedana and Dehra Rose; **Uttar Pradesh**: Rose-scented, Early Large Red, Kalkatia, Gulabi, Swarna Roopa and Late Seedless.
- **Propagation and planting:** Propagated through air layering and planted at 9 m apart in pits during the rainy season.
- **Yield:** A mature tree produces about 110 kg of fruit each year.

FRUITS OF ARID AND SEMI-ARID CONDITIONS

Date-Palm (*Phoenix dactylifera*) 2n = 36

It is native to Iraq and mainly cultivated in Punjab, northern Rajasthan and Kutch region in India. It is also an alternate bearer.

- **Varieties:** Hillawi (Iraq), Khadrawi (Iraq), Shamran (produces uneven ripening), Medjool (Morocco), Barhee, Hayany, Zaidi.
- Date palm variety Medjool produces highest yield. Halawy variety is recommended for fresh fruits and Medjool for dry dates. Date palm fruits of ***khala*** stage of Halawy give quality ***chhuhara*** if they are dipped for 10-15 minutes in boiling water followed by drying in air at 45°C for 60-65 hours. Barhee is used for best quality *pindkhajoor.*
- **Propagation and planting:** Propagated through suckers planted at 6-7 m apart in pits of 1 × 1 × 1 m size to accommodate 202-275 plants/ha.
- **Harvesting:** There are two stages *viz.* **khalal** stage (when the fruit has its most intense red or yellow colour and maximum weight) and **tamar** stage (when it has lost the greater part of its moisture content). Harvested as the choice of stage.

Phalsa (*Grewia asiatica*)

It is indigenous to India. Phalsa is a small bush growing all over the country including Punjab, Haryana, Uttar Pradesh and Andhra Pradesh. The fruit is berry-like, globular, smooth, deep reddish brown and comes in the market in May and June. Fresh phalsa fruit contains 81.5% Pulp, 5.4% Juice, 14% TSS and 4.64% Acidity.

- **Propagated** through seed grown in July-August at the distance of 10-15 cm apart from each other.
- **Fertilizers:** 100:40:25 kg/ha NPK.
- **Harvesting:** Bearing starts from second year. A good commercial crop is usually obtained during third year yielding 5.2 kg/bush.

Custard Apple (*Annona squamosa*)

It is a small tree seldom more than 4.5 metres high. This fruit-tree is propagated through seeds and by inarching and veneer grafting. Bullocks-heart (*Annona reticulata*) rootstock is used for grafting by inarching or budding. Arka Sahan (interspecific hybrid from *A. atemoya* × *A. squamosa*). APK 1 variety is suitable for commercial cultivation. The **yield** per tree varies from 25 to 30 kg.

Aonla (*Emblica officinalis*)

It is indigenous fruit of India. The Banarsi *aonla* is the most important cultivar cultivated in the district of Pratapgarh of U.P. It is the rich source of vitamin C (600 mg/100 g) content.

- It is propagated vegetatively by shield budding during June.
- **Varieties:** Kanchan (NA 4), Krishna (NA 5), Amrit (NA 7), Neelum (NA 9) and Balwant. Aonla NA 10 and NA 7 are aonla varieties superior under rainfed cultivation.
- Lakshmi 52 (seedling selection of aonla) has been identified in the village Bhadausi, Garwara, district Pratapgrah, U.P., which has tree growth of semi-erect and semi-spreading branches. The fruit matures during November-December and is free from necrosis having a yield potential of 2-2.5 q/tree (10 years onwards). The fruit weighs 40-60 g containing 90.4% pulp, 82.5% moisture, 11° Bri× TSS, 1.7 % acids, 512 mg/100g vitamin C and 3.3% tannins.
- **Fruit necrosis** is caused due to boron deficiency. Application of 0.6% boron twice or thrice improves the deficiency.
- Bearing starts from the 10th year; and fruits are fully mature by January-February.

Fig (*Ficus carica*)

It is sparingly cultivated in Maharashtra, Hyderabad and other parts of the country. **Poona** is known **variety** grown in these areas. Propagated through cuttings, Budding, or grafting, planted at spacing of 4.5-5 m. Need 25 kg FYM plus 225: 450:450 g/tree NPK for commercial cultivation.

Jujube (*Ziziphus mauritiana*) $2n = 24$

Jujube, *ber* or bor, is called **poor man's fruit**; it is also called **king of arid fruits**. Ber is cultivated mainly in the northern, eastern and western parts of India on 4000 hectares of land. M.P. is the leading ber producing state.

- **Varieties:** Umran, Sanaur-2, Kaithli, Z.G.-2, Sanaur-5, Sanaur-4, Chhuhara and Laddu. Katha, Tikdi, Sanaur-1, Mehrun and Dodia are resistant to fruit fly. Gola, Seb, Illaichi, Safed Rohtak and Mehrun are resistant to powdery mildew. Kaithali and Gola are recommended for commercial cultivation in rainfed condition.
- Indian aloe was integrated with ber for cultivation.

- **Planting:** Planted in February-March and again in August-September, but the latter produces good crop.
- **Propagation** is done by budding both as Shield or T-budding and ring-budding methods during March-April or August-September. Katha ber (*Zizyphus mauritiana*) and Mallah ber (*Zizyphus numularia*) are used as **rootstocks** for ber.
- FYM of 20 kg and 100 g nitrogen (400 g CAN) is recommended for one-year-old ber tree.
- **Harvesting:** The peak season of harvesting in north India is in February-March to mid-April.

amun (*Syzigium cumini*)

Jamun is successfully grown in the lower range of the Himalayas ıp to an elevation of 1300 metres and in the Kumaon hills up to 600 metres above mean sea level (MSL). **Propagation** is by seed or narching and air layering.

- The average **yield** of fruit from a full-grown seeded jamun tree is about 80-100 kg and from a grafted tree 60-70 kg/year.

EMPERATE FRUITS

pple (*Malus × domestica*)

It is called "**king of temperate fruits**". Apple is cultivated in Punjab, Jttar Pradesh, Himachal Pradesh. and Kashmir and to a small extent n the Nilgiris on 12,141 hectares of land. Fleshy thalamus is the dible portion.

- **Varieties:**

Iimachal Pradesh	Ambred (Red Delicious × Ambri), Ambstarking & Ambroyal (Starking delicious × Ambri), Ambrich, Red Delicious, Golden Delicious, Worester Pearmain, Newton Wonder (all diploids), Coxs Orange Pippen (triploid), King of Pippens, Starking (Royal) Delicious and Richard.
ashmir Valley	Lal Ambri (Red Delicious × Ambri), Sunehari (Ambri × Golden Delicious), Red Delicious (diploid), Baldwin (triploid), Ambri Kashmiri, Akbar, White Dotted Red and Blood Red.
imla Hills	Beauty of Bath (triploid), Red Delicious, Jonathon, Rome Beauty (all diploids), Early Shanburry, Red Astrachan, Red Sudeley, Stayman Winesap, Winter Banana and Yellow Newton.

Kumaon Hills	Chaubattia Princess (Red delicious × Early Shanburry), Chaubattia Anupam (Red delicious × Early Shanburry), James Grieve, Jonathon, Rome Beauty (all diploids), Blenheim Orange Pippen, Delicious, Early Shanburry, Golden Pippen, King of Pippens, Rhymer and Winter Banana.
Kulu Valley	Ben Davis, Red Delicious, Golden Delicious (all diploids), Co×s Orange Tippen, Blenheim Orange, Baldwin (all triploids), Red Astrachan, King of Pippens, Yellow Newton and Granny Smith.
Nilgiri	Rome Beauty (diploid) and Irish Peach.

- Thomas Andrew Knight produced first apple cultivar Parentago.
- **Bitter pit** is a disorder caused by zinc deficiency.
- **Propagation and Planting:** Propagated by shield budding, bench grafting and tongue-grafting on seedlings raised from seed. Clonal **rootstocks** of the Malling-Merton are suitable for woolly aphid.

Apricot (*Prunus armeniaca*) 2*n* = 16

Apricot is propagated by shield budding on wild apricot stock, i.e. *zardalu*.

- **Varieties:** Kaisaha, Moorpark, Shipley Early, Kaisha, New Castle, St. Ambroise, and Royal. Apricot selection, Suka, produces red cheeks grown in Ladakh.

Cherry (*Prunus avium*) 2*n* = 2*x* = 16

It is originated in Europe. Cherries grown mainly in the Simla and Kulu Valley, and Kashmir at elevations above 1,500 m MSL.

- **Varieties:** Early Rivers, Governor Wood, Bigarreau de Schreken, Elton, Bedford Prolific, White Bigarreau, Monstrueuse de Mezel, Bigarreau Napoleaon, Emperor Frencis and Late Black Bigarreau. San, Sue, Windsor, Victor and Van are resistant to fruit cracking.
- **Propagation and planting:** Propagated by whip or tongue grafting on seedlings of wild cherry stock, called *paja* (*P. cerasoides*) and planted at the distance of 9 to 12 m.
- **Manuring:** Sheep manure plus 75-100:55-90:110-165 kg/ha NPK.

Peach (*Prunus persica*)

Peach is cultivated mainly in the Himalayas at various elevations.

- **Varieties:** Shan-e-Punjab, July Elberta, Red Heaven, Florida Sun, Kanto-5, Florida Red, Early Beatrice, Ale×ander, Early Rivers, Duke of York, Peregrime, Noblesse, Late Devonian, Elberta, J.H. Hale and Triumph.
- **Propagation and planting:** Propagated by budding on peach seedlings and planted 6 to 8 m apart in early spring. G 557 and G 677 are important **rootstocks.**
- **Fertilizers:** 55-65:55-65:110-135 kg/ha NPK.

Pear (*Pyrus communis*)

Pear is grown mainly in the hills at elevations ranging from 1,500 to 2,500 m. Italy is the largest producer of pear.

- **Varieties:** Red Blush, Punjab Gold, Punjab Nectar, William Bon Christien (Bartlett), Clappsoil Favourits, Thimpsons, Doyenne du Comice, Easter Beurre, Winter Nalis, Conference, Dr. Jules Guyot, Marie Louise dUccle, *Baggugosha* (Citron des carmes), Emile dHeyst and Nashpati. Waite and Magness are pollen sterile cultivars.
- **Fruit cracking, Calyc end rot** and **Blossom blast** are important disorders and can be managed by 0.4% boron. **Black End** and **Corky tissue** are due to calcium deficiency.
- **Propagation and Planting:** Propagated by shield budding or tongue grafting, which is done in June-July. The stocks are raised on wild pear *shegal* (*Pyrus pashia).*

Persimmon (*Diospyros kaki*)2*n* = 90

Originated from china and grown in the Kulu Valley at elevations ranging from 900 to 1,500 m. Epicarps and mesocarps are edible portion.

- **Varieties:** Fuy, Twentieth century, Hachiya and Hyakume, Dai Dai, Maru, Nightingale and Tenanshi.
- It is **propagated** by grafting on seedlings of *Diospyros lotus* and *D. virginiana* and planted at 6.5-7.5 m distance.

Almond (*Prunus amygdalus*) 2*n* = 16

It is native to the western Asia and now USA is the largest producer. It is **propagated** by tongue grafting and shield budding on Behmi (*P. ira*) **rootstock.**

- **Varieties**: Drake, Dhenbar, Katha, Peerless, Ne Plus Ultra, an mission. **Hybrids:** JK 39, JK 57, Hybrid 29, Hybrid 50 and N 258.

Plum (*Prunus domestica*)

Plum is grown mainly in the Himalayas.

- **Varieties:** Grand Duke, Early Transparent Gage, Victoria, Sant Rosa, Wickson, Beauty, Rubio, Alu Bokhara, Gaviota, Shir Combination, Kelsey, Burmosa, Frontier, Nubiana, Frie Mariposa, Barbank, Aldorado, Formosa, and Hale. Santa Ros is commercial hybrid cultivar.

Strawberry (*Fragaria x ananassa*) $2n = 8x = 56$

Propagated by Runners and transplanting is done in March April in the hills and in January-February in the plains.

- **Varieties:** Laxtons Latest, Royal Sovereign, Early Cambridg Hu×ley Giant, Penomenol, Robinson, Pusa early dwar Brighton, Chandler, Tioga, Taliman and Torrey.

Walnut (*Juglans regia*)

It is native to Iran. USA is the leading producer of walnut. Jamm and Kashmir is leading producing states in India.

- **Varieties:** Eureka, Placentia, Prolific, Govind, Roopa, Kara etc.

Kiwi Fruit or Chinese Gooseberry (*Actinidia deliciosa*)

It is also called **China's miracle fruit** or **horticultural wonder** Newzeland. It is deciduous vine fruit crop, **propagated** through ste cuttings.

- **Varieties:** Abott, Allison, Bruno, Hayward, and Monty a commercial cultivars of kiwifruit.

32

Vegetable Production

Per capita daily requirement of vegetables is 300 g, which includes 125 g of green leafy vegetables, 100 g root and tubers and 75 g other vegetables.

Vegetables are good source of **Carbohydrates** (Tapioca, Sweet potato, Potato, Colocasia, Elephan's foot); **Proteins** (Agathi, Drumstick, Colocasia, Pea, Beans); **Vitamins** like A (Leafy vegetables, Carrot, Sweet potato, Pumpkin, Colocasia, Turnip green, Knol-khol), B_1 (Lettuce, Cabbage, Carrot, Onion), B_5 (Peas, Peppers, Potato, Spinach, Tomato), C (Cauliflower, Cabbage, Knol-khol, Turnip, Tomato, Pepper, Drumstick, Fenugreek leaves, Amaranth), D, E and K (Green vegetables); and **Minerals** including Calcium (Beans, Carrot, Cabbage, Cauliflower, Lettuce, Onion, Spinach, Pea, Tomato, Amaranth, Fenugreek); **Phosphorus** (Potato, Carrot, Tomato, Cucumber, Spinach, Cauliflower, Lettuce); **Iron** (Spinach, Lettuce, Cabbage, Peas, Beans, Tomato, Carrot, Bitter gourd, Onion); **Iodine** (Onion, Okra, Summer squash, Asparagus).

- Characteristic flavour in cole crops is due to dimethyl trisulphide. Pungency in onion and garlic due to allyl propyl disulphide and diallyl disulphide, respectively.
- Pre-harvest application of benzyl adenine @ 25 ppm on broccoli Pusa Broccoli 1 retain green colour.

Newly Released Varieties

Crop	Variety	Remarks
Muskmelon	NDM 15	Northwestern alluvial plains
Garlic	DARL 52	Humid western Himalayan region
	G 323	Arid western plains
Tomato	Arka Meghali	Rainfed cultivation
	Arka Shreshta	Bacterial wilt resistance
	Arka Abhijit	Bacterial wilt resistance
	Pusa Rohini	Determinate tomato, for red colour
Cauliflower	Pusa Sharad	Sharad season (November maturity)
	Pusa Meghna	September maturity

Mustard	Pusa Sag 1	Vegetable mustard
Ash gourd	Pusa Ujwal	*kharif* season
Snapmelon	Pusa Shandar	First variety of released for cultivation
Cucumber	Pusa Uday	Light green, smooth-skinned
Sponge gourd	Pusa Sneh	Dark green fruits

- Tomato genotypes, H 86, H 24, Bilali 1 and 6-11 B, are tolerant to leaf curl. Hybrids, DTEH 2, DTEH 8, DTEH 9, DTEH 18 and DTEH 19, are resistant to early blight. NF 31, VFN 8 and Pusa 120, resistant to root-knot nematode.
- Brinjal hybrids, DBHL 135 and DBHL 137, are tolerant to shoot and fruit borer and phomopsis blight, respectively.
- Cauliflower, selection, Kn 81, BR 2 and 3-5-1 are resistant for downy mildew, black rot and *Sclerotinia* rot.
- **Vegetables are cultivated** into six different garden types, *viz.* home-gardens or kitchen gardens, market gardens, truck-gardens, gardens for processing, gardens for vegetable-forcing, and gardens for seed production.

Vegetable forcing is a technique under which vegetables are grown without the normal season.

Important Growth Regulators in Vegetables

Crop	Growth regulator/Nutrient used
Bottle gaurd	Maleic Hydrazide 40 ppm @ 1 g/20 litre of water at 2 or 4 leaf stage.
	Ethrel 100 ppm @ 4 ml/20 litre of water at 2 or 4 leaf stage.
Round gaurd	Ethrel 100 ppm @ 4 ml/20 litre of water at 2 or 4 leaf stage.
	Maleic Hydrazide 40 ppm @ 1 g/20 litre of water at 2 or 4 leaf stage..
Ribbed gourd	Ethrel 100 ppm @ 4 ml/20 litre of water at 2 or 4 leaf stage.
Ash gourd	Ethrel 240 ppm @ 10 ml/20 litre of water at 2 or 4 leaf stage.
Bitter gourd	Cycoceal 240 ppm @ 10 ml/20 litre of water at 2 or 4 leaf stage.
Cucumber	Ethrel 100 ppm @ 4 ml/20 litre of water at 2 or 4 leaf stage.
	Cycoceal 40 ppm @ 1 g/20 litre of water at 2 or 4 leaf stage.
	Boron 3 ppm @ 6 g/20 litre of water at 2 or 4 leaf stage.
	Molybdenum 3 ppm @ 6 g/20 litre of water at 2 or 4 leaf stage.
Water melon	Gibberellic acid 25 ppm @ 5 g/20 litre of water at 2 or 4 leaf stage.
	TIBA 40 ppm @ 40 ml/20 litre of water at 2 or 4 leaf stage.

SOLANACEOUS VEGETABLES

Potato: Potato is a native of South America, occupies the largest area under any single vegetable in the world. It has a special value as food.

- **Varieties**: Traditional varieties include Satha, Gola, Phulwa, Up-to-date, Darjeeling Red Round, Craigs Defiance, Great Scot and President. The Central Potato Research Institute, Simla, has released a large number of improved varieties which include Kufri Red, Kufri Kuber, Kufri Kisan, Kufri Kundan, Kufri Safed, Kufri Kumar, Kufri Neela, Kufri Sindhuri, Kufri Chandramukhi, Kufri Khasi-garo, Kufri Naveen (resistance to late blight and wart disease), Kufri Chamatkar, Kufri Neelmani, Kufri Sheetman (frost-resistant), Kufri Jyoti (resistant to late blight and wart), Kufri Alankar and Kufri Jeevan.
- **Cultivation**: Seed rate 800-1,500 kg/ha. The sowing time is from the middle of September to the beginning of January. In the Nilgiri Hills, three crops are raised in succession in April, August and January. In the hilly regions of the north, the crop is sown in March-April. A spacing of 45-60 cm × 15-25 cm, according to the variety and the size of tuber is adopted.
- **Fertilizers**: FYM 30 tonnes plus 120:100:70 kg NPK.
- **Yield:** The average yield varies from 20 to 30 t/ha. Potatoes are stored at 2.2°C to 3.3°C with 75- 80% relative humidity.

Tomato (*Lycopersicum esculentum*) is grown in five forms, *viz. Ceraciforme* (Small fruited, Cherry tomato), *Pyriformae* (Pear tomato), *Commune* (Common tomato), *Grandifolium* (Potato leaf type) and *Validium* (Upright tomato).

- **Varieties**: **Determinate type**: HS-101, HS-102, HS-110, Sweet-72, Punjab Chhuhara Roma, KS-1, Punjab Keshri, Sel-7, Sel-32, Sel-152, Sel-12, Pusa Early Dwarf, Pusa Gaurav, Co-1, Co-3, Labonita, Sel-1-6-1-4, Hisar Lalima, Pusa Red Plum, Pusa Sel-4, Pusa Sel-8, Pusa-120, Balkan; **Indeterminate type**: Best of all Pant Bahar, Pusa Ruby, Sel-120, Sioux, T-1, Arka Vikash, Arka Saurabh, DT-10, BT-12, Pant T-3
- Lycopene is responsible for red colour in tomato.

Brinjal (*Solanum melongena*)

Brinjal is grown in different varietal types, *viz. Escutellum* (Round or egg shaped), *Serpentinum* (Long, slender type), and *Depressum* (Early and dwarf cultivars). It is a good source of Vitamin B and C. Arka Shirish is the green coloured cultivar of brinjal. KKM-1 is the white coloured variety.

- **Varieties**: **Long**: Pusa Purple Long, PBR-128-5, PBR-61, Sel-1, Punjab Sadabahar, Neelam, PH-4, Pusa Kranti, Pant Samrat, Azad Kranti, ARU 2C, BB-26, Sel-4, Punjab Barati, KT-4, NDB-25, ARUK, Arka Sheel, Punjab Chamkela, Arka Navneet, PBR-9-1, PBR-91-2, Punjab Bahar; **Round**: Jamuni Gol Baigan, Pant Rituraj, H-8, KS-224, AB 1, K 202-9, DBR-31, DBR-8, T-3, Pusa Purple Round; **Small Round:** PLR-1, Aruna, DBSR-44; **Green Brinjal:** Arka Kushmakar, Arka Shirish, Ramnagar Ziant, Rajendra Baigan.

Chillies (*Capsicum* spp.)

Portuguese brought chilli from Brazil to India in 1584. *C. annum* and *C. frutescence* have white flowers whereas, *C. pubescence* has purple flowers. Powdery mildew resistance is found in *C. baccatum*. Arka Abir variety is used for colour extraction. Pusa Deepti is F_1 hybrid of capsicum.

- **Varieties: Chilli**: Andhra Jyoti (G-5), Bhagyalaxmi (G-4) K-2, K-1, Sel-1, J-218, Muslabadi, LCA 206 B, JCA 283, Phuley C-5, Bhaskar, Co-1, Co-2, MDU-1, NP-46-A, Punjab Lal, Pusa Jawala, Pant C-1, Pant C-2, JCA-154, Kalyanpur Selection, Pusa Sadabahar, X-235, Kalyanpur Red, Chamatkar, Kalyanpur Red, Aparna, G-3; **Capsicum**: California Wonder, Yolo Wonder, King of North, Early Ziant, Bull Nose, Chinese Gaint, World Beater, Arka Mohini, Arka Gaurav, Arka Basant.

COLE CROPS: Cabbage (*Brassica oleracea* var. *capitata*), Cauliflower (*B. oleracea* var. *botrytis*), Knol-khol or Kohlrabi (*B. caulorapa*), Broccoli (*B. oleracea* var. *italica*), Brussels sprouts (*B. oleracea* var. *gemmifera*), and Chinese cabbage ((*B. pekinensis* and *B. chinensis*). All these above crops have developed from wild cabbage, known as Colewart, hence the name cole crops. The seeds of other cole crops are sown from the mid September to the end October.

Cauliflower

Jemson introduced cauliflower in India from Kew garden (London) in 1822. It is grown in three different seasons:

Early	Mid-September to mid-October: Kunwari and Early Patna; October-November: Pusa Kataki
Mid-season	Mid-November to mid-December: Aghani, Poosi, Patna; Mid-December- Mid January: Early Snowball, D-96, Japanese improved
Late	January and February: Dania; January to April: Snowball-16, Suttons Snowball

- **Other varieties**: Punjab Kunwari, Pusa Deepali, Improved Japanese, Pusa Synthetic, Snowball-16, K-1, Early Kunwari, Pant Gobhi-3, Pusa Early Synthetic, Pant Gobi-2, PG-26, PG-35, Hisar-1, IIHR-101, IIHR-105, Pant Subhra, Pusa Subhra, Pusa Himjyoti, Pusa Katki, Pusa Snowball-1, Pusa Snowball-2, Pusa Snowball K-1. Pusa Himjyoti variety can be grown round the year.
- Boron deficiency causes **browning** or **brown rot** of cauliflower. The application of 10-15 kg of Borax per hectare controls browning.
- **Whiptail** is caused by molybdenum deficiency, particularly in acid soils. Liming on acid soils or the application of 1 kg of ammonium molybdate per hectare is recommended.

Cabbage

It has anti-cancer property due to presence of indole-3 carbinol. It is grown in three forms, *viz. B. oleracea* var. *capitata* f. *alba* (white cabbage), *B. oleracea* var. *capitata* f. *rubra* (red cabbage) and *B. oleracea* var. *sabauda* (savoy cabbage).

- Pusa ageti was the first tropical variety. Pusa Sambandh is synthetic variety. Pusa Mukta is resistant variety to black rot. Other varieties include, **Round**: Golden acre, Pride of India, Copenhagen market, express flat, Golden Eve, Golden Acre, Pusa Mukta; **Drumhead**: Pusa Drumhead, Drumhead; **Conical head**: Jersey wakefield; **Savoy type**: Chieftan.

Chinese Cabbage

It is natural hybrid of *B. compestris* ssp. *rapifera* × *B. compestris* ssp. *chinensis*, both found in China.

- Varieties include Chihili, wong bok, pakcholi, Red Cabbage.

Knol-Khol

It is popular in Kashmir. The edible part is swollen stem.

- Varieties include White Vienna, Purple Vienna, King of North, and Large Green.

Broccoli

The term Broccoli has been derived from Latin word, *Brachium*, meaning 'an arm' or 'branch'. USA is the largest producer of Broccoli. It is the rich source of sulphoraphane, a compound associated with reducing cancer.

- **Varieties** include Calabrese, bronzino.

Brussels' Sprout

The edible portion of Brussels' sprout is swollen axillary bud. It can be grown as high winter season crop.

- **Varieties** include Catskill, Long island, Danish prize.

ROOT CROPS: Radish (*Raphanus sativus*, Cruciferae), Turnip (*Brassica rapa*, Cruciferae), Carrot (*Daucus carota*, Umbelliferae) and Beet (*Beta vulgaris*, Chenopodiaceae).

Radish

Akshin is a disorder due to boron deficiency. Hollow root disorder is due to high temperature.

- **Varieties** include White Icicle, Pusa Himani (grown round the year), Rapid Red, White Tipped, Scarlet Globe, French Breakfast, Japanese White, Pusa Desi, Pusa Ketaki, Jaunpuri, Bombay Red, Arka Nisani (resistant to physiological disorders).

Turnip

The edible part of turnip is hypocotyls. Temperature below 10°C force turnip to flower.

- **Varieties:** Purple Top, White Globe, Golden Ball, Snow Ball, Pusa Swarrima. Pusa Kanchan (sets seed in plains), Pusa Sweti.

Carrot

Cavity spot is a physiological disorder due to calcium deficiency. Heavy nitrogen application or moisture level, force carrot to split.

- **Varieties:** Half-long Nantes, Coreless, Chantaney, Pusa Kesar, Pusa Meghali.

Beet

Red colour of beetroot is due to presence of red violet pigment, ß-cyanins and yellow pigment ß-xanthins.

- **Varieties** include Crimson Globe, Detroit Dark Red.

BULB CROPS: Onion (*Allium cepa*), Garlic (*A. sativum*), Leek (*A. porrum*), Shallot (*A. ascalonicum*), Welsh onion (*A. fistulosum*), and Chive (*A. schoenoprasum*).

Onion

It is highly cross-pollinated due to protoandry, which is pollinated by bees. Onion is grown in both *rabi* and *kharif* (South India) season.

- **Varieties** include, Pusa Red, Ratner, Patna Red, Patna White, Poona Red, Nasik Red, Nasik White, and Bellary Red, Arka Niketan, etc. *Kharif*: varieities Arka Kalyan, Agrifound Dark Red, Baswant 780, Nifad 53. **Yellow coloured** varieties Early

Grano and Brown Spanish. **White coloured** varieties Pusa White Flat, Pusa White Round, Udaipur-102, Punjab-48, N-257-9-1. Varieties for **green onion** are Early Grano, Pusa White Flat and Pusa White Round.

- In Maharashtra Lasalgaon is the biggest market for onion in India.
- Netherlands is leading exporter of onion followed by Spain and India.
- Cytoplasmic genetic male sterility was first found in onion.

Leek

It is cultivated for its blanched stem and leaves. The most common varieties of Leek are London Flag and American Flag.

PEAS AND BEANS: Peas (*Pisum sativum*), French bean (*Phaseolus vulgaris*), Cow pea (*Vigna sinensis* savi), Clusterbean (*Cyamopsis tetragonoloba*), Indian bean (*Dolichos lablab*) and Okra (*Abelmoschus esculenstus*).

Pea

Pisum elatius is considered the ancestor of pea. *P. arvense* is known as field pea has coloured flowers, whereas *P. sativum* is called garden or sweet pea produces white flowers.

- Arka Ajit is resistant to powdery mildew (a serious problem in pea). Whole pod edible variety is UN 53 (IIHR). Arkel variety was introduced from England, whereas Bonneville from USA. Ageta-6, Arkel, Early Badger, Little Marvel, Early December, T-19, Lincoln, Delwiche Commado, NP-25, Perfection New Line, Thomas Laxton, Alderman, GC-141, GC-195, Kwari, Sylvia, Harbhajan, GC-477, Pant Uphar, P-88, VL-3, JP-4, Azad Pea-1.

French Bean or Kidney Bean

P. arborigineus is the progenitor for French bean.

- **Varieties**: Pusa Parvati (resistant to mosaic and powdery mildew), Kentucky wonder (from USA), Arka Komal, IIHR 220 (resistant to rust) and IIHR 909, Boundiful-Plantifur, Contender, Premier King Green, Blue Lake Kentucky Wonder, VL Boni-1, Pant Anupma (a hybrid from Contender × Blue crop).

Cow pea

It is rich source of vitamin B. It is usually grown as catch crop.

- **Varieties:** Pusa dofasli, Arka Garima and Arka Suman are photosensitive varieties. Pusa Phalguni, Pusa Barsati, Pusa

Dofasli, C-152, S-1552, S-203, Arka Garima, Sel-2-1, Red Seeded selection.

Cluster Bean or Guar

C. senegalensis is progenitor for cluster bean. Pusa Sadabahar is non-branching type variety.

- **Varieties:** Pusa Navbahar, P-28-1-1, CP-78, Co-160-1.

Indian Bean

D. lablab var. *lignosus* is cultivated as pulse crop, whereas *D. lablab* var. *typicus* for soft edible vegetables.

- **Varieties:** Konkan Bhusan, Pusa Early Prolific, JDL-37, Kalyanpur T-1, Arka Jay, Arka Vijay.

Okra or Lady's Finger

India is the largest producer of bhindi. Roots of bhindi are used for cleaning Jaggery.

- **Varieties:** Prabhani Kranti (resistant to YVMV, a serious disease transmitted by White fly), Varsha Uphar, Punjab Padmini, Punjab 7, Punjab 8, Pusa Sawani, Punjab No.-13, Red Bhindi, Co-1, Perkins Long Green, Ghana Red, Gujarat Bhindi-1, Selection-2, EMS-8.

CUCURBITS: Cucumber (*Cucumis sativus*), Musk-melon (*Cucumis melo*), Water-melon (*Citrullus vulgaris*), Bottle-gourd (*Lagenaria siceraria*), Bitter-gourd (*Momordica charantia*), Sponge-gourd (*Luffa cylindrica*), Ridge-gourd (*Luffa acutangula*), Snake-gourd (*Trichosanthes anguina*), Pointed-gourd or *parwal* (*Trichosanthes dioica*), Round-gourd or *tinda* (*Citrullus vulgaris* var. *fistulosus*), Ash-gourd (*Benincasa hispida*), Pumpkin (*Cucurbita moschata*), Summer squash (*C. pepo*), winter squash (*C. maxima*).

Cucumber

- **Varieties:** Pusa Sanyog (first F_1 hybrid developed in 1971), Himangi, Balam Khira, Khira Poona, Japanese Long Green, Straight Eight, Poinsette, Poona Khira, Balam Khira, Swarn Poorna, DVRM-1, IIHR-177-1.

Musk-melon

- **Varieties:** Pusa Sharbati, Lucknow Safeda, Hara Madhum Kutana, Durgapur, Madhu, Pusa Madhuras, Hara Madhu, Punjab Sunehari, Sel-2, Arka Jeet, Arka Rajhans, Lucknow Safeda, Durgapur Madhu, RM-43, IIHR-352, IIHR-190, Edisto, Honewdew.

Water-melon

A good water-melon should have 9-10% TSS.

- **Varieties:** Sugar Baby, Asahi Yamato, Charleston Grey, Pusa Badana (seedless), Tetra-2, etc. Arka Manik, Asahi Yamato, Pusa Bedana, Durgapur Kesar, Sugarbaby, Durgapur Meetha, Improved Shipper, Special No. 1.

Bottle-gourd

- **Varieties:** Pusa Summer Prolific Long, Pusa Summer Prolific Round, Pusa Meghdut, Pusa Manjari (round fruited F_1 hybrid), Pusa Naveen (cylindrical), Arka Bahar, Co-1, Punjab Round, Punjab Long, Punjab Komal, NDBG-1, KBG-13.

Bitter-gourd

- **Varieties:** Kalianpur Baramasi, Coimbatore White Long, Coimbatore Long, Arka Harit, VK-1, Priya, PMC-84, MDU-1, Co-1, Konkan Tara, Pusa Do Maushmi, Kalyanpur Sona, Pusa Vishesh, Punjab-14, NDB-1, Phule BG-6.

Sponge-gourd

It contains a gelatinous compound called luffein.

- **Varieties:** Pusa Chikni, Phule Prajakta and Pusa Supriya.

Ridge-gourd

It also contains luffein. Satputia is cultivar from Bihar.

- **Varieties:** Pusa Nasdar, Konkan harita, Co-1, Arka Sumeet, PKM-1, Punjab Sadabahar.

Summer Squash

- **Varieties:** Early Yellow Prolific, Australian Green, Butternut, Pusa Alankar (F_1 hybrid), Hisar Sel-1, Patty Pan, Early Yellow Prolific, Australian Green, Punjab Chappan Kaddoo-1, Arka Chandan, Co-1, Co-2.

Pumpkin

- **Varieties:** Arka Suryamukhi, Pusa Vishwas, CM-14.

Long melon

- **Varieties:** Arka Sheetal, Punjab Long melon.

Winter Squash

- **Varieties:** Arkha Suryamukhi, Pink Banana.

Tinda

- **Varieties:** Arka Tinda, Punjab Tinda, S-48.

TUBER CROPS: Colocasia (*Colocasia esculenta*), Yam (*Dioscorea alata*), Tapioca (*Manihot esculenta*) and Elephant's-Foot (*Amorphophallus campanulatus*). They are rich sources of carbohydrates. They are sown in February-March (for summer crop) and June-July (for rainy season crop).

Sweet Potato (*Ipomoea batata*)

The sweet potato has been widely recognized as a 'saviour crop' due to profitable yield for sustaining food and nutritional security in Sujeli village of Kandhamala district in Orissa. It has brought a revolution by minimizing malnutrition and improving nutritional security by popularized high-yielding Gauri, Sankar and Sree Bhadra varieties.

- **Varieties:** Pusa Safed, Pusa Lal, Pusa Sunheri, SP-3, SP-9, Ranger, Bhadrakali, Hosur Red, Gold Rush, Centennial, Pusa Harit are other varieties.

Dioscorea or Yams

- **Varieties:** *Dioscorea alata* (water yam) and *D. esculenta* (Chinese yam), are mostly cultivated in India. Dopsgenin is found in yam used in oral contraceptives. Sree Shilpa is the first hybrid of yam.

Cassava

It originated from Brazil, cultivated for its roots and propagated through cuttings. Cassava is bitter due to presence of cyanogenic glucoside (HCN). It is good source of carotene.

Elephant's Foot, Jimmikand, or Suran

- **Varieties:** *Amorphophallus companulatus* is cultivated for its roots. Gajendra and Satragachi are non-acrid (bitter) varieties.

Colocasia (*Colocasia esculenta*)

C. esculenta var. *antiquorum* is called *arvi*, whereas, *C. esculenta* var. *esculenta* is called *banda*. Africa is the leading producer of colocasia.

- **Varieties:** Satamukhi, Sri Rashmi and Sree Pallavi are the improved varieties.

SALAD CROPS: Lettuce (*Lactuca sativa*), Celery (*Apium graveolens*) ıd Parsley (*Petroselinum crispum*).

ettuce

- **Varieties: Crisp head type**: Great Lakes (resistant to tip burn), Imperial 859; Leaf type: Chinese Yellow, Slobolt; **Butter head type**: White button; **Cos type**: Dark green.

'elery

- **Varieties**: Standard Beared, Wright Grove Giant, Florida Golden, Fort Hook Emperor, etc.

arsley

It is rich source of vitamin C and Iron.

- **Varieties:** Mosscurled and Hamburg.

LEAFY VEGETABLES: These are very rich in minerals and itamins A and C, include Palak (*Beta vulgaris*), Spinach (*Spinacia leracea*), Fenugreek or Methi (*Trigonella foenumgraecum, T. cormiculata* ; used for *Kasuri methi*) and Mustard or *sarson*, (*Brassica* spp.), Chaui *Amaranthus tricolour*), Portulaca (*Portulaca oleracea*) and *Poi* (*Basella lba*) etc.

Spinach

- **Varieties:** Virginia Savoy (prickly seeded), Early Smooth Leaf.

'enugreek

- **Varieties:** Pusa Early Bunching, Kasuri, Rajendra Kranti.

Amaranth

- **Varieties:** Chhoti chaulai, Badi chaulai.

PERENNIAL VEGETABLES: Asparagus (*Asparagus officinalis*), Rhubarb (*Rheum rhabarbarum*), Globe Artichokes (*Cynara scolymus*) Drumstick (*Moringa oleifera*) and Jerusalem Artichoke (*Helianthus uberosus*). Asparagus is cultivated for its tender shoots, commonly known as spears; Rhubarb for its large, thick leaf stalks; Glove artichokes for its flower bud; Jerusalem artichoke is cultivated for its roots.

There are some other perennial vegetables, such as *cho-cho* (*Sechium edule*), sea-kale (*Crambe maritima*) and horse-radish (*Armoracia rusticana*)

Package and Practices of Important Vegetable Crops

Crop	Duration (days)	Season	Spacing (cm)	Seed rate (g/ha)	N:P:K (kg/ha)	Yield (MT/ha)	Important varieties and other information
Tomato	135-150	June-July Aug.-Oct. Nov.-Dec	60 × 45 45 × 45 45 × 40	350-400	150:100:50	35	Co 1, Co 2, Co 3, PKM 1, Pusa Ruby, Pusa Early Dwarf, Sioux, Marglobe, Best-of-All, Slope 120, Rama, Kalyanpur Angurlata, Ponderose.
Brinjal	80-90	Dec.-Jan. May-June	75 × 45	350-400	100:50:50	25-30	Co 1, Co 2, Co 3, MDU 1, PKM 1, Arka Navneet, Pusa Purple Long, Pusa Purple Round, Pusa Purple Cluster and Pusa Kranti, Black Beauty
Bhindi	90-100	June-Aug. Feb.-Mar.	60 × 45 45 × 30	6,000-8,000	80:50:30	12-15	Co 1, Co 2, Co 3, MDU 1, Pusa sawani, Arka anamika, parbhani kranti
Chillies	110-130	Jan.-Feb. June-July	40 × 30	1,000-1,500	120:60:30	2-2.5 (Dry Pods) 10-12 (Green)	K 1, K 2,Co 1, Co 2, Co 3, PKM 1, PKM, California Wonder, Yolo Wonder (Vegetable type)

Crop	Duration (days)	Season	Spacing (cm)	Seed rate (g/ha)	N:P:K (kg/ha)	Yield (MT/ha)	Important varieties and other information
Onion	140-150	October-November.	20 × 10	8,000-12,000 10 kg sulphur	110:50:125	15-18	Bellary Red, Pusa Red, NP 53, Arka Niketan, Arka Kalyan, Light red, Dark red.
Cow pea	75-90	Feb.-March June-July	45 × 15	20,000	25:50:0	2.5-5	Co 2, Co 4, Co 6, Pusa Phalguni, Pusa Dofasali.
French bean	90-100	August-October	45 × 10	30,000	60:100:75	4.5-5	Watex, Premier, Pusa Parvathi, Arka Komal
Cluster beans	90	February-July	45 × 15	10,000	50:50:25	5-7	Pusa Mausami, Pusa Noubahar, Pusa Sadabahar
Broad bean	120	All seasons	60 × 60	25,000	75:50:50	400-500	Local, SRS 1, BR 1, BR 2
Peas	80-110	October-November	10 × 30	150 kg	30:70:50	8-12	Bonnevelle, Arkel, Asauji, Lincoln, Alaska
Beet	120	Sep.-Nov.	10 × 30	5-6 kg	120:160:100	20-25	Crimson, Globe, Detroit, Dark red, Red ball
Potato	120	June-July Oct-Nov	45 × 20	3,000-3,500 kg	120:240:120	15-20	Kufri Jyoti, Muthu, Swarna

Crop	Duration (days)	Season	Spacing (cm)	Seed rate (g/ha)	N:P:K (kg/ha)	Yield (MT/ha)	Important varieties and other information
Sweet potato	110-120 Sep.-Feb.	June-July	60 × 30	80,000 vines	80:50:75	25-30	Co 1, Co 2, Co 3
Radish	45-60	Feb.-Mar. Sept.-Jan.	30 × 10	8-10 kg	50:100:50	20-30	Nilgiris Red, Co 1, Pusa Rashmi, Pusa Chaiti, Pusa Desi, Japanese White, Arka Nishant
Cabbage	70-120	August-Nov.	60 × 45	500	150:80:75	25-30	Golden Acre, Large Solid, Late Drum Head, Maharani
Knol-khol	75-90	August-Nov	30 × 20	1.0-1.5 kg	180:125:100	20-25	White Vienna, Purple Vienna
Cauli-flower	120-150	May-Sept.	60 × 45	375-600	150:80:80	120	Early Kunwari, Pusa Kataki, Marvel, Patna, Midseason, Second Early, Early Synthetic, Pusa Dapoli
Carrot	90-100	Aug-Dec	30 × 10	3-4 kg	80:60:60	25-30	Zeno, Nantes, India Gold, Pusa Kesar, Pusa Meghali, Kashmir Beauty
Bitter	140-150	Jan.-July	2.5 × 2	2.5 kg	20:30:60	14	Co 1, Pusa Do

Crop	Duration (days)	Season	Spacing (cm)	Seed rate (g/ha)	N:P:K (kg/ha)	Yield (MT/ha)	Important varieties and other information
Ribbed gourd	125	Jan.-July	2.5 × 2 Metre	1.5 kg	32:24:24	14-15	Co 1, Co 2, Pkm 1
Snake gourd	70-80	April-July	2.5 × 2 Metre	1,500	32:24:24	18	Long Co 1, Pkm 1, Co 2
Pumpkin	120	Jan.-July	2.5 × 2 Metre	1,000	32:60:24	30	Co 1, Co 2, Arka Suya Mukhi, Arka Chandan
Ash gourd	140	Jan.-Oct., Jan.-May	2.5 × 2	2.5 kg Metre	12:24:24	20	Co 1, Co 2
Bottle gourd	135	Jan.-July	2.5 × 2 Metre	3 kg	32:24:24	15-20	Co 1, Pusa Summer, Prolific Long Round, Pusa Majari, Pusa Meghdoot
Cucumber	120	Jan.-April June-Sept.	1.5 × 0.6 Metre	2.5 kg	35:20:40	8-10 Veg. 25 fruits	Co 1, Japanese Long Green, Straight Eight, Pointsette
Water-melon	120	Jan.-Feb.	2.5 × 0.9 Metre	3.5 kg	55:55:55	25-30	Pkm 1, Sugar Baby, Arka Manik, Ashahi, Yamta, Arka Jyoti, Pusa Badena
Musk melon	120	Nov.-Feb.	1.5 × 0.6 Metre	3.0 kg	70:30:60	20	Pusa Sarbati, Melon, Arka Rajhans, Arka Jeet

Crop	Duration (days)	Season	Spacing (cm)	Seed rate (g/ha)	N:P:K (kg/ha)	Yield (MT/ha)	Important varieties and other information
Round gourd	90	Jan.-Feb.	1.5 × 1.0 Meter	3.5 kg	60:40:40	10	Arka Tinda
Amaranthus	50	All season	15 × 12	2.5 kg	75:25:25	10/25 days	Co 1, Co 2, Co 3, Co 4, Co 5.
Tapioca	270-330	Round the year in irrigated	75 × 7560 × 60	Irrigated: 17777 setts Rainfed: 27777 setts	IR: 60:60:160	IR: 30-40 RF: 50:65: 125 RF: 15-20	Co 1, Co 2, Co 3, H 165, H 226, Sree Vishaham (H 1687), Sree Sahay (H 2304), Nidhi
Elephant yam	240	April-May	90 × 45	3500 kg corms	80:60:100	30-35	Local
Colocasia	160	Feb.-Mar., June-July	45 × 45	800 kg	100:80:80	8-10	H-13 is a promising taro hybrid
Dioscorea	240	May-June	25 × 25	1875-2500 kg tubes	90:60:240	20-25	Sree Shilpa Is The First Hybrid of yam
Palak	30-35	All seasons	30 × 30	20-25 kg	60:60:60	20	All Green, Pusa Jyoti, Pusa Harit, Jobner Green, Pusa Bharati

□□□

33

Post-Harvest Technology

Preservation is a method by which food is kept out from spoilage fter harvest. Modern methods of preservation include canning, asteurization, freezing, irradiation and the addition of chemicals.

- **Nicolas Appert** reported for the first time in 1804, the successful preservation of food in glass containers, for his work the French Government in 1809 awarded him, since then he is recognized as **Father of Food Preservation.**
- In India first food preservation factory was established in Bombay in 1935. Central Food Technological Research Institute was established in 1950 at Mysore (Karnatka). Government of India in 1955 passed Food Product Order (FPO) to control the quality of processed food. Food and Nutrition Board was formed in 1973 for the licensing of the same.
- Storage at low temperatures prolongs the shelf life of many food materials by reducing the growth rates of microbes and slowing down many physical and chemical reactions occurring in foods.
- The typical microorganisms that cause food spoilage are bacteria (*Lactobacillus*), yeasts (*Saccharomyces*), and moulds (*Rhizopus*). Yeasts promote fermentation in fruits by breaking down sugars into alcohol and carbon dioxide.
- The most of chemicals used in food preservation include benzoic acid, sodium benzoate, propionic acid, sorbic acid and sodium diacetate.

Mechanism of Spoilage

Needham in 1749 suggested the cause of spoilage in food. Spoilage occurs following different reactions:

- **Autoxidation:** The unsaturated fatty acids present in the lipids of many foods are susceptible to chemical breakdown when exposed to oxygen. The oxidation of unsaturated fatty acids autocatalytic. This lipid radical reacts with molecular oxygen (O_2) to form a peroxy radical. The peroxy radical removes hydrogen atom from another lipid molecule and the reaction starts over and again. During the propagation steps hydroperoxide molecules are formed that may break down into alkoxy and peroxy radicals plus water (H_2O). The lipid, alkoxy and peroxy radicals may combine with one another to form stable, non-propagating products called termination. These products result in the development of rancid off-flavours in the food. In addition to promoting rancidity, the free radicals and peroxides produced in these reactions may have other negative effects, such as the bleaching of food colour and the destruction of vitamins A, C, and E. This type of deterioration is prevalent in fried snacks, nuts, cooking oils and margarine.

- **Maillard reaction:** Another chemical reaction that causes major food spoilage is non-enzymatic browning known as the Maillard reaction. This reaction takes place between reducing sugars (simple monosaccharides) and the amino group of proteins or amino acids present in foods. The products of the Maillard reaction lead to the darkening of colour, reduced solubility (proteins), development of bitter flavours, and reduced nutritional availability (lysine). Non-enzymatic browning causes spoilage during the storage of dry milk, dry whole eggs and breakfast cereals.
- **Light-induced reactions or photosensitized oxidation:** Light influences a number of chemical reactions that lead to spoilage of foods. These light-induced reactions results into (*i*) the destruction of chlorophyll in certain vegetables; (*ii*) the discoloration of fresh meats; (*iii*) destruction of riboflavin in milk; and (*iv*) oxidation of vitamin C and carotenoid pigments.

Principles of Preservation

The preservation of food material is done following these principles: (1) Prevention or delaying the microbial decomposition (2) Preven-tion or delaying the self-decomposition of the food materials and (3) Prevention of damage by insects, animals and mechanical causes.

Methods of Preservation

There are following methods of preservation of food materials:

- **Asepsis**: It is the prevention of microbes by maintaining general cleanness during picking, grading, packing and transportation of food materials.
- **Pasteurization:** Pasteurization of milk target the pathogenic bacteria *Mycobacterium tuberculosis, Coxiella burnetti,* and *Brucella abortus*. It is carried out as heat treatment food material at 72°C for 15 seconds, or 63°C for 30 minutes, or 90°C for 0.5 second, or 94°C for 0.1 second immediately followed by rapid cooling to 7-4°C. The high-temperature-short-time (HTST) treatments cause less damage to the nutrient composition and sensory characteristics of foods and therefore are preferred over the low-temperature-long-time (LTLT) treatments.
- **Sterilization:** Sterilization is the complete exclusion of microbes. Fruits and acidic vegetables like tomato can be sterilized at 100°C for 30 minutes; whereas, non-acidic vegetables require treatment of 116°C temperature for 30 minutes.
- **Refrigeration:** The shelf life of many food materials may be increased by storage at 4°C or below. Commonly refrigerated foods include fresh fruits and vegetables, eggs, dairy products, and meats. However, some foods, such as tropical fruits (*e.g.*, bananas), are damaged if exposed to low temperatures.
- **Freezing:** Freezing and frozen storage provide an excellent means of preserving the nutritional quality of foods. It is done at –18°C to –40°C. At subfreezing temperatures the nutrient loss is extremely slow for the typical storage period used in commercial trade. Juices are mostly preserved by freezing.
- **Chemicals:** Under the Food Product Order (1955), two chemicals *viz.* Sulphur dioxide and Benzoic acid, are allowed in India to be used as preservatives. **Sulphur dioxide** acts as an antioxidant and bleaching agent. It is used in the form of its salts like sulphite, bisulphite and metabisulphite. Permissible amount in fruit juices including RTS and nectar is 100 ppm whereas in squash, crush and cordial it is 350 ppm. Sulphur dioxide retains the original colour of beverages for longer period than benzoic acid. **Benzoic acid** is used in the form of sodium benzoate and permitted up to 100 ppm in RTS and nectar, 600 ppm in squash, crush and cordial.

- Other **organic compounds** used as preservatives include vanillic acid esters, monochloroacetic acid, propionates, sorbic acid, dehydroacetic acid and glycols.
- **Dehydration:** It is removal of moisture from the food materials for preservation. The initial temperature of dehydration is usually at 43°C, which is gradually increased up to 60-66°C (vegetables) and 66-71°C (fruits).
- Moisture content in dried products should not be more than 6-8% (vegetables) and 10-20% (fruits).
- **Sweating** is the process, which is done to equalize the moisture content by keeping preserved material into bins or boxes.
- **Sulphuring** is process of fuming food materials (particularly potato slices) through sulphur dioxide to prevent discolouration.
- **Freeze-drying**: It is done by employing high vacuum conditions, permitting specific temperature and pressure.
- **Carbonation:** Carbonation is the process of dissolving sufficient carbon dioxide in water or beverages to inhibit the microbial activity. Complete inactivation of microbial activity (moulds including yeast) can be achieved by mixing 14.6 g CO_2 per litre for juice or beverage.
- **Sugars:** Sugars preserve food by the process of osmosis. Approximately 66 per cent or more sugar is necessary for preservation of fruits. Fruit syrup, Jam, Jelly, Marmalade, Preserve, Candy, Cristallised fruit and glazed fruit are preserved using sugars.
- **Salts:** About 15-25 per cent salt (NaOH) concentration is sufficient to preserve most of the food products.
- **Acids:** Acidic environment inhibit the growth of microbes responsible for food spoilage. Acetic acid, Citric acid, and Lactic acid are used for preservation of food materials including fruits.
- **Antibiotics:** Some of the antibiotics are used as preservatives for food materials. Nisin is used for canning of mushrooms, tomatoes and milk products. Pimaricin (used primarily against *Pythium* spp.) is used for treating fruits for fruit juices.

Food Irradiation

Food irradiation involves the use of either high-speed electron beaming or high-energy radiation with wavelengths lesser than 200 nanometers, or 2,000 angstroms (*e.g.*, X-rays and gamma rays). These rays contain sufficient energy to break chemical bonds and ionize molecules that lie in their path. The two most common sources of high-energy radiation used in the food industry are cobalt-60 (^{60}Co) and cesium-137 (^{137}Cs).

Canning

Canning sometimes called Appertizing (after the name of Nicolas Appert). Destruction of spoilage organisms within the sealed container by means of heat is the main principle of canning. A typical canning operation involves cleaning, filling, exhausting, sealing, heat processing, cooking, labelling, casing and storage. A significant loss of nutrients, especially heat-labile vitamins, may occur during the process of canning. Vitamins A, D and ß-carotene are resistant to the effects of heat whereas vitamin B_1 is sensitive to thermal treatment.

- The scientific process of canning was discovered in 1896 when **Emile van Ermengem** discovered *Clostridium botulinum*, with its lethal toxin causing botulism.
- **Peter Durand** received a British patent for use of containers made of glass, pottery, tin, or other metals for the heat preservation of foods.
- Tin-coated steel containers, made from 98.5% sheet steel with a thin coating of tin, are most commonly used cans.

Blanching: Blanching also called **scalding**, parboiling, or precooking is a thermal process used mostly for vegetables prior to freezing, drying, or canning in order to soften the texture. It is carried out at 100°C for 2-5 minutes in either a water bath or steam chamber. It is done to reduce microbial load, remove gases, and wilt the tissues of leafy vegetables so that they can easily be put into the containers. Blanching also inactivates enzymes (*e.g.*, phenoloxidase, which cause browning in banana, apple and potato) that cause deterioration of food materials during storage.

- Retention of ascorbic acid (vitamin C) is markedly improved, if packaging is done at 49°C temperatures.
- Syrup should be canned at 79-82 °C.

Lye peeling: It is the peeling of fruits (Peaches, Apricots, Sweet Oranges, Mandarin, Oranges) and vegetables (Carrot, Sweet Potatoes) before preservation by dipping them in 1-2% boiling caustic soda solution for 0.5 to 2 minutes

Brine solution: Salt (NaOH) dissolved in water is called brine solution, which is used for washing the vegetables before canning at 1-3% concentration.

Important Fruit Beverages

Fruit beverages can be categorized into two categories, *viz.* Unfermented and Fermented.

(*A*) **Unfermented**: Fruit juices, which do not undergo alcoholic fermentation, are usually termed as unfermented beverages, *e.g.* Sweetened juices, RTS (Ready to Serve), Nectar, Cordial, Squash, Crush, Syrup, etc.

(*i*) **Sweetened juice**: Sweetened juice contains 85% juice and 10% soluble solids.

(*ii*) **RTS**: It contains 10% fruit juice and 10% soluble solids. In addition to these it also contains 0.3% acid. It is diluted just before serving.

(*iii*) **Nectar**: Nectar contains 20% fruit juice, 15% total solids and 0.3% acid. It is also diluted while serving. Nectar is prepared from Mango, Papaya, Bel, Aonla, etc.

(*iv*) **Cordial**: It is a clear fruit juice having no traces of pulp and other soluble substances. It contains 25% juice, 30% TSS, 1.5% acid and 350 ppm sulphuric acid. It is used mostly as blend in wines and prepared from Lime and Lemon.

(*v*) **Squash**: Squash contains 25% fruit juice or pulp and 40-50% TSS. It is diluted before serving. It is prepared from Mango, Orange and Pineapple at commercial scale.

(*vi*) **Crush**: Crush contains 25% fruit juice or pulp and 55% TSS. It is also diluted before serving.

(*vii*) **Syrup**: It contains 25% fruit juice or pulp, 65% TSS, and 1.3-1.5% acid. It is also diluted before serving.

(*viii*) **Fruit juice concentrate**: It is a kind of beverage with almost no amount of water, removed either by heating or freezing. It contains pure juice with at least 32% TSS.

(*ix*) **Fruit juice powder:** It is a converted fruit juice into free flowing and highly hygroscopic powder.

(*x*) **Barley water**: Barley water contains 25% fruit juice, 30% TSS, 0.25% barley starch and 1.0% acid. It is prepared from citrus fruits like lime, lemon, grapefruit etc.

(*B*) **Fermented**: Fruit juices, which have undergone alcoholic fermentation by yeasts or other microbe, are called fermented beverages, *e.g.* Wine, Champagne, Port, Slurry, Tokay, *Nira* and Ciders, etc. Fresh fruits and vegetables soften after 24 hours in a watery solution and begin a slow, mixed fermentation-putrefaction. The addition of salt (NaOH) suppresses undesirable microbial activity, creating a favourable environment for the desired fermentation.

Important Post-harvest Products

- **Jam:** It is a product made by boiling fruit pulp with sufficient amount of sugar to a reasonable thick consistency, as to hold fruit tissue in original position. Jam contains 0.5-0.6% acid and 40% invert sugar. It is prepared from Mango, Apple, Pear, Sapota, Peach, Papaya, Karonda, Strawberry, Raspberry, Tomato, Musk melon, etc.
- **Jelly:** It is a semi-solid product prepared by boiling a clear stained solution from pectin containing fruit extract, free from pulp, after the addition of sugar and acid. A perfect jelly should have original flavour of fruit. It is prepared from Guava, Sour apple, Plum, Karonda, Wood apple, Gooseberry, Papaya and Luquat. Only ripe fruits are chosen as they contain pectinic acid (protopectin found in developing fruits) form of pectin. Good quality jelly requires at least 0.5% pectin. It contains 65% TSS. The pH of final jelly should be 3.2.
- **Marmalade:** It is prepared from citrus fruit slices suspended in sugar solution.
- **Candied fruits/vegetables:** A fruit or vegetable impregnated with the cane-sugar or glucose syrup, subsequently draining of syrup leaving it dried, is called candied fruits or vegetables.
- **Tomato Ketchup:** It is clear, soured product made from strain tomato juice, salt, sugar and vinegar, etc. It contains tomato juice 12%, TSS 25% and Acidity 1.2%.
- **Pickle**: The salt concentration in pickle is maintained at 8 to 10 per cent during the first week and increased by 1% in every subsequent week till it reaches to 16 per cent.

Institutions Involved

- Agriculture and Processed Food Product Export Development Authrity (APEDA), New Delhi.
- Central Institute for Post-harvest Engineering and Technology (CIPHET), Ludhiana.
- Central Food Technological Research Institute (CFTRI), Mysore.
- Food and Agriculture Organization (FAO), Rome.
- National Horticultural Board (NHB), Gurgaon.

❑❑❑

34

Ornamental Horticulture

Ornamental horticulture consists of floriculture and landscaping.

- The major **importing countries** of Cut Flowers are Netherlands, USA, Germany, France, UK, Switzerland, Italy and Japan. The major **exporting countries** include Netherlands, Columbia, Ecuador, Israel, Spain and Kenya.
- **International flower market** is located at **Alsmeer** in **Netherlands.** Rose is the most important flower traded in the international market.
- **The contribution** of Netherlands in international floriculture trade is 57% followed by Columbia (14%), Israel (4%), Kenya and Ecuador (3%), Thailand and Spain (2%), India (0.6%).
- **Flower consumption:** Per capita consumption of flowers is highest in Switzerland followed by Norway, Netherlands, Austria and Belgium, whereas per capita consumption of live plants is highest in Norway followed by Germany, Denmark, Sweden and Switzerland.
- **National/International registration centres:** The International Registration authority for Bougainvillea is situated at Indian Agricultural Research Institute (IARI), New Delhi. IARI is also the centre of national registration for roses. National Botanical Research Institute (NBRI) is the National Registration Centre for Chrysanthemum.
- **Flowers and human feelings:** Flowers convey human feelings as love (Rose, Tulip, Carnation), sorrow-jealous (French Marigold), regard (Daffodil), self-esteem (Narcissus), message (Iris), pride (Amyryllis), departure (Sweet pea), luxury (Stock), presumption (Snapdragon) and purity (Lily).
- **Flowers as symbols:** Flowers are also the national symbols as Lotus for India and Egypt; Rose for U.K., U.S.A, Iran, New Zealand; Narcissus for China; Chrysanthemum for Japan;

Tulips for Netherlands; Lily for Italy, Cornflower for Germany; and Daffodil for Wales.

- The **bulb crops** include plants such as the tulip, hyacinth, narcissus, iris, daylily, and dahlia.
- **Non-hardy bulbs** used as potted plants in indoors and summer outdoor plantings include amaryllises, anemones, various tuberous begonias, caladiums, cannas, dahlias, freesias, gladioli, tiger flowers, etc.
- **Hardy bulbs** are those that survive even they are left in soil over a winter, include various crocuses, snowdrops, lilies, daffodils, and tulips. Garden tulips are different from tulips as they arose from crosses between thousands of cultivars representing several species. **Garden tulips** are grouped as early tulips, breeder's tulips, cottage tulips, Darwin tulips, lily-flowered tulips, triumph tulips, Mendel tulips, parrot tulips and others. The garden tulips have been **developed** first in **Turkey**.
- **Shrubs:** Production of ornamental shrubs is the backbone of the nursery trade, is about equally divided between the production of (1) coniferous evergreens such as yew, juniper, spruce and pine; (2) broad-leaved evergreens such as rhododendron, camellia, holly, and boxwood; (3) deciduous plants such as forsythia, viburnum, berberis, privet, lilac and clematis; and (4) roses.

Roses (*Rosa* spp.) Family: Rosaceae

Roses are the prickly shrubs with scrambling or trailing stems. The leaves are pinnately compounded with stipules (leaf-like appendages) fused to the base of the leaf stalk. The flowers have five sepals (wild species) and five petals, numerous stamens and pistils. The flowers come in various colours and shades, including red, pink, yellow, and white. The fruit is the well-known hip, a swollen and thinly fleshed hypanthium (cup-shaped receptacle) enclosing the dry achenes.

The modern roses have been derived from crosses between the Chinese roses (*Rosa chinensis*) and the European roses (*R. gigantea, R. damascena, R. moschata*).

- **New released varieties:** Six new rose varieties, Pusa Mohit, Pusa Abhishek, Pusa Manhar, Pusa Muskan, Pusa Urmil and Pusa Ranjana, developed at IARI, New Delhi, released for cultivation. Pusa Mohit is a Hybrid Tea, which produces red coloured flowers suitable for cut flowers while others 5 are floribundas.

- **Promising varieties:** The plants of Pusa Abhishek are hardy and tolerant to powdery mildew and black spots. Pusa Manhar is medium growing floribunda type, produces creamy white flowers with magenta shade. It is also tolerant to powdery mildew and black spot.
- Pusa Muskan produces creamy white flowers in clusters having pink shade and red coloured edges. Pusa Urmil is a bud sport Jantar Mantar that produces large clusters of 40-45 brown pink coloured flowers. Pusa Ranjana, a dwarf floribunda, produces dark pink flowers in a big cluster. It is suitable for pots and bedding purposes. Pusa Gaurav for cut flower, Neelambari and Arunima for loose flowers and Arunima and Banjaran for garden displays.

ackage and Practices

lowers	Season	Spacing	Seed Rate (cm)	N: P: Kg/plant	Yield
ose	Sep.-Oct.	2 × 1 M	5000 Layers	60:12:12 Twice a year	6-7.5 M Flowers
ybrid ose	July-Aug.	75 × 75	17777 Buds	60:12:12 Every 3 months	60-70 Flowers/ Year/plant

Scientific classification: Hybrid perpetuals, or remontant roses, re derived mainly from the hybrid species *Rosa × borboniana*; olyantha roses from the hybrid species *Rosa × rehderana*; tea roses rom *Rosa × odorata*; and China roses from *Rosa × odorata* and *Rosa hinensis*.

Hybrid-tea type: The flowers in the hybrid-tea are well shaped nd borne singly. **Varieties** of hybrid-tea include Avon, Papa Meilland, Mister Lincoln, Oklahoma, Christian dior and happiness red and dark red); Hawaii and super-star (Orange); summer sunshine, ing's Ransom, Kiss of fire, Golden splendor and golden giant (yellow); Eiffel tower, Michelle Meilland, Peter Frankenfeldt, First Prize, Montezuma south seas (pink and coral pink); Virgo, Matterhorn, John F. Kennedy, Dr. Homi Bhabha (white); Bajazzo, Ingo Hortsmann, Rose Gaujard, Granada (Bicoloured); Blue Moon, Lady X (Lavender or Mauve); Thais, Vienna Charm, Whisky Mac (Copper colour); Anvil

Sparks (red with yellow streaks); Careless Love (pink with whi streaks); Crimson Glory (red with fragrance), Papa Meillan Oklahoma, Fragrant cloud, Charles Mallerin (Velvety red) (Fragran

Floribunda type: In floribunda flowers are large and produced clusters. **Varieties** include Charleston (yellow and crimson), Flam neo (salmon), Orange Sensation (deep orange), Banjaran (red and gol Iceberg (white), Arthur Bell (yellow), Africa Star (mauve), Else Pouls (pink, single), Delhi Princess (pink), Himangini (white), Prema (so pink with deep-pink edges), Summer Snow (white), Dearest (ro salmon), Zorina (red) and Zambra (orange), Queen Elizabeth (pinl Sea pearl (pink), Pink Parfait (light pink), Tiki (shell pink).

Polyantha type: Produce smaller flowers in larger trusse **Varieties**: Chatillon Rose (deep pink, single), Vater Tag (vermillior Echo (pink changing to white).

Climbing and rambling type: They are climbing type rose **Varieties:** Clg. Show Girl (pink), Clg. Virgo (white), Clg. Summer Sno (white), Prosperity (white), Marechal Niel (lemon), Golden Showe (yellow), Lamarque (white), Mardan White (white), Mardan Pir (pink), Cocktail (red with yellow centre), Josephs Cat (red and yellow

Miniature type: They are dwarf, having small leaves and flowe suitable for pots. **Varieties:** Cri Cri (salmon coral), Baby Masquera (lemon chrome), Little Buckaroo (velvety red), Rosemarin (silver rose Coralin (red orange).

Propagation

Roses are propagated by both budding and cuttings. The ramble polyantha and miniature roses are successfully multiplied fro cuttings. The cuttings are inserted into the soil or sand from Decemb to February. The commonly used rootstock is the Edouard rose f North and *R. multiflora* for Southern India. Transplanting is done July or August.

Rose Perfume

The oil of rose is extracted from *Rosa damascena* var. *triginipetala*

($2n = 14$), popularly called **Kazanlik Rose** or 30 petalled ros Bulgaria produces the largest quantity and best quality of rose-oil the world.

- In India, the Damask rose (*Rosa damascena*) or the Bushra ro similar to the kazanlik rose of Bulgaria, is grown in sever areas of U.P. The largest being grown in Aligarh (400 ha). *damascena* var. *bifera* is commonly cultivated in Kannauj (U.I and gives a second flush of flowering in September.

- The oil percentage in a rose flower is about 0.045%. The common products prepared are rose-oil, *gulkand*, rose water and rose concrete.
- The Edouard Rose (*R. borboniana*) or Chiniya *gulab* is grown for making *gulkand*. The species *R. centipetala* is also grown in some parts of India for making *gulkand* and rose water.

Jasmine (*Jasminum* spp.) Family: Oleaceae

The jasmines are primarily used for the preparation of perfume and concrete. Different species grown include *Jasminum officinale*, *J. grandiflorum* (chameli or janti), *J. sambac* (bela, motia, mogra), *J. auriculatum*, *J. augustifolium*, *J. paniculatum*, *J. pubescens*, *J. arborescens* and the yellow-flowered *J. primulinum* and *J. humile*. The flowers of *J. grandiflorum* are used for extracting the essential oil. *J. sambac* is most commonly grown in the gardens. Almost all species flower during summer and rainy season. *J. pubescens* flowers during winter in Northern India.

- **Varieties**: *J. auriculatum*: Co 1, Mullai, Parimullai, Large Round, Large Point, Short Point; *J. grandiflorum*: Co 1 Pichi, Co 2 Pichi; *J. sambac*: Addukaumalli, Elusuttumallige, Iruvatchi, Mohra, Madanban, Ramabanam, Virupakshi, etc.
- The yield of flowers is about 1,000-1,500 (erect) and 2000 (climbing type) kg/acre.

Chrysanthemum (*Chrysanthemum* spp.) Family: Compositae

When tubular rays are open and flattened at the tips, the plants are then called **spoon chrysanthemums**.

The terms "**pompon**" and "**button**" are applied to small, globular flowers; "**anemone**" to the flowers with twisted rays; and "**decorative**" to loose, open flowers with flat, grooved, or tubular rays. Based on above terminology chrysanthemum has been divided into several groups, *viz.* **incurved** (a perfect ball, incurving petals loosely or irregularly); **reflexed** (dropping florets); **anemone** (single petals with a tubular central disc);, **Pompon** (very small flowers, without any visible centre); **Singles** (five petals with a central disc), **Spider** (petals with a hook at the tip); **Spoon** (spoon-like tip of petals); **Koreans** (small single, semi-double or double flowers with a visible disc) and **Rayonnantes** (with quelled petals).

- **Varieties:** Mahatma Gandhi, Modinagar, Pride of Jamshedpur, Red carpet, Steel city beauty, Sri Ganga, Anokha, Rangamahal,

Chanderkant, Chandrika, Indira, Kanak, Kumkum, Nirbhaya, Pingal, Rohit, Shefali, Shveta, Baggi, Basanti, Gul-e-Shair, Punjab Gold, MDU Chrysanthemum 1, Co Chrysanthemum, Co 2 Chrysanthemum. **Small mutant flowered:** Agnishiksha, Alankar, Anamika, Basanti, Hemanthi, Lohit, Manbhavan, Navneet, Sharadhar, Shanti Sheela, Sonali, Surekha yellow, Y2K: **Off season cultivars:** Ajaya, Haldi Ghati, Himansu, Jaya, Jwala, Jyoti, Maghi, Mayday, Meghdoot, Phuhar, Sarad Mala, Sarad Singar, Tushar, Usha, Vasantika, etc.

- In India *Chrysanthemum indicum* (small-flowers of yellow or white) is used as cut flowers in Coimbatore, Madurai and Bangalore.

Dahlia (*Dahlia pinnata*) Asteraceae

Dahlia is a tuberous-rooted perennial plant native to Central America and Mexico. Genus Dahalia has been so named after Swedish botanist Anders Dahl (a pupil of Carolus Linnaeus), who cultivated Dahlia for the first time in Europe. The dahlias introduced into cultivation grew to a height of about 2 m and produces single flowers with a yellow disc and scarlet rays. **Flowers of every shade except blue** have been produced through hybridization.

- **Varieties**: Kenya Blue, Kenya White, Kenya Yellow, Manali, Manjushri, Lord Budha, Prabodh, Vivek, Jyotsna, Jayanti, Chitchor, etc.

Orchids (*Renanthera* spp., *Aerides* spp. and *Saccolabium* spp.)

Orchidaceae is largest family among flowering plants having 35,000 species. Orchid flowers are borne on stalks called pedicels, during the growth and development pedicel rotates 180°, therefore mature flower is borne upside down. Of the total sepals and petals of flower's, three sepals and three petals are usually similar both in colour and shape; remaining petals are distinct from each other called the labellum or lip.

- The sexual organs of the orchid flower are fused together into a structure called the column, which lies opposite the labellum. Orchids have usually one stamen with single anther. In a few orchids, however, two anthers are produced.
- Orchids are propagated by psedo-bulbs or stem cuttings and mostly cultivated in Assam, Darjeeling, Andhra Pradesh, Meghalaya, Tripura, Sikkim, Bhutan, Kodaikanal, Bangalore, Pune and Bombay during November to February, which flower in March-April.

- The orchids that flower in the plains year after year include *Aerides multiflora, A. odoratum, Cymbidium aloifolium, Phaius wallichii* (terrestrial), *Saccolabium guttatum, Dendrobium pierardii, D. moschatum, Pholidota imbricata* and *Vanda tessellata* var. *unicolor*.

Gladiolus (*Gladiolus* spp.) Family: Iridaceae

The earliest known species, which laid the discovery of gladiolus is *Gladiolus primulinus* found growing as wild near the Victoria Falls (Zimbabwe). Other species include *G. byzantinus, G. psittacinus, G. cardinalis, G. childsii, G. colvillii* and *G. gandavensis*.

- **New release:** Five new varieties, *viz.* Urmi, Jyotsana, Gulal, Shabnam and Urvashi have been released from IARI.
- **Other varieties:** George Mazure, Fay, Gold Dust, Tunia's Yellow Triumph, Elizabeth the Queen, Jo Wagenear, Spic and Span, Spotlight, Dream Girl, Goeff Whiteman, Blaur Dominos, Polygoon, Banaras, Mary House, Snow Princess, Ratnas, Butterfly, Masholra Butterfly, Sylvia, Apple Blossom; **IARI**: Agnirekha, Anjali, Archana, Chirag, Dhanvantari, Gunjan, Kamini, Mayur, Neelam, Neelkanth, Noopur, Pusa Suhagin, Rangmahal, Sanjeevni, Sarang, Shweta, Suchitra, Sukanya, Sunayana, Swapnil, Urmil; **IIHR:** Aarti, Apsara, Darshan, Dhiraj (resistant to Fusarium), Poonam, etc.

Bougainvillea (*Bougainvillea* spp.) Family: Nyctaginaceae

The Bougainvillea is so named after Louis Antoine de Bougainvillea (a French navigator), includes several species cultivated for glory

B. glabra, B. spectabilis, B. peruviana and ***B. buttiana.***

- **Varieties:** Snow Queen (white), Shubhra (white), Sanderiana (deep mauve), Trinidad (pale mauve), Mrs. H.C. Buck (deep rose), Louis Wathen (orange), Enid Lancaster (yellow with shades of rose), Ladt Marry Baring (yellow), Mrs. Butt (deep crimson), Sonnet (light rosy purple), Spring Festival (medium magenta purple), Summer Time (bright red), Partha (young bracts orange changing to pink purple), Tomato Red (terracotta), Sensation (deep magenta), Blondie (orange turning light rose), Isabel Greensmith (coppery changing to rose), Bois due Rose (biscuit colour), Begum Sikander (white with rose edges) and Wajid Ali Shah (rose). **Multi-bract cultivars:** Mahara (red), Roseville's Delight (orange), Cherry Blossom (white), Los Banos Beauty (rose). **Varieties with variegated leaves**: Rao (white and green, bracts red), Louis Wathen (variegated white and green, bracts orange) and Glabra (variegated white magenta green).

Tuberose (*Polianthes tuberosa*) Family: Amarylidaceae

The tuberose is a native of Mexico. Its leaves are long, narrow, linear and grass-like. The flowering stalk emerges from the centre of the leaves. The flowers are tubular, single or double, white and highly fragrant. The white, waxy, funnel-shaped flowers, borne in pairs in a loose spike, have three sepals, numerous petals, six stamens, and a solitary pistil. The fruit is a many-seeded capsule. The plant is commonly raised from tubers and grows to a height of 90 cm.

- Tuberose is commercially grown for cut flowers near Madurai (Tamil Nadu) and Bangalore.
- Chemical treatment of tuberose spikes with sucrose 2% + Al_2SO_4 300 ppm and wrapping them in newspapers increase post-harvest life of tuberose.
- The bulbs are planted in September-October in the plains. The flowering takes place during summer and rainy season (April to September) in the northern plains and in May-June in the hills.
- **Varieties:** Shringar (single), Suvasini (double), Rajat Rekha (single), Swarna Rekha (double).

Marigold (*Tagetes* spp.) Family: Compositae

True marigolds are also known as calendulas, are annual herb growing up to 1 m tall and producing large, globular, golden-yellow or orange flower heads.

- **African marigold** (*T. erecta*): It is generally tall with large double globular flowers, which are lemon, golden yellow, primrose, orange or bright yellow in colour. **Varieties**: Pusa Basanti Gainda, Pusa Narangi Gainda, Pusa Sankar 1, MDU-1 Marigold.
- **French marigold** (*T. patula*): It is mostly dwarf, early-flowering and compact with dainty single or double blooms, borne freely and almost covering the entire plant. The flowers may be yellow, orange, golden yellow, primrose, mahogany, rusty red, tangerine or deep scarlet or combination of these colours. The flowers may be self-coloured, spotted, striped or botched. **Varieties:** Jhumka, Karana Pali, Lalita, Mukta, Ratnam and Vibhuti.
- **The Single Signet** (*T. tenuifolia*): This is a dwarf type of marigold having small single orange, yellow or lemon flowers, *e.g.* Pumila compact variety.

□□□

35

Spices And Condiments

The name spice has been derived from the word *species,* which was applied to groups of exotic foodstuffs in the middle Ages.

- India is the largest producer, consumer and exporter of spices in the world.
- The Spices Board India was established in 1987 under Ministry of Commerce, Government of India, is the apex body dealing with the promotion and export of Indian spices.
- The Arabs develop the spices trade bringing Pepper and Cloves from India; Cinnamon and Nutmeg from the Spice Islands; and Ginger from China through "*the Golden Road of Samarkand*" and selling them in markets of Nineveh, Babylon, Carthage, Egypt and Rome.
- There are about 35 spices and condiments included in the Indian culinary.

Common Spice Crops and Their Parts Used as Spices/Condiments

Spices (part used)	Species and family
Cinnamon (bark)	*Cinnamomum verum* (= *C. zeylanicumts*) *C. cassia* (Lauraceae)
Mace (aril), **nutmeg** (endosperm)	*Myristica fragrans*
Cloves (flower buds)	*Syzygium aromaticum* = *Eugenia caryophyllus* (Myrtaceae)
Small cardamom (pods)	*Elettaria cardamomum* (Zingiberaceae)
Large cardamom (pods)	***Amomum subulatum*** (Zingiberaceae)
Pepper (drupes)	*Piper nigrum* (Piperaceae)
Turmeric (root)	*Cucurma longa* (Zingiberaceae)
Ginger (rhizome)	*Zingiber officinale* (Zingiberaceae)
Star anise (immature fruit)	*Illicium verum* (Illiciaceae)

Bay leaf (leaves)	*Laurus nobilis* (Lauraceae)
Caper (flower buds)	*Capparis spinosa* (Capparidaceae)
Poppy (seeds)	*Papaver somniferum* (Papaveraceae)
Saffron (stigma)	*Crocus sativus* (Iridaceae)
Allspice (fruits)	*Pimenta dioica* (Myrtaceae)
Pepper (berries)	*Capsicum annum C. frutescen* (Solanaceae)
Vanilla (berries)	*Vanilla planifolia, V. pompona* (West Indian Vanilla), *V. tahitensis* (Tahitian Vanilla): Orchidaceae
Cumin (seeds)	*Cuminum cyminum,* Apiaceae (Umbelliferae)
Basil (leaves and seeds)	(*Ocimum basilicum,* Lamiaceae (Labiatae
Celery (seeds)	*Apium graveolens* (Apiaceae)
Coriander (leaves and seeds)	*Coriandrum sativum* (Apiaceae)
Fenugreek (seeds)	*Trigonella foenum graecum* (Fabaceae)
Garlic (bulb)	*Allium sativum* (Alliaceae)
Fennel (seeds)	*Foeniculum* vulgarisa (Apiacae)
Sage (leaves)	*Salvia officinalis*: Lamiaceae (Labiatae
Savory (dried leaves)	*Satureia hortensis*: Lamiaceae or Labiatae
Cambodge (rind)	*Garcinia gummi-gutta* (Clusiaceae)
Rosemary (leaves)	*Rosmarinus officinalis*: Laminaceae
Parsley	***Petroselinum crispum*: Apiaceae**

Important Flavour Compounds in Spices

Eugenol, found in cinnamon, clove and pimento, enhances sexual feelings. Menthol, from mints, has a cooling effect as well as characteristic fresh taste and smell. Ginger contains gingerol zingiberene are good sources of aphrodiasc. Saffron contain picrocrocin causes erotic sensations. Vanilla contains vanillin.

Spices	Flavour compounds
Allspice	Eugenol, β-caryophyllene
Anise	(E)-anethole, methyl chavicol
Black pepper	Piperine, S-3-Carene, β-caryophyllene
Caraway	d-carvone, carone derivatives
Cardamom	a-terpinyl acetate, 1-8-cineole, linalool
Cinnamon, Cassia	Cinnamaldehyde, eugenol
Chilli	Capsaicin, dihydro capsaicin
Clove	Eugenol, eugenyl acetate

Coriander	d-linalool, C10-C14-2-alkenals
Cumin	Cuminaldehyde
Dill	d-carvone
Fennel	e-anethole, e-fenchone
Ginger	Gingerol, Shogaol, Neral, Geranial
Mace	a-pinene, Sabinene, 1-terpenin-4-ol.
Nutmeg	Sabinine, a-pinene, myristicin
Parsley	Apiol
Saffron	Safranol
Turmeric	Turmerone, Zingeberene, 1, 8-cineole
Vanilla	Vanillin, p-OH-benzyl-methyl ether
Basil, Sweet	Methylchavicol, linalool, methyl eugenol
Rosemary	Verbenone, 1-8-cineole, camphor, linanool
Savory	Carvacrol
Peppermint	1-menthol, menthone, menthfuran
Spear mint	1-carvone, carvone derivatives

Cinnamon

Cinnamon is a bushy evergreen tree native to Malabar Coast of India. It has 0.5-1.0% essential oil. Cinnamon is used in many dishes from around the world. Ground cinnamon is used with traditional spices in baking rich cakes, pastries and biscuits.

Mace

Mace is sold either as whole blades or ground spice, used in savoury dishes; flavouring milk-based sauces like bechamel; and processed meats, such as sausages and charcuterie. Pickles and chutney can be seasoned with mace.

Nutmeg

Nutmeg is a traditional flavouring for cakes, gingerbreads, biscuits, fruit and milk puddings. Mulled alcoholic drinks are enhanced with the addition of little nutmeg. Nutmeg can be used in risotto, tomato sauce or fish sauces, chicken pies, lamb chops and mashed potatoes. It can also enhance the flavour of hot milk drinks.

Cloves

It is a reddish-brown unopened flower bud of a tropical evergreen tree. Clove originated in Moluccas (called Spice Island in Indonesia) and now cultivated in the islands of Zanzibar and Pemba (parts of Tanzania), Indonesia, Madagascar, Sri Lanka and Malayasia, etc. The

East India Company first introduced clove to India around 1800 AD, into its spice garden in Courtallam, Tamil Nadu.

- Clove plantations in India started from a few seedlings obtained originally from Mauritius. Since, 1850 it is cultivated in Nilgiris, Tiruneiveli, Kanyakumari, Nagercoil and Ramanathapuram districts of Tamil Nadu, Kozhikode, Kottayam. Kollam and Thiruvananthapuram districts of Kerala and South Kanara district of Karnataka.
- **Climate and soil:** Clove is a tropical plant and requires warm humid climate and deep loam forest soil having high humus.
- It is propagated through seed obtained from ripened fruit called '**mother of clove**'. Seeds with pink radicle are ideal for sowing. Seeds sown with a spacing of 12-15 cm. 25-30 cm seedlings are then grown in pots for another 12-18 months and planted in pits (75 × 75 × 75 cm size, at spacing of 7 m) in May-June.
- **Manuring:** About 15 kg FYM plus 20:18:50 g NPK/plant for first year, applied in May-June; double of this amount in second year, increasing gradually to attain 300:250:750 g NPK/plant for 15 year- old trees.
- **Harvesting:** Clove tree begins to yield from the 7th year of planting and full bearing stage is attained after 15 to 20 years. The flowering season is September to October (in plains) and December to February (hills). Buds mature, the base of the calyx has turned from green to pink colour, in five to six months for harvest.
- **Yield:** The average annual yield from 15th year onward is usually 2 kg/tree or 400 kg/ ha.

Small Cardamom

Cardamom is considered to be the '**queen of spices**'. The seeds have a warm, slightly pungent, and highly aromatic flavour somewhat reminiscent of camphor. In the Middle East countries, cardamom is mainly used for preparation of *Gahwa* (cardamom flavoured coffee).

- India is the home of cardamom grown in evergreen forests of Western Ghats in South India. Till recently India was the main producer and exporter of this commodity, but now Guatemala has emerged as a keen competitor to Indian cardamom in the international market.
- It is basically a pseophytic plant growing under shade in evergreen forests. Grows well in forest loamy soils having pH 4.2 to 6.8.

- It is propagated through seeds, suckers and tissue culture plantlets.
- **Varieties: Varieties are grouped into the major and minor categories.** Major comprised of wild indigenous types of Sri Lanka and minor comprising of cultivars like, Mysore, Malabar and Vazhukka. **Malabar cultivars include ICRI 1, ICRI 2, ICRI 3, TDK-4, TQK-11, PV-1, CCS-1, Mudigere-1, etc.**
- **Propagation and planting: Propagated through seed and rhizomes.** Rhizome multiplication is done during March to October planted at 1.80 m × 0.60 m spacing in filled trenches of 45 cm width, 45 cm deep and 1.8 m apart. In field Mysore and Vazhukka cultivars are generally planted at 3 × 3 m or 2.4 × 2.4 m for irrigated crop, whereas in Karnataka 1.8 × 1.8 m or 1.2 × 1.8 m spacing is followed.
- Plant goes up to 2-4 metres height, matures in about 20-22 months and economic yield starts from 3rd year onwards after planting, and it continues up to 8-10 years. The peak period of panicle emergence is from Nov.-March. Flowers normally in May-August.
- **Curing:** The moisture of freshly harvested capsule is reduced from 80% to 10-12% at 50ºC to retain green colour.

Large Cardamom

It contains 2 to 3% of essential oil and medicinal properties like carminative, stomachic, diuretic, cardiac stimulant, antiemetic, etc. It is cultivated in the sub-Himalayan state of Sikkim and Darjeeling district of West Bengal. Soil rich in organic matter and having pH with 4.5 to 6.0 are suitable for cultivation.

- **Cultivars and selections**: Ramsey, Sawney, Golsey, Varlangey and Seremna. Bebo, Boklok Tali, Jaker, Belak are the other cultivars found in Arunachal Pradesh. **Selection:** SBLC 5, SBLC 47, SBLC 42, SBLC 44, SBLC 50, SBLC 51.

Propagated through seeds and suckers. Seeds are collected from capsules from bottom and middle position. Seeds are generally sown in September-October.

Planting is done during June-July in the pits of 30 × 30 × 30 cm size prepared on contour at a spacing of 1.5 × 1.5 m.

Shade trees: It performs well under shade trees like Utis (*Alnus nepalensis*), Panisaj (*Termalia myriocarpa*), Pipli (*Bucklandia* spp.), Malito (*Macaranga denticulate*), Argeli (*Edgeworthes gardneri*), Asare (*viburnus eruberens*), Bilaune (*Maesa cheria*), Kharane

(*Symplocos* spp.), Siris (*Albizzia lebbeck*), etc.

Manuring: 20:30:40 kg NPK/ha applied during April to Sept.

- **Leaf eating caterpillar** (*Artona chorista*) causes **infestation** on the leaf lamina from under surface of the leaf in May-July and Oct.-March. Spraying with Quinalphos 25 EC @ 0.05% or Endosulfan 35 EC @ 0.05% controls pest.
- **Harvesting and Curing:** The spikes are harvested by using special knives known as *Elaichichhuri*, and cured at 45-50°C

Pepper

The alkaloid piperine forms 5 to 8 per cent by weight of the seed and the volatile pepper oil forms 1 to 3 per cent of the unripe berries. Pepper cultivation is mainly confined to Kerala, Karnataka, Tamil Nadu., Assam and West Bengal, Andhra Pradesh and the Andamans.

- The International Pepper Community (IPC) has estimated that India with more than 40% share of the world area under pepper, contributes about 23% of the total production of pepper in the world.
- **Soil:** Soil for black pepper cultivation require 0.26% N, 0.25% P_2O_5, 0.41% K_2O, 0.18% MgO and 0.5%CaO. Soils with pH above 7.5 inhibit the growth.
- **Propagation:** Propagated best from cuttings of the runner shoots. Cuttings are separated from the vine in February-March.
- **Planting** is done on onset of the southwesterly monsoon (May-June) in the pits of 0.5 × 0.5 × 0.5 m at 3-4 m apart in each direction.
- **Cultivars and hybrids:** Over 75 cultivars are cultivated in India. **Famous in Kerala**: Karimunda, Kottanadan, Narayakkodi, Aimpiriyan, Neelamundi, Kuthiravally, Balancotta, Kalluvally. **Karnataka:** Billimalligesara, Karimalligesara, Doddiga, Mottakare and Uddagare. Panniyur-1 and Panniyur-3 have the highest oleoresin (17.8%) followed by Aimpiriyan (15.7%). **Hybrids** like HP34, HP105, HP813 etc. are suitable for the high altitudes.
- Black pepper needs a reliable support tree called **'standards'** *e.g. Erythrina indica, Garuga pinnata* (Indian coral tree), *Gravillea robusta* (Silver Oak), *Glyricidia sepium, Leucaena leucocephala*, etc.
- **Harvesting:** The pepper vines commence bearing from third year. Flowering starts during May-June and takes 6 to 8 months maturing in Nov.-Feb. (plains) and Jan.-March (hills).

- **White pepper** is prepared from fully ripened berries by removing the outer rind and the pulp before drying.
- **Yield:** 600-800 kg/ha of black pepper. The recovery of the white pepper is 25 per cent and black pepper is 33 per cent out of total yield of spike.

Turmeric

Turmeric is an herbaceous tropical perennial plant of India. The primary rhizomes round in shape are called **bulbs** while the thin long secondary rhizomes called **fingers**. Turmeric is an important spice and a useful **dye** for drugs and cosmetic industries. **Kumkum** is a by-product of turmeric, which is used in offerings on religious and ceremonial occasions. Anti-microbial property of turmeric comes from curcumin. Turmeric marketed from the Alleppey market (Kerala) is called as Alleppey turmeric contains higher percentage of curcumin and is preferred in foreign markets for its colour. Turmeric can be raised as mixed crop with Chillies, Colocasia, Onion, Brinjal and Cereals like Maize, Ragi, etc. It is grown in well drained sandy or clay loam soils.

- **Varieties:** Duggirala, Tekkurpet, Sugandham, Amalapuram, Erode local, Alleppey, Muvattupuzha, Lakadong.
- Planting is done in small pits with a spacing of 25 × 30 cm during April-May using 25 q/ha rhizomes followed by mulching with green leaves @ 12-15 t/ha.
- It requires 40 t FYM plus 30:30:60 kg NPK/ha.
- **Curing**: Boiling of fresh rhizomes in water and drying in the sun.
- **Yield:** The yield of dry turmeric varies from 20-30% of production. In addition to dry turmeric fingers are also separated from mother rhizomes used as seed materials

Ginger

Ginger is a slender herbaceous perennial plant. It is cultivated in Kerala, Karnataka, Tami Nadu, West Bengal, Bihar, Himachal Pradesh, Uttar Pradesh and Maharashtra. India is the largest producer of dry ginger of which one-third is exported to middle east. Sandy or clay loam, red loam or lateritic loam, friable loamy soil rich in humus is ideal.

- **Varieties:** Rio-de-Janeiro (exotic), China, Maran, Thingpuri, Nadia, Narasapattam, Wynad Manantoddy, Karkal, Vengara, Ernad Manjeri, Burdwan.

- Planting is done during first fortnight of May with seed rhizomes weighing 20-25 g each finger having one or two good buds. The seed rate varies from 15-18 q/ha.
- Crop requires 25-30 t compost and neem cake @ 2 t/ha plus 75:50:50 kg NPK/ha. Mulching the ginger beds with green leaves is essential to enhance germination.
- Ginger should be dried to a safe moisture level of 8-10% after harvesting. The recovery of dry ginger varies from 16-25% of fresh ginger.
- **Yield:** The average yield of green ginger is about 50-100 q/ha. In India the grading in ginger is done only in H.P. Grade 'A' ginger is called **gola** and grade 'B' is called **gatti**.

Star Anise

Star anise is one of the most important spices in Chinese cooking and Chinese five-spice powder. It is also used in sweet and savoury cooking, in spicy dishes from India, as well as lightly flavoured cuisines like confectionery, bread, cakes, biscuits and sauces.

Capers

Chopped capers are included in a wide variety of classic sauces including, Tartare, Remoulade and Ravigote. Sauces using capers are traditionally served with boiled mutton, salmon, pan-fried or grilled fish, with the addition of a little grated lemon rind. Capers are also widely used in Italian cuisine, as flavouring in antipasyta salads and as a topping on pizza.

Poppy Seeds

The creamy coloured poppy seeds are more common in India, where they are ground and used as a thickening agent in curries and sauces, biscuits, savoury and sweet. Dry-fried seeds are used in salads and salad dressings, *e.g.* in Potato, Tomato, Egg or Pasta salads or Coleslaw.

Saffron

Saffron is added to special dishes in many cuisines, for its distinctive flavour and striking colour. It is also used in sweet and milk recipes like milky rice, vermicelli puddings and sweet custard like desserts from India.

Allspice

It is also known as **pimento** or **Jamaican pepper**, grown primarily in Jamaica. The berry is a sort of reddish greenish brown and is about the size of a pea. Allspice smells of cloves, cinnamon and nutmeg, and some people even detect a hint of mace and peppercorns in its aroma. In Jamaica, a local drink, known as Jamaica dram, is made from allspice and rum. The whole berries are a popular ingredient for mulled wine and Christmas puddings.

Chilli

It is a native of Mexico with secondary origin in Gautemala. The Portuguese introduced chillies to India. It is also called as hot pepper, red pepper, cayenne pepper, etc. Commercial product of chilli is the dried pod having two commercial qualities, the **red colour due to pigment casanthin** and **biting pungency attributed by capsaicin** (contained in skin and the septa of the fruit). It is a rich source of Vitamins A, C and E and assists in digestion. It also prevents heart diseases by dilating blood vessels. It is the universal spice of India, grown in almost all the states. It is mostly cultivated in Andhra Pradesh, Maharashtra, Karnataka and Tamil Nadu Chilli requires warm and humid climate for its best growth and dry weather during the maturation of fruits. Black soils are suitable for rainfed crop whereas well drained chalka soils and sandy loams are good under irrigated condition.

- Sowing starts from July-August using 6.25 kg/ha seed with 15 × 56 cm spacing maintained after thinning. *Rabi* crop is transplanted during first fortnight of September at a spacing of 56 × 56 cm or 60 × 60 cm or 90 × 60 cm depending upon the soil fertility.
- **Manures and fertilizers:** 10 t FYM plus neem cake @ 3-4 q/ha. Rainfed crop needs 60:30:50 kg NPK/ha, whereas irrigated crop requires 60: 60: 30 kg NPK/ha. In case of Zinc deficiency, apply Zinc sulphate @ 25 kg/ha also.
- The moisture content of dry pods should be kept at 8-10 %.

Vanilla

Vanilla originated in Mexico, now cultivated well in warm and moist climatic conditions with annual rainfall of 150-300 cm and 25-32°C temperature. It is the **second most expensive spice** traded in the world market, added to cakes, biscuits, desserts, puddings, confectionery and chocolates. Vanillin is mainly responsible for the fragrance, flavour and aroma of vanilla essence. Synthetic products such as ethyl vanillin and synthetic vanillin are used alternatively for the above purposes. Forest soil rich in humus is ideal for vanilla.

- **Propagation:** Vanilla is propagated by stem cuttings having 10-12 internodes in each cutting, planted **during** August-September in South India.
- **Support and shade trees:** Vanilla being a climbing orchid needs support and shade, of Glyricidia, Plumeria, Casuarina, Mulberry and *Erythrina lithosperma*, for growth.
- **Flowering: Normally** vanilla flowers from third year onwards during December to April. Flowers are large, pale greenish yellow and bisexual.
- **Harvesting:** Harvested when beans are fully mature developing yellow colour at the lower end.

Cumin

It is a small, slender annual herb with finely dissected leaves and white or rose-coloured flowers. Ground cumin is very popular in cuisines and essential ingredient in most curry powders and *garam masala.* Cumin upon frying releases its flavour. It is cultivated in Gujarat, Rajasthan and in some parts of M.P. and U.P. as *rabi* crop. Well drained sandy loam and medium soils are suitable for the crop.

- **Varieties**: S-404, MC-43. Gujarat Cumin-1 (GC-1), GC-2, GC-3, RS-1, UC-198, RZ-19, etc. The maturity ranges from 110-115 days.
- **Sowing and seed rate:** Sowing commences during November and December using 12-15 kg/ha of seed at 30 cm depth.
- It requires 15-20 t FYM plus 30:15:00 kg NPK/ ha.
- **Irrigation:** 1st light irrigation is given immediately after sowing and second after 6-10 days; subsequent irrigations should be given after 30, 45, 65 and 80 days from 1st irrigation. Irrigations at the time of flowering and fruit set are essential.
- **Aphid** is a major pest of cumin crop; it sucks the sap of tender parts and reduces the yield. Spraying of 0.03% Dimethoate or 0.025% Methyl demetone or 0.04% Monocrotophos is recommended.
- **Harvesting and yield:** After 110-115 days crop becomes ready for harvest. **Yield:** 600 to 700 kg/ha.

Basil

In ancient times it was known as the **herb of kings**. It is indigenous to India. The essential oil content is 0.1% in which methyl chavicol and d-linalool present as principal compounds. Most of the volatile oils are found on the underneath the leaf. The heart-shaped basil leaf is a symbol of love in Italy.

Ajwain

It is also known as **Bishop's Weed**, particularly popular in Indian savoury recipes, pastries, and snacks, bean and pulse recipes. Upon crushing it releases a powerful thyme aroma and flavour.

Celery

Whole celery seeds are added to bread dough and biscuits. Celery seed is used in ground form as dry seasoning powder and for extraction of oleoresin. It is cultivated in *Rabi* season in Punjab and some districts of U.P. Well-drained loamy soil required for cultivation. Nursery is raised (using 2.0 kg seed for 200 m^2) during November and transplanted at a spacing of 45 cm × 20 cm during January. Flowering takes place in March and seeds mature by end of April.

- **Manures and fertilizers:** 5-6 q FYM plus 1.6:0.8:0.4 kg NPK/ 200 sq. m for nursery and 25-30 t FYM plus 80: 40: 20 kg NPK/ ha for main field.
- **Irrigation:** First irrigation should be applied on the day of transplanting and subsequent at an interval of 15-20 days up to 1st fortnight of April.
- **Yield:** 10 to 12 q/ha.

Coriander

It is also known as **Chinese parsley**, or **cilantro**. Fresh coriander is a very versatile herb used in meat, fish, poultry dishes and vegetables. It is cultivated in Rajasthan, Gujarat, M.P., T.N., U.P. It is grown under *Rabi* season in well-drained loamy soil.

- **Varieties:** Guj. Coriander-1, Guj. Coriander-2, RCr-41, UD-20, Rajendra Swati (RD-44), CS-287, Co-1, Co-2, Co-3, Sadhana, Swati and Sindhu, etc.
- **Seed rate and sowing:** 15 to 20 kg/ha. The best time for sowing of coriander is 15 October to 15 November, at a spacing of 30 cm.
- It requires 15-20 t FYM plus 20:30:20 kg/ha NPK for rainfed crop and 20 t FYM plus 60:30:20 kg NPK/ha for irrigated crop.
- **Irrigation:** First irrigation is given within 30-35 DAS then with interval of 25-30 days.
- **Aphid** infestation occurs during flowering resulting in heavy loss. Spraying with 0.3% solution of Malathion or 0.1% solution of Dimethoate controls the aphid.
- **Harvesting:** After 110 to 140 DAS. **Yield:** About 5-8 q/ha rainfed crop and 12-20 q/ha from irrigated crop.

Curry Leaves

These small oval leaves come from the *Murraya koenigi* plant, which eventually grows into a tree. It has a powerful aroma, used as fresh or dry in Madras style curry powders and pastes. It gives best flavour when used with asafoetida.

Fenugreek

It is rich in protein, minerals and vitamins. It has small oval bitter tasting leaves and has a powerful curry flavour. Kasuri or Champa Methi (*Trigonella corniculata*) is another species of methi. It is cultivated in *rabi* season in Rajasthan, M.P., Gujarat, U.P., and T.N. on loamy soil having 6.0-7.0 pH.

- **Varieties:** Guj. Methi-1, Rmt-1 (Rajasthan Methi), Prabha (NLM), Methi No. 47, Methi No. 14, Rajendra Kranti (RM-16), Co-1, UM-34, UM-35, Kasuri, and Kasuri Selection.
- Sowing is done in first fortnight of November with 10-15 kg/ ha of seed at the spacing of 8-10 × 30 cm.
- It requires 10-15 t of FYM plus 40:20:00 kg/ha NPK.
- **Irrigation:** First irrigation is given at the time of thinning and subsequent irrigation at an interval of 20-25 days to the total 4-5 irrigations.
- **Harvesting:** After 120-150 days pods become yellowish and leaves start falling. **Yield:** 18 to 20 q/ha.

Five Spice

Five spice is a mixture of equal quantities of Szechwan pepper, Cinnamon or cassia, Cloves, Fennel seeds and Star anise. Grind all ingredients to a fine powder. The aroma of this spice always seems to dominate the Chinese supermarket. This mixture is used in chicken, red-cooked meat and pork dishes with Soy sauce.

Garlic

It is an essential ingredient in a variety of dishes around the world. It is cultivated during *rabi* season in M.P., Gujarat, Rajasthan, Orissa, U.P., Maharashtra, Punjab and Haryana. Garlic is a frost tolerant crop requires loamy soil for cultivation.

- **Planting and spacing:** Planting is done during August (central India) September (Northern India) to October (Gujarat) at 10 × 15 cm spacing.
- **Varieties:** Godavari, Sweta, HG-1, HG-6, Pusa Sel-10, LCG-1, ARU-52, Agrifound White (G-41), Yamuna Safed (G-1), Yamuna

Safed-2 (G-50), G-282 and Agrifound Parvati, G-282 and Agrifound Parvati are suitable for export.

- **Manures and fertilizers:** 50 t FYM plus 100:50:50 kg/ha NPK.
- **Yield:** 10-20 q/ ha.

nnel

There are two main types of fennel, *viz.* Florence and common nnel. **Florence fennel**, also called finocchio, is cultivated throughout e Mediterranean region and USA. It has a broad, bulbous base at's treated like a vegetable. Common fennel is the variety from which e greenish-brown fennel seeds are used. It is mainly cultivated in ıjarat, Rajasthan and U.P. and used as condiment and culinary ice. Fennel requires cool dry climate and well-drained loam soil to ack cotton soils. **Varieties** include PF-35, Guj. F-1, Guj. F-2. It is ltivated as ***kharif*** as well as ***rabi*** **crop.**

ckage and Practices of Fennel

	Kharif crop	*Rabi* crop
wing time	15th June	Last week of August to 1st week of September
ed rate	2-2.5 kg seeds/100 m^2	2.5-3.0 kg seed/ 150–200 m^2
anures dFertilizers nursery	250 kg FYM plus 0.6:0.3:00 kg/ 100 m^2 NPK.	375 to 500 kg FYM plus 1.0:0.5-0.6:00 kg/150–200 m^2 NPK.
anures and tilizers for in field	20t FYM plus 100: 60: 00 kg /ha NPK.	20 t FYM plus 90:45:00 kg / ha NPK.
acing	Transplanted at 90 × 60 cm or 100 × 60 cm.	45 x 10 cm.
ld	2000 to 2500 Kg/ha.	1800 to 2000 Kg/ha

ge

It is an aromatic perennial herb cultivated for its leaves, which are d fresh or dried as a flavouring in many foods, particularly in ffing's for poultry and pork and in sausages. The bushes grow up 2 feet. The principal components of sage are thujone and borneol.

Savory

Savory is an aromatic annual herb of the mint group. The drie leaves and flowering tops of savory are used for flavouring man foods.

Cambodge

It is glabrous and evergreen tree seen in the Western Ghats Kerala (the travencore tract), Karnataka (Konkan tract). Its mature frui are highly acidic having Hydroxy Citric Acid; rind is used a condiments in fish and prawn preparations. Planting is done durin July-Octobers. Both sole and perennial intercrop with Coconu Arecanut etc., planted in pits of 75 × 75 × 75 cm (hard and laterit soil) or 50 × 50 × 50 cm (sandy and alluvial soils) size, at a spacing 4 m × 4 m for grafting and 7 m × 7 m for seedlings.

- **Propagated** through soft grafting or seedlings.
- **Manuring and fertilizers:** 10 kg FYM/seedling/graft plu 20:18:50 g/plant NPK during the first year.
- **Harvesting:** Graft start bearing from the third year and Seec grown plants start bearing at the age of 10-12 years. Flowerir occurs in January-March and fruits mature in July.
- **Processing:** The dried rind is mixed with common salt @ 150 and coconut oil @ 50 ml/kg of dried rind.

Rosemary

The plant gives pungent, resinous taste with a delightful perfume. is a small perennial evergreen ritual herb indigenous to th Mediterranean region used in weddings, chastening and funerals. adds flavour to everyday dishes of meat, eggs and vegetables. Fresh chopped leaves give flavour to Jam, sweet sauces and butter.

Parsley

Universal biennial herbal spice is a native of Mediterranean lanc Dwarf Parsley is 15-20 cm tall whereas Hamburg Parsley is up to cm tall. Parsley gives a characteristics flavour to the food. The leav are rich in Vitamins A, B, C, F, and minerals like Iron, Calciu Magnesium and Sodium, which add value to the food. Parsl stimulates the digestive glands improving digestive system. **Gri water** is made from Parsley. It is cultivated by seeds, which are sov in the Nilgiris during April-May, using 70 g/ha seed. Curled Parsl leaves with long petiole are formed in rosette, are harvested 90 da after planting.

Institution Involved

- Indian Institute of Spices Research, Calicut, Kerala.

36

Plantation Crops

Plantation crops are generally associated with tropical and ubtropical areas producing products like Tea, Coffee, Cacao, Rubber, Coconut, Arecanut, Palm oil, and Palmyra oil.

Tea (*Camellia* spp.)

Tea is an evergreen tree with broad, simple, resin-containing leaves. A product of tea plantation, the 'Tea' is an important beverage used all around the world, therefore it is called "**queen of beverages**". Tea is made from the tender or young leaves and unopened buds of the tea-plant, popular as a 'healthful herb'. The important tea growing countries are India, Sri Lanka, East Africa, Japan, Indonesia, Bangladesh, China, Georgia, Argentina, etc. In India it is cultivated in Assam, West Bengal, Kerala, Karnataka and T.N. on 0.358 Mha of land producing over 4.68 MT of Tea; India is the largest producer.

- Two distinct varieties of tea-plant, *viz.* small-leaved China (*C. sinensis*) and the large-leaved Assam (*C. assamica*) are called China Jat and India Jat, respectively.
- **Climate**: Tea is grown in warm and moist climate, up to 2,460 m MSL and requires rainfall of 125-750 cm.
- **Varieties**: Sundaram, Singara, Anthrey.
- **Soil**: Well-drained, deep and friable loam or forest land rich in organic matter having acidic (pH 4 to 6) nature, low in calcium and rich in iron and manganese are suitable for tea plantation.
- **Cultivation**: Cultivated both from seed and clonal propagation or soft woodcutting. The plants are raised in nurseries up to 1-1½ year to produce healthy plants, which are planted in pits of 30-45 cm deep and 24 cm wide with the spacing of 120 × 75 cm accommodating 10,000 plants in a hectare.
- **Training, pruning and plucking**: The tea-plant is initially trained into a small bush of 40 to 50 cm height. **Tipping** is the

removal of terminal portion of shoot. **Skiffing** is lightest forı of pruning.

- The tea leaves are sorted into different grades, *e.g.* Pekoe, Orang pekoe, Flowery pekoe, Broken Orange pekoe and Fanning.
- Tea research is carried out in the country at two centres: Tockl Experimental Station of the Tea Research Association, Jorh (Assam) and the Tea Research Station of the United Plante Association of South India (UPASI) Cinchona, Coimbator district, Tamil Nadu.

Coffee (*Coffea* spp.)

It is native to Ethiopia. There are two species of Coffee (*C. Arabic* $2n = 44$, *C. robusta* $2n = 22$) cultivated commercially in the four souther states of Karnataka, Tamil Nadu, Kerala, Andhra Pradesh, Oriss West Bengal, Assam and Madhya Pradesh. Arabica grows well elevations between 900-1,200 m MSL and robusta grows luxuriant at the lower elevations (about 150 metres). Coffee grows well in th red and lateritic soils. It is picked when the fruits are just ripe.

- **Varieties:** *C. arabica*: Old Chiks, Coorgs, Kents, S-288, S-795, S 1934; from *C. robusta*: S-274, S-270. Cauvery (caturra × hibrid de-timor) is a hybrid variety.
- There are two kinds of coffee, *viz*. **Parchment coffee** (prepare by wet method, generally favoured by the market) and **Cherr coffee** (associated with a characteristic fermenting flavour).
- United Planters' Association of South India (UPASI) wa organized to look after coffee industry in 1992.
- Coffee Board of India (1946) under Ministry of Commerc Government of India, was constituted under the Coffee Act, V of 1942.

Cacao or Cocoa (*Theobroma cacao*) $2n = 20$

It is the perennial dicotyledonous plant belonging to famil sterculiaceae native to Amazon Valley in South America. It is a sma evergreen tree growing to a height of 9 m having two types of branche *viz*. 1. **Jorquette** (forked), 2. **Chupon** (arises below the jorquette). It cultivated in Kanyakumari, Tirunelveli, Palni Hills (T.N.); Nyna Trivandrum, Quilon and Kottayam in Kerela; Chikmagalur, Kana in Karnataka.

- Brazil is the leading producer of cocoa.
- It is a rich source of fat (37%) and protein (7%). Active compou is Theobromin. Theobromin is extracted from the cake.

- Cocoa is propagated through seed or soft woodcutting.
- **Varieties:** Forstero, CCRP I, CCRP IV, V, VI, VII, etc.
- Flowering in cacao begins in the second year of planting. The pods mature in 6-8 months. The pods when ripe are yellow to orange red. There are 2 main flushes every year, *i.e.* in September-February and May-August.
- The cake is powdered to prepare the cocoa powder.
- Cacao is both a beverage and a food crop. It is used in manufacturing chocolate, cocoa and other foods. The rind of the pods is used as cattle feed. On an average 600 kg/ha beans are produced.

Rubber (*Hevea* spp.)

Natural rubber is extracted from para rubber tree *Hevea brasiliensis*, the most important source of rubber; *H. glaziovii*, *Ficus elastica*, *Parthenium argentatum* and *Taraxacum kok-saghyz*, *Euphorbia intisy*, *Cryptostegia grandiflora* etc. *H. brasiliensis* was originated from Brazil to tropical Asia in 1876 through the Kew Gardens (England).

- Hevea is propagated through seeds and vegetative methods. The seedlings are usually transplanted in the fields in June-July.
- Majority of the rubber trees grown in a narrow belt from Kanyakumari to Coorg district of Karnataka and in the west of the Western Ghats on lateritic soils.
- **Tapping** is a process of wounding during which thin shavings of the bark are removed to induce flow of latex. It commences early in the morning when latex flow is high. The tapping should be deep without chopping the cambium. It should be done in alternate days. A higher intensity of tapping often leads to **brown bast**, physiological disorder.
- An application of **Ethrel** stimulates the yield of rubber.
- **Processing** of rubber is done to obtain the different forms of rubber for marketing, *viz.* preserve latex and latex concentrates (having 50-60% latex); dry ribbed sheet rubber; dry creped rubber; and dry solid block rubber. Latex is concentrated through centrifugation.
- The major quantity of natural rubber produced in the country is marketed in the sheet form.
- Rubber Research Institute, Kottayam, Kerala, is looking of research in rubber.

- Rubber Board of India (H.Q. Kottayam) is supreme body for rubber industry and products.

Coconut (*Cocos nucifera*)

It is a majestic monoecious perennial palm is also called '*kalpa-vriksha*'. It is mainly cultivated in Kerala, Tamil Nadu, Karnataka and Andhra Pradesh India ranks second in the world production of coconuts. It is cultivated for the nuts from which two important products copra and fibre are obtained. Coconut is propagated through seed. Horizontal planting is better than the vertical planting.

- **Varieties:** Fiji, S.S. Green, San Roman, Philippines and West coast.
- COGENT (Coconut Genetic Resource Network) under IPGRI, restricts the movement of germplasm of coconut.
- The unopened spathe is tapped for **toddy**, which can be converted into Jaggery. Fermented toddy is a mild alcoholic drink as well as used for making vinegar. Water from tender coconut is a refreshing drink.
- Husk is used to extract coir, used in mattresses. The shell flour is used as filler for plastics.
- The average yield of coconut is 10,000-14,000 nuts/ha/annum.
- Coconut Development Board was established in 1981.

Arecanut or Betel Nut (*Areca catechu*) **$2n = 32$**

It is native to Malay Archipelago and extensively cultivated as tropical palm tree forming a popular masticatory in India. India is the largest producer of arecanut in the world. Arecanut thrives well in a variety of soils including laterite soils of the West Coast, the red loamy soils of the Mettupalayam (T.N.), the alluvials of Assam and W.B., and the loams of Orissa. Arecanut is consumed both as a raw/ripenut (Kacha tamul) as dried ripenut (supari).

- **Varieties:** Mangla, Sumangala, Sree Mangala, Mohitnagar, Calicut-17 (Suitable for Andaman Islands).
- The cup shaped nuts are prepared by boiling tender arecanuts after de-husking and cutting into halves.
- Tender arecanut contains tannins of 30-37 per cent, which reduces with the increase of age.
- Directorate of Arecanut and Spices Development under Ministry of Agriculture, Government of India, is nodal agency for formulation of research schemes.

- Price stabilization for arecanut is the responsibility of Central Arecanut and Cocoa Marketing and Processing Cooperative Limited (CAMPCO), head quartered at Mangalore.

Oil Palm (*Elaeis guineensis*) 2*n* = 32

This species of oil palm is called **African oil palm** (the American being *E. oleifera, E. odera,*). Portuguese introduced oil palm to India, from New Guinea. It is also called "**small holders irrigated crop**" cultivated for edible oil. Oil palm based on absence or presences of shell are grouped into two. The *Dura* type has shell, whereas *Pisifera* type does not possess the same. It is propagated by seed. Oil is extracted from mesocarp and kernel. The oil from mesocarp is called palm oil and kernel oil is called palm kernel oil. Mesocarp yields 70-90% oil, whereas kernels yield 10-30% oil. Palm oil is rich in palmitic acid. Commercial orchard produces 4-6 t/ha oil.

- It is mainly cultivated in Andhra Pradesh, Karnataka, Tamil Nadu., and Kerala, Gujarat, Goa, Maharashtra, Orissa, Assam, Tripura and West Bengal.
- Pulp comprised of 35-95% containing 10-20% fibre.
- Nursery is sown with 5 kg/ha seeds and transplanted during May-June in the pits of 60 × 60 × 60 cm size accommodating 140 plants/ha.
- **Oil palm decorticator** is used for separation of fibres from empty fruit bunches. The fibre obtained from decorticator can be used for various value-added products like blended yarn, fibreboard and rubberized mattresses.
- **Palm oil processing:** Processing of palm oil completes in three different stages, *viz.* Extraction (Stripping, Digestion, Pressing, Clarification), Refining (Degumming, Bleaching, Deodorizing and Polishing, Physical Refining), and Fractionation.
- **Palm kernel oil:** It is obtained from the endosperm or kernel, which contains about 50% oil.
- **Palm cake:** It is the rich source of protein and amino acids.

Palmyrah Palm (*Borassus flabellifier*)

Since the all parts of this tree are used therefore it is called "**tree of life**" and "**Poor men's beverage**". Next to coconut palmyrah is the most abundant palm found in the world. It is mostly cultivated in Tamil Nadu (except in Nilgiris district). The fruit is drupe yellow to light orange in colour with black bottom. It is the deciduous tree, flowering occurs during March-July. It is propagated through seeds.

- **Neera**: It is the tapped juice of palmyrah smelling pleasant and sweet, used as stimulant and antiphlegmatic.
- **Toddy**: It is the fermented sugary sap having alcohol percentage of 5%. **Palmyrah arrack** is recovered from toddy.
- **Palm jaggery**: It is processed from Neera contains about 8.97% moisture, 3.25% ash, 73.78% sugars, 1.41% proteins.
- **Nangu**: The tender palmyrah fruits are called Nangu.

Institutions involved

- NRC on OilPalm, Pedavegi, Andhra Pradesh.
- Central Plantation Crops Research Institute, Kasaragod, Kerala.

❑❑❑

37

Medicinal And Aromatic Plants

MEDICINAL PLANTS

Charak Samhita (1000 BC) provides records for the use of over 340 drugs of vegetable origin. The curative properties of drugs are due to the presence of complex chemical substances (secondary metabolites), which are grouped as alkaloids, glycosides, corticosteroids, essential oils, etc.

Important Secondary Metabolites and Their Sources

Metabolites	Source
Alkaloids	
Morphine, Codein	Poppy
Strychnine, Brucine	Nux vomica
Quinine	Cinchona
Ergotamine	Ergots (a disease caused by Fungi)
Hypocyamine	Belladonna
Scolapomine	Datura
Emetine	Ipecac
Cocaine	Coco
Ephedrine	Ephedra
Reserpine	Rauwolfia
Caffeine	Tea dust
Aconitine	Aconite
Vascine	Vasaca
Santonin	Aremisia
Lobelin	Lobelia

Glycosides	
Digoxin	Foxglove
Stropanthin	Strophanthus
Glycyrrhizin	Liquorice
Barbolin	Aloe
Sennocides	Senna
Corticosteroids	
Diosgenin	Dioscorea
Solasodin	Solanum

- Essential oils including valerian *kutch* and peppermint possess medicating properties and used in pharmaceutical industry.

Cinchona (*Cinchona ledgeriana, C. officinalis, C. calisaya, C. succirubra*)

It is mainly cultivated in Peru, Bolivia, Columbia and Ecuador. In India cinchona is cultivated mainly in W.B., Nilgiris and the Annamalai Hills (T.N.) on 1,600 hectare of land.

- Bark of cinchona yields quinine ($C_{20}H_{24}O_2N_2$), which is used as a treatment against malaria.
- Quinine salts are now increasingly used in soft drinks as bitters. Quinidine sulphate, a constituent, is used in the treatment of heart troubles like auricular fibrillation and ventricular trachycardia.
- The average total alkaloid content of 10-12 year old *Cinchona ledgeriana* plant in the root (7.21%), stem (6.01%) and branch (4.0%) of which the quinine content is 5, 4 and 1.98 per cent respectively.

Isabgol (*Plantago ovata*)

It is an annual stemless herb, a native of Persia, grown as a cash crop in the Mehsana, Palampur and Banaskantha districts of Northern Gujarat. India is the largest producer and exporter (Rs. 25 million) of isabgol. The husk is the rosy-white membranous covering of the seed, which constitutes the drug and is given as a safe laxative, particularly beneficial in habitual constipation, chronic diarrhoea and dysentery.

- It is cultivated in *rabi* season, which remains in the field for about 4 months on well-drained sandy-loam to loamy soils having pH between 7 to 8.

- The seed rate is 7.8 kg/ha. It requires a cool climate and dry sunny weather.

Opium Poppy (*Papaver somniferum*)

Poppy is a native of the western Mediterranean region, introduced into India in the early 16th century. India produces about 70% of the world's production of which 90 per cent is exported annually. It is cultivated with valid licence from Excise Department in Neemuch, Mandsaur and Ratlam districts of M.P.; Faizabad, Bara Banki, Bareilly and Shahjahanpur districts of U.P.; Chittoor, Jhaḷawar and Kota districts of Rajasthan. Poppy is a *rabi* crop, remains for about 150-160 days in the fields. **Seed-rate** is 2.5 to 3.5 kg/ha.

- The green unripe capsules contain the maximum amount of morphine, whereas codeine and narcotine is found in aged plant.
- **Lancing** is the making slit into the capsule longitudinally in bright sunlight, through which the latex (crude opium) oozes out. This oozed out crude opium dries during night and is scrapped with a sharp kitchen-knife in the early hours of the succeeding morning and collected in earthen pots. Each capsule is lanced for 4-6 times. On an average yield of raw opium varies from 13 to 33 kg/ha and 3 to 4 q/ha of seeds. The seeds contain up to 50 per cent of golden-yellow fatty oil that is devoid of narcotic properties.
- There are 25 opium alkaloids identified, of these morphine, theabine, codeine, narcotine and papaverine, are important. Among these morphine is still most important.
- Poppy produced in India contains on an average 20% (9 to 14% of morphine, 5-7% narcotine, 1.25-3.75% codeine, 0.4-1% papverine and 0.2-0.5% theabine) of the total alkaloids by weight.

Senna (*Cassia angustifolia*)

Senna is a native of South Arabia. India is the main producer of senna in the world and exports senna leaves and pods worth over Rs. 6 million annually. Senna is a small, perennial, branched under-shrub, remaining in field for 5-7 months. Generally two crops are taken from February to March (irrigated) and November (rainfed).

- **Seed-rate:** 27 kg/ha (rainfed) and 15 kg/ha (irrigated).
- Senna leaves and the pod-shell contain **sennocide** used as a laxative in medicine.

Belladonna (*Atropa belladonna*)

It is originated in Europe and now cultivated in Kashmir. The plant is a small perennial herb, which grows up to 1.5 m in height. The leaves and roots of belladonna constitute the commercial drug, which contains atropine, hyocyamine and hyocine, used in pharmacy for their mydriatic, analgesic and antispasmodic properties. The crop prefers a well-drained slightly acidic, silty loam to clayey-loam soil, rich in humus.

Rauwolfia (*Rouwolfia serpentina*)

It is an evergreen, perennial indigenous herb found in the Himalayan foothills and Peninsular India. The root constitutes the drug and important medicine. Rauwolfia grows well in sandy-loam to clayey-loam acidic soils, rich in humus and prefers heavy monsoon rains between June and August. The **seed rate** is 8-10 kg/ha.

Ipecac (*Cephaelis ipecacuanha*)

The root bark is the drug used as an expectorant and emetic, mainly in the treatment of amoebic dysentery. It is cultivated in Darjeeling, Sikkim and parts of Assam. The roots contain emetine, caphaeline and psychotrine. The average alkaloid content in the Indian crop is 2.5 per cent of which 1.3-1.4 per cent is emetine (the most important). The alkaloids are extracted in the form of their salts, *viz.* emetine sulphate and emetine hydrochloride.

Foxglove (*Digitals lanata*)

It is a biennial herb containing glycosides, used for heart stimulation.

The crop prefers silty-loam to clayey-loam soils, rich in organic matter and temperate climate. The **seed-rate** used is 500 g/ha.

Leaves contain 0.1% glycoside (digoxin, digitoxin, gitoxin, etc.).

Dill or Sowa (*Anethum graveolens*)

Sowa is a *rabi* crop grown almost throughout the country for its fresh aromatic leaves used in cooking. The fruits contain essential oil, rich in carvone used in pharmacy for the preparation of **dill water** to treat flatulence, abdominal and colic pain. India exports dill fruits worth about Rs. 2 million annually.

- There are two known species, *viz.* the East Indian Dill (*A. graveolens* var. *sowa*) and European Dill (*A. graveolens*).

Liquorice or Mulhati (*Glycyrrhiza glabra*)

Liquorice is a hardy perennial legume, about 0.6 m tall. Its underground stems and roots constitute the drug used for demulcent, mild laxative, expectorant, all cough and catarrh syrups, throat lozenges and pastilles. Liquorice grows well in fertile sandy-loamy soils in a warm and dry climate. Its extract containing glycyrrhizin (2.14%) has a healing effect on peptic ulcers.

Dioscorea (*Dioscorea composita, D. floribunda, D. prazeri*)

The tubers produce corticosteroids. **Yield:** 7.5 t/ha (dry), containing, on an average, 3 per cent diogenin. For details refer Chapter 32, Vegetable Production).

AROMATIC PLANTS

The aromatic plants possess odoriferous and volatile substances, which occur as essential oils, gum exudates, balsam and oleoresin.

Lemon Grass (*Cymbopogon flexuosus*)

It is a stemless perennial grass, found wild in the southern states of India particularly Kerala. The leaves yield aromatic oil (containing 75-85% **citral**) used in soaps, cosmetics and disinfectants. The herbage contains 0.35% oil on fresh-weight basis. The grass yield ranges from 18-25 t/ha, giving 60-72 kg of oil.

- There are two types of grasses, *viz.* the red-stemmed grass is the true lemon-grass, produces high quality essential oil, and white-stemmed yields oil having low citral content.

Citronella Grass (*Cymobopogon winteriaruns*)

It is also a stemless perennial grass. The oil is mainly used in soaps, cosmetics, deodorants and mosquito-repellent creams. It is mainly cultivated in lower hills of Assam, Karnataka and Southern Gujarat.

Celery (*Apium graveolens*)

India is now the principal grower (annual type) and exports large quantities of celery seeds (worth Rs. 17.5 millions to the American and European markets). The celery seeds upon distillation yield 2.1 to 2.3% essential oil containing selinene, d-limonene and sesquiterpenes, glycoside opine. Also refer Chapter 35, Spices and Condiments.

Geranium (*Pelargonium graveolens*)

It is native of the hilly tracts of Cape Colony (South Africa). The highly aromatic Rose Geranium is a hybrid (*P. graveolens* × *P. radens*). It is grown in Tamil Nadu, Bangalore, Yercaud and in the Nilgiri Hills. The oil of geranium has a refreshingly delicate rose like aroma containing 66-78% alcohols calculated as geraniol, used for scenting ointments, pharmaceutical and tobacco products. It is suitable in a slightly alkaline medium and, therefore, it is widely used in the manufacture of high-grade soaps and cosmetic products.

Patchouli (*Pogostemon cablin*)

Patchouli is a native of humid Indo-Malayan tropics. The plant is small bushy herb, which yields fragrant leaves containing very sweet smelling oil used to manufacture soaps and cosmetics. It is grown in small pockets mainly in Karnataka and Tamil Nadu.

Vetiver or Khus (*Vetiveria zizanioides*)

Khus is a tall perennial grass found wild in the drier tracts of Western India including Bharatpur (Rajasthan), Musanagar, Biswan and Nawabganj and some parts of western U.P. Also it is grown with little amount in Trichur, Palghat, Kozikode, Wynad and Trivandrum district of Kerala; Tirunelvelly, Madhrai and Coimbatore districts of T.N. and Kurnool and East Godavari districts of Andhra Pradesh. Spongy roots contain fragrant oil, which itself is a perfume. The dry aromatic roots are made into curtains, mats, fans, etc. to emit scented cool aroma when moistened. The oil is used as a valuable fixative for blending perfumes and cosmetics. In southern states, khus is grown as a rainfed crop in well-drained sandy-loam soils with moderately humid localities. The yield is 3-5 tonnes of fresh root, yielding about 20 kg of oil per hectare.

Kewara (*Pandanus odoratissimus*)

Kewara is a large indigenous shrub up to 3-6 m tall having white or creamy dioecious flowers. Its enclosing spathe contains fragrant oil. The kewara attar and kewara water are commonly used at ceremonial functions in perfuming aerated waters, other drinks and confectionery products. Most of the cultivation is confined to the Ganjam district (400 ha) in Orissa. The blossom contains 0.1-0.3% oil. The attar is mostly produced over sandalwood oil or paraffin base.

Davana (*Artemisia pallens*)

It is a small annual indigenous herb up to 50 cm tall. It is a 4-month *rabi* crop cultivated on a limited scale in Karnataka for making bouquets and producing oil. The yield of fresh herbage is about 30 t/ha producing 10-12 kg of brownish viscous oil.

Henna or Mehandi (*Lawsonia inermis*)

It is a perennial hedge plant, native to North Africa. It is cultivated in the Pali, Sojat and Nagor districts of Rajasthan; Gurgaon and Faridabad district of Haryana. The crop is grown in sandy loam to loamy soils in the hot and dry climate on marginal land. Two varieties are known, *viz*. Hinna (odorous) and Rajni (more colouring).

Sweet Flag or Bach (*Acorus calamus*)

It is a perennial indigenous undershrub grows wild in stagnant pools and shallow creaks all over the country. Its long aromatic rhizomes contain aromatic oil (Ascerone 82%) used for lending oriental notes in perfumery. Oil has germicidal properties also therefore used in insecticidal formulations. It is a 10-month crop cultivated in Koratgere Taluk of the Tumkur district in Karnataka on 500 ha clayey to clayey loam soils.

Linaloe (*Bursera delpechianum*)

It is a small tree native to Mexico. The wood of linaloe and berries yield 7-9% and 3% sweet smelling essential oil respectively, on steam distillation. The characteristic odour of lavender oil is due to the presence of 35-44% Easter (linalyll acetate) and 32-48% of free alcohols (linalool). The oil is used in the manufacturing of high quality soaps and cosmetic products. They **yield** 2.5 to 3% oil on fresh weight basis comprising 20 kg/ha oil from the sixth year onwards.

Lemon Gum (*Eucalyptus citriodora*)

It is an Australian tree, about 25 m tall, with a clean silvery green trunk and strongly scented narrow leaves. The plant is coppiced at a height of 90 cm to get a larger yield of foliage. The foliage has up to 0.8% of oil, containing 60-80 percent of citronellal (attributed to lemon colour). It is commercially cultivated in the Nilgiri Hills.

Institutions Involved

- Central Institute of Medicinal and Aromatic Plants (CIMAP) Lucknow.
- NRC on Medicinal and Aromatic Plants, Boriavi, Gujarat.

□□□

38

Forest Trees

Neem (*Azadirchta indica*)

It is one of the important indigenous trees as potential timber. The wood is relatively heavy with specific gravity varying from 0.56 to 0.85. Nim seed is a rich source of anti-insect, anti-fungal and anti-viral activities, due to presence of azadirachtin.

Poplar (*Populus deltoides*)

Poplar is among the first growing industrial soft woods. The wood being light, homogeneous used for paper and pulp, plywood, match sticks, packing cases, sports goods, light constructional timber and furniture. Poplar is a winter deciduous and adds tremendous amount of leaf litter to the soil.

- **Clones**: PL-1, PL-2, PL-3, PL-4, PL-5, PL-6, PL-7.
- **Propagated** through stem cuttings of 20-25 cm length and 2-3 cm diameter prepared from one year old plants. Cuttings are soaked in fresh water for 24 hours before planting. Cuttings are planted in the beds (5 × 15 m) at 50 × 50 cm distance during the first fortnight of February. Apply light irrigation at 7-10 days interval.
- Plants are ready for transplanting after one year.

Safeda (*Eucalyptus tereticornis*)

Safeda is the most widely exploited exotic genus in the world. It is native of Australia and now grown in different soils and climatic zones. It has features like fast growth, straightness, self-pruning and wide utility of wood. The wood is used for furniture, doors, windows, crates, packing cases, fuel, and pulpwood and a source of rayon. Tree itself is used as windbreak especially for the protection of fruit crops.

Sagwan or Teak (*Tectona grandis*)

Teak grows well in a fairly moist, warm tropical climate with annual rainfall of 125-400 cm in well-drained sandy loam soil. It produces soft wood for various purposes.

Dek (*Melia azedarach*)

It is grown primarily for shade purpose in dry reasons. It is propagated through seeds, cuttings and root suckers during July and planted at 15 × 15 cm distance.

- Dek grows well under dry conditions with rainfall of 60-100 cm and 8 to 40°C temperature. It prefers well-drained deep soils including saline and alkaline.
- The wood is comparable to that of neem and is widely accepted in the market for furniture, doors and windows, packing cases etc. The leaves and fruits of Melia contain pest-repellant qualities.

Kikar or Babool (*Acacia nilotica* spp. *indica*)

It is a valuable source of fuel, timber, fodder and tannin. The wood is used for making furniture, doors, windows, carts, trolleys, agricultural implements and other household articles. The pods and leaves contain digestible protein. The bark is a rich source of tannin. Kikar is grown in semi-arid and Kandi regions.

Subabul (*Luecaena leucocephala*)

It is also called **miracle tree** as it provides fodder, fuel, pulpwood and timber. The forage is highly palatable, digestible and rich in proteins. Subabul helps to enrich soil and aid fertility to neighbouring plants. Bushes pruned and mowed in soil can add up to 500 kg/ha of nitrogen. The wood is good source of fuel, charcoal, pole and pulp. **Varieties**: K-8, Cunningham.

Sisso or Shisham (*Dalbergia sissoo*)

It is a native of Indo-Gangetic plain of India. Heartwood provides excellent timber and leaves provide a nutritious fodder during lean period. It is a winter deciduous, and fixes atmospheric nitrogen to enrich the soil.

Mulberry (*Morus* spp.)

It is a native of Japan and now it is cultivated in almost all parts of India, particularly in Karnataka and W.B. There are several species grown in India, *viz. M. alba, M. indica, M. serrata* and *M. laevigata* (Silk), *M. nigra* (fruit) and *M. rubra* (timber) for different purposes. Silkworm thrives well on this tree and produces silk of international standards. The wood is yellowish-brown used for furniture, turney, hockey sticks and boats. Twigs are used for baskets and as fuel wood.

- Mulberry is propagated through root grafting and bud grafting.
- In rainfed areas, mulberry is planted at a distance of 7.6 × 7.6cm whereas under irrigated condition with the spacing of 5 × 5 cm.
- **Varieties:** Kanva-2, MR-2, S-30, S-36, S-41, S-54 for irrigated condition. S-3, S-13, S-14, S-25, S-34, V 1, S-1635, S-36, S-146, BG-259 and S-28 for rainfed.

□□□

39

Animal Husbandry

Raising of animals including Dairy Cattle, Pigs, Sheep, Goats, Horses, Mules, Asses, Buffaloes, and Camels; Chickens, ducks, Geese, Guinea Fowl, Quail, and Squabs, for draught, milk or pleasure, is known as Animal Husbandry.

- India occupies first position in the world having a total bovine population of 95.1 million compared to the world's total bovine population of 167.13 million. The present cattle population in India is 221.9 million and in world it is 1366.67 million (2003-2004). The cross-bred cattle are predominant in Kerala, Maharashtra, Tamil Nadu, Punjab and Uttar Pradesh, while buffaloes are very common in Uttar Pradesh, Andhra Pradesh, Rajasthan, Madhya Pradesh, Maharashtra, Gujarat, Punjab, Bihar, Karnataka, Haryana and Tamil Nadu.
- The census for livestock is carried out in every five years.

Cattle

In the whole world there exist 277 breeds of cattle, which include 33 for beef; 18 for draft; 39 for meat and draft; 54 for meat and dairy; 21 for dairy and draft; 61 for meat, dairy and draft; and 51 as dairy breeds.

- The term oxen are used only for castrated bulls.

Beef Cattle Feed

Beef cattle can utilize roughages of both low and high quality including pasture forage, hay, silage, maize fodder, straw, and grain by-products. Cattle also utilize non-protein nitrogen in the form of urea and biuret feed supplements, which can supply from one-third to one-half of all the protein needs of beef animals.

Characteristics of Indian Breeds

Breed	Milk prod./ lactation	Origin/ distribution	Identification and characteristics
Milch cows (*Bos taurus, B. indicus*)			
Sahiwal	4,000-5,000 litre	Mont-gomery	Weighing 340 kgs having various shades of red, pale, dark brown; deep body short legs, massive hump voluminous dew-lap, long tail and stumpy horns.
Sindhi	5,440 litre	Karanchi and Hyderabad	290 kg wt; dark red to dim yellow colour, well proportionate body, heavy hump; heavy milker.
Gir	1,740 litre	Gir forest of Gujarat	Approx. 380 kg wt; red to black in colour, well proportionate body, long tail and long head.
Deoni	1,650 litre	Northwest and western Hyderabad.	Most resembling to Gir but less pronounced forehead.
Dual purpose cow breeds			
Haryana	1,400 litre	Hissar and Karnal	400 kg body wt.; white to light grey; proportionate body, long legs and lean bones.
Tharparkar	1,500 litre	Tharparkar (Sindh)	400 kg wt.; white to light grey; medium size, strong built including strong limb.
Kankrej	1,400 litre	Rann of Kutchh	500 kg wt.; silver grey to iron grey; heaviest body, energetic, moderate milk producer.
Exotic cow breeds:			
Holstein Friesian	5,500-6,100	Nether-lands	It is black and white in colour and large in size. Holsteins give more milk than any other breed. The average fat content is 3.7 per cent.

Ayrshire	4,600 litre	Scotland	Red or brown and white colour, and they are strong, vigorous, and good foragers; milk contains 4.1% fat.
Brown Swiss	5,000-5,200 litre	Switzer-land	Silver to dark brown in colour, with a black nose and tongue; strong and vigorous having fat percentage of 4.1.
Jersey	4,000 Litre	Islands of Jersey, in Great Britain	Fawn in colour, with or without white markings; smallest of the major dairy breeds, but their milk is the richest in fat with an average of 5.2 per cent.

Buffalo

The name buffalo is applied to several different cud-chewing (ruminant) mammals of the ox family *Bovidae*. The true, or Indian buffalo (*Bubalus bubalis*), also known as **water buffalo**, used for draft, as well as milk and butter.

Buffalo breeds (*Bubalus bubalis*)

Breed	Milk prod./ loctation	Origin/ distribution	Identification and characteristics
Murrah	1,600 litre	Rohtak, Karnal	Weighing 430 kg, massive body, jet-black colour, scanty hair, tightly curved horns, developed udder.
Bhadawari	1,100 litre	Agra, Etawah	Medium wedge shaped body, copper coloured, moderate udder. Famous for high fat contents all over the world.
Surti	1,770 litre	Anand, Baroda	Sickle shaped horns, black to brown colour, medium body.
Nili	1,850 litre	Firozpur	White patches on forehead, depression between eyes, small coiled horns, developed udder.
Jafrabadi	1,360litre	Kathiawar	Proportionally longer body, black colour, horn inclined toward neck, developed udder.
Mehsana	1,750 litre	Gujarat	Body longer than murrah, longer head, well shaped udder.

Goats

Goat is used primarily for milk, cheese, mohair and meat. Its skin has been used as a source for leather. The Angora and Kashmiri breeds are famous for their fine wool or mohair.

Indian Goat Breeds

Breeds	Origin/ distribution	Characteristics and utility
Kashmiri or Pashmina	H.P., Lahaul valley, Laddakh	White silky hair of 4-5" long used for Pashmina Shawl, Undercoat, firs, etc. Kidding after 22 months.
Gaddi	H.P., Kangra, Kullu valley	White grey red colour, horns pointed at apex, hairs 7-10" long, yields 0.5-kg wool/ combing.
Jamunapari	Etawah, U.P.	Biggest and Majestic breeds of India; White with tan markings; short flat horns; Roman nose. Produce 2.5-3.0 kg milk/day.
Beetal	Sialkot, Jhelum, Gurdaspur, Amritsar	Except size resembles Jamunapari breed; horns horizontally backward and spirally twisted.
Black Bengal	West Bengal	Ears upright, small legged, short and soft hair, black colour, used principally for meat.
Barbari	Etwah, Etah, Aligarh and Mathura	Small with short ears; white coloured with few tan spots. Kidding twice in a year, generally in twins and triplets.
Exotic breeds of Goats reared in India		
Alpine	France	White to black with white spots; short pointed ears; 900-1300 g milk/day.
Anglo-Nubian	Indian Jamunapari × Egyptian Nubians	Called Jersey cow; dual purpose for both milk (with 5% fat) and meat; black dark brown with white spots; developed udder.
Saanen	Switzerland	Called milk queen of goats; sensitive to sunlight; dull white colour; upright erect ears.
Angora	Middle China	Short stature, small head, white colour, long ear with lobe, flat pointed horns, small udder, body covered with mohair.

Sheep

The gestation period for sheep is 150 days with 16-17 days between periods of estrus, which last 29 hours. The average number of lambs raised per hundred ewes is 91, and the average fleece weight per shearing is 3.78 kg.

Breeds of sheep (*Ovis aries*)

Breeds	Origin/ distribution	Characteristics and utility
Gurez	Kashmir	Hornless, white coloured, biggest among Kashmiri breeds. Produce (1.5 kg/year) good quality wool.
Bhakarwal	Kashmir	Ewes hornless and rams horned. Produce (2.5 kg/year) long coarse wool.
Bikaneri	Bikaner	Short ears, white, small head. Produce (1.5 kg/year) carpet type wool.
Marwari	Jodhpur	Black faced, twisted ears, thin and long legs. Produce 1.5-2.5 kg/year white coarse wool.
Deccani	Border of Maharashtra, Andhra Pradesh, Karnataka	Black to grey colour and tan face; rams horned. Produce (700-1,500 gm/year) rough wool.
Exotic breeds of sheep		
Merino	Spain	White coloured, rams with twisted horns. Produce (3.5-4.0 kg/year) fine quality wool.
Lincoln	England	Massive body. Produce (3.5-4.0 kg/ year) coarse wool.

Camels

The term camel usually applied for two species of the genus *Camelus*. The Arabian camel, *Camelus dromedarius* has one hump, the Bactrian camel, *Camelus bactrianus,* has two humps. The females produce one birth after a gestation of 11 months and suckle it for a year; maturity is reached at the age of 10-12 years, and the life-span is 30 to 40 years.

Pigs

Pigs have a gestation period of 114 days with a 21-day interval between periods of estrus. A boar can mate with 15-45 sows per year. The average litter consists of seven pigs, each with a birth weight of 1.1 kg. Sows have usually 80% conception rate on first mating, about eight or more pigs per litre, and on an average 1.6 litres per year.

- The Hampshire pig, which originated from the Norfolk thin-rind breed of England, is black with a white belt completely encircling its body and both front legs and feet. There is no white on the head or on the ham. The Yorkshire pig is also originated in England.
- Pigs are subjected to transmissible gastroenteritis, an infectious disease often fatal to young pigs.

Breeds of Pigs (*Sus scrofa, S. vittatus*)

Breeds	Origin/ distribution	Characteristics and utility
Large white Yorkshire	England	Longer face, broad snout, erect ears, black spots on white body, fine skin. Boar 300-400 kg; Sow 230-320 kg.
Landrace	Denmark	Longer snout, drooping ears, straight face, short legs, black spots on white body. Boar 300-350 kg; Sow 200-250 kg.
Middle white Yorkshire	England	Straight jaw, white in colour, fine skin without wrinkles. Boar 270-360 kg; Sow 200-250 kg.

Poultry

Indians first domesticated chicken for the purpose of cockfighting.

Development of Egg: The male sperm lives in the hen's oviduct for two to three weeks. Eggs are fertilized within 24 hours after mating. Yolks originate in the ovary and grow to about 4.0 cm in diameter, after which they are released into the oviduct, where the thick white and two shell membranes are added. The egg then moves into the uterus where the thin white and the shell are added. This process requires a total of 24 hours per egg. The hatching of fertilized eggs requires about 21 days and hatching takes place at 38^0C temperature.

- An egg contains 67% water, 13% protein, 9% fat and 11% minerals.
- Poultry diseases include fowl typhoid, pullorum, fowl cholera, chronic respiratory disease, infectious sinusitis, infectious coryza, avian infectious hepatitis, infectious synovitis, bluecomb, Newcastle disease, fowl pox, avian leukosis complex, coccidiosis, blackhead, infectious laryngotracheitis, infectious bronchitis and erysipelas.

Names of Different Stages of Animals and Their Groups

Animal	Adult Male	Adult female	Child	Group	Child production
Cow	Bull	Heifer	Calf	Herd	Calving
Goat	Buck	Doe	Kid	Trip	Kidding
Sheep	Ram	Ewe	Lamb	Hertle	Lambing
Pig	Boar	Sow	Piglet	Drove	Furrowing
Horse	Stallion Or stud	Mare Or Ewe	Foal	Herd	Foaling
Dog	Dog	Bitch	Puppy	Kennel	Whelping
Fowl	Cock Or Rooster	Hen Or Pullet	Chick	Flock	Hatching

- **Gestation period** in Buffalo (310 days), Cow (283 days), Mare (336 days), Ewe/Doe (150 days), Swine (114 days) and Bitch (60 days).
- **Heat period** in Buffalo (18-38 hours), Cow (12-24 hours), Mare (4-7 days), Ewe (36 hours), Doe (48-72 hours), Swine (2-3 days) and Bitch (7-9 days). Heat period in bitch is noticed usually once in a year (September-October.).
- **Body temperature of healthy animals in degree Fahrenheit** for cow/buffalo (101-102), Sheep/Goat (101.5-104), Pig (101-103.5), Chicken (105-109.5), Horse (99.4-101.2), Camel (97-101) and Dog (100-102).
- ***2n* chromosome numbers** in cattle (60), buffalo (50), sheep (54), goat (60), horse (64), pig (38), dog (78), fowl (78) etc.

Ration:

Ration is an amount given to animal in 24 hours (in parts).

- **Feed:** Single article in food is called feed. Mixture of two or more feeds is known as **food.**
- **Maintenance ration** is given to animal of non-producing nature, which is comprised of 0.254 kg DCP (Digestible Crude Protein) and 3.0 kg TDN (Total Digestible Nutrients) for a 400 kg animal.
- Growing animals need 2-3 kg, pregnant animal 1-2 kg, breeding bull 1-2 kg and working bullocks 1.5-2 kg of concentrate in their ration.
- **Production ration** is given to animal of producing in nature. It is required as per the need of animal, *e.g.* a milch cow yielding 4% fat in milk require 0.045 kg DCP and 0.316 kg TDN per kg of milk.
- For milk producing cow, 1 kg of grains for every 3 kg of milk, plus 1 kg of concentrate as a maintenance ration, is given in addition to dry matter (2.5 kg for every 100 kg body weight).
- Buffalo need 1.5 kg concentrate for every 2.5 kg of milk plus 1.5 kg concentrate as maintenance ration is given in addition to dry matter (3 kg for every 100 kg body weight).

Important Schemes Launched in India

- **Key village scheme:** The scheme was started in the first five-year (from 1952) plan for all round development of cattle industry in India.
- **Intensive cattle development programme (ICDP):** It was started in the second five-year plan to provide balance nutrition, controlled breeding and better veterinary facilities. Out of the scheme so far, the milk production has increased from 11-17% in cow and 4-10% in buffalo.
- ***Goshala* development:** This scheme was launched after the formation of Central *Goshala* Board, Chennai, under Ministry of Agriculture in 1948. However, scheme could not achieve much the objective was meant for.
- ***Gosadan* scheme:** The scheme was launched (1952) in view of creation of good herd of animals, by collecting all the old age and non-producing animal and castrate them to check the further developments unproductive population.

- **Milk colony:** The milk colony scheme was launched in 1946 to collect milk from the total catchment area and supply it to metros. First milk colony in Asia was developed at Mumbai (Array Milk Colony) with the capacity of 10-lakh litres milk.

Chronology of Important Livestock Development Programmes

Year	Programme
1892	Establishment of Civil Veterinary Department (CVD).
1944	Establishment of Serum Institute (VBRI).
.1948	C.V.D. renamed as Animal Husbandry Department.
1949	Supply of Breeding Bulls under Premium Bull Scheme.
1955	Introduction of Key Village Scheme and Artificial Insemination.
1959	Introduction of Cross Breeding Programme.
1961	Establishment of Semen Banks.
1964	Introduction of Intensive Cattle Development Blocks.
1971	Launching of Operation Flood I.
1974	Starting of Intensive Sheep Development Projects.
1975	Functioning of Indo Swiss Project.
1976	Reorganisation of the Animal Husbandry Department.
1976	Introduction of Livestock Projection Programmes for Weaker Sections.
1977	Formation of Andhra Pradesh Meat and Poultry Development Corporation.
1981	Operation Flood II.
1981	Formation of Andhra Pradesh Dairy Development Co-operative Federation.
1984	Introduction of Frozen Semen Technology.
1985	Upgradation of Taluk Level Hospitals.
1985	Operation Flood III.
1988	Technological Mission for Dairy Development.
1991	Launching of National Project on Rinderpest Eradication.
1995	Control of Rinderpest Disease by Mass Vaccination.

Vaccination Schedule for Cattle and Buffaloes

Name of the disease	Age at 1st vaccination	Booster dose months	Time of vaccination
Foot and Mouth Disease	2 months	Once in 6M	Mar.–Apr. Aug.– Sep.
Rinder Pest	6 months	Once in a year	Jan.–Feb.
Haemorrhagic Septicaemia	5 months	Once in a year	May–June
Black-Quarter (Black-leg)	7 months	Once in a year	May–June
Anthrax	6 months	Once in a year	August–Sep.
Brucellosis	4.6 months	Once in a life period	August
Theileriasis	After 4 months	Once in a year	August

Important Diseases of Livestock

Contagious diseases are those, which spread through contact. Such diseases are caused either by bacteria (*e.g.* Anthrax, B.Q., Hemorrhagic Septicemia, Tuberculosis, Mastitis, etc.) or viruses (*e.g.* Rinderpest, Foot and Mouth Disease, Cowpox, Rabies, Ephemeral fever, etc.). **Non-contagious** diseases include Parasitic (either due to Ectoparasites, *e.g.* Ticks, Lice, Mites, Fleas; or Endoparasites, *e.g.* Roundworm, Tapeworm, Hookworm, Lungworm, etc.), Non-Parasitic (either due to nutritional deficiency, *e.g.* Avitaminosis, Constipation, Milk fever, Goiter; faulty ration, *e.g.* Impaction, Tympanites, Diarrhoea etc.; and due to Poisoning or Toxicity) and Non-specific (*e.g.* Mestritis, Retained Placenta, Dystokia, Prolapse of Uterus).

- **Anthrax (*Bacillus anthracis*):** Anthrax is an acute, infectious febrile disease of virtually all animals and men. In India, it is well known as the cause of sudden death of cattle, sheep and goats. Treatment is of use in cases showing sub-acute form of the disease.
- **Black-quarter (Black-leg):** Young animals in the prime of condition and six months to three years old are affected more than others. True black-quarter is caused by *Clostridium chauvoei*.
- There is high fever with a hot, tense, painful swelling usually in one of the quarters, more often a hindquarter. Crepitating sound on pressing the affected part of muscle. Death may occur in severe cases within 1 or 2 days.

- Use of black-quarter vaccine protects animals against the disease for about a year. Animals should be vaccinated with this about three to one month before the onset of rains.
- **Contagious bovine abortion:** This disease of cattle and buffaloes, usually termed brucellosis, is caused by *Brucella abortus,* a small gram-negative coccobacillus, also known as Bang's bacillus.
- **Bovine mastitis:** This disease is characterized by the inflammation of the udder, resulting in changes in the udder tissue and its secretion. The milk is affected both in quality and in quantity, and as a result of permanent impairment of the function of one or more quarters, milk production may cease altogether.
- Drugs as acriflavine, gramicidin and tyrothricin, sulphonamides, penicillin and streptomycin are used to control the disease.
- **Cowpox:** Under natural conditions the infection takes place through inoculation by the cutaneous route and readily spreads from one animal to another through the agency of milkers.
- **Foot-and-mouth disease:** The food-and-mouth disease is a highly communicable disease affecting cloven-footed animals. It is characterized by fever (up to 104-105°F), formation of vesicles and blisters in the mouth, udder, teats and on the skin between the toes and above the hoofs. A profuse salivation rope of stringy saliva hangs from mouth.
- **Haemorrhagic Septicaemia:** This acute septicaemic disease of cattle and buffaloes is widely prevalent in India. The causal organism, *Pasteurella multocida* (*P. boviseptica* for cattle, and *P. bubaliseptica* for buffaloes) is a small gram-negative cocco-bacillus, commonly called bipolar organism on account of the intensity with which is stains at the poles.
- Redness of eye and painful swelling at head, jowl region or brisket region with high fever. The lesions comprise haemorrhagic spots in the lymph nodes including the inner lining of the heart; spleen is normal in size.
- Disease can be treated well in early stage with sulphonamides, sulphadimidine coupled with antibiotics, such as penicillin.
- **Rinder pest:** Rinderpest is the most destructive of the virus diseases of cloven-footed animals. The virus is found in the

saliva, discharge from eyes and nostrils, and in the urine and faeces. The virus is usually spread by contaminated feed and water.

- Rise in temperature up to 104-107°F, lacrimation and redness of eye, foul odour from mouth are symptoms.

Institutions Involved

- Central Goat Research Institute, Makhdum, Mathura, U.P.
- Central Buffalo Research Institute, Hisar, Haryana.
- Central Avian Research Institute, Izzatnagar (Bareilly), U.P.
- Indian Veterinary Research Institute (IVRI), Izzatnagar, U.P.
- Central Sheep and Wool Research Institute, Malpura, Avikanagar, Rajasthan.
- National Institute of Animal Nutrition and Physiology, (Adugodi) Bangaluru, Karnataka.

❏❏❏

40

Forage and Fodders

Grasses comprising most of the forage are the primary source of food for animals, which offered either directly or through conservation in form of hay and silage. **Fodder** is the general term used for food of animals. The term **forage** is applied for the fodder from the grasses.

- Area under forage and fodder crops is 4.4 per cent of the total area. The area under permanent pastures and cultivable wastelands is approximately 13 and 15 Mha, respectively. The total area under forests is 25.1 Mha of which 21.0 Mha is open for grazing.

Some Cultivated Fodder Species for Different Regions

Regions	Rainfed	Irrigated
Arid tracts	Jowar, Bajra, Moth, Guar, Lobia.	Lucerne, Berseem, Oats, Maize, Jowar, Bajra.
Semi-dry	Bajra, Jowar, Lobia, Moth, Guar, Velvet Bean, Field Bean, Moong.	Jowar, Maize, Lobia, Teosinte, Lucerne, Berseem, Sarson, Turnips, Hybrid Napier, Oats, Sudan Grass, Guinea Grass, Rhodes.
Semi-wet	Dinanath Grass, Jowar, Lobia, Rice Bean, Velvet Bean, Teosinte, Sunnhemp.	Berseem, Oats, Sudan Grass, Hybrid Napier, Guar, Jowar, Maize, Para, Rhodes, Setaria.
Wet regions	Jowar, Dinanath Grass, Rice Bean.	Berseem, Oats, Hybrid Napier, Guinea, Lucerne, Berseem, Sarson, Turnips, Hybrid Napier, Oats, Setaria , Para, Jowar.
Lower hills	Jowar, Lobia, Bajra, Velvet Bean, Field Bean, Guar	Maize, Jowar, Oats, Berseem, Lucerne, Hybrid Napier, Sudan, Setaria, Rhodes.

FODDER CONSERVATION

In order to regulate the supply of palatable and nutritive fodder during the lean periods both in October and November and May to July, there is a need of conserving the surplus fodder in the form of hay and silage.

Silage

Silage is the product obtained by packing fresh fodder in a suitable container, and allowing it to ferment under anaerobic conditions, without loss of nutrients. Fermentation under anaerobic conditions preserves the nutritive value and enhances the keeping quality of the fodder. The process of conserving green fodder in this way is termed as **ensiling**.

Qualities of Good Silage

Good silage is greenish or yellowish brown, with pleasant odour, and possesses a high acid content (butyric acid). Shephered *et al*. (1948) classified the silage into the following categories:

(*i*) **Very good silage**: Silage with acidic taste and odour, being free from butyric acid, moulds, sliminess having 3.4-4.2 pH and less than 10% ammoniacal nitrogen of the total nitrogen.

(*ii*) **Good silage:** Silage possessing acidic taste and odour, traces of butyric acid, pH 4.2-4.5 and ammonical nitrogen 10-15% of the total nitrogen.

(*iii*) **Fair silage:** Ensiled material with some butyric acid, a slight proteolyses, some moulds, >4.8 pH and >20% ammonical nitrogen of the total nitrogen.

Crops Suitable for Silage Making

Fodder crops rich in soluble carbohydrates and low protein content are suitable for silage making. A high content of soluble carbohydrate provides an excellent growth medium for the anaerobic bacteria to form abundant acids, which increase the keeping quality of the silage. Maize, Jowar, Bajra, Guinea Grass, Para Grass and Napier Grass are highly suitable for making good-quality silage.

Steps for Making Silage

(*i*) The fodder crops chaffed (1-2 cm) at the proper stage (at least 30-35% dry matter).

(*ii*) The silo pits must be filled quickly (within 3-4 days) and the material must be compacted in such a way as to remove maximum air. Urea @ 3-4 kg/t of the chaffed material can be mixed, if necessary.

(*iii*) The silo pits, after filling and compacting the material carefully should appear like dome.

(*iv*) The ensiled material is then covered with a polythene sheet or a tarpaulin from all sides so as to protect it from the direct rays of the sun and rains.

(*v*) After a week, the polythene sheet is removed and the material is compacted again to consolidate the chaffed material. The polythene sheet is then placed back.

(*vi*) The chaffed material ensiled by the above procedure is ready for feeding to the livestock after 2-3 months.

Hay

Hay is the conversion of green forage into dry form without affecting the quality of the original material. The cured hay should have a natural green colour, pleasant aroma, optimum moisture content and freedom from microbes.

Crops Suitable for Hay Making

The efficiency and quality of haymaking are determined by the moisture content. All the thin-stemmed grasses, *viz.* Anjan, Sain, Moshi, Dhaulu, Spear, Blue Panic, Sewan, Marvel, Dinanath, Oat, Rhodes Grass, Thin Guinea, Thin Napier; and Lucerne, Berseem, Senji, Peas, Methi, Vetches, Cow pea, Field Bean, Rice Bean and Velvet Bean, can be conveniently and quickly dried.

Hay Making

Cut the crop at the flowering stage, chaff into small pieces and spread evenly in thin layers allowing two or three turnings daily, till the final moisture remained to 15 per cent. It should preferably be stored at a low temperature and humidity so as to prevent losses owing to the oxidation of the carbohydrates.

Crop Residues Improvement

The straw of Paddy, Wheat, Barley, Maize, *Jowar*, *Bajra* and *Ragi* crops are highly deficient in protein and minerals, but are fairly rich in carbohydrates. **Haylage** is the product after enriching the fodder with urea (1-2%), molasses (10-15%), salt (2%) and mineral mixture (1%).

Institutions Involved

- Indian Grassland and Fodder Research Institute, Jhansi, Uttar Pradesh.
- Central Arid Zone Research Institute, Jodhpur, Rajasthan.
- National Dairy Research Institute, Karnal, Haryana.
- National Seeds Corporation, New Delhi.

Package and Practices of Important Forage and Fodder Crops

Crop and duration (days)	Sowing time	Seed-rate (kg/ha)	Spacing (cm)	FYM (t/ha) fertilizers kg/ha	Varieties and special features	Yield (q/ha)
Jowar 70-90	March-July (North) Feb.-Nov. (South)	40-50	25-30	FYM 20-25 60:30:30	J.S.-20, J.S.-29/1, J.S.-263, J3/53, Swarna, S.L.-44, Pusa Chari, Haryana Chari, T-3, T-4, M.P. Chari, S-700, H_1, H_2, Rio, Sundhia 1049, Chhastia 10-2, Dudhia, Red Khaki, Nilwa, Nandyal, M-35-1, Gwalior-82, Gwalior-304, Vidisha 60-1, Ujjain-6, Ujjain-8, J-195, K 3, Co 11, Co 18, Co 19, Rungu 1.	300-400 500-700
Maize 70-80	April-Aug. (North) Feb.-Nov. (South)	40-40 60-75 (Hybrid)	25-30	FYM 25 50-60:30:20	Ganga-Safed-2, Ganga-3, Ganga-5, Ganga-7; Jawahar, Amber, Kisan, Vijay, Sona, Vikram; N.P. Yellow-2, K-41, Bassi, Jaunpur, Emenillo de cuba, Kalimpong.	350-450
Bajra 50-60	Mar.-Aug. Feb-Nov	10-12 (Rain fed)	30-40 50-60	FYM 10-12 40:30:00	A-1/3, H.B. 3, S-530, T-55, D 1941, D 2291.	300-400
Cowpea 60-70	Mar.-Aug. Feb.-Nov.	30-40	40-50	FYM 10 20:40: 120	FOS-1, FOS-10, K-395, K-585, EC 4216, IGFRI-S-450, IGFRI-S-457, IGFRI-S-978, IGFRI-S-985, Russian Giant, E.C. 4216, Chhrodi 14-20, Chhrodi 26-28, Co 1.	450 250-300

Crop and duration (days)	Sowing time	Seed-rate (kg/ha)	Spacing (cm)	FYM (t/ha) fertilizers kg/ha	Varieties and special features	Yield (q/ha)
Guar 60-70	Apr.-Aug. Mar.-Nov.	25-30	30-40	FYM 5 10:30:10	FOS 1, FOS 2, F.S. 277, IGFRI-S 212	250-300
Oats 70-75	Mid-Oct. to mid-Nov.	80-90 80:30:20	20-25	FYM 20	**Early**: Western-11; Mid-season: Kent, Craig, Afterlee, Green Mountain, A-17, Flaminagolds, Fulgham, Bamboo-966, IGFRI-Soil-3021, IGFRI-Soil-2688; **Late**: Algerian, FOS-1/29, Kharsai.	400-450
Berseem 60-70	Oct.-Nov.	20-25	Broad-cast	FYM 25 20:60:30	Meskawi-Diploid, Pusa Giant-Tetraploid, IGFRI-S-29-1, Chhindwara; First cutting in 60-70 days and subsequent cuttings after 40 days interval.	750-800
Lucerne 70-80	Oct first week	15-20	Broad-cast	FYM 20 80:30:00	Type-8, Type-9, Anand II, IGFRI-S-244, Moopa, IGFRI-S-54, N.D.R.I.-170-80 days subsequent cuttings at 30-40-day intervals.	800-1000
Senji 80-90	End of Sept to Oct.	25-30	Broad-cast	FYM 10 10:30:20	FOS-1, F.S. 14, F.S. 18.	250-300

Crop and duration (days)	Sowing time	Seed-rate (kg/ha)	Spacing (cm)	FYM (t/ha) fertilizers kg/ha	Varieties and special features	Yield (q/ha)
Hybrid Napier	Mar.-Aug. (North) Feb.-Nov. (South)	10,000 rooted slips	60 × 60	FYM 25 40:30:20	Pusa Giant Napier, NB 21, EB 4, or Gajraj, N.B. 5, Coimbatore1st cut-75 days subsequent cuts at 45 day intervals.	2,000-2,800
Sudan grass	Mid Mar. to mid July	20-25	25-30	FYM 15-20 30:20:00	SS-59-3, G 287, Piper, J-691st cut 50-60 days later cuts at 40-45 days intervals	500-1, 000
Mustard 60-65	1st week of Sept. to 1st week of Oct.	6-8	30-40	FYM10-15 Nitrogen-30	Japan sarson, IM-98, IM-100, Laha 101, Chinese cabbage	300-350
Turnip 70-80	1st week of Sept. to 1st week of Oct.	4-5	25-30	FYM 10-12 Nitroen-60	Green Top, Purple Top, Kenshin – Kaba	300-400

❒❒❒

41

Dairy Technology

Dairy technology deals with the milking, production and handling of milk with improved technologies. Milk is one of the most complete and oldest known animal foods. Hippocrates, the Greek physician, recommended milk as a medicine in the 5th century BC. Sanskrit writings from ancient India refer to milk as one of the most essential human foods.

- There has been a major improvement in milk production, which increased from 17 MT in 1951 to 88 MT in 2003.
- U.P., Punjab, M.P., Rajasthan, Maharashtra, Gujarat, A.P., Haryana, T.N. and Bihar contribute to the extent of 85 per cent of the total milk production in the country.
- Indian dairy industry is one of the fastest growing (@ 4.5 per cent per annum) sectors in India.
- India holds number one position in the world in milk production with 112·5 MT (2009-2010) against global milk production at 600 MT (2003, FAO report). More than half of the milk (54%) of Indian milk comes from buffalo.
- The present per capita availability of milk is 237 g as against the recommended (ICMR, New Delhi) requirement of 250 g.
- Prevention of food adulteration Act (PFA), 1954 and Milk and Milk products order, 1992; ensures the quality milk to the public.

Milking

There are three methods of milking, *viz.* full hand or fisting method, stripping method and knuckling method; among these fisting method is best. Let down effect of oxytocin hormone remains for 6-7 minutes therefore, milking in cows should be completed within this period.

Milk

Milk in normal sense called **'whole food'** as it contains almost all the constituents required for human beings. Normal milk on an average contains 5.1% fat, 4.78% lactose and 3.5% protein; and it supplies 78 calories/100 g of milk.

Comparative Composition (%) of Milk of Different Species

Constituents	Cow	Buffalo	Goat	Sheep	Human
Water	87.20	82.75	86.50	83.70	87.43
Fat	3.70	7.38	4.50	6.00	3.75
Protein	3.50	3.60	3.50	4.80	1.63
Lactose	4.90	5.48	4.70	4.90	6.98
Ash	0.70	0.78	0.80	0.80	0.21
S.N.F.	9.10	9.86	9.00	10.30	8.82

- Milk has vitamin A from 160 IU (Cow) to 170 IU (Buffalo) in 100 g of milk. Toned milk contains 60 IU (36 IU in double toned) vitamin A per 100 g of milk. Standardized milk contains 90 IU vitamin A in 100 g of milk.
- The protein content of milk is highest in Jersey (3.92%) followed by Guernsey (3.91%) and lowest being in Holstein (3.23%).
- The cow from her blood produces milk, and a large amount of food is necessary for maintenance of a high milking cow. Each time the blood passes through the udder a small fraction of the components is removed to make the milk. ***About 200 litres of blood must pass through the udder to make about 0.45 liters of milk.***

Colostrum

It is the milk secretion during first 3-5 days of calving. Colostrum is rich in vitamins A, B, Iron, Tryptophan and globulins (carrier for antibodies). It acts as laxative helping movement of bowels in newly born calf.

Comparison of Normal Milk with Colostrum

Parameters	Normal milk	Colostrum
Taste	Sweet	Bitter
Odour	Normal	Abnormal
Acidity	0.12-0.14	0.2-0.4
Freezing point	–0.52°C to –0.56°C	–0.605 °C
Specific gravity	1.028-1.032	1.048-1.080
Refractive index	1.344-1.348 at 20 °C	More than milk
Electrical conductivity	0.005 mho	More than milk

Physical Properties of Milk

Colour: Cow's milk is light yellow due to presence of carotene. Buffalo's milk is devoid of carotene hence it is white in colour. When casein and fat are removed by addition of rannet, the colour of whey remains light blue due to presence of riboflavin.

- **Specific gravity:** Specific gravity at 60 °F is 1.028 (cow milk) and 1.031 (buffalo milk). It is 1.667 for lactose, 1.346 for protein, 5.500 for mineral matters and 0.900 for fat. It is measured by lactometer.
- **Freezing point:** The freezing point of milk ranges from minus (-) 0.525–minus (-) 0.565 °C with an average at minus (-) 0.55°C. It is measured by Hortvet cryscope.
- **Refractive index:** It ranges from 1.344 to 1.348 at 20°C . It is measured using refractometer.
- **Buffer value:** It is 0.24 at pH 6.0 and 0.018 at 6.6 pH. Buffer value is due to presence of CO_2, citrate, albumin, casein and phosphates.
- **Acidity:** Acidity in milk may be natural or developed. The natural acidity is due to presence of CO_2, citrate, albumin, casein and phosphates. Developed acidity is due to development of lactic acid in milk. Normal milk has acidity of 0.12-0.14%.
- **pH value:** pH is the scale for measuring acidity/alkalinity. The pH in the fresh milk is 6.6.
- **Viscosity:** It is measured in 'poise' and ranges in normal milk from 1.5 to 2.0 centipoise at 20 °C.
- **Surface tension:** It is measured in dynes and ranges in normal milk from 40 to 60 dynes/sec at 20 °C.
- **Electrical conductivity:** It is due to presence of sodium, potassium and chlorides in milk. It is measured using ammeter. In normal milk it is 0.005 mho.

Pasteurization of Milk

Extensive studies have determined that heating milk to 63°C for 30 minutes or 72 °C for 15 seconds followed by immediate cooling at 7-4 °C inactivate to most of the resistant harmful bacteria. High-temperature short-time (HTST) method at 72 °C for 15 seconds is most widely used.

- The shelf life for high-quality pasteurized milk is about 14 days when properly refrigerated. It may be extended (up to 45 days) through ultra-pasteurization, in which milk is heated to 138°C for two seconds and aseptically placed in sterile conventional milk containers.

Milk Types According to Consumers

- **Whole milk:** The milk obtained from animal and supplied to consumers called 'whole milk' without any adulteration or alteration in composition. As per the PFA rules whole milk should contain 3.5% fat, 8.5% SNF for cow and 6% fat and 9% SNF for buffalo.
- **Standardized milk:** When the composition of milk is altered as per the predetermined level of composition. As per the PFA rules standardized milk should contain a minimum of 4.5% fat and 8.5% SNF.
- **Toned milk:** Such milk is made using skimmed milk powder with addition of water. As per the PFA rules toned milk should contain a minimum of 3% fat and 8.5% SNF.
- **Double toned milk:** It is also prepared as toned milk and according to PFA rules it should contain a minimum of 1.5% fat and 9% SNF.
- **Reconstituted milk:** It is made using whole milk powder and addition of water into the ration of 1:7-8.
- **Filled milk:** When the fat of natural milk is substituted by vegetable fat, the milk with vegetable fat is called filled milk.

MILK PRODUCTS

In India 46% of the milk produced is consumed as whole milk, 28% as ghee, 7% as butter, 8% as curd, 7% as Khoa and 4% as milk powder/ice-creams.

Curd or *Dahi*

Dahi making involves the partial conversion of lactose to lactic acid, by lactic-acid bacteria *Streptococcus* and *Lactobacillus* incubated at 28-32°C. It is produced by heating milk (72-75°C for 60 minutes), cooling (29 °C), adding starter (*Streptococus lactis*, or *Lactobacillus acidophilus* or *L. bulgaricus*) into milk and incubating at 28-32°C temperature for 8-10 hours. Milk used for curd making may be whole or skimmed, but water percentage is more in *dahi* from skimmed than that of whole milk.

Cream

Due to lighter weight, fat globules rise to the top forming upper layer of milk, called cream (proportion of milk having not less than 20% fat). With increase in fat percentage usually SNF percentage is reduced, being 7.2 at 20% fat, 6.7 at 25% fat, etc. Cream is separated either by gravity method or centrifugal method; in these two methods centrifugal method is mostly adopted.

- Separation of cream by gravity method depends upon the size of fat globules. The separation rate may be assessed as,

$$V = \frac{2r^2 \ (d_s - d_f) \ g}{9N}$$ Where, V = velocity of fat globules.

d_s = density of milk serum.
d_f = density of fat globules.
r^2 = square radius of fat globules.
g = force of gravity (980.616 dynes).
N = velocity of milk serum.

- **Separator slime** is a thick smooth substance, present in bowl hood of cream separator. It contains several foreign matters and 66.3% water, 0.5% fat, 22% casein, 0.5% lactose, 10.7% etc.

Butter

Butter is obtained from churning of cream. It contains 80% of fat and less than 16% moisture. Before churning, cream is standardized to have 35% fat, pasteurized at 62°C for 30 minutes (or 71°C for 20 seconds). To incorporate better aroma, cream is ripened at 27-32 °C for 8 hours and added with diacetyl ($CH_3COCOCH_3$).

- Overrun is the difference between amount of cream churned and amount of butter produced.
- Margarine is a substance often confused with butter. It is prepared from vegetable oil having same taste, odour like butter. Skimmed milk is used to produce flavour of butter in margarine.

Ghee

Ghee is obtained from cream or butter. It should have 99% fat, 0.5% moisture. Ghee making from cream is done to manufacture butter first and then to ghee. Butter is filtered through muslin cloth and heated to 115°C.

Khoa

It is a partially desiccated milk product following rapid evaporation of moisture from milk to 70-75% solids. The recovery percentage is 18-20 per cent in cow milk and 20-23 per cent in buffalo milk.

Chhaina

Chhaina is prepared by coagulating milk with the help of acid. The milk is boiled, cooled, 0.5% citric acid added, coagulation achieved, whey drained, finally Chhaina achieved. Recovery percentage of Chhania is 15-20 per cent in cow milk and 20-22% in buffalo milk.

Quality Tests in Milk and Milk Products

Acidity test: Test is carried out to check whether the acidity is present in milk. It is measured by titration of 10 ml milk against N/10 sodium hydroxide (NaOH) using 4-5 drops of phenolphthalein indicator. Milk showing less than 0.18 per cent acidity is said to be satisfactory. Acidity percentage is measured as:

$$\text{Titrable acidity percentage} = \frac{9 \times \text{amount of 0.1 NaOH used}}{\text{Volume of milk taken}}$$

- **Clot on boiling test:** If the acidity in milk is more than 0.2% the milk upon boiling clots. In other words, if we boil milk and acidity percentage is more than 0.2%, which is not acceptable, milk will clot upon boiling.
- **Fat test:** It is done to assess the amount of fat in milk. To test the fat, take 10 ml of sulphuric acid in butyrometer. Pipette out 10.75 ml of milk and transfer it to same butyrometer. Add one ml amyl alcohol. Centrifuge at 1,000-1,200 RPM for 5 minutes. After settle, keep butyrometer in water bath at 70°C for two minutes and read the column of fat. Pure cow milk shows 4% fat and buffalo milk 7% fat.
- **Hansa test:** This is done to test adulteration of cow milk with buffalo milk. In the test, skim milk is injected into rabbits and antibodies are collected, purified, and specific antiserum is made. When this antiserum is added to buffalo milk produces a clump of tiny casein particles, which easily can be diagnosed.
- **Bromocresol purple test:** This test is carried out to test the alkalinity present in milk due to mastitis in animals. It is tested by taking a little amount of milk and placing on bromocresol paper. If the paper turns bright purple it indicates the alkalinity in milk.

- **Test for urea in milk:** This test is conducted to test whether milk is adulterated with urea. To test it, take 5 ml milk in conical flask. Add 5 ml buffer (sodium acetate: Acetic acid in the ratio of 1:1) and boil for 3 minutes in water bath. Filter through Whatman filter (No. 42). Take one ml of filtrate and add one ml of sodium hydroxide (2%) solution plus 0.5 ml sodium hypochlorite (2%) solution, mix it thoroughly. Add 0.5 ml phenol (5%) solution. If there is appearance of blue colour, it indicates adulteration with urea in milk. No colour develops in pure milk.
- **Moisture test in butter:** This is conducted to test the moisture in butter. For testing, take 10 g of butter in buttercup. Heat it on Bunsen burner till brown colour is achieved. Cool and weigh the same. Assess moisture (Moisture %= Loss of weight × 10).
- **Methylene blue reduction (MBR) test:** The test is conducted to check the bacterial population in milk; as bacteria utilize the oxygen present in milk; in result oxidation reduction potential is reduced from normal (+0.2 volts) to minus. To test it, take 10 ml of milk in sterile test-tube. Add one ml of methylene blue dye. Mix it properly. Add two drops of liquid paraffin to prevent air contact. Keep it at 37°C in the water bath. Observe the time and condition of discoloration of methylene blue dye. Both time and conditions in observation are the important factors.

Dairy Development in India

- **Milk-cooperative Federations:** The federations were formed to accelerate the milk production, collection and distribution to urban mass from rural areas for providing employment to rural mass and better supply to urban mass. **The first such federation was founded in 1931 at Allahabad.**
- National Dairy Research Institute (NDRI) Karnal started its bachelor degree programme in dairying in 1957. It is popularly called **'Mecca in dairy sciences'**.
- **AMUL (Anand Milk Union Limited):** This cooperative union was formed in late 1940s, in Anand, a small town of Kaira district (Gujarat).
- **National Dairy Development Board (NDDB):** It was set-up in 1965 under the chairmanship of Dr. Vergese Kurian, at Anand (Gujarat).

- **Operation Flood:** The first phase of programme was launched in 1970-81 and second phase from 1981-85 and third from 1985-96 for production of milk and milk product to make India self sufficient in dairy products. Operation flood brought India into new avenue of milk industry.
- **Indian Dairy Corporation:** It was founded in 1970 at Anand (Gujarat) for successfully launch of operation flood programme.
- **Technology Mission on Dairy Development:** It was launched in September 1989 to consolidate the achievement of the cooperative dairy sector after operation flood.

Institutions Involved

- Central Institute of Research on Buffaloes, Hisar, Haryana.
- National Dairy Research Institute Karnal, Haryana.

42

Sericulture

Sericulture is the technique of silk production. Silk-fibre is a protein produced from the silk glands of silkworms.

- Sericulture was introduced for the first time, into China by Hoshomin, the Queen of China. Then, it was introduced into Europe and Japan.
- A strong demand for the local production of raw silk arose in the Mediterranean area. Justinian I, Byzantine emperor during 527 to 565 persuaded two Persian monks who had lived in China, to return there and smuggle silkworms to Constantinople in the hollows of their bamboo canes (*c.* AD 550). These few hardy silkworms were the beginning of all the varieties that stocked and supplied to European sericulture until the 19th century.
- In India the silk was introduced about 400 years back and the industry was established by 1857, with an annual production of two million pounds of silk fibre. Japan is the leading producer of silk followed by China, South Korea and India.

Type of Silk and Distribution

1. *Bombyx mori*, feeds on the leaves of mulberry plants to produce the best quality of fibre among the different varieties of silk produced in the country. **Mulberry silk** is produced extensively in the states of Karnataka, West Bengal and Jammu and Kashmir.
2. *Antherea assama* is confined to only Brahmaputra Valley of India in the world. It produces the famous **Muga silk**. *Muga* silk is produced exclusively in Assam and it is still considered to be a ceremonial dress by the local population.
3. **Tasar silk** is a product of *A. mylitta,* which feeds on *Terminalia tomentosa* grown in the thick jungles of Bihar, M.P. and Orissa. The recent introductions of *Antherea royeli* and *A. perniyi* have

enabled the country to produce the **oak** (*Philosamia ricini*) **tasar silk** in the sub-Himalayan belt and in Manipur.

4. Eri silkworm (*P. ricini*), which feeds on Castor (*Ricinus communis*) is raised commercially in Assam and Orissa. Assam produces as much as 90% of **eri silk**.

- About 85% of the country's production is contributed by the Karnataka state alone through multivoltine hybrids of silkworm that allow growers to harvest five to six crops in a year.

Presently Andhra Pradesh, Bihar (Tasar); Assam (Mulberry, Eri, Muga); Himachal, Jammu and Kashmir, Karnataka, Punjab, Tamil Nadu, Uttar Pradesh, Meghalaya (Mulberry); Madhya Pradesh, West Bengal. (Mulberry, Tasar); Maharashtra, Orissa (Tasar); and Tripura (Eri), are engaged in production of silk in India.

Mulberry Silk

Production of silk involves (1) the care of the domesticated silkworm (*Bombyx mori*) from the egg stage through completion of the cocoon and (2) the production of mulberry trees that provide leaves upon which the worms feed. The silkworm caterpillar builds its cocoon by producing and surrounding itself with a long, continuous fibre, or filament. Liquid secretions from two large glands within the insect emerge from the spinneret, a single exit tube in the head, hardening upon exposure to air and forming twin filaments composed of **fibroin,** a protein material. A second pair of glands secretes **sericin**, a gummy substance cementing the two filaments together. Because an emerging moth would break the cocoon filament, the larva is killed in the cocoon by steam or hot air at the chrysalis stage. Silk containing sericin is called **raw silk.**

- The thickness of silk filament yarn is expressed in terms of **denier**, the number of grams of weight per 9,000 metre of length. Silk with good strength is assumed if it resists breakage, when subjected to weights of about 4 g per denier.
- Technically, the silkworm is actually a caterpillar rather than a worm.

Silkworm-Rearing

B. mori is an insect belonging to family Bombycidae (order Lepidoptera). Out of a life-span of 50 days, the egg stage lasts for 10 days; the larval stage for 25-30 days; pupal stage 10 days. At the end of the larval duration, the silkworm emits silk from its mouth and constructs a cocoon on scaffolding. The silkworm pass 4 moults during growth. The silkworms consume as much as 95% of the food after the third and fourth moults. **Silkworm races:** PM, TW (Multivoltine); NB 7, KA, NB 18, NB 4, D 2 (Bivoltine); NB 4, D 2 × PCN, NB 7 × NB 18, CCI × NB I8 (Hybrids).

- The average annual yield of cocoons in India is as low as 150 kg and 400 kg under rainfed and irrigated conditions, respectively.
- The cocoons are cooked in hot water and the silk fibre is unwound from the cocoons. This process is called **'reeling'**. During reeling cocoons are processed in hot water at 95-97°C for 10-15 minutes, this process is called **cooking**. The cooking enables the sericin portion to get softened and make unwinding easy without breaks.
- The **silk** consists of **two proteins**, the inner core of **fibroin** and an outer cover of gum **sericin**.
- The silk produced by the **bivoltine** races of silkworms possesses superior quality silk and stands to the international 'A' grade. New technique for rearing bivoltine silkworm is practised in Karnataka.

Tasar Silk

Three species of *Antherea*, *viz. A. mylitta*, *A. perniyi* and *A. royeli* are reared, on trees of *Terminalia tomentosa*, *T. arjuna* found in the jungles of central and north-eastern parts, for tasar silk in India. The first crop, usually called the seed crop, is raised during May to July; commercial crop is raised during October-November.

- Most of the tasar silk is produced in M.P., Orissa and Bihar.
- Tasar silkworms are usually green, however, yellow, blue are also found. Larvae are white in colour. The cocoons are cooked in caustic potash and reeled to extract the fibre. They are also spun for manufacturing coarse fibre.

Tasar Rearing

The cocoons spun by the *A. perniyi* are superior-quality fibre, founds in the oak jungles of the sub-Himalayan belt. The cocoons are made up of two layers, an outer layer of **thin floss** and an inner thick shell of **silk**. The silk is extracted only from the inner layer. Hybrids of *A. perniyi* and *A. royeli* are being exploited commercially for the production of quality tasar silk in India.

Muga Silk

The golden-yellow silk produced by *A. assama* is found only in the Brahmaputra Valley of India. The worms are raised on Som *(Machilus bombycina)* and *Litsaea polyantha* trees. The cocoon has a very weak peduncle having golden-yellow colour, are boiled in soap and soda solution. Boiled cocoon are reeled on an appliance called "***bhir***". It is a tradition in Assam to raise *muga* silk.

Eri Silk

Eri silkworm (*Philosamia ricini*) produces eri silk. It is grown in Assam and eastern parts of India. The heavy rainfall and humid atmosphere in these areas are suited for eri cultivation. The food plants for *P. ricini* are castor, *Plumeria* spp., *Ailanthus papaya, Carica utilissima,* and *Manihot fragans,* etc. The cocoons are usually white, however, brick red cocoons have also been seen. The cocoons cannot be reeled, as they are made up of uneven fibres. Usually, after the emergence of the moths, the cocoons are used for producing spun yarn.

Enemy of Silkworms

1. **Pebrine disease:** It is a protozoan disease caused by *Nosema bombycis* affecting all the stages of worm.
2. **Flachere:** It is bacterial disease (*Bacillus thuringiensis*) affecting larvae of silkworm.
3. **Grasserie:** Borilia virus is the causal organism, affecting on larvae.
4. **Muscardine:** It is caused by *Beauveria bassiana* fungus, affecting all the stages of worm.
5. **Uzy fly** (*Tricholyga bombycis*) is the parasitoid of larvae.

Institution Involved

1. Agriculture Produce Export Dev. Agency (APEDA) Mumbai.
2. Mahatma Phule Krishi Vidyapeeth (MPKV) Rahuri (Ahmednagar) Maharastra.

43

Apiculture

Apiculture is science dealing with care and management of colonies of honey bees. Honey bees belong to the order Hymenoptera with the genus Apis. The females of most species of bees are equipped with a venom sting. Honey bees collect nectar from nectaries in blossoms or leaves or stems of plants. Nectar may consist of 50 to 80% water whereas honey contains only 16-18% water. A colony in a year's time collects and carries into the hive as much as 450 kg of nectar, water, and pollen grains.

- Bee keeping originated in the Middle East. China, Mexico, and Argentina are the world's leading honey-exporting countries; Germany and Japan are the leading importers.

Honey Bee Species Reared in India

1. *Apis dorsata*: **Rock bee or Giant bee** is 20 mm in length produces high amount of honey (27-28 kg from one comb).
2. *Apis crana indica:* **Indian bee** is smaller than dorsata produces combs in trees, trunks, walls and earthen pots. The species is gentle in nature.
3. *Apis florae*: **Little bee** is smaller than both dorsata and indica. It produces comb of palm size and yield very small amount of honey.

- *Apis mellifera*: **European bee or Italian bee** produces high quality of honey (less in amount) and easily domesticated at any place.

Honey Bee Colony

A colony of honey bees is a highly complex cluster of 30-40 individuals that functions virtually as a single organism. The colony consists of the queen bee, a fertilized female capable of laying a thousand or more eggs per day, the worker bees and drones.

1. **Queen bee:** The week old surviving virgin queen start mating while flight with more than one drone. She stores sufficient sperm in her spermatheca to fertilize all the eggs she will lay for the rest of her life. The drones die in the act of mating.
2. **Worker bees:** Worker bees live about six weeks during the active season. Worker bees do all of the work of the hive, except the egg laying.
3. **Drones:** Drones are reared only when the colony is populous and there are plentiful sources of nectar and pollen. The only duty of the drone is to mate with the queen.

- Sometimes queen lays eggs in the drone cells, if she is not allowed to mate or if her supply of sperm is exhausted. The development of unfertilized eggs into adult drones is known as **parthenogenesis.**

Swarming

Swarming is the bees' natural method of propagation or multiplication. When the colony becomes crowded with adult bees and there are insufficient cells in which the queen can lay large numbers of eggs, the worker bees select a dozen or so tiny larvae that would otherwise develop into worker bees, is drawn out downward to permit more space for development of the queen. These drawn out larvae are fed copiously with royal jelly produced.

Beekeeping Equipment

- The **smoker** to quell the bees.
- A **veil** to protect the face.
- **Gloves** for the novice or the person sensitive to stings.
- A blunt steel **blade** called a hive tool, for separating the frames and other hive parts for examination.
- The uncapping **knife**, for opening the cells of honey.
- The **extractor** to centrifuge the honey from the cells.

Types of Honey

Liquid honey: It is the honey extracted directly from beehive by the uncapping of cells with uncapping knife. The removed honey is immediately heated to about 60°C in order to destroy yeasts, which cause fermentation.

Comb honey: It is the honey extracted after breaking the comb. Process of extraction is same as above.

Creamed honey: Creamed honey is produced same as liquid honey but processing is done at 66°C. Properly processed honey has fine granules, smooth, creamy appearance, is referred to as creamed honey.

Floral type honey: It is the honey produced from bees visiting floral nectaries. Different flowers produce different colours and flavours of honey. It may be heavy-bodied or thin-bodied, dark or light, mild-flavoured or strong-flavoured.

Beeswax

Beeswax is a by-product of beekeeping. The wax is recovered just after the extraction of honey from comb. The comb material heated in water to slightly over 66°C, after this treatment wax comes over the surface. Upon cooling it hardens and collected for use in quality candles, cosmetics, agriculture, art and industry.

Honey Bee Disease

1. **American foul brood** (*Bacillus larvae*) is the most serious brood disease. The spores are highly resistant to heat and chemicals. Broods affected with this disease have a mottled appearance. Sulfathiazole and Terramycin are used to manage the disease.
2. **European foul brood** (*Streptococcus pluton*): This disease is similar in appearance to American foul brood. Terramycin is used to control the disease.
3. **Sac brood** (viral): It is also similar to the foul brood diseases. It can be managed only by requeening the hive.
4. **Chalk brood** (*Ascosphaera apis*). The larvae victims of this disease have a chalky, white appearance.
5. **Stone brood**, caused by *Aspergillus flavus*.
6. **Nosema disease**, caused by a protozoan *Nosema apis*, is the most serious disease of adult bees. It is widespread, causes heavy losses in honey production, and severely weakens colonies. It can be managed by feeding the colony with the drug fumagillin.
7. **Acarine** disease is caused by the mite *Acarapis woodi* that gets into the tracheae of the bees through breathing. Bees affected by this mite are unable to fly, have disjointed wings and distended abdomens.

Pests of Honey Bee

1. **The greater wax moth** (*Galleria mellonella*): The larval stage of insect destroys combs as well as larvae of bees when they are ready to pupate. Fumigate combs for management of pest.
2. **Lesser wax moth** (*Achroia grisella*): The larvae of moth cause damage to stored combs similar to that of the greater wax moth.
3. **The bee louse** (*Braula caeca*): It is a tiny, wingless member of the fly family that is occasionally found on bees, but feeds on nectar or honey. Its larvae burrow in the capping of honeycombs.

Institution Involved

1. All india Coordinated Project on Honeybeen Research and Tranning Nagraita (H.P.)
2. APEDA (Ag. Processed Food Product Export Development Authority, (New Delhi).

□□□

44

Mushroom Cultivation

Mushroom is the conspicuous umbrella-shaped fruiting body (sporophore) of certain fungi, typically of the order Agaricales in the class Basidiomycetes of fungi. By fresh weight, the common commercially mushroom is more than 90% water, less than 3% protein, less than 5% carbohydrate, less than 1% fat (0.2 g/100 g), and about 1% mineral salts and vitamins. Since very less amount of fat they serve as the food for diabetic person. Presently several varieties are cultivated out of which *Agaricus bisporus* comprised 56% area followed by *Lentinus edodes* (14%), *Volvariella volvacea* (8%), *Pleurotus* spp. (7.7%) and others 13%.

At present three mushrooms, *viz Agaricus bisporus* (white mushroom), *Volvariella volvacea* (paddy-straw mushroom) and *Pleurotus sajor-caju* (oyster mushroom), are cultivated in India. Among them the white button mushroom, is the most popular and economically sound species extensively cultivated throughout the world. SSI-689 and SSI-17 are single spore selections of *Agaricus bisporus.*

Historical Background

First record on cultivation of mushroom was found during the reign of Loius XIV (1638-1715). The earliest description and method of growing of Mushroom was written by Turnforte, which was published from Paris in 1707 by Royal Society of Science.

- In 1886 some fine specimens of mushroom were grown by N.W. Newton and exhibited at Annual show of Horticultural Society of India (Kolkata).
- B.C. Roy explained nutritional value of mushrooms in 1896 by collecting mushrooms at Calcutta Medical College, Kolkata.
- In 1902, Miss Ferguson of Crone explained the technique of germinating the spores in detail.
- In 1905, American scientist Duggar invented the pure suspension culture from the mushroom tissue.
- Bose 1921 was first successful man to culture *Agaricus* mushrooms. The details were published in Indian Science Congress held at Nagpur (Maharashtra) during 1926.

- Lambart in 1929 introduced the technique of spawn production.
- Bose and Bose 1940 discussed the method of growing of mushroom on horse manure in detail.
- Paddy straw mushroom (*V. volvacea*) was first time cultivated by department of Agriculture Madras during 1939 and 1945. Su and Sath 1940 outlined the Spawn production and Thomas in 1943 gave the detail method of cultivation.
- In 1965, F.A.O. specialist E.F.K. Mental and W.A. Hays gave detailed technical help for development of mushrooms in India.
- The ICAR created a centre named "National Centre for Mushroom Research and Training" (NCMRT) in 1982 in Solan (H.P.) and "All India Coordinated Mushroom Improvement Project" (AICMIP) at six different centres in 1983.

Year-wise Production Schedule for Mushrooms

Mid-November to mid-March	: *Agaricus bisporus*
February to mid-April	: *Pleurotus sajor-caju*
Mid-June to mid-September	: *Volvariella volvacea*
September to November	: *Pleurotus sajor-caju*

Spawn: The propagating material used for mushroom cultivation is called spawn. There are several kinds of spawn, but mostly **grain spawn** is being used for commercial cultivation.

- **Grain spawn**: Equal amount of wheat grains and water (w/w) are boiled for 15 min, and then allowed to soak for another 15 min without heating. The excess water is drained off and the grains are cooled in sieves. The cooled grains are mixed with calcium carbonate and gypsum ($CaSO_4.2H_2O$). The gypsum prevents the grains from sticking together and calcium carbonate is necessary to correct the pH. The prepared grains are filled into half-litre bottles or polypropylene bags (@ 150-200 g/bottle or bag) and sterilized in autoclave at 15-pound pressure (per square inch) for 2 hours. The bottles are inoculated with mycelium and incubated at 22° -24°C in a dark place.

Compost

The white-button mushroom is grown on a selected substrate, which provides adequate levels of nutrients to support the crop.

Ingredients of Compost and Their Functions

1. **Base materials** include wheat straw, maize cobs and other similar cellulosic plant wastes with or without horse-manure, to provide celluloses, hemicelluloses and lignin in bulk materials.

2. **Supplements:** These activate fermentation.

(*i*) **Animal dung:** This includes horse and chicken-manure having nitrogen content from 1-5%. Cow manure is not suitable.

(*ii*) **Carbohydrate nutrients:** Such nutrients are added from molasses and malt sprouts etc.

(*iii*) **Concentration meals** include wheat or rice bran, the seed meals of cotton, soya, castor and linseed. Nitrogen content may vary from 3-12%.

(*iv*) **Nitrogen fertilizers** like ammonium sulphate, calcium ammonium nitrate and urea are rapidly released for the quick growth of microbial population.

(*v*) **Materials to correct mineral deficiencies**: Muriate of potash and calcium superphosphate.

(*vi*) **Materials to correct greasiness:** Gypsum and calcium carbonate serve to precipitate suspended colloidal materials and neutralize greasiness.

- Finally compost should have 2.0-2.3% N at the completion of the process, which corresponds to 17:1, C-N ratio.

Method of composting: There are two methods for preparing mushroom compost, the long and the short method.

Composting by long method

(*i*) **Wetting the straw:** The straw is spread thinly over cemented floor. The wetting straw is done by sprinkling water. Several turnings are given for uniform distribution of water.

(*ii*) **Mixing and heaping:** After the straw is wetted, the supplements excluding the gypsum are uniformly scattered over the straw and mixed and the mixture is finally stacked in one metre high, one metre wide a heap.

(*iii*) **Detailed Schedule of Composting:**

Schedule	Work to be done	Remarks
Day zero	Wet, mix the stack the heap	Supplement nitrogen and carbohydrates.
4th day	First turning	
8th day	Second turning	
12th day	Third turning	Add Gypsum.
16th day	Fourth turning	
20th day	Final turning and filling of the trays.	Add 40 ml Malathion diluted in 20 litres of water.

Composting by short method:

This short method was developed by Sinden and Hauser (1950), consists of two phases: phase I and phase II. The procedure for phase

I is similar to the initial stages of the long method except, that turnings are given sooner, the first on day 3, the second on day 6 and the third day on 9 or 10 when gypsum is added. The compost is now ready for the phase II or the peak heating. This is recognised as the microbial-composting stage and is an integral part of the total composting process. The phase II of composting is comprised of pasteurization of the compost in order to kill microbes. It is done by heating the compost, at 60°C for a brief period through warm air.

Morphology of Mushroom

- There are following different parts of a sporophore.

1. **The cap or pileus:** It is an expanded portion of the sporophore which may be thick fleshy membranous or corky and varies in different shape and size and colour.
2. **Gills or lamellae:** They are situated on the under side of the pileus starting from the apex of the stalk and radiate out towards the margin. These gills bear spores on their surface and exhibit a change in colour corresponding to that of spores.
3. **Veil and veil annulus:** The young fruiting bodies and gills remain covered by a tissue that extends from the margin of cap to the stipe. This tissue is called the veil. As the cap expands this tissue breaks away, leaving some portion attached to the margin of cap and other to the stipe forming a ring like structure known as veil annulus.
4. **Stipe/stalk:** Stipe is an organ, which supports cap, its presence or absence makes the important character for that particular spp.
5. **Rhizoids:** Rhizoids are the organ of food absorbing usually attached below corresponding to the stalk/ stipe.

Nutritional Value of Mushroom

Name	Calories	Moisture	Fat	Carbohydrate	Protein
Beet root	42	87.6	0.1	9.6	12.9
Brinjal	24	92.7	0.2	5.5	15.1
Cabbage	24	92.4	0.2	5.3	18.4
Cauliflower	25	91.7	0.2	4.9	28.8
Celery	18	93.4	0.2	7.7	21.6
Green beans	98	74.3	0.2	7.7	21.6
Lima beans	128	66.5	0.8	23.5	22.2
Mushroom	16	91.1	0.3	4.4	26.9
Potato	83	73.8	0.1	19.1	7.6

Comparison on Nutritional Values of Different Edible Mushrooms

Mushrooms	Moisture	Ash	Protein	Fat	Carbohydrate
A. bisporus	*89.5*	*1.25*	*3.94*	*0.19*	*1.09*
Pleurotus spp.	90.0	0.97	2.78	0.65	1.08
V. diplasia	90.4	1.10	3.90	0.25	1.57
V. volvacea	88.4	1.46	4.98	0.74	1.38

Source: FAO report 1972.

Energy value of mushroom: Mushrooms are good source of energy as 454 g of fresh mushroom provide 120 kcal of energy.

Other Uses of Mushroom:

1. The fruit body of *Fomentarius* and *Ganoderma appalatum* is used for producing Suede like materials.
2. Bottle corks are made from *polyporus squasmosus.*
3. *Polyporus formentarius* also known as timber mushroom is used for cigar light.
4. *Polyporus nigricans* is used for preparing snuffing agents.
5. *Polyporus bispidus* is used for making dye for colouring silk, cotton and wool.
6. *Polyporus sulphurus* and *Fomes ignarius* are used to prepare yellow and blackish brown colour, respectively.
7. *Daedalea quercika* is used as a comb to rub the body of a horse.
8. *Coprinus comatus* is used for making black ink.
9. *Amanita muscaria* is used for making hallucinogenic material (Som ras) and drug for epilepsy.
10. *Polyporus officinalis* is used for medicinal purpose as purgative.

Diseases of mushrooms

1. **Bacterial blotch:** *Pseudomonas tolassi*: Disease appears as brown slightly sunken blotch on the mushroom cap of irregular yellowish to dark brown in colour. Spraying with Terramycin @ 9 mg/ft^2 manages the disease.
2. **Brown plaster mould:** *Populospora byssina*: This disease usually occurs in spawning and cropping trays. Infection occurs through the compost. Disinfection with 2% formalin manages disease.

3. **Inky cap:** *Coprinus lagopus* or *C. comatus*: The disease characterised by long slender stalk with a small thin cap, which dissolves to inky liquid. Proper removal of ammonia is necessary to avoid this disease.
4. **Olive green mould:** *Chaetomium olivaceaum*: Initially it is white but in due course of time changes to olive green colour. It occurs inadequate ventilation. Disease can also be checked by treatment of tray with thiram @ 0.2% and captan/benlate @ 0.05%.
5. **Soft mildew or cobweb:** *Dactylium dendroides*: A fluffy, white cobweb like mould grows over the surface of casing soil. Initially it is white but later changes to pink. A good ventilation and prevention of excess humidity; application of Dithane-Z 78 @ 0.2% can check to disease.
6. **White plaster mould:** *Scopulariopsis fumicola*: This disease is closely related to brown plaster mould in the initial stages but later it changes from white to delegate pink shade. Control as above.

Preservation of Mushrooms

Mushrooms like other fruits and vegetable are highly perishable. They are preserved as,

Short-term storage: Fresh mushrooms can be preserved for 3 days if they are kept at or below 4°C temperature in plastic packets of 100 gauze. For the same after harvest mushroom is washed in potassium metabisulphite @ 0.05% for 30 minutes, and then packets of mushroom weighing 200-400 g are made and stored at 4°C. The shelf life can be extended from 3 days to one month if the packets are kept in 10-12% brine solution.

Long-term storage: There are several methods, including canning, freeze-drying, pickling, drying, vacuum cooling. Among these above procedures canning and freeze-drying are most preferably used. (For details refer Chapter 33, Post Harvest Technology).

❑❑❑

45

Extension Education

Extension education is an applied behavioural science dealing with the desirable changes in the behavioural complex of human beings, through various strategies and programmes, by applying the latest scientific and technological innovations.

The term 'extension' was incorporated for the first time in the Extension University, Britain in 1940 and the term 'extension education' was coined by the Cambridge University, England in 1873. The present form of extension was primarily started in the USA, during 1908 where President Roosevelt appointed a Country Life Commission to stop the Migration of people by connoting the knowledge of extension from the Land Grant Colleges to the farmers through the process of informal education. The Smith Level Act of 1914 provided the foundation for the cooperative extension system in USA.

- James Stuart is called the **father of extension education**.
- In India, extension work was primarily started with Gurgaon project, organized by F.L. Brayne (1920) from Punjab. Community Development Programme (1952) led the establishment of the National Extension Service in 1953.

Principles of Extension Education

1. Principle of interest and need.
2. Principle of cultural difference.
3. Principle of participation.
4. Principle of adaptability.
5. The grass roots principle of organisation.
6. The leadership principle.
7. The whole-family principle.
8. Principle of co-operation.
9. Principle of satisfaction.
10. The evaluation principle.

LEARNING TEACHING PROCESS

'Learning' is the process by which an individual, through his own activity, attains a change in his behaviour. It is an active process on the part of the learner. The essential role of an extension worker is to create effective '**learning situations**', which requires the following essential elements, *viz.* an Instructor, Learners, Subject matter, Teaching aids and Physical facilities.

'Teaching' is the process of arranging situations in which the things to be learnt are brought to the notice of the learners, and their interest is developed and desire aroused.

Steps in Teaching

1. Attention ⟶ 2. Interest ⟶ 3. Desire
4. Conviction⟶ 5. Action ⟶ 6. Satisfaction

Classification of Teaching Methods

Written	Spoken	Objective or visual
• Bulletins • Leaflets • Folders • News articles • Personal letters • Circular letters	• General and special meetings • Farm and home visits • Official calls • Telephone calls • Radio	• Result demonstration • Demonstration posters • Motion-picture or movies • Charts • Slide, Film-strips • Models, Exhibits

Brief Description of Important Teaching Methods

The extension-teaching methods are the tools and techniques used to create situations in which communication can take place between the rural people and the extension workers. These methods include,

1. **Individual-contact methods:** In this method face-to-face or person-to-person contact between the rural people and extension workers is held.
2. **Group-contact methods:** In such method rural people or farmers are contacted in a group, which usually consists of 20 to 25 persons. These groups are usually formed around a common interest.

3. **Mass or community-contact methods:** In such approach a large number of people are contacted for dissemination of new information.

Media Used in Above Three Methods

Individual contacts	Group contacts	Mass contacts
Farm and home visits	Method and result demonstration	Bulletins
Office calls	National demonstration leader-training meetings	Leaflets
Telephone calls	Conferences, meetings, workshops and discussions	Circular letters and radio
Personal letters	Field trips	Television, fairs, exhibitions, posters

4. **Farm and home visits:** Such visits provide an opportunity for two-way communication.
5. **Result demonstration:** This method is based on seeing by doing. This method is used to show the superiority of practices, such as the use of fertilisers, insecticides, pesticides, performance of high yielding varieties.
6. **Method demonstration:** It is used to show the technique of doing things or carrying out new practices, *e.g.* preparing a nursery-bed, treating seed with pesticides, method of sowing, soil sampling, grafting fruit trees, etc.
7. **National demonstrations:** National demonstrations are the "**front-line demonstrations** (FLDs)", conducted by researchers on the farmers' field for increased production. Such demonstrations were first initiated on a modest scale in 1965.
8. **Group discussions:** Extension workers contact all the farmers in groups. The method is used to encourage and stimulate the people to learn more about the problems that concern the community through discussion.
9. **Exhibitions:** An exhibition is a systematic display of information, actual specimens, models, posters, photographs, and charts, etc. in a logical sequence.
10. **General meetings:** These are usually held for passing on certain information to the people for future action.

11. **Campaigns:** Campaigns are used to focus the attention of the people on a particular problem, *e.g.* rat control, village sanitation, plant protection, the production of *rabi* crops and family planning.
12. **Tours and field days:** Tours are arranged to visit different institution of agriculture production for improvement of knowledge.
13. **Literature:** Newspapers, magazines, bulletins, leaflets, folders, pamphlets and wall newssheets are another set of mass media for communicating information to a large number of literate people.
14. **Radio:** It is a mass medium of communication and can reach a large number of people at any given time.
15. **Television**: It is one of the most powerful media of communication combining both audio and visual impacts. It was used for the first time in agriculture for communication in 1967.

Classification of Audio Visual Aids

Audio Aids	Visual Aids		Audio Visual Aids	
	Non-Projected	Projected	Non-Projected	Projected
• Radio • Telephone • Tape recorder • Song • PA system	• Posters • Charts • Flip book • Photograph • Flash cards • Flannel graph • Chalk board • Bulletin board	• Film strips • Slides • Silent films	• Drama • Puppet show • Dance with songs	• Television • Motion picture

16. **Motion pictures (movies):** Movies are an effective tool for arousing interest among the people. They are the most suitable medium for attracting bigger audience. A film show is followed by a discussion with the villagers.

Brief Description Visual Aids

- **Posters**: A poster should not be less than 50 × 75 cm size.
- **Flannelgraphs:** It is graph adhered to thick flannel cloth fixed on a board. Flannelgraphs serve as a good teaching aid.

- **Flash cards**. Flash cards are a set of small compact cards of 30-45 cm size used for used for transmitting a unique idea, *viz.* benefits of a smokeless *chulha* or the cultivation of hybrid maize etc.
- **Puppets:** It is a media to communicate with farmers. Puppets are suitable for village people.
- **Slides***:* A slide is a transparent picture or photograph in an individual mount, projected through slide projector.
- **Film strips:** These are a kind of slides depicting a single idea in the form of story, mounted and printed on a single length of 35-mm strip film.
- **Models:** Models are the virtual forms of the actual things for a sense of realization in people, used for, *e.g.* farm equipments.
- **Bulletin boards:** It's a kind of simple board serving the purpose of making announcements, displaying events of short duration.
- **Photographs:** It shows some action and catches the feelings, emotions of the people. They are arranged in a way that depicts a story.
- **Blackboards***:* Blackboards are most useful in group-teaching methods.
- **Cultural programmes:** In order to collect the people several folk songs and dramas are organized for effectively communicating the message of development programmes. Dramatization of a theme or story creates a lively interest among the audience.

ROGRAMME-PLANNING AND EVALUATION

Programme planning is the process of making decisions about the irection and intensity of extension programme to make effective.

rinciples of Programme Planning

1. The programme planning should be based upon a careful analysis of a factual situation.
2. In a good programme planning, problems for action are selected on the basis of recognized needs.
3. A good programme planning determines objectives and solutions, which are feasible and offer satisfaction.
4. The programme should be permanent, flexible to meet a long-term situation, short-time changes, and emergencies.

5. A sound programme should have both balance and emphasis.
6. Programme planning should be educationally directed towards bringing about improvement in the ability of the people to solve their own problems individually and collectively.
7. A good programme planning provides for the evaluation of results.

The Programme-Planning Process

1. **Collection of facts:** It is collection of relevant information subject matter through questionnaires, interviews, surveys, existing governmental records, census reports, reports of the Planning Commission, Central Bureau of Statistics and survey on past experiences of people.
2. **Analysis of the situation**: After facts collected, they are analyzed, and interpreted to find out the problems and solution for the people.
3. **Identification of problems**: As a result of the analysis of facts the important gaps between 'what is', 'what should be' are identified, and lacunae are identified.
4. **Determination of objectives:** Once the needs and problems of the people have been identified, they are stated in terms of objectives and goals.
5. **Developing the plan of work:** With availability of information and vision a detailed plan of work made in order to achieve the stated objectives and goals.
6. **Execution of the plan of work:** The execution of the plan of work is done through available extension methods.
7. **Evaluation:** Evaluation is done to measure the degree of success of the programme against objectives and goals thereof.
8. **Reconsideration:** The weaknesses and strong points of the programme are reconsidered based on systematic and periodic evaluation of the programme.

COMMUNICATION

Communication is the interchange of ideas between two persons, in such a way that they act on the existing knowledge to achieve some useful results. The transfer of message through suitable medium performs the communication.

’re-Existing Models of Communication

hannon and Veaver (1947)	Lasswell (1948)	Berlo (1960)	Fano (1963)
• Source • Transmitter • Signal • Receiver • Destination	• Who say • What say • Channel • To whom Concern • Under what circumstances • With what effect	• Communication source • Encoder • Message • Channel • Decoder • Communication receiver	• Source • Source encoder • Channel encoder • Channel • Source decoder • User

·agen (1963)	Letterer (1965)	Hertley Ebrenel
Communicator Message Channel Treatment Audience Audience response	• Sender • Channel • Receiver • Noise	• Communicator • Communicant • Content • Effect • Intent

ages of adoption

1. **The awareness stage:** Individual knows of the new idea but lacks information, which need to be provided.
2. **The interest stage:** Individual becomes interested in the new idea and seeks more information.
3. **The evaluation stage:** Individual evaluates the idea with information, and plans future course of action.
4. **The trial stage:** Individual uses the new idea on a small scale into to determine its utility in his own situations.
5. **Adoption stage:** Individual uses new ideas continuously on a full scale.

JRAL SOCIOLOGY

Rural sociology is the science of dealing interaction among the ·al society. It is composed of the important members by virtue of tus, and wealth, etc.

mponents of Rural Society

1. A group of people,
2. Living together long enough to become organized,

3. Organized,
4. Sharing common interests values,
5. Considered as unit by themselves.

Five Main Institutions of Rural Society

1. **The family**: Family is the most important, primary and multi-functional unit of the society. It plays a decisive role in the material and cultural life of the rural people. The families based on the members can be classified into two categories:

(*i*) **Conjugal or nuclear or primary family:** Such family consists of husband, wife and their children.

(*ii*) **Consanguine or extended or joint family:** It is a grouping of more than one primary family on the basis of close blood relative (Joint family). When members of some relatives are added to the family it is said 'Extended family'. The consanguine families are further classified into:

Based on dominance:

(*a*) **Patriachal or Patrillineal:** Man, from the lineage of male side, is the dominant person over family. Mostly found in North India.

(*b*) **Matriachal or Matrillineal:** Women, from the lineage of females, dominant families. Children brought up in the house of mother's parents. Husband do not live with his wife, rather he visits periodically. Such type of families are common in Assam.

Based on relatives joining into the family:

(*a*) **Patrilocal:** Wife joins the relatives of husband.

(*b*) **Matrilocal:** Husband joins the relative of wife.

Other type families

- **Polyandrous:** More than one husband.
- **Polygynous:** More than one wife in the family.

2. **Religion:** The second main institution in the society is the religion or forms of worship, rituals and belief.
3. **Government:** Government maintains law and order in the society, according to norms of particular society.
4. **Economy:** The basic needs like food, clothing and shelter are fulfilled based on the economy of the society.
5. **Education:** Education introduces the members of society for their social and cultural work.

Terminology Related to Rural Sociology

Community: It is the group of mutually dependent people; living in a compact geographical area sharing common values, interest acting collectively to perform social works.

Neighbourhood: It is smaller than community, living in limited area as to reach each other to perform work together.

Group: It is the unit of two or more people together for reciprocal interaction or communication with each other.

- Family is the basic unit of society and civilization.
- Village is the basic unit of rural society.

Rural (Community) Development Programmes

Stage I: Pre-independence Era (1866-1947)

1903 **Adarsh Gram Yojna**: Daniel Hamilton started the programme for creation of model villages.

1908 **Light through Learning**: The programme was started from the villages in the Kaligram Paragana, **Sriniketan** (Bengal) with the organization of Youth for apathy of privileged class of villages towards downtrodden people. This programme led the construction of schools, dispensaries, adult schools, demonstrations farms, etc. at Shantiniketan in 1921.

1920 Gurgaon Experiments by F.L. Brayne (the deputy commissioner of Gurgaon) for poverty alleviation and improving backwardness of people of Gurgaon district.

1921 Rural Reconstruction Institute was established at Shantiniketan.

1926 Sevagram Project by Mahatma Gandhi, for social change.

1928 Marthandam Project by Spencer Hatch (Now called Young Men Christian Association) for social change.

1929 Adarsh Seva Sangh, Pohri (Gwalior) by Col. Shitle.

1932 Rural Reconstruction Movement by N.T. Krishnamachari in Baroda.

1942 Grow more food campaign.

1945 Indian Village Service by A.T. Mosher and B.N. Gupta.

1946 Firka Development Scheme by T. Prakashan was started from Madras. Basic idea for this programme was from Mr. Raj Gopalachari.

1947 Mazdoor Manzil at Nilokheri by S.D. Dey.

Stage II: Post-Independent Era (1947-1953)

1948
- **Etawah Pilot Project** by Albert Mayer (American Engineer): Etawah district was chosen, as it was the most typical district in the country for its geographical locations. USA and state government provided the funds for this project, jointly.
- **Sarvodaya Programme**: This programme was started by Acharya Vinoba Bhave for the upliftment of villages, based on Bhudan and Gramdan, etc.

1952 Grow more food campaign enquiry committee

Stage III: Community Development and Extension Service Era (1953-1960)

1952 Community Development Project was started (2.10.1952) in 55 blocks under the dynamic leadership of S.K. Dey.

1953 National Extension Service Scheme was inaugurated on 2.10.1953

1954 National Extension Service Programme.

1957 **Balwantrai G. Mehta Committee** on Community development project recommended democratic decentralization, the Panchayati Raj.

1958 Rajasthan became first state to adopt Panchayati Raj on October 2, 1959 followed by Andhra Pradesh, Bihar, Gujarat, Himachal Pradesh, Maharastra, Punjab, Tamil Nadu, Uttar Pradesh and West Bengal.

Ashok Mehta Committee was appointed to study the decay in the system of Panchayati Raj, which submitted its report in 1978.

G.V.K. Rao Committee was appointed on 25 October 1985 which recommended as basic unit in Panchayati Raj to be district level.

L. M. Singhvi Committee was instituted in 1986, which recommended for organisation of villages in more prominent form for easy implementation of Panchayati Raj.

After several committees' reports by the amendment 73rd and 74th in Indian constitution, a new part IX was inserted containing Articles 243 to 243-O. The amendments came into force on 25.04.1993 and 1.6.1993, respectively.

Stage IV: Intensive Agriculture Development Era (1960 onwards)

1960 IADP (Intensive Agriculture District Programme also called as Package Programme in seven districts, later extended to nine more districts.

1970 IAAP (Intensive Agricultural Area Programme.

1964 ICDP (Intensive Cattle Development Project).

1966
- HYVP (High Yielding Varieties Programme).
- MCP (Multiple Cropping Programme).

1969 SFDA (Small Farmers Development Agency).

1971 MKP (**Minikit Programme**) for Rice was started and later extended to wheat, maize and other millets etc.

Stage V: Development Programme with Social Justice Era

1970
- MFAL (Marginal Farmers and Agricultural Labourers Programme).
- DPAP (Drought Prone Area Programme).

1972 MNP (Minimum Need Programme).

1974
- **FWP** (Food for Work Programme).
- **T&V** (Training and Visit) System formulated by Daniel Boner and Baxtor of Israel. Turkey was the first country to adopt the T&V system. In India, Rajasthan canal area and Chambal area in Madhya Pradesh started first T&V system.
- **KVK** (Krishi Vigyan Kendra); Mohan Singh Mehta committee recommended KVKs and first KVK was established by TNAU at Pondicherry. By the end of IX plan(2001-2002) there were 276 KVKs and moreover, 178 have been sanctioned including 128 during 2004-2005, covering 488 rural districts.
- CAD (Command Area Development Programme).

1979
- IRDP (Integrated Rural Development Programme).
- TRYSEM (Training Rural Youth for Self-employment).
- LLP (Lab to Land Programme).

1980
- NREP (National Rural Employment Programme).
- NARP (National Agricultural Research Project).
- DRDA (District Rural Development Agency).
- IRDP (Integrated Rural Development Programme).

1982
- DWCRA (Development of Women and Children in Rural Areas).
- CAPART (Council for Advancement of People Action and Rural Technology).

1985 IPM (Integrated Pest Management) Programme.

1986 TMO (Technology Mission on Oilseeds).

1989 JRY (Jawahar Rozgar Yojna) farmed after merging NREP and RLEGP.

1992 Integrated Krishi Vigyan Kendra.

1993
- EAS (Employment Assurance Scheme).
- Mahila Samridhi Yojna.

1994
- IVLP (Institute Village Linkage Programme).
- PMRY (Prime Minister Rozgar Yojna).

1995 NSAS (National Social Assistance Scheme).

1997
- Ganga Kalyan Yojna.
- Kasturba Gandhi Education Scheme.
- Swarn Jayanti Shahari Rozjar Yojna.

1998 Rajrajeshwari Mahila Kalyan Yojna.

1999
- NATP (National Agriculture Technology Project).
- JGSY (Jawahar Gram Samuridhi Yojna) after merging JRY.
- SGSY (Swarnjayanti Gram Swarozgar Yojna) after merging IRDP, TRYSEM, DWACRA, SITRA.
- Annapurna Yojna.

2000
- Janashri Bima Yojna.
- Antyodaya Anna Yojna.
- Pradhan Mantri Gram Sadak Yojna.

2001
- Ashray Bima Yojna.
- Khetihar Majdoor Bima Yojna.
- Sampoorna Gramin Rozgar Yojna.
- Shiksha Sahyog Yojna.

2002 Pradhan Mantri Grameena Jal Samvardhan Yojna.

2003
- Varishtha Pension Yojna (in collaboration with LIC).
- Pradhanmantri Swasthya Suraksha Yojna (AIIMS has been given the assignment).
- Vidya Vahini (Computerization Programme).

2004
- Vishesh Krishi Upaj Yojna (to promote export of fruits, vegetables, flowers, minor forest produce, and their value added products).
- Launch of *Krishi* (Agriculture) television channel.

2005 Rozgar Guarantee Programme.

2007-08 National Food Security Mission

2007 Rastriya Krishi Vikas Yojna.

2008-09 Food Security and Quality Year by GOI.

2009 Integrated Child Protection Scheme started

2010 Pilot Weather Based Crop Insurance Scheme started.

Institution Involved

- National Research Centre for Women in Agriculture Bhubaneshwar (Orissa).

46

Agricultural Marketing

Market is a place where buyer and seller, buy and sell their goods. Agricultural marketing involves its simplest form of buying and selling the agricultural produce. In modern marketing agricultural produce has to pass through several stages and exchanges till it reaches to consumer. The transfer of produce or goods takes place through a chain of middlemen or agencies.

- **Main functions of market:** Main functions of agriculture market are (*a*) assembling, (*b*) preparation for consumption, and (*c*) distribution.

Types of Markets

1. **Primary market:** The main functionaries of such markets are the producer, the village merchant, pre-harvest contractors, commission agents, transport agents etc.
2. **Secondary market:** In this market the processing and manufacturing agents are the additional functionaries other than above. Sometimes, financing agents like shroffs, banks and co-operatives also take part in the function of market.
3. **Terminal or export market:** In this type of market the commercial analyst and shipping agent are involved in the transfer of goods in addition to above functionaries.

- India being a primary producing country, agriculture plays a vital role contributing 25% of Gross Domestic Product (GDP), both as an essential infrastructure and a development component in generating and sustaining a higher national income.
- It is estimated that about 50% of the agricultural produce is available as marketable surplus.

Government Regulatory Programmes

Directorate of Marketing and Inspection looks after the functions and shortcomings in the country's marketing system. Directorate is aimed to increase the farmers' income by ensuring a fair price system.

Regulation of Markets

The markets are regulated through an Act of legislation called **Agricultural Produce Markets Act, 1937**.

- Act provides for the removal of various malpractices widely prevalent in the markets for the settlement of disputes between sellers and buyers.
- **Marketing Committee:** The committee consisting of the representatives of growers, traders, merchants, local bodies and Government. nominee administers the marketing system. The committee is generally empowered to raise funds for its working by levying a small fee on the produce bought and sold in the market in addition to the licence fees received from the functionaries.
- **First market to be regulated** was Karanja in 1886. So far Andhra Pradesh (335), Bihar (62), Chandigarh (1), Delhi (3), Gujarat (212), Mysore (102), Madhya Pradesh (233), Haryana (80), Kerala (6), Maharashtra (212), Orissa (34), Punjab (95), Rajasthan (90), Tamil Nadu (136), Tripura (1), Uttar Pradesh (264), Goa, Daman and Diu (1), West Bengal (15), and Himachal Pradesh (5) have regulated markets.
- Some states and union territories which are yet to regulate markets include Assam, Andaman and Nicobar Islands, Arunachal Pradesh, Dadra and Nagar Haveli, Jammu and Kashmir, Lakshadweep and Minicoy islands, Meghalaya, Mizoram, Nagaland and Pondicherry.
- **Contract terms:** The contract terms specify the quality and quantity of the produce, the time and place of delivery, the price and terms of payment, handling and incidental charges, the procedure for settlement of disputes and penalties.
- **Agricultural Produce (Grading and Marking) Act, 1937:** The act was formulated to achieve grading of the produce in conformity with certain standards of agricultural produce. The grades are designated as the '**Agmark**' grades. Presently the commodities like cotton, ghee, butter, rice, wheat (including flour), gur (Jaggery), eggs, arecanut, potato, fruits, bura, pulses, vegetable oils and ground spices are presently being graded under 'Agmark' on voluntary basis.
- A **central Agmark Laboratory at Nagpur** with sixteen regional laboratories at Guntur, Madras, Bombay, Kanpur, Cochin, Rajkot, Calcutta, Sahibabad, Jamnagar, Bangalore, Patna,

Tuticorin, Virudhunagar, Mangalore, Alleppey and Kozhikode, is functioning to provide adequate laboratory facilities for fixing grade standards.

- **Grade for export:** Grading of agricultural produce under the **Agricultural Produce (Grading and Marking) Act, 1937** is voluntary with some prohibitions. The Directorate of Marketing and Inspection exercises a three-tier control on the quality of agricultural commodities that are graded under 'Agmark' before they are exported, through inspection.
- **Grading of fruits and vegetable products:** The Government. promulgated the **Fruits Product Order** under the **Essential Commodities Act, 1955**. The act specifies the preservatives and colours to be used for vegetables and fruits. The order clearly stipulates the hygienic and sanitary methods, which must be adopted by the manufacturers.
- The Executive Director, Food and Nutrition Board, issues the license for all such work.

Regulation of Cold Storage

- The first cold storage in India was established in Kolkata in 1892.
- **Cold storage order, 1964:** Government. of India and the ministry of agriculture promulgated an order under **Section 3 of the Essential Commodities Act, 1955**, to regulate the cold storages. The order is applicable to every cold storage having 8.4 m^3 or more capacity. The jurisdiction of this order extends to the whole of India except West Bengal. Execution of this order is vested in the directorate of marketing and inspection for enforcing the cold storage order.
- In obligation to this order, every operator of the cold storage has to obtain a licence from the Licensing Officer before using the installation for storing any foodstuffs like fruits, vegetables, meat, fish, and dairy products, etc. The Agricultural Marketing Advisor to the Government. of India is the Licensing Officer.
- Uttar Pradesh has the maximum number of cold storage followed by Bihar and West Bengal.
- The **National Co-operative Development Corporation (NCDC)** provides financial assistance for setting up new cold stores in the co-operative sector.

- Potato is the most important commodity, which is presently placed in the cold storages accounting for as much as 92% of the total capacity in the country. The remaining 8% is being utilized for other perishables, *viz.* fruits, vegetables, meat, seafoods, dairy and poultry products.

Consumer Protection

The Agmark attempts to provide a third party guarantee for the consumer. It not only certifies the purity of the product but also gives an indication of their quality by the grade-designating mark.

- The **Consumers' Guidance Society** has been established with the objective of educating the consumers about their rights and responsibilities and advising them on the quality of products available in the market.

Co-operative Marketing

Co-operatives are functioning at the primary level, at the secondary level (taluka or district) and at the state level. **Dantwala Committee** was set up to persuade the state governments to put middle tier (the district marketing federations) into function.

- **National Agricultural Co-operative Marketing Federation (NAFED)** is the national level cooperative. Gujarat has two societies dealing with cotton and fruits and vegetables. U.P. has one society dealing with sugarcane crop.
- National Agricultural Cooperative Marketing Federation Ltd. is carrying out bulk exports. Other societies like Gujarat State Cooperative Marketing Federation Ltd., Khanna Cooperative Marketing Federation Ltd., Kerala State Cooperative Marketing Federation Ltd., Jalgaon district fruit sales societies and the Coconut Oil Millers Society also cooperated to exports to the countries like Kuwait, Malaysia, Ceylon, Singapore, Bahrain, Doha, Dubai, Iran, Muscat.
- Pulses are exported to Cuba and onions to Malaysia and Singapore.

Market Extension

The Directorate of marketing and inspection has in collaboration with the directorate of extension launched a series of 'Agmark' exhibitions known as '**vital link between farm and home**' since 1969.

❏❏❏

47

Glossary

Acaricide: Any chemical that kills members of order Acarina (Mites).

Acclimatization: The physiological and behavioural adjustment of living organisms according to change in their immediate environment.

Acedophiles: The weeds that grow under acidic soil conditions.

Acid rain: Rainwater containing excessive concentration of NO_3, SO_4, and H^+, having pH range from 5-7.

AFLP: Amplified Fragment Length Polymorphism: A sensitive method for detecting DNA polymorphism.

Agrology: The study of applied phases of soil science and soil management.

Agrostology: Deals with study, classification, management and utilization of grasses.

Akiochi soil: Sulphide containing soils.

Allozymes: Codominant protein variants (alleles) that can be visualized by appropriate staining and starch-gel electrophoresis.

Androgenesis: Development of plants from male gametophyte.

Angstrom: A unit of length equal to 10^{-10} metre.

Antibody: Protein produced in response to an antigen and capable of specifically binding with the same.

Antidote: A substance that counteracts the effect of poison.

Antigen: Substance that stimulates an immune response when introduced into the body.

Apomixis: Apomixes are a naturally occurring form of asexual reproduction in which plant embryos grow from egg cells without fertilisation.

Aquaculture: Farming in water that includes fish, algae, etc.

Aquifer: A structure that contains large water in grounds.

Arboriculture: Deals with cultivation of woody plants, woody ornamentals and shade trees.

Aroma: A special smell in rice produced due to essential oils and oleoresin extracts.

Arrowing: The flowering in sugarcane.

Attenuated vaccine: Whole pathogenic organism treated with chemical, radioactive, or other means to render it incapable of producing infection.

Autoclave: High temperature equipment for sterilizing and cleaning laboratory equipment and media.

Autosome: Chromosome other than a sex chromosome.

Auxins: A group of hormones of plants which are synthesized by growing tips of stems and roots and regulate many aspects of plant growth, *e.g.* IAA.

Awn: A stiff bristle like appendages occurring frequently on the flowering glumes of grasses and cereals.

Baggase: The crushed stalk of canes after juice extraction.

Barrage: A large structure erected across a river in order to store water, usually for irrigation.

Base sequence: The specific order of purine and pyrimidine bases in polynucleotide.

Batch culture: A suspension culture in which cells grow in a finite volume of nutrient medium and follow a sigmoid pattern.

Batch processing: Method in which bioreactor is loaded with raw materials and microorganisms; and the process is turned to completion at which time products are removed.

Beer's law: Law describing light penetration in crop canopy.

Benchmark: A reference point used for the survey of elevations.

Bioassay: Method of measuring the concentration or activity of a substance by determining its effect on a living organism.

Biodegradable: Organic compounds that can be broken down by microorganisms.

Biofertilization: Nutrient enrichment of soil as a result of microbial activity.

Biomass: Weight of organisms per unit area.

Biome: An ecological community of organisms maintained under a particular climate zone.

Biosynthesis: The formation of organic compounds by living organisms.

Bog soils: Soil developed under swamp and marsh type vegetation, composed of peat.

Booting: Stage of plant growth indicated by swelling of the flag leaf.

Brix: Unit of brix hydrometer for the percentage of total solids in sugarcane juice.

C_3 plants: A plant type in which the first product is 3-carbon compound (Phosphoglyceric acid) in CO_2 fixation, *e.g.* Wheat, Rice, Barley.

C_4 plants: A plant type in which the first product is 4-carbon compound (Oxaloacetic acid) in CO_2 fixation, *e.g.* Sugarcane, Maize.

Callus: A tissue consisting of dedifferentiated cells generally produced as a result of tissue wounding or of culturing tissues in the presence of auxins in particular.

CAM (Crassulacean Acid Metabolism).

Plants: A plant in which the CO_2 is fixed in the night. Such plants are adapted to arid climate, *e.g.*Pineapple, Cactus, etc.

cDNA: Complementary DNA, which is produced by reverse transcription from mRNA.

Cell differentiation: The process whereby descendants of a common parental cell achieves, and maintains specialization of structure and function.

Clone: Asexually cultured cells designed to produce multiple copies of a single gene or segment of DNA.

Cloning vector: DNA molecule originating from a virus, plasmid, into which another DNA fragment of appropriate size can be integrated without loss of the vector's capacity for self-replication; vectors introduce foreign DNA into host cells, where it is replicated autonomously in large quantities.

Complementary DNA: DNA synthesized by reverse transcriptase from an RNA template.

Concatamer: DNA made up of repeated unit length DNAs.

Cosmid: Artificially constructed cloning vector containing the *cos* gene of phagelambda.

Cryophyte: A plant growing in ice or snow.

Cultivar: A category of plants of the same species, but with a characteristic phenotype, generated through cultivation by man.

Cultivar: It is a group of crop plants having similar but distinguishable characteristics.

Cusec: The quantity of water flowing @ 1 cubic feet/second. The term day cusec is used for this water flowing for 24 hrs.

Cybrid: Plant or cell, which is a cytoplasmic hybrid produced by fusion of a protoplast and cytoplast.

Cycocel (CCC): 2-Chloroethyl trimethyl ammonium-choride, is a plant growth regulator.

Cytokinins: A group of hormones with stimulatory effect on divisions of plant cells, *e.g.*kinetin and zeatin.

Denaturation: Alteration of material, usually protein, through heating or chemical treatment, so it loses its characteristic activity.

Differentiation: Modification in structure and function of the parts of an organism, owing to increase in specialization.

DNA probe: Sequence of DNA used to detect presence of particular nucleotide sequence.

Drizzle: A type of precipitation where water drops are less than 0.2-0.5 mm.

EDTA: Ethylene diamine tetra-acetate. A food preservative, anticoagulant and common laboratory buffer component.

Electrophoresis: Separation of molecules based on their differing electrical charges.

Embryogenesis: A pathway of differentiation, which is characterized by the formation of organized structures that resemble zygotic embryos.

Embryoids: Embryo-like structures produced as a consequence of differentiation processes such as embryogenesis and androgenesis.

Endonuclease: An enzyme that hydrolyses DNA by breaking bonds in the middle of the chain.

Enriched compost: Compost fortified with the addition of fertilizers (Urea, SSP, rock Phosphate) in order to narrow down C:N ratio and raise nutrients.

Enzyme: Enzymes are kind of protein which, acts as catalyst in the metabolic reactions.

Epigeal germination: It is a type of germination in which the cotyledons appear above the soil surface.

Eppendorf: Small flip-top plastic vial for storing reagents, samples etc.

***Escherichia coli*:** A bacterium on which much genetic work has been done and which is a colon bacillus.

Eukaryotic: Refers to organism having membrane bound nuclei, genetic material organized into chromosomes and membrane bound cytoplasmic organelles.

Exon: Section of the DNA that codes for amino acids.

Exonuclease: An enzyme that can attack DNA from the ends without needing a recognition site.

Explant: A plant organ or piece of tissue used to initiate a tissue culture.

Fermentation: Decomposition occurring in organic compounds, usually carbohydrates, brought about by enzymes either directly or in microorganisms, resulting in the production of other compounds such as alcohol or lactic acid, often with heat and gases.

Fuzz: Non-separable part of fibre attached to cottonseeds.

Gametoclonal variation: Variation observed among plants regenerated from gametic cultures.

Gene library: Collection of DNA fragments (DNA, genomic DNA), which have been cloned in a vector.

Gene: Segment of a DNA molecule that contains information directing a cell to synthesize a specific protein product.

Genetic drift: A force that reduces heterozygosity by the random loss of alleles.

Genetic engineering: The experimental manipulation of DNA (or RNA) of different species producing recombinant DNA, which includes some genes from both species.

Genetic information: The information contained in a sequence of nucleotide base in a DNA (or RNA) molecule.

Genome: Genome consists of all the chromosomes of a diploid species that are distinct from each other with respect to their gene content, and often morphology. Members of a genome do not pair.

Genotype: Genetic constitution of an organism.

Genotype: The set of DNA variants found at one or more loci in an individual.

Germplasm: Total genetic variability available to species.

Gossipol: A phenolic pigment in cottonseed that is toxic to some animals.

Gram-negative: In the Gram stain, bacteria that do not retain the crystal violet dye after decolorization with alcohol.

Gram-positive: In the gram stain, bacteria that retain the crystal violet dye after decolorization with alcohol.

Haploid: Having a set of unpaired chromosomes in each nucleus.

Harvest index: The economic yield of plant with reference to biological yield in terms of percentage dry matter.

HCN (Hydrocyanic acid): Released through Cyanogenesis in a relatively short period, during drought in Sorghum, Sudan grass, white Clover, is a poison for ruminants, if increases more than 20 mg/100 g of plant tissue.

Heavy water (D_2O): Water in which hydrogen has been replaced by deuterium (hydrogen isotope of mass 2).

Herbarium: Collection of plant specimen by classifying, pressing, drying and mounting on the sheet of paper.

Herbigation: Application of herbicide with irrigation water.

Heterokaryon: A cell in which two or more nuclei of unlike genetic make-up are present.

Homokaryon: Protoplast or cell with two, genetically identical nuclei, a product of somatic hybridization.

Huller: A machine, which used for the purpose of hulling (removal of husk from paddy).

Hybrid: Offspring of two genetically dissimilar parents.

Hybridoma: A method of creating pure and uniform antibodies against a specific antigen.

Hypogeal germination: A type of germination in which the cotyledons remain below the soil surface.

Immunization: Administration of antigen to animal or organism to stimulate production of antibodies by that organism, also administration of antigens, antibodies or lymphocytes to organism to produce corresponding active, passive or adoptive immunity.

Immunology: The science that deals with resistance to disease.

***In vitro*:** (In Latin language meaning is 'in glass') any process carried out in sterile cultures.

***In vivo*:** (In Latin language meaning is 'in life' or natural) any process occurring in whole organism.

Inoculum: The part of microbes, which can initiate disease (or used for inoculation).

Interferon: Glycoprotein, important in immune function and thought to inhibit viral infections.

Intron: Intron is a sequence of DNA interrupting the coding sequence of gene.

Inventory: It is a detailed list of farm properties claimed for debt.

Jhum cultivation: It is a shifting cultivation usually followed in angladesh and Assam tract; remains at one place till the fertility is ere otherwise change the place.

Kilobase: A chain of nucleotides 1,000 monomers in size.

Lapse rate: The rate at which temperature decreases at the rise or ll of altitudes (air mass) in the atmosphere.

Lenticel: An opening in the cork of roots and stem for exchange of ses.

Ligase: Enzyme used to join nucleic acid fragments together.

Ligation: Enzyme-mediated procedure for joining segments of DNA.

Lithophyte: Plants growing on the rock surfaces.

Litmus: Some lichens produce colouring (blue or red) matter used identify pH of a medium, if impregnated into a paper.

Lopping: Pruning of shrubs or trees.

Lumen: A unit for measurement of radiant energy per second in e visible part of the spectrum (1 lumen sq. ft = 10.764 lux) derived om SI unit of luminous flux.

Lux: A unit for measurement of illumination by solar radiation.

Meristem culture: Culture of apical meristems, particularly shoot ical meristem, for production of shoots and plantlets.

Messenger RNA (RNA): RNA that serves as a template for protein nthesis.

Molar solution: A solution containing one g molecular weight of substance maintained to one litre.

Monoclonal antibodies: Those antibodies, which, are derived from, ingle source clone of cells and which recognize only one kind of tigen.

Morphogenesis: Developmental pathways in differentiation, ich, result in the formation of, recognised tissues.

Mower: A machine used for trimming grasses in the lawns or ks.

Mulch: Any material including straw, plant residue, leaves, plastic n, used for covering soil surface in order to reduce evaporation.

Mull: When humus contains appreciable amount of mineral bases, s called mull.

Myeloma: Antibody-producing tumour cells.

Nick translation: A procedure for radio labelling DNA *in vitro*.

Operon: A genetic unit consisting of adjacent genes that functions coordinately under the joint control of an operator and a repressor.

Organogenesis: Type of morphogenesis, which results in the formation of roots, shoots and /or floral organs.

Organoleptia: The common term used to describe sensory impression for spice, aroma, flavour, pungency and bitterness by the nose and mouth etc.

Oxylophytes: Plant tolerant to high acidic soil conditions.

P^{32}: A radioactive isotope of phosphorus, which emits strong beta particles and has a half-life of 14.3 days.

PAGE (Poly acrylamide Gel Electrophoresis): A technique for separating DNA fragments based on differential mobility in a gel.

Penicillin: The collective name for salts of a series of antibiotic organic acids produced by a number of *Penicillium* and *Aspergillus* species; active against most gram-positive bacteria and some gram-negative cocci having cell wall.

pH: A measure of the acidity of a substance, specifically, the logarithm of the reciprocal of the hydrogen ion concentration.

Photosynthetic number: The number of gram CO_2 absorbed against each gram molecule of chlorophyll.

Phytotrons: Greenhouses with precise environmental controls are known as phytotrons.

Plasmids: Small, circular piece of extrachromosomal DNA in bacteria. Some plasmids can integrate into a bacterial chromosome.

Platelet: A small rooted shoot or germinated ember.

Pressmud: It is the by-product of sugar industry, contains 1.25 N, 2% P_2O_5, 20% organic matter and 45% lime, used in acid soils.

Protoclonal variation: Variation observed among plants regenerated from protoplast cultures.

Protoplast: A cell, which lacks wall.

Recombinant DNA (rDNA): Hybrid DNA produced by joining pieces of DNA from different organisms together *in vitro*.

Recombinant DNA technology: Use of recombinant DNA for specific purpose, such as formation of product and study of gene.

Restriction endonuclease: Enzyme that cleaves DNA at specific nucleotide sequences, often leaving single-stranded region (sticky ends).

Restriction enzyme: Enzyme that cuts DNA at specific DNA sequence.

Reverse transcriptase: Enzyme that polymerizes a molecule of DNA using RNA as the template for determining sequence.

Sandy clay loam soil: Contains 20-35% clay, 28% silt and 45% sand.

Sandy clay soil: Contains 35% clay and 45% sand.

Sandy loam soil: Contains 50% sand and 20% clay.

Sandy soil: Contains 70% sand and less than 15% clay.

Sapling: Seedling of tree plant having age up to 1 year called saplings.

Silvics: Deals with the life history and general characters of trees or crops.

Silviculture: Cultivation of trees and crops together.

Sludge: Semi-solid phase of sewage water.

Somaclonal variation: Variation observed among plants regenerated from somatic cultures.

Somatic embryogenesis: Development of embryos from somatic cells in culture whose structure is to zygotic embryos found in seeds and with analogous embryonic organs such as cotyledons or cotyledonary leaves.

Somatic hybridization: A technique of fusing protoplasts from two contrasting genotypes for production of hybrids or cybrids, which contain various mixtures of nuclear and/or cytoplasmic genomes, respectively.

Splicing: A stage in RNA processing, in which introns are removed and exons are joined to form a continuous coding sequence of RNA.

Spray drift: This is the movement of pesticide particles with the air current while application, into area not covered for application.

Sprigging: It is a kind of vegetative propagation using rhizomes or stolon planted into furrows or dibbled into soil.

Steppe: The grass covered plains with light wood trees in the semi-arid areas.

Stirred tank bioreactor: Agitated vessel in which bioprocess takes place, mixing is provided by mechanical action of impeller/agitator.

Stover: Matured stalks of maize, sorghum, bajra used as fodder after removal of grains.

Synthetic seeds: Embryoids preserved in a thin layer of calcium alginate.

Template: The macromolecular mould for the synthesis of anothe macromolecule.

Ti-plasmid: Plasmid from *Agrobacterium tumefaciens,* used as plar vector.

Tissue culture: Culture of plant cells and tissues *in vitro* o artificial media.

Totipotency: Potentiality or property of a cell to produce a who organism.

Transcription: A process involving base pairing whereby th genetic information contained in DNA is used to order complementary sequence of bases in an RNA chain.

Transduction: The transfer of bacterial genes from one bacteriu to another by a bacteriophage particle.

Transformation: The genetic modification induced by th incorporation into a cell of DNA purified from cells or viruses.

Transgenic organisms: A genetically manipulated organis containing in its genome one or more inserted genes of another specie

Translation: The process where the genetic information present an RNA molecule directs the order of the specific amino acids durir protein synthesis.

Trashing: Stripping of lower leaves of sugarcane.

Vaccine: A preparation of a pathogenic microorganism which treated to destroy its virulence when introduced into the body, causir the body to produce antibodies and so conferring immunity.

Virgin soil: The soil, which has not been used for cultivation.

Viruses: Infectious disease causing agents, smaller than bacteri which always require intact host cells for replication and whi contain either DNA or RNA as their genetic component.

Vitamin: An organic compound essential in small amounts for t normal metabolism of other nutrients.

Windrower: A machine used for the purpose of crop harvestin

Appendices

Appendix 1: Important Journals

	Name of Journal	Period	Published by
1.	Agricultural Research	Monthly	Agricultural Research Services, IARI, New Delhi
2.	Annals of Agricultural Research	Quarterly	Indian Society of Agricultural Sciences, New Delhi
3.	Current Research	Monthly	UAS, Dharwad
4.	Journal of Maharastra Agricultural Universities	Quarterly	College of Agriculture, Pune
5.	Journal of Research	Half Yearly	Rajendra Agriculture University, Bihar
6.	PKV Research Journal	Half Yearly	Punjabrao Krishi Vishwavidyalaya, Akola
7.	Vayu Mandal	Half Yearly	Indian Meteorological Society, Mausam Bhavan, New Delhi
8.	Haryana Journal of Agronomy	Half Yearly	Haryana Agronomists Association, Dept of Agronomy, HAU, Hisar
9.	Madras Agricultural Journal	Monthly	MASU, TNAU, Coimbatore
10.	Mysore Journal of Agricultural Sciences	Quarterly	UAS, Bangalore
11.	JNKV Research Journal	Biannual	JNKV, Jabalpur, M.P
12.	Indian Journal of Agricultural Sciences	Monthly	ICAR, New Delhi
13.	Indian Journal of Agricultural Research	Quarterly	Agricultural Research Communication Centre, Karnal
14.	Indian Journal of Sugarcane Technology	Half Yearly	Association of Sugarcane Technologists of India, Lucknow
15.	Tobacco research	Half Yearly	Indian Society of Tobacco Sciences, Rajamundry
16.	Intensive Agriculture	Monthly	Directorate of Extension, IASRI Campus, New Delhi
17.	Journal of Indian Society of Coastal Agricultural Research	Half Yearly	Indian Society of Coastal Agricultural Research, West Bengal

18.	Fertilizer News	Monthly	Fertilizers Association of India, New Delhi
19.	Clay Research	Half Yearly	Clay Mineral Society of India, IARI, New Delhi
20.	Journal of Indian Society of Soil Sciences	Quarterly	Journal of Indian Society of Soil Sciences, IARI, New Delhi
21.	Journal of Nuclear Agriculture and Biology	Quarterly	Nuclear Research Laboratory, IARI, New Delhi
22.	Indian Journal of Agricultural Chemistry	Quarterly	Indian Society of Agricultural Chesmists, Allahabad
23.	Farming System	Quarterly	Institute of Studies on Agricultural Rural Development, Dharwad
24.	*Mausam*	Quarterly	IMD, India Habitat Centre, New Delhi
25.	Indian Journal of Agronomy	Quarterly	Indian Society of Agronomy, IARI, New Delhi
26.	Research and Development Reporter	Biannual	Rajasthan Fertilizers Trading Corporation, Jammu and Kashmir
27.	Indian Journal of Dry Land Agricultural Research and Development	Half Yearly	CRIDA, Hyderabad
28.	Indian Farming	Quarterly	ICAR, New Delhi
29.	Crop Research	Bimonthly	Agricultural Research Information Centre, Hissar
30.	Crop Improvement	Half Yearly	Crop Improvement Society of India, Ludhiana
31.	International Chick/pea Newsletter	Half Yearly	ICRISAT, Hyderabad
32.	International Arachis Newsletter	Half Yearly	ICRISAT, Hyderabad
33.	International Pigeon Pea Newsletter	Half Yearly	ICRISAT, Hyderabad
34.	Jute Development Journal	Quarterly	Directorate of Jute Development, Kolkata
35.	Agricultural Review	Quarterly	Agricultural Research Communication Centre,Karnal
36.	Indian Phytopathology	Quarterly	Indian Society of Phytopathology, Division of Plant Pathology, IARI, New Delhi

Appendix 2: Important International Agencies Dealing with Agriculture

AVRDC Asian Vegetable Research and Development Centre, Taiwan.

CGIAR Consultative Group of International Agricultural Research, Washington DC (USA)

CABI Commonwealth Agricultural Bureaux International

CIAT *Centro International de Agricultura Tropical* (International Centre for Tropical Agriculture), Coli-Columbia (South America)

CIDA Canadian International Development Agency, Cubac

CIMMYT *Centro International de Mejorimiento de Maiz y Trigo* (International Centre for Improvement of Maize and Wheat), Mexico

CIP *Centro International de la papa* (International Potato Research Centre), Peru (South America)

FAO Food and Agricultural Organisation, Rome, Italy

IBPGR International Board for Plant Genetic Resources, Rome, Italy

IBRD International Bank for Reconstruction and Development (the World Bank), Washington DC (USA)

IBSNAT International Benchmark Soils Network for Agrotechnology Transfer, Hawai

ICARDA International Centre for Agricultural Research in Dry Area, Allepo, Syria

IVRAF International Council for Research in Agroforestry, Nairobi, Kenya

ICRISAT International Crops Research Institute for Semi-Arid Tropics, Patancheru, Hyderabad, Andhra Pradesh, India

IFAD International Fund for Agricultural Development, Cubac

IFDC International Fertilizer Development Centre, Albania (USA)

IFPRI International Food Policy Research Institute, Washington, DC

IIMI International Irrigation Management Institute, Digana Village, Sri Lanka

IITA International Institute of Tropical Agriculture, Ibadan, Nigeria

ILCA International Livestock Centre for Africa, Addis Ababa, Ethiopia

ILRAD	International Laboratory for Research on Animal Diseases, Nairobi, Kenya
IRRI	International Rice Research Institute, Manila, Philippines
ISNAR	International Service for National Agricultural Research, The Hague, Netherlands
ISRIC	International Soils Reference and Information Centre, Netherlands.
TPRI	Tropical Pesticides Research Institute, Arusha, Tanzania.
WARDA	West African Rice Development Association, Monnrovia, Liberia.
WMO	World Meteorological Organisation, Geneva, Switzerland

Appendix 3: Important Institutes, Bureaus and Project Directorates.

Institution

1. Bhabha Atomic Research Centre, Trombay, Mumbai, Maharashtra.
2. Central Arid Zone Research Institute, Jodhpur, Rajasthan.
3. Central Food Technological Research Institute, Mysore, Karnataka.
4. Central Agricultural Research Institute, Port Blair
5. Central Inland Fisheries Research Institute, Barrackpore, West Bengal.
6. Central Institute for Cotton Research, Nagpur, Maharashtra.
7. Central Institute for Research on Goats, Farah, Uttar Pradesh.
8. Central Institute for Research on Cotton Technology, Mumbai
9. Central Institute of Agricultural Engineering, Bhopal, Madhya Pradesh.
10. Central Institute for Arid Horticulture, Bikaner, Rajasthan
11. Central Institute of Brakishwater Aquaculture, Chennai, Tamil Nadu.
12. Central Institute of Freshwater Aquaculture, Bhubaneswar, Orissa
13. Central Institue of Fisheries Education, Mumbai, Maharashtra.
14. Central Institute of Fisheries Technology, Willingdon Island, Cochin, Kerala

15. Central Institute of Post-Harvest Engineering and Technology, PAU, Ludhiana, Panjab.
16. Central Marine Fisheries Research Institute, Kochin, Kerala
17. Central Institute of Horticulture for Northern Plains, Lucknow, Uttar Pradesh.
18. Central Institute of Medicinal and Aromatic Plants, Lucknow, Uttar Pradesh.
19. Central Institute for Research on Buffaloes, Hisar, Haryana.
20. Central Institute for Research on Goats, Makdoom, Mathura, Uttar Pradesh.
21. Central Plantation Crops Research Institute, Kasargod, Kerala.
22. Central Research Institute for Dry Land Agriculture, Hyderabad, Andhra Pradesh.
23. Central Research Institute for Jute and Allied Fiber, Barrackpore
24. Central Rice Research Institute, Cuttack, Orissa
25. Central Sheep and Wool Research Institute, Avikanagar, Rajasthan
26. Central Soil Salinity Research Institute, Karnal, Haryana
27. Central Tuber Crops Research Institute, Thiruvananthapuram
28. Indian Agricultural Statistics Research Institute, New Delhi
29. ICAR Research Complex For Goa, Ela Old, Goa
30. Indian Grassland and Fodder Research Institute, Jhansi
31. Indian Institute of Horticultural Research, Bangalore, Karnataka
32. Indian Institute of Pulses Research, Kanpur, Uttar Pradesh.
33. Indian Institute of Soil Science, Bhopal, Madhya Pradesh.
34. Indian Institute of Spices Research, Calicut, Kerala
35. Indian Institute of Sugarcane Research, Lucknow, Uttar Pradesh.
36. Indian Institute of Vegetable Research, Varanasi, Uttar Pradesh.
37. Indian Lac Research Institute, Namkum, Ranchi
38. National Academy of Agricultural Research Management (Manage), Hyderabad, Andhra Pradesh.
39. National Institute of Animal Nutrition and Physiology, Bangalore, Karnataka
40. National Institute for Research on Jute and Allied Fibres Technology, West Bengal (formerly JTRL)

41. Sugarcane Breeding Institute, Coimbatore, Tamil Nadu.
42. Vivekanand Parvatiya Krishi Anusandhan Sansthan, Almora, Uttaranchal

Deemed universities cum institutes

1. Indian Agricultural Research Institute, New Delhi
2. National Dairy Research Institute, Karnal, Haryana
3. National Veterinary Research Institute, Izzatnagar, Uttar Pradesh.
4. Central Institute of Fisheries Education, Mumbai

Bureaus

1. National Bureau of Animal Genetic Resources, Karnal, Haryana
2. National Bureau of Fish Genetic Resources, Lucknow, Uttar Pradesh.
3. National Bureau of Plant Genetic Resource, New Delhi
4. National Bureau of Soil Survey and Land Use Planning, Nagpur, Maharashtra.
5. National Bureau of Agriculturally Important Microorganisms, Distt. Mau, Uttar Pradesh.

Project Directorates

1. Project Directorate of Biological Control, Bangalore
2. Project Directorate on Cattle, Meerut, Uttar Pradesh.
3. Project Directorate of Cropping System Research, Modipuram, Uttar Pradesh.
4. Project Directorate of Oilseed Research, Rajendranagar, Hyderabad
5. Project Directorate of Poultry, Rajendranagar, Hyderabad, Andhra Pradesh
6. Project Directorate of Maize Research, IARI, New Delhi
7. Project Directorate of Rice Research, Hyderabad
8. Water Technology Centre for Eastern Region, Bhubaneswar, Orissa

Appendix 4: List of Agricultural and Veterinary universities.

1. Acharya NG Ranga Agricultural University, Hyderabad, Andhra Pradesh
2. Anand Agricultural University, Anand, Gujarat
3. Assam Agricultural University, Jorhat, Assam
4. Bidhan Chandra Krishi Viswavidyalaya, Mohanpur, West Bengal
5. Birsa Agricultural University, Ranchi, Jharkhand
6. Central Agricultural University, Imphal, Manipur
7. Chandra Shekar Azad University of Agriculture & Technology, Kanpur, Uttar Pradesh
8. Chaudhary Charan Singh Haryana Agricultural University, Hisar, Haryana
9. CSK Himachal Pradesh Krishi Vishvavidyalaya, Palampur, Himachal Pradesh
10. Dr. Balasaheb Sawant Konkan Krishi Vidyapeeth, Dapoll, Maharashtra
11. Dr. Paniabrao Deshmukh Krishi Vidyapeeth, Akola, Maharashtra
12. Dr. Yashwant Singh Parmar University of Horticulture & Forestry, Solan, Himachal Pradesh
13. Govind Ballabh Pant University of Agriculture and Technology, Pantnagar, (Nainital) Uttarakhand
14. Guru Angad Dev Veterinary and Animal Science University, Ludhiana, Punjab
15. Indira Gandhi Krishi Vishwavidyalaya, Raipur, Chhattisgarh
16. Jawaharlal Nehru Krishi Viswavidyalaya, Jabalpur, Madhya Pradesh
17. Junagadh Agricultural University, Junagadh, Gujarat
18. Kerala Agricultural University, Trichur, Kerala
19. Maharana Pratap Univ. of Agriculture & Technology, Udaipur, Rajasthan
20. Maharashtra Animal Science & Fishery University, Nagpur, Maharashtra
21. Mahatma Phule Krishi Vidyapeeth, Rahuri, Maharashtra
22. Marathwada Agricultural University, Parbhani, Maharashtra
23. Narendra Deva University of Agriculture & Technology, Faizabad, Uttar Pradesh

24. Navsari Agricultural University, Navsari, Gujarat
25. Orissa Univ. of Agriculture & Technology, Bhubaneshwar, Orissa
26. Punjab Agricultural University, Ludhiana, Punjab
27. Rajasthan Agricultural University, Bikaner, Rajasthan
28. Rajendra Agricultural University, Pusa, Samastipur, Bihar
29. Sardarkrushinagar-Dantiwada Agricultural University, Sardar Krushinagar, Gujarat
30. Sardar Vallabh Bhai Patel University of Agriculture and Technology, Meerut , Uttar Pradesh
31. Sher-E-Kashmir University of Agricultural Sciences and Technology, Jammu, Jammu & Kashmir
32. Sher-E-Kashmir University of Agricultural Sciences and Technology of Kashmir, Shrinagar, Jammu & Kashmir
33. Sri Venkateswara Veterinary University, Tirupati, Andhra Pradesh
34. Tamil Nadu Agricultural University, Coimbatore, Tamil Nadu
35. Tamil Nadu Veterinary and Animal Science University, Chennai, Tamilnadu
36. University of Agricultural Sciences, Bangalore, Bangalooru, Karnataka
37. University of Agricultural Sciences, Dharwad, Dharwad, Karnataka
38. UP Pandit Deen Dayal Upadhaya Pashu Chikitsa Vigyan Vishwa Vidhyalaya evam Go Anusandhan, Mathura, Uttar Pradesh
39. Uttar Banga Krishi Viswavidvalava, Pundibari, West Bengal
40. West Bengal University of Animal & Fishery Sciences, Kolkata, West Bengal
41. Karnataka Veterinary, Animal and Fisheries Sciences University Bidar, Karnataka
42. University of Agricultural Sciences, Raichur, Karnataka
43. University of Horticultural Sciences, Navanaciar, Bagalkot Karnataka
44. Andhra Pradesh Horticultural University, Tadepailigudem, Andhra Pradesh
45. Rajmata Vijayraje Sciendia Krishi Vishwa Vidyalaya, Gwalior, Madhya Pradesh
46. Rajasthan University of Veterinary and Animal Sciences, Bikaner, Rajasthan

Important Abbreviations

A.P.E.D.A.	Agriculture and Processed Products Development Authority
A.U.	Agricultural Universities
AGMARK	Agricultural Marketing
AMA	Agricultural Co-Marketing Advisor
APC	Agricultural Price Commission
ARDC	Agriculture Refinance and Development Corporation
ATMA	Agricultural Technology Management Agency
C.A.D.	Command Area Development
CAPART	Council for Advancement of Peoples and Actions Rural Technology
C.B.	Co-operative Bank
C.D.D.	Cattle and Dairy Development
CDP	Community Development Programme
D.P.A.P.	Drought Prone Area Programme
EEC	European Economic Community
F.A.O.	Food and Agricultural Organisation
F.T.C.	Farmers Training Centre
FCI	Food Corporation of India
FSS	Farmers Service Society
GNP	Gross National Product
H.A.D.	Hill Area Development Programme
H.Y.V.P.	High Yielding Varieties Programme
I.A.A.P.	Intensive Agricultural Area Programme
I.A.D.A.	Intensive Agricultural District Programme
I.C.D.P.	Intensive Cattle Development Programme

I.O.D.P.	Intensive Oil Seed Development Programme
I.D.A.D.	Integrated Dryland Agricultural Development
ICRISAT	International Crop Research Institute for Semi Arid and Tropics
IDBI	Industrial Development Bank of India
IFFCO	Indian Farmers Fertilizer Co-operative Ltd.
IMF	International Monetory Fund
IPCC	Intergovernal Panel on Climate Change
IRDP	Integrated Rural Development Programme
IVLP	Institute Village Link Programme
JRY	Jawahar Rozgar Yojana
KCC	Kissan Call Centre
KCCS	Kishan credit card scheme
K.V.K.	Krishi Vigyan Kendra
LBS	Lead Bank Scheme
LDB	Land Development Bank
M.F.A.L.	Marginal Farmers and Agricultural Labour Programme
MCP	Multiple Cropping Programme
MSY	Mahila Samridhi Yojana
NABARD	National Bank for Agriculture and Rural Development
NAEP	National Agriculture Extension Project
NAFED	National Agriculture Co-operative Marketing Federation
NASA	National Aeronauts & Space Administration (USA)
NCA	National Commission on Agriculture
NCAER	National Council for Agricultural Economics and Research.
NCAP	National Centre for Agricultural Planning.
NCDC	National Co-operative Development Corporation

NES	National Extension Service
NFSM	National Food Security Mission.
NHM	National Horticulture Mission.
NIAM	National Institute of Agricultural Marketing
NOAA	National Oceanic & Atmospheric Administration (USA).
NOVOD	National Oilseeds and Vegetable Oils Develo-pment Board.
NREGA	(Mahatma Ghandhi) National Rural Employment Guarantee Act
NSC	National Seed Corporation
NSRTC	National Seeds Research and Traning Centre
P.D.	Poultry Development
PPTD	Pilot Project for Tribal Development
RKVY	Rashtriya Krishi Vikas Yojana
RLEGP	Rural Landless Employment Guarantee Programme
RMK	Rashtriya Mahila Kosh
RRB	Regional Rural Banks
RUCHI	Rural Centre for Human Interests
S.D.	Sheep Development
SFAC	Small Farmers Agri-Business Consortium
S.F.D.A.	Small Farmers Development Agency
S.G.S.Y.	Swaran Jyanti Gram Swarojgar Yojana
SRI	System of Rice Intensification.
T.A.D.	Tribal Area Development
T.E.R.I.	Tata Energy Research Institute
T.T.C.	Trainer's Training Centre
TRYSEM	Training of Rural Youth for Self Employment
UTI	Unit Trust of India
UNDP	United Nations Development Programme

UNEP	United Nations Environment Programme
WBCIS	Weather Based Crop Insurance Scheme
W.V.D.P.	Whole Village Development Programme
WHO	World Health Organization
WTO	World Trade Organisation

Tsunami and Impact on Agriculture

The term Tsunami was almost unknown to common man before the black event of 26th December, 2004, but upon show it has swallow the lives of thousand of people and Trillions of rupees property. *Tsunami* is a Japanese word means "harbour wave" and used as the scientific term for a seismic sea wave, a large ocean wave generated by an undersea earthquake. A tsunami is triggered when the ocean floor is tilted or offset during the quake, creating a set of waves similar to the concentric waves generated by an object dropped into water. The least possible cause sometimes is an undersea landslide or volcanic eruption. Most tsunamis originate along the so-called Ring of Fire, a zone of volcanoes and seismic activity, 32,500 km long that encircles the Pacific Ocean.

- Since 1819 about 40 tsunamis have struck the Hawaiian Islands.
- Tsunamis are sometimes confused with tidal waves, but they do not have diurnal pattern of high and low tides as occurs in tidal waves.

IMPACT OF TSUNAMI ON AGRICULTURE

The tsunami waves approached from the East, having sufficient tide to sweep over some lands simultaneously to crops and trees. The impact of Tsunami was quite heavy causing a loss of food, feed, fibre and livestock depending upon the topography.

Young Fruit-trees Dying From Salt Stress

The agricultural impact of the tsunami was generally limited to the loss of field crops and the dying of fruit trees due to osmotic stress and toxicity of the floodwater. Very little erosion of the agricultural fields or deposition of sediments was observed. Damage to infrastructure (irrigation/ drainage/road systems, fences, farm buildings, etc.) also appeared to be negligible, as little infrastructure had been constructed. All field crops in the flooded areas were lost beyond rescue. Almost all fruit trees shed their leaves and many appeared to be dead. Most mango trees showed no sign of life. Young trees (especially seedlings) had suffered more than the mature trees.

Impacts on the Soils

The "*FAO Soil Salinity Assessment Mission*" has briefed that most of the saline flood water eventually drained back to the sea and the period of flooding in some cases was quite short, enough seawater infiltrated or remained on the land to leave a considerable salt load in the soil. After the retreat of the saline flood water, most of this salt remained in the root zone, raising the soil salinity in this zone to an estimated level as high as EC e =50-60 dS/m (thresholds for most crops and fruit trees is EC e <4 dS/m)[2] . These high soil salinity values prevailed until the arrival of the first rain. Post-tsunami rainfall has been varied and is in line with the decreasing trend in total rainfall in a South to North direction. Due to topographic differences and variance in rainfall salinity is still a problem in some areas.

Impact on Groundwater

The saline floodwater has raised the water- table and salinized the upper groundwater. Many of the wells have been flooded and salinized the surrounding ground water. Sea water intruded laterally into the ground water aquifer, thereby salinizing the fresh water.

Salinity levels in flooded wells were found to be mostly in the rang of EC = 5-7 dS/m (as compared to pre-tsunami salinity levels of EC = 0.5-0.6 dS/m).

EMMERGING OUT OF TRAGEDY

Affected tree showing new sprouts. In areas where the rains we on time, some of the trees survived. Post-tsunami rainfall has cleane most of the affected area and it is expected that after two-thre monsoon seasons, all salinity problems will be eradicate Nevertheless, farmers can take to ensure crop and fruit tree surviv by opting relevant measures, such as they should not irrigate fie crops with well water having EC > 5 dS/m (deci-Siemens per metr and water conservation should be promoted through mulching a run-off reducing measures.

POST-TSUNAMI MEASURES

Foremost among the issues thrown up by the December 26, 2004 trage asked for the need of tsunami warning system and a permane protective shield along the coast to minimise the loss of lives a property in the event of a future killer wave attack.

A protective shield is to be constructed as "sea wall" along the 1,000-km Tamil Nadu coastline. However, fishermen, agriculturists, political leaders and activists working in the fields of environment and coastal safeguards are interested for natural fence of mangroves and other trees along the coastline over the preference to a concrete or stone structure. At present, only about 10 per cent of the TN coastline has the protection of mangroves including Pichavaram mangrove forest.

M.S. Swaminathan has suggested for the environmental defence systems as a long-term post-tsunami programme, called for steps to initiate a "coastal bio-shield movement" involving the raising of mangrove forests, plantations of *Casuarina, Salicornia, Laucaena, Atriplex*, palms, bamboo and other tree species, and halophytes that can grow near the sea. These will serve as speed-breakers under conditions of coastal storms, cyclones, and tsunami. In addition these bio-shield will serve as carbon sinks, enhancing carbon sequestration thereby contributing to reducing the growing imbalance between carbon emissions and absorption.

Agriculture Insurance for Tsunami-hit Farmers

The Agriculture Insurance Company of India Ltd (AIC), has taken the responsibility to insure crops in Nagapatnam, Thiruvallur and Cudallore districts in Tamil Nadu and Konkal in Pondicherry. About Rs. 10-15 crore is likely to be paid as compensation for damages done to insured crops in Tamil Nadu and Pondicherry. AIC is expecting to cover 180 lakh farmers in 2004-05.

- During 2003-04, 44 lakh farmers were paid compensation of Rs 19,000 crore.
- Rajasthan, Haryana and Jammu & Kashmir accepted the NAIS (National Agricultural Insurance Scheme) in 2004-05.
- NAIS covers more than 30 crops in *Kharif* season and over 20 crops in *Rabi* season.
- An AIC scheme Varsha Bima for rainfall launched during 2004 covered 1,000 farmers in 20 rain gauge stations in Andhra Pradesh, Karnataka, Rajasthan and Uttar Pradesh.

- AIC has launched as CRIAY (Coffee Rainfall Index and Area Yield) Insurance Scheme covering 75% of rainfall risk and 25% of yield risk for coffee growers in Hassan, Chikmagalore and Kodagu districts in Karnataka from 2005.
- Another scheme "Sookha Suraksha Kavach" will become operational in 12 districts of Rajasthan from *kharif* 2005.
- The " Farm Income Insurance Scheme" has been suspended.
- A scheme for Insurance covers for "Basmati rice and poppy crop" grown under the supervision of Narcotics Bureau will also be operational in 2005.

Tsunami-hit Farmers to Grow Salt-tolerant rice

The International Rice Research Institute (IRRI) has sent Rice varieties that can grow in salty conditions where rice-growing regions were badly affected by the tsunami. M.S. Swaminathan Research Foundation is working on the aspects of salt tolerance varieties and their possibilities in the tsunami hit area.

Famous Books and Authors

S.No.	Books	Authors
1.	Soil Fertility and Fertilizers	– S.L. Tisdale & W.L. Nelson
2.	Nature and Properties of Soils	– N.C. Brady and Weil
3.	Garden Flowers	– Vishnu Swaroop
4.	Vegetables	– B. Chaudhry
5.	Fruits	– Ranjeet Singh
6.	Floriculture in India	– M.S. Randhawa
7.	Handbook of Horticulture	– K.L. Chadha (ICAR)
8.	Entomology and Pest Management	– L.P. Peddigo
9.	Extension Education	– A. Reddy
10.	Spices and Condiments	– J.S. Pruthi
11.	General Texbook of Entomology (Vol.I and II)	– Imm's
12.	Principles of Biochemistry	– Lehninger
13.	Plant Pathology	– G.N. Agrios
14.	Principles of Agricultural Engg. (Vol.I and II)	– A.M. Micheal and T.P. Ojha
15.	Wings of Fire	– A.P.J. Abdul Kalam
16.	India 2020	– A.P.J. Abdul Kalam
17.	Ignited Minds	– A.P.J. Abdul Kalam
18.	Indomitable spirit	– A.P.J. Abdul Kalam
19.	The Wonder that was India	– Bhasam
20.	History of Indian Agriculture	– M.S. Randhawa

21. It's Always Possible – *Kiran Bedi*
22. Indian Philosophy – *Dr. S. Radhakrishanan*
23. Long Walk to Freedom – *Nelson Mandela*
24. India's Struggle for Independence – *Bipin Chandra*
25. The God of Small Things – *Arundhati Roy*
26. You Can Win – *Shiv Khera*
27. Discovery of India – *Jawahar Lal Nehru*
28. Glimpses of World History – *Jawahar Lal Nehru*
29. My Experiment with Truth – *M.K. Gandhi*
30. The Augmentative Indian – *Amartya Sen*
31. The Good Earth – *Pearls Buck*
32. The Name Shake – *Jhumpha Lahiri*
33. The Song of India – *Sarojini Naidu*
34. The Time Machine – *H. G. Wells*
35. The White Tiger – *Arvind Adiga*
36. Origin of Species – *Charles Darwin* **(ARS 2010)**
37. Wealth of Nations – *Adam Smith*
38. Rose in India, – *B.P. Pal*
39. Horticulture at a Glance (Vol. I, II, III) – *A.S. Salaria & Babita Salaria*
40. Insects Structure and Function – *Chapman*
41. Revolutions : to Green the Environment to Glow the Human Heart – *M.S. Swaminathan*
42. Unaccoustomed Earth – *Jhumpha Lahiri*

Index

V

W

X

Y

Z

experience" is a plain fact, observable in our daily selves. Our subjective selves are "much more to be compared to a rising and falling tide," continually expanding and contracting, rather than "isolated pillars with their fixed circumferences".

This perspective profoundly alters the debate around Monism versus Pluralism.

Pluralism, seen as a "verticaldivision, into pillars and not into strata," becomes "relatively unimportant and superseded," though not entirely false. Instead, "Multiplicism, the variety of levels of experience, each possessing its peculiar range and area, becomes the obvious truth". Dualism loses its prominence as the sole antithesis of Monism. The question of Monism and the Absolute then simply becomes: "how far we are able to maintain a unity within multiplicism while following it out into its higher, which are also necessarily its deeper, ranges".

The "general formula of the Absolute" – the "transmutation and rearrangement of particular experiences, and also of the contents of particular finite minds, by inclusion in a completer whole of experience" – is a matter of "everyday verification". Our experiences are transmuted by changes in work or scene, and in the co-operation of minds, their elements are modified into "members of the new and common mind which arises".

This is not a mere abstraction; minds in a working whole supplement, widen, and reinforce each other, deepening and widening together. The fear, pain, and perplexities of individual consciousness take on a different value and coloring. Our mere changes in mood throughout the day demonstrate this constant fluctuation in the value and significance of existence's details.

This process, therefore, is not an "idealistic chimera" but the "common law and fact of experience," verifiable daily within our private consciousness and on a larger scale in creations like the State, fine art, and religion. The precise number of "levels of experience" is less important than the "character of the transmutations" themselves, which are not just intellectual but also "moral, aesthetic, and religious". They form different worlds with varying degrees of reality, yet are "nothing but one and the same world, more and less fully experienced". Plato, too, emphasized this: we "live in different worlds according to the differing energy of our minds," yet it is only "according to the differing energy of our minds that we do live in different worlds". The "real point is in the transmuting or expanding power of common finite mind".

When these facts are given their due weight, the difficulties in conceiving the Absolute are removed. Its positive proof rests logically on the principle of non-contradiction, specifically in its positive bearing: "a complete unification in which all contradictions are destroyed, though diversity or a negative aspect of course remain". From navigating mountains to managing daily business or discerning beauty through ugliness, we find "how contradictory aspects blend into harmony as linking and distinguishing contents come into view".

One might object: "Does not greater knowledge bring greater suffering and the highest effort encounter the most insuperable obstacles?". The lecture responds that this does not invalidate the principle. Every finite being has limits and ill-balanced properties; it is not a perfect microcosm of the universe. But even so, "so far as the finite being lives a life at all, it affirms in its whole existence the principle of the Absolute". It "transmutes toil into happiness by seeing it as a pledge of devotion, and pain into love by the depth of the tenderness it evokes, and hardship into courage by its revelation of what a man is able to be". The failure in degree is not an argument against this analysis of nature once finiteness is accepted. This is not optimism, but a critical observation that "transmutation of experience, in accordance with the law of non-contradiction in its positive bearing, is the principle of daily life". If admitted here, there is "no reason for making it a fundamental difficulty when we come to deal with ultimate reality".

The lecture expresses amazement that the significance of these daily facts, though commonplaces in literature and practice, is"never to be noted". It argues that a careful analysis of a single day in a typical human life would "establish triumphantly all that is needed in principle for the affirmation of the Absolute". The hard and fast limits often attributed to our self or personality are "not to be found anywhere in the real world". In the great achievements of knowledge, morality, beauty, and religion, the argument that the limits of our normal self cannot restrict our ultimate self becomes "irresistible". The "expansive power of the common mind is really the crux". Regarded from this point of view, the Absolute is simply the "high-water mark of fluctuation in an experience which is deeper as well as wider than our minimum self". The transmutation of externality and obstruction into "instruments and factors of more complete living" are familiar facts. The "technical point" is to focus on the "levels of experience, as determined by the logical criterion," rather than being obsessed with divisions into partially exclusive centers. While finite excellence is often broken up (division of labor), the "philosophic" spirit in Plato leaves room for "the Treasure of the Humble". Our experience becomes "more human and valuable, as well as more solid and more verifiable, in proportion as we approach the Absolute". We don't experience anything perfectly, but "we experience the Absolute better than we experience anything else, because it is greater and because everything else we only experience among other things, the Absolute we experience in everything".

To provide a concrete analogue, the lecture invites us to consider Dante's mind as uttered in the *Divine Comedy*. First, externality—Italy, and the wider universe—is present in Dante's experience. It is not destroyed but appears as "expression, character, emotion," deeply rooted in real externality. Dante is, in a sense, Italy "come alive," transforming external Nature into concrete emotion through his genius. Second, the selvesportrayed in the poem "have all rendered up their content to the great experience which was the poet's mind, and are constituent parts of it". Yet, for the poem's effectiveness, they are also depicted as acting and thinking beings "for themselves and in the outer world". These selves are not pure, separate objects merely mirrored by Dante's mind; rather, they are "in their degree participants in the moods, volitions, and perceptions which, taken as a whole of experience, are the substance and tissue of the poet's mind in the poem". They are seen as extending beyond their minimum historical attachment, embodying varieties of being up to the poem's own level.

Finite selves, then, reveal themselves as the "copula," the "living tension," by which the full experience affirms itself through externality. Each self is a "representative centre of an external world"; some aspect of nature "comes alive" in it. Every self participates in experiences beyond its own minimum, thus expanding "from its place in nature to a more or less wide and deep participation in the Absolute," where some degree of transmutation occurs.

Finally, the Absolute is remotely suggested by the whole experience of the poem itself—the poem in its "fullest completeness". It is a "perfect union of mind and nature, absorbing the world of Nature by and through the world of selves". Every self is a "meeting point of tension and fulfilment," where the one life maintains itself through a portion of the external world, and the external world is centered in a case of the one life. The complete experience of the Absolute includes "all the selves, with nothing omitted, but transformed and expanded by the place they hold and the illumination they receive in it". Episodes like Paolo and Francesca or Ugolino serve to illustrate how an actual historical self can be "transformed and expanded in the reality".

However, the lecture cautions that phrases like "transformed, transmuted, expanded," though convenient, can be misleading. The "true normal" is the real, and the self as we know it in space and time is actually a "figure deformed and diminished" by our "impotence to attain the grasp which holds all being in one".

Our individual being is narrowed down into an "appearance, incomplete and successive, in actual history". This "dissociation of the Absolute" in daily life, though never complete, is the "rule and essence of finite life". There is always something in the world of time and space that represents the fusion of the Absolute. The analogy with Dante, despite its illustrative power, faces an obstacle: the "stubborn dissociation" of the Absolute in actual existence.

In reality, Dante's poem was an imaginative creation *within* a human mind, and the nature and history it dealt with were "separate and independent facts, outside it". The analogy, therefore, uses only the reflection or interpretation of these facts within Dante's imaginative product, which might lead to the impression that reality is just "somebody's dream".

But this misunderstanding misses the point. Our meaning depends on placing ourselves within Dante's imaginative world, taking its nature and figures as the "actual scenery and inhabitants of that "actual" world".

The lesson is to understand the true relation between actual Nature and personalities (as Dante's imagination presents them) and the "spiritual interpretation which exhibits all these facts as, without detriment to their actuality, elements in a Vast unitary vision and experience constituting a single spiritual world".

This is more profound than a mere spiritual interpretation; it shows actual persons moving freely and self-determined, yet simultaneously, through a deeper insight into their selves, exhibited as elements within an embracing spiritual universe—Dante's vision. This spiritual world is a "revelation of the true appearance which such a history might yield under intense illumination, without detriment to its factual objectivity for the common eye".

In the "ultimate reality—known to us as our everyday world"—we face a far more "stubborn dissociation," a "huge obstinate plurality of independent facts".

Yet, the lecture insists that our life, within the realm of genuine fact, contains "uncounted degrees of power and insight".

Without denying that things are what they are, we can begin to frame a positive conception of "what more they must be," and realize that if we take them as such a "more," "they are at once more themselves, and plainly indicate their dissociation to be a character of partial reality, and their full nature to lie in the universe of a single experience". This concludes our general theory of the self-interpretation of the real through the fundamental principle of individuality. It is a journey that, as we've seen, asks us to reconsider our most basic assumptions about the self, nature, and the interconnectedness of all experience, moving us towards a more unified and profound understanding of reality.